High-risk newborn infants

The basis for intensive nursing care

High-risk newborn infants

The basis for intensive nursing care

SHELDON B. KORONES, M.D.

Professor of Pediatrics, University of Tennessee College
of Medicine; Director, Newborn Center, City of Memphis Hospital,
Memphis, Tennessee

With the editorial assistance of, and a chapter by

JEAN LANCASTER, R.N., M.N.

Associate Professor of Nursing of Children, University of
Tennessee College of Nursing; Clinical Supervisor of Nurses,
Newborn Center, City of Memphis Hospital,
Memphis, Tennessee

SECOND EDITION

with 113 illustrations

The C. V. Mosby Company

Saint Louis 1976

Second edition

Copyright © 1976 by The C. V. Mosby Company

Previous edition copyrighted 1972

Printed in the United States of America

Distributed in Great Britain by Henry Kimpton, London

Library of Congress Cataloging in Publication Data

Korones, Sheldon B
   High-risk newborn infants.

   Bibliography: p.
   Includes index.
   1. Infants (Newborn)—Diseases. 2. Pediatric
nursing. 3. Intensive care nursing. I. Title.
[DNLM: 1. Intensive care units. 2. Infant, Newborn,
Diseases—Nursing. WS420 K84h]
RJ254.K67 1976   618.9'201   75-43615
ISBN 0-8016-2736-2

CB/CB/B 9 8 7 6 5 4 3 2 1

To

The infants who suffered from our past inadequacies
and to those who will benefit from our newly acquired skills

AND

Judy and David and Susan, who motivate me;
and to my parents, who started everything

Preface

This second edition was written because advances in perinatal medicine have unfolded at a dizzy pace since publication of the first edition. It was also written to meet the increasingly sophisticated requirements of nurses in educational programs and those already in the field. The book is thus presented to keep its readers apace of recent developments and to keep apace of the development of its readers.

Like the first edition, the second is not intended as a "how-to-do-it" manual; neither is it offered as an encyclopedic reference. I have discussed the major topics of neonatal medicine with the unchanged conviction that although nurses are eager to know *what* must be done, they are more eager to know *why*. As in the first edition, I have attempted to maintain a narrative that is as conversational as the subject permits. Tables of data are presented when reasonably full exposition of a topic is impractical or when a tabulated summary of the accompanying narrative serves to implement the learning process.

This new edition is longer than its predecessor because material has been added throughout. Discussions are more extensive in the chapters devoted to the fetus, the relationship of birth weight and gestational age, and physical examination of the neonate. The chapter on respiration was virtually rewritten and considerably expanded. The discussion of thermoregulation, which appeared as a section in the first edition, has now been expanded into a separate chapter. I particularly enjoyed adding a substantial number of illustrations to enhance the effectiveness of corresponding discussions. The great majority of them were taken in our own unit. If there are any inadequacies in the photographs, I accept full responsibility for them; a long-standing compulsion to take all kinds of pictures was simply uncontrollable.

The preface is an appropriate place to record some personal observations on the role of the nurses for whom this book is written. Although the drama and genuine importance of equipment are inescapable, the reader will note throughout the book a relentless emphasis on the role of personnel. The role of the nurse cannot be an ancillary one. Intensive care is primarily a nursing activity. Without superb nursing, effective intensive care is impossible, the caliber of medical supervision notwithstanding. One need not work long in a neonatal intensive care unit to be fully convinced. I have been repeatedly gratified by the success of my own efforts when working with nurses whose performance was admirable by any standard. On the other hand, I have been frustrated by the futility of the same effort while working with nurses who could not perform at such a level.

The nurse is in a better position than anyone else to detect the subtle signs that often herald catastrophe. No one else can continuously provide and monitor the multiple facets of therapy that support the infant through critical illness. This is a big job. It cannot be done without understanding the bases of intensive care. Ventilatory support, oxygen therapy, and manipulation of the thermal environment, for example, cannot be performed reliably unless nurses have adequate knowledge of fundamentals. Without such knowledge, today's correct maneuvers may be performed only by chance and for the wrong reasons, whereas tomorrow the baby may not be so lucky; the maneuver may not be correct, for whatever reasons. The nurse's need to be well informed is no different from the physician's; in neonatal intensive care they are indeed colleagues.

The job is being done daily. It can be seen in hundreds of units in this country and in others, and more babies are now surviving because of it. The uninitiated nurse generally approaches the task with fear and trepidation; yet if scrupulous guidance is provided in a well-structured training program, nursing responsibilities are ultimately well met. The apprehensive and insecure become calm and confident. The uninformed become knowledgeable. The metamorphosis is something to behold, and this book is intended to implement it.

Books cannot be written or revised without the kindness and help of others. The task was eased and the deadline met because a number of individuals provided much-needed support.

Only a rare physician (and I am not one of them) could write a book like this without the guidance of an exemplary nurse such as Jean Lancaster, R.N., M.N. Her expert advice is an indispensable contribution for which I am deeply grateful. It is derived from her effective activities as Clinical Supervisor of Nurses in our unit. In this position she functions as teacher of nurses, caretaker of babies, counselor of parents, and mollifier of the unit's Director—for all of which I am even more grateful.

Drs. Loraine Evans, Fabien Eyal, and Charles Sarasohn relieved me of clinical responsibilities during the protracted period of time that was required to complete this revision. The numerous extra sleepless nights for which they spontaneously volunteered are reason enough for profound appreciation, but the friendship that motivated them was a particularly moving experience.

Through her capacity for gentle leadership, Ann Lamb, R.N., has steadfastly brought cohesion and stability to all the nursing functions in our unit. As Head Nurse, even before the inception of intensive care at this institution, she was the one primarily responsible for bringing to sick babies the best care that was then available. An unsurpassed intensive care nurse, the intelligent and compassionate example she sets has long been an object of my admiration.

I am indebted to Kathleen Ambrose and Marion Haynes for their expert handling of all the details that comprised the actual preparation of this manuscript. I am thankful for their forbearance in the face of repeated impositions and for the impressive, well-ordered manuscript they produced. Their uncanny ability to decipher hundreds of pages of my scribblings is a noteworthy feat in itself.

I mention Patti Lechman's art work because it is perfect and was produced just a few days after my urgent request.

Without exception, the comments of reviewers of the first edition were constructive. I have attempted to respond to most of their suggestions whenever possible.

My thanks to Doll. And thanks, too, to Susan Poo.

Sheldon B. Korones

Contents

Chapter 1
The fetus

NEONATAL DISORDERS, especially those which occur soon after birth, are usually the result of prenatal difficulties. Effective management of these illnesses requires familiarity with the intrauterine events that give rise to them. This chapter is concerned with the important aspects of fetal growth and function and the maternofetal relationships on which they depend.

THE PLACENTA: JUXTAPOSITION OF FETAL AND MATERNAL CIRCULATION

Fundamentally, the placenta provides bidirectional passage of substances between the mother and the fetus, whose circulations are contiguous but separate. The placenta is comprised of a maternal contribution called the decidua basalis and an embryonic one called the chorion. The maternal tissue contains uterine blood vessels, endometrial stroma, and glands; the embryonic tissue is composed of chorionic villi anchored to the chorionic plate.

The placenta (from Latin for "flat cake") is shaped like a round biscuit. At term it is about 15% of the fetal weight, approximately 6 to 8 inches in diameter, and 1 inch thick. Throughout pregnancy it occupies approximately one third of the inner surface of the uterus. One side, the fetal surface, is covered by glistening amniotic membrane, which receives the umbilical cord near its center. The

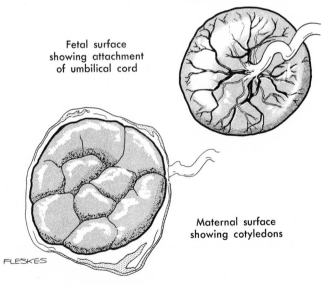

Fetal surface showing attachment of umbilical cord

Maternal surface showing cotyledons

FLESKES

Fig. 1-1. Maternal and fetal surfaces of the placenta. The cotyledons are visible on the maternal surface, which is implanted into the uterine wall. The fetal surface glistens, being covered by amnion. Branches of the umbilical vessels are on the fetal surface. (Modified from Netter: In Oppenheim, E., editor: Ciba collection of medical illustrations, vol. 2, Reproductive system, 1965.)

1

Fig. 1-2. Microscopic appearance of the villi in an intervillous space. Fetal capillaries permeate the villi, which are immersed in maternal blood within the intervillous spaces.

opposite side, the maternal surface, remains embedded in the uterine wall until it begins to separate during labor and is extruded during the third stage (Chapter 2). The placenta is composed of fifteen to twenty-eight grossly visible segments called cotyledons (Fig. 1-1), which are of identical structure and are separated from each other by connective tissue septa. Each cotyledon contains fetal vessels, chorionic villi, and an intervillous space. The dark red color of the placenta is due to fetal hemoglobin rather than to maternal blood, which is usually drained by the time the placenta is delivered. Thus, if the placenta appears pale, the fetus was significantly anemic.

Chorionic villi, intervillous space, and placental circulation

Within a week after implantation the embryo elaborates fingerlike projections of tissue known as the chorionic villi, which invade uterine endometrium at the site of implantation. They enlarge and branch considerably, becoming more deeply embedded into uterine tissue as they grow. Each of these projections is ultimately comprised of an outer layer of epithelial cells and a connective tissue core that contains fetal capillaries. During villous invasion of the endometrium, erosion of uterine vessels and supporting tissue occurs, and as a result irregular spaces are formed in the uterine wall. They are filled with maternal blood and surround the chorionic villi. These comprise the intervillous space, and the exchange of substances between maternal and fetal blood takes place at these sites. Transfer of any given substance from the maternal to the fetal circulation thus requires sequential passage from the mother's blood through the outer epithelial layer of the chorionic villus, through the connective tissue, and then through the endothelial wall of the capillary into fetal blood (Fig. 1-2). As pregnancy progresses, the villi decrease in size but increase considerably in number. This change in both size and number of villi provides a progressive increase in fetal surface area within the placenta for the greater needs of the growing fetus. The villous surface at term is estimated at 13 to 14 sq M, an area that is ten times greater than the total skin surface of the adult. This enhanced capacity for maternofetal exchange is further implemented by simultaneous thinning of the tissue layer in the villus, thus reducing the distance between fetal capillaries and the intervillous space.

Maternal blood in the uterine arteries enters the base of the intervillous spaces through spiral arterioles. At term there are approximately 100 arteries supplying the placenta. Spurting jets of oxygenated blood diffuse upward and laterally to surround the villi, passing out of the intervillous spaces in a deoxygenated state by way of venous orifices that are situated at the base of the

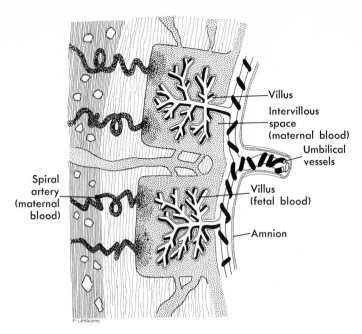

Fig. 1-3. Section through the placenta, showing the spiral arteries that supply maternal blood to the intervillous space, the branching villi immersed in the intervillous space, and the umbilical vessels that branch repeatedly to terminate as villous capillaries. (Modified from Netter: In Oppenheim, E., editor: Ciba collection of medical illustrations, vol. 2, Reproductive system, 1965.)

intervillous space adjacent to the spiral arteries. The direction of blood flow is normally maintained by an arteriovenous pressure gradient, that is, from higher arterial pressure to lower venous pressure (Fig. 1-3). Pressure in the spiral arteries is about 70 to 80 mm Hg. In the draining veins it is 8 mm Hg. Lateral flow between cotyledons is negligible.

Fetal blood leaves the body through two umbilical arteries that course through the umbilical cord to the placenta. Once they contact the fetal surface of the placenta, the arteries branch to supply each of the cotyledons. After continued branching and diminution in size, the vessels finally terminate in capillary loops within each chorionic villus. Villous blood receives oxygen from the maternal circulation, returns from capillary loops to venules, and goes thence to larger veins that leave each of the placental cotyledons. Coalescence of veins results in the formation of a single umbilical vein, which

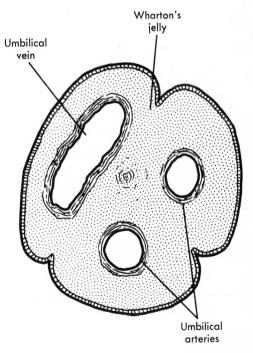

Fig. 1-4. Cross section of umbilical cord. The arteries have thick walls; the lumen of the vein is larger than those of the arteries, and its wall is thin.

passes from the placenta through the length of the umbilical cord to the body of the fetus. A cross section of the umbilical cord reveals two thick-walled muscular arteries and one vein. The vein is noticeably larger than the arteries, although it has a considerably thinner wall (Fig. 1-4). The umbilical vessels are surrounded by a white gelatinous material called Wharton's jelly.

FETAL CIRCULATION

Two major circuits, pulmonary and systemic, comprise the circulation in the fetus as well as in the adult. A third component, the placental circuit, is peculiar to the fetus. Pulmonary circulation begins at the pulmonic valve at the origin of the main pulmonary artery, which arises from the right ventricle. It continues through the lungs and terminates at the pulmonary vein orifices in the wall of the left atrium. The systemic circulation includes all other arterial and venous channels elsewhere in the body. The placental circuit is comprised of the umbilical and placental vessels as described earlier.

In any discussion of circulatory patterns a conceptual subdivision into "right" and "left" sides is often invoked. In the mature individual the right-sided circulation contains venous blood and the left side, arterial blood. Anatomically the right side begins at the venous end of capillary beds in all organs except the lungs. It continues through progressively enlarging veins to the inferior vena cava into the right atrium, to the right ventricle, into the pulmonary arteries, and finally to the pulmonary alveolar capillaries, where oxygenation occurs. Blood now continues on to the left side, which begins at the alveolar capillaries and progresses through the pulmonary veins into the left side of the heart, through the aorta to smaller arteries, and to the arterial side of capillary beds in all organs except the lungs. At the arterial side of the capillaries, blood gives up oxygen and continues to the venous side, where it reenters the right side of the circulation.

The normal mature circulation is characterized by flow of unoxygenated (venous) blood into the right side of the heart, which continues into the pulmonary circuit, where oxygenation occurs, and then returns to the left side of the heart for distribution to the rest of the body by way of the aorta. Thus the only connections between the right and left circulations are at the capillary beds in the lungs and in the capillaries of other organs of the body.

When, as in certain cardiovascular malformations, a connection between the right and left sides exists at sites other than the capillaries, an anatomic shunt is said to be present. Examples of such anomalies are persistent patency of the ductus arteriosus, arteriovenous aneurysm, and numerous malformations of the heart itself. Blood flow through an abnormal vascular channel from the venous to the arterial circulation constitutes a right-to-left shunt. Conversely, flow of blood through an anomalous channel from artery to vein is a left-to-right shunt. In either case blood enters one side of the circulation from the other before reaching the capillary bed for which it is normally destined, and the result is an admixture of oxygenated and unoxygenated blood.

Fetal circulation differs from the neonatal or adult pattern in three major respects: (1) presence of anatomic shunts, one within the heart at the foramen ovale, one immediately outside the heart in the ductus arteriosus, and another at the juncture of the ductus venosus and the inferior vena cava; (2) presence of a placental circulation; and (3) minimal blood flow through the lungs (3% to 7% of cardiac output).

The course of fetal circulation is as follows (Fig. 1-5): Blood that has been oxygenated in the chorionic villi leaves the placenta through the umbilical vein, which enters the fetal abdomen at the umbilicus and then courses between the right and left lobes of the liver. Some of this blood perfuses the liver through branches of the umbilical vein, whereas the rest continues past it to the ductus venosus and empties into the inferior vena cava at a point just below the diaphragm. Blood now enters the heart through

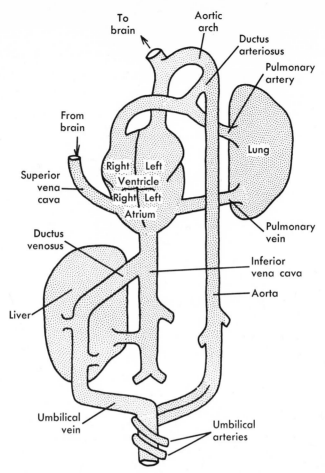

Fig. 1-5. Fetal circulation. (Modified from Lind, J., Stern, L., and Wegelius, C.: Human foetal and neonatal circulation, Springfield, Ill., 1964, Charles C Thomas, Publisher.)

the inferior vena caval orifice, where a direct communication exists between the right and left atria (foramen ovale). Here the caval bloodstream is divided, the major portion flowing directly into the left atrium, whereas the remainder enters the right atrium to join blood from the superior vena cava, which drains the head, neck, and upper extremities. The left atrium also receives blood that has perfused the lungs from pulmonary veins, and this mixture enters successively the left ventricle, the ascending aorta, and the aortic arch, from whence most of it is distributed to the coronary arteries and the vessels of the head and upper extremities.

The smaller quantity of blood directed to

the right atrium from the inferior vena cava is added to the superior vena caval flow, enters the right ventricle and then the main pulmonary artery. Most of it is conveyed to the descending aorta through the ductus arteriosus. Some continues through the pulmonary circuit to perfuse the lungs and return to the left atrium by way of the pulmonary veins. The descending aorta bifurcates at the lower end of the body into the right and left iliac arteries. The two hypogastric arteries are branches off the latter vessels. They each course upward around the bladder and leave the abdomen through the umbilical cord, where they are called the umbilical arteries.

Admixture of blood occurs at three sites

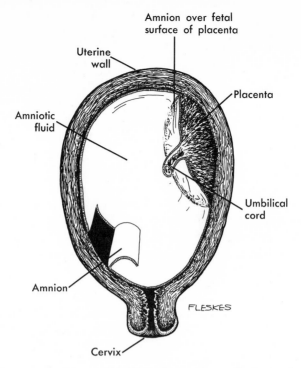

Fig. 1-6. Uterine cavity at term. The amnion lines the uterine wall. It continues over the placenta and reflects from it to envelop the umbilical cord. Amniotic fluid surrounds the fetus to fill the cavity. (Modified from Hillman, L. M., and Pritchard, J. A.: Williams obstetrics, ed. 14, New York, 1971, Appleton-Century-Crofts.)

in the fetal circulation: (1) the foramen ovale, (2) from the pulmonary artery to the descending aorta through the ductus arteriosus, and (3) at the junction of the ductus venosus and inferior vena cava.

THE AMNION AND AMNIOTIC FLUID

The amnion and the amniotic cavity develop in the embryo during the first week, appearing as a small elongated sac adjacent to the dorsal embryonic surface. As the fluid-filled cavity enlarges, it spreads around the embryo in all directions and ultimately comes to surround the fetus. This cavity is traversed only by the umbilical cord, which courses from the umbilicus to its insertion into the placenta. The amniotic membrane is 0.5 mm or less in thickness and is comprised of five microscopic layers. Fully developed, it lines the entire inner surface of the uterine wall, except at the site of placental attachment, where it covers the fetal surface of that

organ, reflects onto the umbilical cord, and completely envelops it (Fig. 1-6). The fluid that surrounds the fetus (amniotic fluid) is contained by this membrane, and when the latter ruptures at the onset of labor, the fluid is released.

Amniotic fluid accumulates progressively throughout pregnancy, attaining a volume of approximately 1000 ml at term (normal range: 400 to 1500 ml). It continuously enters and leaves the amniotic cavity, creating a constant turnover of approximately 600 ml/hr involving complex water and solute exchanges that have yet to be precisely delineated. Amniotic fluid is derived primarily from maternal serum and fetal urine. The latter constitutes the major source of amniotic fluid during the last half of pregnancy. Some fluid originates in the fetal lung. Egress of fluid occurs largely by absorption into the fetal bloodstream from the gastrointestinal tract, into which it gains entry as a result of repeated fetal swallowing. That the fetus swallows effectively has been shown often by amniography, a procedure that entails injection of radiopaque dye into the amniotic fluid for the primary purpose of demonstrating the site of placental implantation for the possible presence of placenta previa. At term, the fetus swallows 500 ml of amniotic fluid per hour. Normal volumes of amniotic fluid are thus largely regulated by contributions of the fetal urinary tract and evacuation through the gastrointestinal tract. Thus, if the elimination of fluid is obstructed, as in esophageal atresia, the quantity of fluid may be abnormally increased to more than 2000 ml. This increase is called *hydramnios* or *polyhydramnios*. Conversely, if little or no urine is excreted, as in renal agenesis, amniotic fluid may be virtually absent or greatly reduced in quantity. This abnormality is known as *oligohydramnios*.

Amniotic fluid affords a milieu that allows relatively free fetal movement. It protects the fetus from externally inflicted trauma, and it contributes to the stability of fetal body temperature. During early labor, hydrostatic forces created by uterine contractions are mediated by the fluid to aid in normal dilatation of the cervix and descent of the fetus.

MATERNOFETAL EXCHANGE OF GAS ACROSS THE PLACENTA

Fetal respiration occurs by transfer of oxygen from maternal blood in the intervillous space to fetal blood in the villous capillaries and by release of carbon dioxide in the opposite direction from fetus to mother. The normal flow of these gases is governed by their respective partial pressures in maternal and fetal blood and by unimpeded fetal and maternal blood flow in the placenta.

Gases have a tendency to expand, and they exert measurable pressure in the process. This pressure is expressed in millimeters of mercury (mm Hg). Thus pressure exerted by gases in the atmosphere at sea level is 760 mm Hg. In any mixture of two or more gases the pressure exerted by each of them is termed their partial pressure. The sum of

Table 1-1. Mean quantitative changes in fetal blood gases resulting from fetomaternal exchange*

	Umbilical artery (blood from fetus)	Intervillous space (maternal blood)	Umbilical vein (blood to fetus)
P_{O_2} (mm Hg)	16	40	29
P_{CO_2} (mm Hg)	46	38	42

*Based on data from Seeds, A. E.: Pediatr. Clin. North Am. 17:811, 1970.

the partial pressures of each constituent gas in a mixture is the total pressure exerted by that mixture. The expression symbolizing partial pressure of a gas is written P (or p) preceding its chemical formula. The partial pressures of oxygen and of carbon dioxide are written as P_{O_2} and P_{CO_2}. This terminology is utilized routinely in reports from clinical and research laboratories.

Assuming normal placental blood flow, the differences in the partial pressures of gases (P_{O_2}, P_{CO_2}) that exist between maternal and fetal blood determine the direction in which these gases move. Gases are transferred in response to pressure gradients, that is, from a higher pressure to a lower one. Tissues intervening between the maternal and fetal circulations (normally 3.5 to 5.5 microns in total thickness) seem to offer more resistance to the movement of oxygen than to carbon dioxide; the latter is thus considerably more diffusable. Table 1-1 gives P_{O_2} and P_{CO_2} values of fetal blood in the umbilical artery, maternal blood in the intervillous space, and fetal blood in the umbilical vein as reported by a number of investigators. The acquisition of oxygen and the surrender of carbon dioxide by fetal blood are indicated in the alterations of P_{O_2} and P_{CO_2} that result from the exchange of gases with maternal blood in the intervillous space. The influence of partial pressure gradients can be appreciated by noting, in Table 1-1, that a higher maternal P_{O_2} in the intervillous space moves oxygen into the fetal circulation to raise P_{O_2} from 16 mm Hg in the umbilical artery to 29 mm Hg in blood returning to the fetus via the umbilical vein. The flow of oxygen is therefore from mother to fetus. The direction of carbon dioxide transfer is from fetus to mother because P_{CO_2} in the intervillous space (38 mm Hg in maternal blood) is lower than in the umbilical artery (46 mm Hg in fetal blood) ; thus carbon dioxide moves from fetus to mother with a resultant diminution of P_{CO_2} in the umbilical vein (42 mm Hg) compared to that in the umbilical artery (46 mm Hg).

Maintenance of these pressure gradients depends on normal maternal blood gas levels and normal blood flow in the mother and fetus. A number of disorders may alter maternal blood gas levels sufficiently to hamper gas exchange at the intervillous space. Thus severe pneumonia, asthma, congestive heart failure, and apnea during convulsions (epilepsy, eclampsia) may result in maternal hypoxemia that endangers the fetus. Impairment of blood flow to the intervillous space may occur as a consequence of maternal shock or congestive heart failure. Local impediment to placental perfusion may result from abnormally intense and frequent uterine contractions during labor or from compression of the inferior vena cava by the overlying heavy uterus when the mother is supine (supine hypotension syndrome).

FETAL GROWTH

Growth of the fetus involves an increase in the number of cells (hyperplasia) and an increase in their size (hypertrophy). Growth progresses through three stages: (1) hyperplasia, (2) a declining rate of hyperplasia with increasing hypertrophy, and (3) predominant hypertrophy. Embryonic growth is largely hyperplastic; hypertrophy becomes increasingly prominent later in pregnancy. Growth may be impeded during any or all of these progressive stages, resulting in different types of growth failure. Thus the number of cells may be diminished although their size remains relatively normal, or cell size rather than quantity may be reduced, or

both size and number may be diminished. The net result is subnormal size and weight of affected organs. These effects are dependent on the stage of growth during which an insult is inflicted. For example, intrauterine rubella infection, which occurs early in pregnancy, produces a severe reduction in the quantity of cells in many organs. On the other hand, the effects of toxemia, which often appear late in pregnancy, are characterized by a significant reduction in cell size, although cell number is relatively normal. All these changes have been produced in pregnant animals that were starved at various stages of pregnancy. Interference with cellular proliferation (hyperplastic growth) may cause a permanent diminution in the quantity of cells, although impaired hypertrophy is apparently reversible to some extent if proper feeding is instituted after birth. There is evidence that these phenomena may also be operative in humans. The human brain continues to grow by cellular proliferation for at least 8 postnatal months after 40 gestational weeks. Postnatal malnutrition impairs this process. Whether maternal malnutrition permanently limits organ growth in humans has yet to be documented. Data from animal studies and clinical observations of human infants suggest that permanent limitation of growth does indeed occur.

The characteristics of normal cellular growth are of importance in understanding the abnormalities of birth weight and size that are peculiar to prematurity and intrauterine growth retardation. (These details are discussed in Chapter 5.)

ASSESSMENT OF FETAL STATUS (FETAL DIAGNOSIS)

The growing ability to assess fetal conditions in utero continues to be one of the most exciting areas of advance in perinatology. The diagnosis of certain disorders of the fetus is feasible; approximation of fetal maturation is aided significantly by examination of chemical and cellular constituents of amniotic fluid and by accurate estimation of fetal head size. Identification of hypoxic stress in utero is possible by monitoring fetal heart rate and by sampling specimens for blood gas and pH determinations. The overall health of the fetus is assessable by estriol determination. The diagnosis of placenta previa can be made by amniography (injection of radiopaque dye into the amniotic cavity) or by ultrasound to demonstrate placental position. Postnatal microscopic examination of the amniotic membrane and the umbilical cord for the presence of neutrophilic infiltration has been used to determine the presence of fetal exposure to intrauterine bacterial infection (Chapter 12). Insofar as intrauterine therapy is concerned, transfusion is the only procedure currently in common use. A description of the most widely utilized methods for fetal diagnosis and assessment follows.

Examination of amniotic fluid

Amniocentesis. Amniotic fluid may be withdrawn simply and safely by amniocentesis, that is, insertion of a needle through the abdominal and uterine walls into the amniotic cavity. Amniocentesis has been performed as early as the twelfth gestational week. Amniotic fluid components can be analyzed for the severity of erythroblastosis (Rh incompatibility); for predictions of postnatal appearance of hyaline membrane disease, certain genetic disorders, and inborn errors of metabolism; and for fetal age. Although the complications of amniocentesis are uncommon, a variety of them have been reported. These risks include abortion, maternal hemorrhage, infection, fetal puncture wounds, pneumothorax, laceration of the fetal spleen, damage to placental and umbilical vessels, and sudden death from fetal exsanguination.

Bilirubin. Determination of bilirubin in amniotic fluid is valuable for assessment of the severity of Rh disease. Bilirubin is derived from the breakdown of red blood cells (Chapter 10), and it is thus present at certain levels in normal amniotic fluid. Peak levels are attained between 16 and 30 weeks of gestation, and a steady decline thereafter usually culminates in its disappearance by 36 weeks. In most instances there is no bilirubin in amniotic fluid beyond 36 weeks of gestation. This finding is variable, however, and bilirubin determination is not valuable for estimation of fetal maturity. If, as in fetal erythroblastosis, an excessive rate of hemolysis occurs, bilirubin levels in amniotic fluid rise abnormally. These values are plotted on a graph that delineates three zones of fetal involvement (mild, moderate, and severe), depending on the bilirubin concentration. If the results indicate severe disease, an intrauterine transfusion or an immediate termination of pregnancy is urgently indicated. If moderate involvement is present, repeated frequent determinations are required to monitor the course of fetal disease. Values falling into the zone of mild involvement contraindicate intrauterine transfusion or interruption of pregnancy, since postnatal therapy is effective in these circumstances. The amniotic fluid of hyperbilirubinemic mothers often contains abnormally increased amounts of bilirubin, even in the absence of Rh disease.

Creatinine. Levels of creatinine in the amniotic fluid increase with gestational age and are thus useful in the assessment of fetal maturity. Creatinine in amniotic fluid is derived from fetal urine. It is excreted through the kidneys across the glomeruli, which increase substantially in number during the third trimester. Thus it is reasonable to expect that creatinine levels will rise steadily as pregnancy progresses. In normal pregnancies, 1.6 to 1.8 mg/100 ml of creatinine is indicative of 36 or 37 gestational weeks in approximately 94% of patients. However, the usefulness of this determination for estimation of fetal age is unfortunately limited in complicated pregnancies. Thus, in toxemic mothers, amniotic fluid creatinine concentrations are often misleadingly higher than in normal pregnancies of like duration. The toxemic gravida's impaired kidney function causes some degree of creatinine retention, and therefore her serum level is elevated. This increase is reflected in amniotic fluid as an inappropriately high creatinine concentration, which may suggest fetal maturity when in fact the fetus is premature. Higher-than-expected values have been observed in diabetic mothers. On the other hand in Rh disease amniotic fluid creatinine concentration may be lower than expected. For these reasons *the critical question of fetal age cannot be consistently answered solely by determination of amniotic fluid-creatinine concentration.*

Lecithin-sphingomyelin ratio (L/S ratio). In the fetal lung, fluid is secreted into the alveoli, and it is ultimately deposited into amniotic fluid after migration up the respiratory tract and out the glottic opening into the posterior pharynx. This secretion contains surfactant, a complex substance that is comprised of several phospholipids, which lowers surface tension forces of alveolar walls (Chapter 8). This function is indispensable for initial opening of the alveoli during the first breath and for prevention of alveolar collapse (atelectasis) subsequently. Deficiency of sur-

factant results in the widespread atelectasis that characterizes hyaline membrane disease. The demonstration, in amniotic fluid prenatally, of sufficient surfactant to preclude hyaline membrane disease postnatally is one of the most helpful and reliable of all intrauterine tests for fetal maturity. This procedure actually indicates the maturational status of fetal lungs—that is, the capacity of the lungs to accommodate normal ventilation after birth. There is no consistent relationship between fetal weight, age, and pulmonary maturity. Up to 10% of mature fetuses have been reported to have low L/S ratios, whereas normal ratios have been reported in premature fetuses.

The principal constituent of surfactant is lecithin; it comprises 50% to 75% of surfactant phospholipids. Its presence in relation to sphingomyelin is expressed as a ratio that usually changes predictability as pregnancy progresses. Surface-active lecithin appears in significant quantities at 22 to 24 weeks of gestation, at which time concentra-

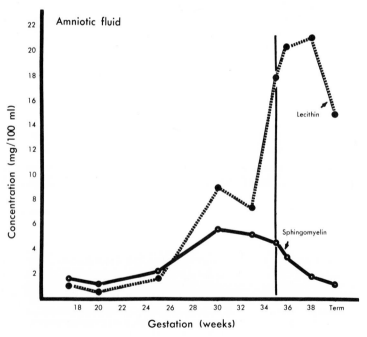

Fig. 1-7. Lecithin (broken line) and sphingomyelin (solid line) concentrations plotted against gestational age. L/S ratio rises to 1.2 at 28 weeks, and to 2 or more at 35 weeks, indicating little chance of hyaline membrane disease postnatally. (From Gluck, L., Kulovich, M. V., Borer, R. C., Jr., Brenner, P. H., Anderson, G. G., and Spellacy, W. N.: Am. J. Obstet. Gynecol. **109:**440, 1971.)

tions are very slightly above those of sphingomyelin. Before this time, very little lecithin is measurable; afterward lecithin increases while sphingomyelin concentration remains relatively unchanged. Between 28 and 32 weeks lecithin concentrations rise slightly to 1.2 times greater than that of sphingomyelin (L/S ratio = 1.2). At 35 weeks an abrupt rise in lecithin to at least twice the concentration of sphingomyelin (ratio = 2 or more) signifies pulmonary maturity; this virtually assures that hyaline membrane disease will not occur after birth. Fig. 1-7 depicts the quantitative changes of lecithin and sphingomyelin. It illustrates that the relationship between lecithin and sphingomyelin in amniotic fluid provides a basis for the assessment of fetal pulmonary maturity.

L/S ratios correlate well with gestational age in normal pregnancies. In high-risk pregnancies the correlation is not so straightforward. Lung maturity, as indicated by L/S ratio, may occur early or late in gestation, depending on the existing maternal disorder. For example, a 3300-gram infant at 38 weeks of gestation has been reported with a ratio of only 0.75, whereas a 920-gram infant at 28 weeks had a normal mature ratio. The older and larger infant had severe hyaline membrane disease, but the smaller infant did not. Following is a list of maternal diseases that have been shown to alter the normal developmental schedule of pulmonary maturity; that is, the attainment of an L/S ratio of 2 or more was either accelerated (pulmonary maturity before 35 weeks) or delayed (pulmonary maturity after 35 weeks).

DISORDERS ASSOCIATED WITH ALTERATION FROM NORMAL TIME OF APPEARANCE OF MATURE L/S RATIO*

Mature ratio before 35 gestational weeks (accelerated maturation)
A. Maternal disorders
    1. Toxemia (early onset)
    2. Hypertensive renal disease

    3. Hypertensive cardiovascular disease
    4. Sickle cell disease
    5. Narcotic addiction
    6. Diabetes, class D, E, F (p. 207)
    7. Chronic retroplacental hemorrhage
B. Fetal disorders
    1. Premature rupture of membranes

Mature ratio after 35 gestational weeks (delayed maturation)
A. Maternal disorders
    1. Diabetes, class A, B, C (p. 207)
    2. Chronic glomerulonephritis
B. Fetal disorders
    1. Hydrops fetalis
    2. Smaller of identical twins (nonparasitic)

Numerous variables may affect the outcome of predictions of pulmonary maturity based on the L/S ratio. Some have already been demonstrated, and extensive investigation will no doubt unearth others. The presence of maternal blood in amniotic fluid tends to lower the L/S ratio. Thus a mature ratio in bloody fluid is a valid result; an immature ratio may be artifactual. In some instances a ratio of 2 or more may be associated with postnatal hyaline membrane disease due to events that transpire after collection of the sample. Thus among 425 pregnancies observed in one study, 13 infants whose ratios were normal had respiratory distress after birth nevertheless. Twelve of these babies had a low Apgar score at 5 minutes (less than 7), reflecting intrauterine or intrapartum stress that occurred subsequent to the L/S ratio determination. This acute distress may have impaired surfactant activity and therefore induced the occurrence of hyaline membrane disease.

As data accumulate, new insights will evolve regarding accuracies and errors in the predictive value of the ratio. This amniotic fluid analysis is currently indispensable as an aid in deciding whether or not the fetus of a high-risk pregnancy is safer in the uterus or outside of it. In general, a ratio of 2 or more predicts the absence of hyaline membrane disease with only occasional inaccuracy. An Apgar score of less than 7 at 5 minutes may be an important influence on such erroneous predictions. On the other

*Modified from Gluck, L., and Kulovich, M. V.: Am. J. Obstet. Gynecol. 115:589, 1973.

hand, a ratio of less than 2 does not predict the occurrence of hyaline membrane disease as reliably as the ratio greater than 2 predicts its absence. Hyaline membrane disease does not occur in a substantial number of premature infants whose ratios are low.

Shake test. The shake test, or foam test, is a simple procedure that attempts to correlate mature or immature L/S ratios (or absolute lecithin content) with the presence or absence of foam in prepared samples of amniotic fluid. The sample is mixed with ethanol and shaken for 15 seconds; a reading is made 15 minutes later. The test depends on the ability of lecithin to create a stable foam in ethanol. A positive result is produced by a complete ring of bubbles at the surface that persists for 15 minutes. It appears to be a reliable indication of pulmonary maturity. Hyaline membrane disease has rarely followed a positive foam test. The absence of foam suggests that hyaline membrane disease will occur, but such absence is not as reliably predictive as the low L/S ratio itself. Therefore the shake test is a good screening procedure for maturity (positive for foam), but in the absence of foam an L/S ratio should be performed.

Cellular examination to assess fetal maturity. Toward the latter phase of pregnancy, fat-laden cells from fetal skin are exfoliated into amniotic fluid in increasing numbers as term is approached. These cells are thought to originate from the sebaceous glands of fetal skin. Lipid in cells is identified by the presence of orange-red droplets on microscopic examination after application of 0.1% Nile blue sulfate solution. Gross groupings according to the percentage of fat-laden cells have been correlated with gestational ages. There is general agreement that differing results from numerous investigations cast doubt on the value of the test. Several investigators have combined the cellular analysis with other tests, such as those for creatinine and bilirubin, with some improvement in results. In one report, when 20% or more of the counted cells contained fat, all infants were mature at birth. In another investiga-

tion, all infants were over 36 weeks when the percentage was 10 or greater; however, low percentages of lipid-laden cells falsely indicated prematurity in a number of infants who were actually mature. The technique of staining may itself alter results considerably. Individual laboratories should carefully analyze their experience before placing reliance on this procedure.

Cellular examination for genetic abnormalities. Since the cells in amniotic fluid are of fetal origin, they have been subjected to intensive study in efforts to identify certain genetically transmitted disorders as early in gestation as possible. Fetal involvement, or absence of it, has been correctly predicted in case reports of galactosemia, cystic fibrosis, glycogen storage disease, Marfan's syndrome, and numerous other infrequently encountered disorders. In addition, fetal sex determination is valuable in assessing the risk of sex-linked hereditary abnormalities such as hemophilia, which is manifest only in males. By demonstrating chromatin bodies in the nuclei, and thus identifying a female, the risk of hemophilia can be excluded; the absence of chromatin bodies in a sufficient number of cells indicates a male fetus and thus a 50% risk of having an affected baby.

Meconium-stained fluid. The incidence of meconium staining of amniotic fluid is reported to vary from 0.5% to 10.9% of all births. It occurs most often in babies delivered at term; premature infants are infrequently involved. Stained fluid usually indicates intrauterine stress.

The release of meconium by the fetus is said to occur in response to hypoxia, but this has not been confirmed since it was reported in 1954. The hypothesized mechanism of release involves increased peristalsis of the intestine and relaxation of the anal sphincter in response to hypoxic stress.

The most direct postnatal consequence of meconium release into amniotic fluid is the massive aspiration syndrome. Particles of meconium are drawn deeply into the respiratory tract in utero; the resultant postnatal distress is often sufficiently severe to require mechanical ventilatory support. Prolonged illness is not unusual; occasionally death ensues. The syndrome occurs predominantly in term infants (p. 164).

Presence of meconium in the amniotic fluid of an apparently healthy infant sometimes indicates transient intrauterine hypoxia that is of no ultimate significance to the infant's status at birth. The staining of fetal tissue (nails, skin, umbilical cord) probably indicates that meconium was released into the amniotic fluid at least 4 to 6 hours previously.

Estriol levels in maternal urine

Estriol, a major metabolite of estrogen, is found in relatively large quantities in maternal urine during the latter half of pregnancy. The fetal contribution to maternal urinary estriol concentration is ten times as great as the maternal contribution. Estriol is a valuable indicator of fetal health because its synthesis requires a normal placenta and fetal adrenal cortex. From the placenta it crosses into the maternal blood and eventually is excreted through the kidneys as estriol glucuronide. Intact function of both the fetal adrenal and the placenta are required for excretion of normal quantities of estriol. In pregnancies that are complicated by hypertension, renal disease, or preeclampsia, normal estriol values are a good indication that the fetus is in no danger at the moment. In Rh sensitization, low values are a particularly ominous finding; perinatal mortality up to 65% has been reported in such circumstances. In diabetes low values are a sign of fetal jeopardy, but here the correlation is not always straightforward, since normal findings do not necessarily indicate fetal health. Estriol concentrations are lowest when the fetus is dead or anencephalic. Anencephaly is regularly associated with absence of the fetal adrenal cortex; since there is no fetal adrenocortical function even if the placenta is intact, maternal urinary estriol is absent. Administered to the mother during gestation, steroids cross the placenta to depress fetal adrenal function. Intact activity of the adrenal-placental axis is impaired, and estriol formation is reduced by as much as 50%.

Urinary estriol increases as pregnancy progresses. There is some correlation between length of gestation and estriol determinations, but exceptions are sufficiently frequent to impair utilization of this test for determination of fetal maturity. Its use for monitoring fetal well-being is widespread and valid.

Urinary estriol assay has a significant logistic disadvantage in that a 24-hour urine collection is required. The time consumed in collection and the dependence on recovery of complete daily output impose some limitation on the procedure. Plasma determination may well replace urinary assay because only a single specimen is essential, and serial determinations on several blood samples are possible over a short time interval. At present, laboratory methods for plasma determination are cumbersome and time-consuming; this is the principal obstacle to widespread use of plasma for this purpose. Together with other laboratory determinations and careful clinical evaluations, urinary estriol determination is a valuable *adjunct* for identification of fetal illness.

Fetal heart rate monitoring

Although 60% to 75% of the fetuses who have difficulty during labor can be identified beforehand on the basis of the high-risk grouping of their mothers, the remainder cannot be similarly anticipated. Thus any healthy fetus of a healthy mother can be sufficiently stressed during labor as to threaten intact survival. The realization that electronic surveillance can rapidly detect the inception of fetal distress has resulted in widespread efforts to monitor the labor of as many women as possible for unanticipated fetal difficulty, regardless of their normal histories. It has been estimated that continuous fetal monitoring can reduce perinatal mortality and brain damage among survivors by 50% and that universal intrapartum monitoring in a hospital of 3000 deliveries annually would cost each maternity patient only $35.50. Monitoring of fetal heart rate (FHR) is currently the most valuable available method for this purpose. Continuous beat-to-beat recording of fetal heart action in relation to uterine contractions provides reliable data on the status of the fetus during labor. Ultimately this information furnishes a basis on which the obstetrician can decide whether to allow labor to progress to delivery from below, or whether to perform a cesarean section. The traditional intermittent auscul-

tation of fetal heart tones with stethoscope to ears is grossly inadequate by contemporary standards, even when performed every 10 or 15 minutes.

As usually performed, the monitoring procedure involves placement of an electrode on the presenting fetal part (usually the scalp) for reception of a cardiac signal, and insertion of a catheter into the amniotic space for recording uterine contractions. This internal technique is limited to women in

Fig. 1-8. The three major patterns of decelerated fetal heart rates. Note the relationship of onset and end of bradycardia to increased intrauterine pressures (contractions). *FHR,* Fetal heart rate; *UC,* uterine contraction; *HC,* head compression; *UPI,* uteroplacental insufficiency; *CC,* cord compression. See text for full explanation. (From Hon, E. H.: An introduction to fetal heart rate monitoring, Los Angeles, 1973, University of Southern California Press.)

labor. Both measurements can be made externally, from the maternal abdominal wall, but the internal method is more accurate. As external methods have improved, however, monitoring of the fetus has become more feasible earlier in labor or prior to its onset. Early evaluation of the fetal heart rate before the inception of labor predicts the fetus' capacity to withstand it.

Records of fetal heart rate patterns during labor reflect transient acceleration, transient deceleration, tachycardia, bradycardia, and variability of millisecond intervals between each heartbeat.

The most frequent significant heart rate changes involve three types of deceleration that are categorized according to their timing with uterine contractions and the shape of the recorded waveform (Fig. 1-8).

Early deceleration (Type I dip). Early deceleration (Type I dip) is probably due to fetal head compression (HC) during contractions. The resultant increased intracranial pressure activates impulses from the medulla through the vagus nerve to the heart, with consequent slowing of cardiac rate. The deceleration begins simultaneously with the onset of uterine contractions; it ceases at the end of the contraction. The waveform on the tracing is similar from one period of deceleration to the next. The heart rate remains in the normal range (120 to 160 beats/min). This pattern does not seem to have clinical significance. It usually occurs when the cervix is dilated 4 to 7 cm. It has not been associated with increased neonatal mortality or morbidity, or with alterations in fetal blood pH that would indicate distress. This fetal response to uterine contraction has been modified experimentally by administration of atropine, which is known to block the transmission of impulses through the vagus nerve.

Late deceleration (Type II dip). *Late deceleration* (Type II dip) is thought to indicate uteroplacental insufficiency (UPI). It is an ominous pattern in which the onset of decelerated fetal heart rate occurs *after* the onset of contraction, reaching its slowest rate after the contraction has ended. Thus the temporal relationship of this deceleration to uterine contraction differs from that of *early deceleration*. The shape of the waveform is similar, however. Even though diminished from baseline, the heart rate is usually within normal limits. This type of recording indicates fetal hypoxia due to diminished maternal blood flow through the intervillous space. Animal experiments have demonstrated the association of late deceleration with lowered fetal arterial P_{O_2}. The deceleration can be abolished or diminished by administering high oxygen concentrations to the mother. The *late deceleration* pattern is often noted in pregnancies that are complicated by diabetes, toxemia, hypertension, Rh disease, maternal hypotension in the supine position, and hypertonicity of the uterus due to excessive oxytocin. Delay in the appearance of fetal cardiac deceleration relative to a uterine contraction ("lag time") is probably a function of the transit time of poorly oxygenated blood from fetal villi to the placenta to the central fetal circulation. In *early deceleration* there is no such delay. Pressure exerted on the fetal head by the uterine contraction stimulates impulses through the vagus nerve that are instantaneously transmitted to the heart. Deceleration and contraction are thus synchronous, since the circulation is not involved and there is no transit or "lag" time. Also, in contrast to *early deceleration,* this delayed variety is often associated with fetal acidosis, lowered P_{O_2}, elevated P_{CO_2}, and low Apgar scores. *Late deceleration* cannot be eliminated by atropine, but it can be improved by oxygen administration to the mother or by correction of any of the detectable causes of diminished placental blood flow. The lowered cardiac rate that characterizes *late deceleration* is directly related to suboptimal oxygenation of fetal blood, however transient it may be.

Variable deceleration (Type 0 dip). *Variable deceleration* (Type 0 dip) bears no temporal relation to uterine contractions. It is the most common deceleration pattern, occurring in approximately 50% of all records. Its onset may be early or late in relation to uterine contractions. In contrast to the two previously described patterns, this waveform is irregular. The record shows an abrupt fall in heart rate to below 100 beats/min and an equally abrupt rise to preexisting levels (baseline). *Variable deceleration* is thought to result from intermittent compression of the cord between fetal parts. Short periods of compression seem to be benign, but prolonged periods of obstructed blood flow through the cord may cause severe hypoxia and acidosis. These episodes of deceleration can often be eliminated by change in maternal position to alter the relationships between the cord, the fetal parts involved in compression, and the uterine wall.

• • •

The usefulness of assessment according to the above categories is indicated by the reported predictive value of the data. Normal heart rate patterns recorded 30 minutes or less before delivery are associated with normal 5-minute Apgar scores in approximately 99% of the babies studied. Abnormal patterns are not as specifically predictive. Although virtually every baby who is depressed at birth has had an abnormal fetal heart rate, only 20% of the ominous deceleration patterns (late and severe variable decelerations) were associated with low Apgar scores. In many instances, therefore, an abnormal record is not indicative of poor fetal outcome. The significance of such records can be verified by pH analysis of fetal blood. Currently there seems to be little disagreement that all high-risk pregnancies should be monitored during labor and that all women who receive oxytocin should also be monitored. Since equipment for noninvasive (external) monitoring seems to be effective, universal monitoring of the apparently normal fetus is feasible. How much benefit will be derived therefrom has not yet been documented.

Oxytocin challenge test (contraction stress test)

The oxytocin challenge test (OCT) is widely used in the prelabor patient to deter-

mine the extent of reserve placental function during uterine contractions. By assessing fetal heart rate patterns in response to this stress test, a prediction can be made in regard to the safety with which the fetus will withstand labor.

Each uterine contraction during normal spontaneous or stimulated labor decreases blood flow in the intervillous space to some degree. If placental reserve is adequate, the normal fetus will not be stressed significantly, since in this instance diminished blood flow in the intervillous space does not impair fetal oxygen supply. The fetal heart rate patterns will thus be normal. If, however, placental circulation is marginal or impaired in the resting state, decreased blood flow in the intervillous space during uterine contractions will diminish fetal oxygen supply. The resultant stress is reflected in a fetal heart rate pattern of *late deceleration.*

The adult cardiologist has for years tested reserve function of the heart by subjecting the patient to exercise while recording the electrocardiogram. Potential catastrophe is demonstrable during such stress even though a perfectly normal electrocardiogram is produced in the resting state. The oxytocin challenge test imposes the same conditions on the fetus before the onset of labor, in an attempt to predict whether there will be jeopardy after labor begins. During the procedure, fetal heart rate is recorded for 15 to 30 minutes in the maternal resting state. Oxytocin is then administered intravenously to the mother at a constant rate of 0.5 mU/min, after which it is gradually increased until three firm uterine contractions occur within 10 minutes. The test is positive (indicating impending fetal danger during labor) if at least two episodes of *late deceleration* are produced. The test is negative if the fetal heart rate is stable and there is no evidence of deceleration. If labor begins within 6 or 7 days after the test, a negative result predicts fetal survival in all instances, and absence of asphyxia during labor in the vast majority. One study demonstrated a low 1-minute Apgar score in only 10% and survival in 100% of infants whose prelabor test was negative. Of the tests that were positive, 78% of the outcomes were abnormal (stillbirth, asphyxia at birth, and signs of chronic placental insufficiency). It appears at this time that the oxytocin challenge test is safe and reliable, even though final conclusions must await accumulation of a considerably greater amount of data.

Studies of the *fetus at rest,* without stimulating uterine contractions before onset of labor, have also been encouraging. The appearance of evanescent acceleration of the heart rate during fetal movement has in itself predicted a negative oxytocin challenge test in all instances. The fetus is compromised if there are no heart rate accelerations during periods of spontaneous movement; the subsequent oxytocin challenge test is usually positive.

Fetal blood sampling

Fetal acid-base balance and blood gas content depend on the status of gas exchange across the placenta. When fetoplacental exchange is disrupted for any reason, blood oxygen tension (P_{O_2}) falls, carbon dioxide tension (P_{CO_2}) rises, and pH falls. Usually disruption of gas exchange is the result of inadequate placental blood flow (hypoperfusion). The disorders that are most frequently associated with diminished placental perfusion are toxemia, maternal hypotension due to supine hypotension syndrome, hemorrhage, anesthesia, umbilical cord compression, and hyperactive uterine contractions. The decline in pH is a consequence of fetal attempts to maintain energy needs by metabolizing glycogen to glucose in hypoxic circumstances (anaerobic glycolysis). This emergency metabolic pathway causes lactic acid accumulation, which results in metabolic acidosis. The decline in fetal blood pH is also due to accumulation of carbon dioxide because of impaired placental gas exchange, and the result is respiratory acidosis. These acid-base imbalances are discussed in Chapter 7. These changes can be demonstrated and usefully applied to fetal management during labor by sampling capillary blood from the presenting fetal part, usually the scalp. The pH, rather than blood gas content, has been found to correlate best with intrauterine status and with the infant's condition at birth because blood gas changes have a greater tendency to be transient. Several studies have established the comparability of fetal capillary blood pH with that of the umbilical vessels; the collection of capillary blood from the presenting fetal part (usually the scalp) is thus a valid sampling procedure. The technique is simple, and undesirable side effects are rare. Excessive bleeding from the scalp may occur in utero and postnatally, occasionally requiring sutures to the scalp incision after birth. Compression of the collection site usually controls bleeding. Scalp abscess has also been reported as a complication.

Normally, fetal capillary blood pH is approximately 7.35 during the first stage of labor and approximately 7.25 during the second stage. Values below 7.20 correlate with fetal and neonatal distress. Normal P_{O_2} is 18 to 22 mm Hg, P_{CO_2} is 40 to 50 mm Hg, and base deficit may vary from 0 to 10 mEq/L. Serial determinations are required during all stages of labor if the dynamic changes of fetal distress are to be appreciated; single values are misleading. If a pH between 7.20 and 7.25 is present, repeated sampling is necessary. If pH is below 7.20 in two or more specimens, interference with labor is usually required. In approximately 10% of fetuses, blood pH does not accurately predict condition at birth; that is, a low pH in utero may be followed by normal postnatal status, or a normal pH may be followed by the birth of a distressed infant. Maternal acidosis (transmitted to the fetus) is the most frequent misleading circumstance in which a low fetal pH is followed by delivery of a normal infant. Maternal acidosis may result from inadequate fluid therapy during labor or from prolonged labor and excessive muscular effort. Thus, if fetal pH is low, maternal acid-base status must be determined before interference with labor is seriously contemplated.

Obviously all labors cannot be monitored by fetal blood sampling. Preselection of pa-

Fig. 1-9. Ultrasonic picture (longitudinal scan) of breech presentation at 30 weeks. *FH,* Fetal head; *ML,* midline of head; *SP,* sacral promontory; *S,* sacrum. (From Thompson, H. E.: Clin. Obstet. Gynecol. **17:**1, 1974.)

Fig. 1-10. Transverse scan of twin pregnancy taken at level of fetal thoraces *(FT).* The heads are not shown, since they are 12 cm above the level of the thoraces on this transverse view. (From Thompson, H. E.: Clin. Obstet. Gynecol. **17:**1, 1974.)

Fig. 1-11. Anencephaly, breech position. Echoes from the small cranial structure *(C)* are seen with the fetal trunk and thorax *(FT)* because this scan is longitudinal. (From Thompson, H. E.: Clin. Obstet. Gynecol. **17:**1, 1974.)

tients for this procedure is based on a history that suggests high-risk pregnancy or on the sudden unanticipated appearance of fetal stress during labor, as indicated by abnormal fetal heart rate patterns. Ominous fetal heart rate patterns plus abnormalities of fetal scalp blood pH are often associated with poor fetal outcome (low Apgar scores), diminished neonatal survival, and increased incidence of subsequent neurologic deficit among survivors.

Fetal scalp sampling and continuous fetal heart monitoring together comprise the most effective available procedures for intrapartum surveillance. Fetal heart responses may be an indication for scalp blood analysis, which in turn provides critical information for interpretation of the significance of abnormal heart rate patterns.

Ultrasound

Ultrasonic diagnosis is a useful method for assessment of fetal maturity and growth. It is also helpful in the demonstration of fetal presentation (Fig. 1-9), multiple pregnancy (Fig. 1-10), certain fetal anomalies (Fig. 1-11), fetal death, and localization of the placenta. It is an attractive diagnostic tool because the need for radiologic diagnosis (and its radiation hazards) is eliminated; it produces no maternal discomfort, and it is apparently not harmful to the fetus.

The procedure involves rebound (echo) of very high frequency sound waves from the interfaces of various tissue layers. The reflected sound waves are converted to visible signals on a screen and are then photographed for a permanent record. The sound waves are transmitted at extremely short intervals (pulses) from an ultrasound scanner that is in direct contact with the maternal abdominal wall. Parts of these waves are reflected back to the apparatus as they cross boundaries of different tissues; the remainder continue to penetrate more deeply, and they in turn are reflected as they cross deeper tissue interfaces. Echoes of sound waves are displayed as hundreds of spots of light that

Fig. 1-12. Normal nonpregnant structures, transverse scan. *Aw,* Abdominal wall; *Ub,* urinary bladder; *Ut,* uterus; *V,* vertebral body. The urinary bladder and uterus are non–echo-producing structures. The vertebra is an inverted U. (From Thompson, H. E.: Clin. Obstet. Gynecol. **17:**1, 1974.)

Fig. 1-13. Normal nonpregnant structures, longitudinal scan. *Ut,* Uterus; *Ub,* urinary bladder; *S,* symphysis pubis; *B,* bowel. Bladder and uterus are cystic and non–echo-producing; they are situated below the symphysis pubis. Bowel is nondescript pattern. (From Thompson, H. E.: Clin. Obstet. Gynecol. **17:**1, 1974.)

Fig. 1-14. Echogram (longitudinal section) of embryo at 9 weeks' menstrual age. *CRL* indicates correct crown-rump length for accurate measurement. (From Campbell, S.: Clin. Perinatol. **1:**507, 1974.)

coalesce to make up the image of the tissue that is being scanned. The resultant scans show, in transverse (Fig. 1-12) or longitudinal (Fig. 1-13) views the anterior abdominal wall, symphysis pubis, urinary bladder, the uterus and its contents, and the sacrum and vertebrae. The bladder appears as a non–echo-producing image (black), as does the nongravid uterus beneath it. Pregnancy is identifiable as early as 5 weeks, when a group of dense circular echoes (white) form the "pregnancy ring," also called the gestational sac, which completely fills the uterus by the twelfth or thirteenth week. Embryonic structures within the sac are visible some time before. Gestational (menstrual) age may be estimated at about this time by measuring the sac and referring to an appropriate chart that relates sac size to age. Later, the fetal head becomes visible, and at 20 to 24 weeks the thorax can be identified.

Assessment of maturity is quite accurate by echo visualization. The earlier the scan is made, the higher is the percentage of ac-

curacy. During the embryonic period (first trimester), the crown-rump length of the embryo is measured (Fig. 1-14). If this is done before the fourteenth week, the date of a term delivery is predictable within 3 days in 97% of patients. Beyond the embryonic period, maturity is assessed by measuring the biparietal diameter of the fetal head (ultrasound cephalometry). A true cross section of the head must be visualized before the biparietal measurement can be made. This point of optimal visualization identified by the presence of a straight midline echo that runs in an anteroposterior direction, representing the space between cerebral hemispheres (Fig. 1-15). After 34 weeks, interpretation of head measurements becomes less reliable because of an increased variation in the rate of growth. The biparietal diameter is used alone or in combination with the thoracic diameter for estimation of fetal age by reference to one of several charts available for the purpose. It would seem that in the absence of serial scans, a single measurement relating fetal

Fig. 1-15. Echogram at 24 weeks menstrual age. The midline echo indicates correct transverse section of fetal head for accurate measurement of biparietal diameter. *Pa,* Parietal bone; *Ml,* midline echo. (From Campbell, S.: Clin. Perinatol. **1:**507, 1974.)

head and chest would be more accurate than measurement of the head alone for identification of growth abnormalities—retardation or acceleration. For example, the fetal growth failure that is associated with maternal toxemia typically involves preferential sparing of the brain with curtailed growth of the rest of the body. Thus the biparietal diameter may be normal, and the thoracic diameter may be small. One could estimate fetal age because the head is unaffected, but estimation of weight and identification of fetal growth retardation would be inaccurate unless a thoracic measurement was also made. Growth failure cannot be diagnosed unless both age and weight are known. If there has been normal growth, weight can be estimated by head measurement alone. In these circumstances it has been found that a biparietal diameter of 8.3 cm or more, taken a week before delivery, indicates a birth weight of at least 2000 grams; at 8.7 cm or more, birth weight is at least 2500 grams. However, if there has been fetal growth failure, these predictions miss the mark grossly because the disproportionately smaller body cannot be perceived without measurement of the thorax.

In contrast, diabetic pregnancies require consideration of fetal growth acceleration. The biparietal diameter does not become larger than normal, in a diabetic pregnancy, until after the thirty-seventh week. Before this time, head measurements alone would miss the fetal overgrowth that is so characteristic of most diabetic pregnancies.

The use of ultrasound has considerably enhanced the effectiveness of fetal diagnosis. Interpretation of results is often subject to the same pitfalls that are encountered when measurements are obtained postnatally. Early ultrasound examination does, however, provide the best available estimate of fetal age.

Considerations of fetal growth and its implications in management of the neonate are presented in Chapter 5.

Radiologic diagnosis

Fetal maturity may be ascertained when an ossification center is present at the distal end of the femur or proximal tibia (Fig. 1-16). However, if these small opacities are absent, the fetus is not necessarily immature because growth retardation in a mature fetus may result in absence of these ossification

Fig. 1-16. Postnatal x-ray film of lower extremities. Small, round ossification centers at distal femurs are visible bilaterally. This neonate was at least 36 weeks at birth. Proximal tibial centers are not present.

centers. Calcification of fetal teeth has also been used to estimate fetal maturity. Multiple births, hydrocephalus, anencephalus, conjoined twinning, and fetal death are identifiable on plain films. Severe erythroblastosis with hydrops fetalis is demonstrable by extensive edema, which elevates fat layers beneath the skin to produce a "halo sign." The so-called "Buddha position" is also indicative of hydrops fetalis. Because most of these procedures are often not reliable and because of concern for the risk of radiation, ultrasound will largely replace x-ray films as a procedure for fetal diagnosis.

Microscopy of the amniotic membrane and the umbilical cord

A number of diagnostic tests have been devised to ascertain at birth the presence of bacterial infections that were acquired in utero. The pathogenesis of these infections and the rationale for these diagnostic procedures are discussed in Chapter 12. Within the context of the present discussion on fetal diagnosis it is appropriate to mention examination of the amnion and umbilical cord. The cellular response of these structures to invasion by bacterial agents is characterized by infiltrations of polymorphonuclear leukocytes. If these cells are noted, the fetus may have an infectious disease, but more often there has merely been exposure to infected amniotic fluid (amnionitis), although the fetus is unaffected. Thus a positive result is most often associated with a normal infant who was exposed to infection before delivery. Infection occurs most frequently after early rupture of membranes. High-risk infants with such findings are often given antibiotics, whether or not they are symptomatic. Although inflammatory cells do not necessarily indicate an affected infant, it is almost always true that among diseased babies amnionitis and inflammation of the umbilical cord are the rule.

HIGH-RISK PREGNANCY

Neonatal intensive care programs have diminished mortality and the incidence of brain damage among survivors, but much if not most of their activity could be eliminated by optimal delivery of prenatal care. Usually the sick neonate was a distressed fetus whose mother's vulnerability to perinatal misadventure could have been identified in 60% to 75% of cases. The ideal medical facility for the management of reproductive events is not a neonatal center nor an obstetric center, but it is rather a *perinatal center* capable of providing continuous care for the well-known biologic continuum that is comprised of conception, gestation, labor, birth, and neonatal life.

Identification and special care of patients

at high risk early in pregnancy have constituted a fruitful approach to the diminution of perinatal misadventure. The high-risk pregnancy is characterized by one or more maternal conditions that impose considerable hazard to intact survival of the fetus or newborn infant. A list of the most common antepartum factors that identify such pregnancies is presented below. A similar but more extensive tabulation of maternal disorders and their associated fetal or neonatal effects is presented in Chapter 2.

Preselection is most effectively accomplished early by considering the historic factors with which a woman enters gestation. The following is a listing of most of these factors.

ANTEPARTUM MATERNAL FACTORS THAT
INDICATE HIGH RISK FOR ADVERSE
FETAL OUTCOME

Previous pregnancy misadventure
Grand multiparity (more than 5 pregnancies)
Cesarean section
Midforceps delivery
Prolonged labor
Fetal loss before 28 weeks (two such)
Fetal loss after 28 weeks
Premature infant
Post-term infant (42 weeks or over)
Abnormal fetal position
Polyhydramnios
Multiple pregnancy
Neonatal death
Infant over 10 pounds at birth
Fetal or neonatal exchange transfusion
Congenital anomalies
Bleeding in second or third trimester
Toxemia, eclampsia

Abnormalities of reproductive anatomy
Uterine malformation
Incompetent cervix
Small bony pelvis

Metabolic and endocrine disorders
Family history of diabetes
Gestational diabetes
Diabetes
Thyroid disorder
Hyperparathyroidism

Cardiovascular disorders
Toxemia

Chronic hypertension
Rheumatic heart disease
Congenital heart disease
Congestive heart failure

Renal disorders
Chronic glomerulonephritis
Acute pyelonephritis
Acute cystitis
Renal insufficiency

Hematologic disorders
Sickle cell disease
Rh sensitization
Anemia (hemoglobin less than 10 grams)
Idiopathic thrombocytopenic purpura

Other factors
Age: Under 16 or over 35 years
     Over 30 years (primipara)
Weight: Less than 100 or more than 200
     pounds
Syphilis
Tuberculosis
Hereditary CNS disorder
Epilepsy
Drug addiction
Smoking (more than one pack daily)
Alcoholism
Maternal malnutrition

Neonatal mortality is lowest if the mother is between 20 and 30 years of age. The risk of poor outcome is considerably increased below 16 and over 40 years of age. Neonatal mortality and morbidity are significantly greater among diabetic gravidas. Prematurity, stillbirth, and low birth weight for gestational age (Chapter 4) are considerably more common among mothers with toxemia and hypertensive cardiovascular disease. Neonatal thyroid difficulty is more often associated with maternal thyroid disorder as a consequence of treatment than as a result of the maternal dysfunction itself. Previous Rh sensitization increases the possibility that an erythroblastotic infant will result from the current pregnancy. Hydramnios may be associated with congenital malformations of the gastrointestinal tract or the brain. It is also common in diabetic pregnancies. Bleeding during the second and third trimesters usually follows disruption of placental attachment, which then poses a serious threat to fetomaternal gas exchange. Multiple pregnancy (twins, triplets) may be fraught with difficulty because at least one of the twins is often delivered from the breech position or is retarded in the rate of intrauterine growth. Excessive cigarette smoking (consumption of more than twenty cigarettes daily), is associated with an increased incidence of low birth weight. Rubella is responsible for severe congenital anomalies and for other tissue changes that are usually incompatible with survival or with a normal postnatal course (p. 225). Maternal hyperparathyroidism may cause severe hypocalcemia in the neonate. Idiopathic thrombocytopenic purpura often results in severe thrombocytopenia in the fetus and newborn.

Although these are only some of the conditions that impose a high risk on pregnancy, they involve the majority of high-risk gravidas. In separating these special pregnancies from the uncomplicated ones, it becomes possible to refer a relatively small number of patients (among whom the bulk of perinatal deaths occur) to medical centers that are equipped and staffed to manage them. There remain the unanticipated events for which preparation is difficult, such as the sudden appearance of complications during labor or delivery in a previously uneventful pregnancy or the first occurrence of premature labor, fetal loss, and neonatal death. Nevertheless, with optimal prenatal management, perinatal mortality can be reduced considerably. This has been demonstrated repeatedly in organized programs of prenatal and postnatal care.

References

Abramovici, H., Brandes, J. M., Fuchs, K., and Timor-Tritsch, I.: Meconium during delivery: a sign of compensated fetal distress, Am. J. Obstet. Gynecol. **118:**251, 1974.

Amarose, A. P., Wallingford, A. J., and Plotz, E. J.: Prediction of fetal sex from cytologic examination of amniotic fluid, N. Engl. J. Med. **275:**715, 1966.

Aubry, R. H., and Pennington, J. C.: Identification and evaluation of high-risk pregnancy: the perinatal concept, Clin. Obstet. Gynecol. **16:**3, 1973.

Battaglia, F. C.: The placenta. In Cooke, R. E., editor: The biologic basis of pediatric practice, New York, 1968, McGraw-Hill Book Co.

Beard, R. W.: The detection of fetal asphyxia in labor, Pediatrics **53:**157, 1974.

Beard, R. W., Morris, E. D., and Clayton, S. G.: pH of foetal capillary blood as an indicator of the condition of the fetus, J. Obstet. Gynaecol. Br. Commonw. **74:**812, 1967.

Behrman, R. E., Parer, J. T., and deLannoy, C. W.: Placental growth and the formation of amniotic fluid, Nature **214:**678, 1967.

Benirschke, K.: What pediatricians should know about the placenta. In Gluck, L., editor: Current problems in pediatrics, Chicago, 1971, Year Book Medical Publishers, Inc.

Biggs, J. S. G.: Progress in fetal assessment, Obstet. Gynecol. **45:**227, 1975.

Bishop, E. H., and Corson, S.: Estimation of fetal maturity by cytologic examination of amniotic fluid, Am. J. Obstet. Gynecol. **102:**654, 1968.

Bowe, E. T.: Fetal blood sampling: maternal-fetal relationships. In Waisman, H. A., and Kerr, G., editors: Fetal growth and development, New York, 1970, McGraw-Hill Book Co.

Brown, J. B.: The value of plasma estrogen estimations in the management of pregnancy, Clin. Perinatol. **1:**273, 1974.

Campbell, S.: The assessment of fetal development by diagnostic ultrasound, Clin. Perinatol. **1:**507, 1974.

Campbell, S.: Fetal growth, Clin. Obstet. Gynecol. **1:**41, 1974.

Clements, J. A., Platzker, A. C. G., Tierney, D. F., et al.: Assessment of the risk of the respiratory distress syndrome by a rapid test for surfactant in amniotic fluid, N. Engl. J. Med. **286:**1077, 1972.

Committee on Maternal and Fetal Medicine and Committee on Technical Bulletins of the American College of Obstetricians and Gynecologists: Fetal heart rate monitoring: guidelines for monitoring, terminology, and instrumentation, ACOG Technical Bulletin no. 32, June, 1975.

Cook, L. N., Shott, R. J., and Andrews, B. F.: Fetal complications of diagnostic amniocentesis: a review and report of a case with pneumothorax, Pediatrics **53:**421, 1974.

Dawes, G. S.: Foetal and neonatal physiology, Chicago, 1968, Year Book Medical Publishers, Inc.

Desmond, M. M., Lindley, J. E., Moore, J., and Brown, C. A.: Meconium staining of newborn infants, J. Pediatr. **49:**540, 1956.

Donald, I. R., Freeman, R. K., Goebelsmann, U., et al.: Clinical experience with the amniotic fluid lecithin/sphingomyelin ratio, Am. J. Obstet. Gynecol. **115:**547, 1975.

Freeman, R. K.: Intrapartum fetal evaluation, Clin. Obstet. Gynecol. **17:**83, 1974.

Fuchs, F.: Volume of amniotic fluid at various stages of pregnancy, Clin. Obstet. Gynecol. **9:**449, 1966.

Gardner, L. I.: Genetically expressed abnormalities in the fetus, Clin. Obstet. Gynecol. **17:**171, 1974.

Gauthier, C., Jr., Desjardins, P., and McLean, F.: Fetal maturity: amniotic fluid analysis correlated with neonatal assessment, Am. J. Obstet. Gynecol. **112:**344, 1972.

Gibbons, J. M., Jr., Huntley, T. E., and Corral, A. G.: Effect of maternal blood contamination on amniotic fluid analysis, Obstet. Gynecol. **44:**657, 1974.

Gluck, L.: Biochemical development of the lung: clinical aspects of surfactant development, RDS and the intrauterine assessment of lung maturity, Clin. Obstet. Gynecol. **14:**710, 1971.

Gluck, L., and Kulovich, M. V.: Lecithin/sphingomyelin ratios in amniotic fluid in normal and abnormal pregnancy, Am. J. Obstet. Gynecol. **115:**539, 1973.

Gluck, L., Kulovich, M. V., Borer, R. C., Jr., et al.: Diagnosis of the respiratory distress syndrome by amniocentesis, Am. J. Obstet. Gynecol. **109:**440, 1971.

Gluck, L., Kulovich, M. V., Eidelman, A. I., et al.: Biochemical development of surface activity in mammalian lung. IV. Pulmonary lecithin synthesis in the human fetus and newborn and etiology of the respiratory distress syndrome, Pediatr. Res. **6:**81, 1972.

Goldstein, A. S., Fukunaga, K., Malachowski, N., and Johnson, J. D.: A comparison of lecithin/sphingomyelin ratio and shake test for estimating fetal pulmonary maturity, Am. J. Obstet. Gynecol. **118:**1132, 1974.

Goodlin, R. C., and Clewell, W. H.: Sudden fetal death following diagnostic amniocentesis, Am. J. Obstet. Gynecol. **118:**285, 1974.

Gore, D. J., Whetham, J. C., and Henry, J. D.: The validity of scalp sampling, Am. J. Obstet. Gynecol. **99:**722, 1967.

Greene, J. W., Jr., and Beargie, R. A.: The use of urinary estriol excretion studies in the assessment of the high-risk pregnancy, Pediatr. Clin. North Am. **17:**43, 1970.

Gruenwald, P.: Fetal malnutrition. In Waisman, H. A., and Kerr, G., editors: Fetal growth and development, New York, 1970, McGraw-Hill Book Co.

Harbert, G. M., Jr.: Evaluation of fetal maturity, Clin. Obstet. Gynecol. **16:**171, 1973.

Hinkley, C., O'Neil, L., and Cassady, G.: Amniotic fluid creatinine in the Rh-sensitized pregnancy, Am. J. Obstet. Gynecol. **117:**544, 1973.

Hobel, C. J., Hyvarinen, M. A., Okada, D. M., and Oh, W.: Prenatal and intrapartum high-risk screening, Am. J. Obstet. Gynecol. **117:**1, 1973.

Hon, E. H.: An introduction to fetal heart rate monitoring, New Haven, Conn., 1969, Hearty Press, Inc.

Hon, E. H.: Physiological procedures for the study of the fetus. In Waisman, H. A., and Kerr, G., editors: Fetal growth and development, New York, 1970, McGraw-Hill Book Co.

Horger, E. O., III, and Hutchinson, D. L.: Diagnostic use of amniotic fluid, J. Pediatr. **75:**503, 1969.

James, L. S., Morishima, H. O., Daniel, S. S., et al.: Mechanism of late deceleration of the fetal heart rate, Am. J. Obstet. Gynecol. **113:**578, 1972.

Jepson, J. H.: Factors influencing oxygenation in mother and fetus, Obstet. Gynecol. **44:**906, 1974.

Kelly, J. V.: Diagnostic techniques in prepartal fetal evaluation, Clin. Obstet. Gynecol. **17:**53, 1974.

Lemons, J. A., Kuhns, L. R., and Poznanski, A.: Calcification of fetal teeth as an index of fetal maturation, Am. J. Obstet. Gynecol. **114:**628, 1972.

Liley, A. W.: Intrauterine transfusion of foetus in haemolytic disease, Br. Med. J. **2:**1107, 1963.

Lind, J., Stern, L., and Wegelius, C.: Human foetal and neonatal circulation, Springfield, Ill., 1964, Charles C Thomas, Publisher.

Lucey, J. F.: The diagnostic uses of amniotic fluid. In Waisman, H. A., and Kerr, G., editors: Fetal growth and development, New York, 1970, McGraw-Hill Book Co.

Magendantz, H. G., Klausner, D., Ryan, K. S., et al.: Estriol determinations in the management of high-risk pregnancies, Obstet. Gynecol. **32:**610, 1968.

McAllister, C. J., Stull, C. G., and Courey, N. G.: Amniotic fluid levels of uric acid and creatinine in toxemic patients: possible relation to diuretic use, Am. J. Obstet. Gynecol. **115:**560, 1973.

McCrann, D. J., Jr., and Schifrin, B. S.: Fetal monitoring in high-risk pregnancy, Clin. Perinatol. **1:**229, 1974.

Mendez-Bauer, C., et al.: A practical approach for evaluating fetal condition during labor by the fetal heart rate. In Waisman, H. A., and Kerr, G., editors: Fetal growth and development, New York, 1970, McGraw-Hill Book Co.

Mendez-Bauer, C., et al.: Fetal acid-base balance and heart rate under physiological and pathological conditions. In Waisman, H. A., and Kerr, G., editors: Fetal growth and development, New York, 1970, McGraw-Hill Book Co.

Mendez-Bauer, C., Poseiro, J. J., Arellano-Hernandez, G., et al.: Effects of atropine on the heart rate of the human fetus during labor, Am. J. Obstet. Gynecol. **85:**1033, 1963.

Meyer, R. A.: Interaction of ultrasound and biologic tissues: potential hazards, Pediatrics **54:**266, 1974.

Murata, Y., and Martin, C. B., Jr.: Am. J. Obstet. Gynecol. **115:**252, 1973.

Myers, R. E., Mueller-Heubach, E., and Adamsons, K.: Predictability of the state of fetal oxygenation from a quantitative analysis of the components of late deceleration, Am. J. Obstet. Gynecol. **115:**1083, 1973.

Nader, H. L.: Fetal diagnosis utilizing amniotic fluid cells. In Waisman, H. A., and Kerr, G., editors: Fetal growth and development, New York, 1970, McGraw-Hill Book Co.

Naeye, R. L.: Structural correlates of fetal undernutrition. In Waisman, H. A., and Kerr, G., editors: Fetal growth and development, New York, 1970, McGraw-Hill Book Co.

Nesbitt, R. E. L., Jr.: Prenatal identification of the fetus at risk, Clin. Perinatol. **1:**213, 1974.

Paul, R. H., and Hon, E. H.: Clinical fetal monitoring, Am. J. Obstet. Gynecol. **118:**529, 1974.

Pernoll, M. L., Prescott, G. H., Hecht, F., and Olson, C. L.: Prenatal diagnosis, Obstet. Gynecol. **44:**773, 1974.

Pitkin, R. M., and Zwirek, S. J.: Amniotic fluid creatinine, Am. J. Obstet. Gynecol. **98:**1135, 1967.

Potter, E. L.: Bilateral absence of ureters and kidneys, Obstet. Gynecol. **25:**3, 1965.

Quilligan, E. J., and Paul, R. H.: Fetal monitoring: is it worth it? Obstet. Gynecol. **45:**96, 1975.

Reid, D. E., Ryan, K. J., and Benirschke, K.: Principles and management of human repro-

duction, Philadelphia, 1972, W. B. Saunders Co.

Renou, P., and Wood, C.: Interpretation of the continuous fetal heart rate record, Clin. Obstet. Gynecol. **1:**191, 1974.

Roopnarinesingh, S.: Amniotic fluid creatinine in normal and abnormal pregnancies, Obstet. Gynaecol. Br. **77:**785, 1970.

Roux, J. F., Nakamura, J., and Brown, E.: Assessment of fetal maturation by the foam test, Am. J. Obstet. Gynecol. **117:**280, 1973.

Saling, E.: Blood chemistry as a method of detection of fetal distress. In Wood, C., and Walter, W. A. A., editors: Fifth World Congress of Gynecology and Obstetrics, Sydney, 1967, Butterworth & Co. (Australia), Ltd.

Schifrin, B. S., Lapidus, M., Doctor, G. S., and Leviton, A.: Contraction stress test for antepartum fetal evaluation, Obstet. Gynecol. **45:**433, 1975.

Seeds, A. E., and Behrman, R. E.: Acid-base monitoring of the fetus during labor with blood obtained from the scalp, J. Pediatr. **74:**804, 1969.

Shenker, L.: Clinical experiences with fetal heart rate monitoring of one thousand patients in labor, Am. J. Obstet. Gynecol. **115:**1111, 1973.

Spellacy, W. N., Buhi, W. C., Birk, S. A., and Holsinger, K. K.: Human placental lactogen levels and intrapartum fetal distress: meconium-stained amniotic fluid, fetal heart rate patterns, and Apgar scores, Am. J. Obstet. Gynecol. **114:**803, 1972.

Stocker, J., Mawad, R., Deleon, A., and Desjardins, P.: Ultrasonic cephalometry, Obstet. Gynecol. **45:**275, 1975.

Thompson, H. E.: Evaluation of the obstetric and gynecologic patient by the use of diagnostic ultrasound, Clin. Obset. Gynecol. **17:**1, 1974.

Weiss, R. R., Duchin, S., Evans, M. I., et al.: Amniotic fluid uric acid and creatinine as measures of fetal maturity, Obstet. Gynecol. **44:**208, 1974.

Willoughby, H. W., Desjardins, P. D., Lee, T. K., and Wood, N.: The contribution of maternal hyperbilirubinemia to amniotic fluid pigmentation, Am. J. Obstet. Gynecol. **115:**11, 1973.

Winick, M.: Cellular growth of the fetus and placenta. In Waisman, H. A., and Kerr, G., editors: Fetal growth and development, New York, 1970, McGraw-Hill Book Co.

Winick, M.: Cellular growth in intrauterine malnutrition, Pediatr. Clin. North Am. **17:**69, 1970.

Chapter 2

Fetal and neonatal consequences of abnormal labor and delivery

THE CONDITION OF AN INFANT AT BIRTH is determined by numerous antecedent factors such as genetic endowment, maternal health before and during gestation, maternal complications of pregnancy, development of the embryo, growth of the fetus, and the course of labor and delivery. This chapter addresses itself to the fetal effects of labor and delivery, normal and abnormal. Although some of the abnormal conditions have their inception well before the onset of labor (placenta previa, for instance), they are discussed here because their presence usually becomes manifest during the birth process. No attempt is made to discuss maternal medical disorders such as diabetes, toxemia, or infectious diseases. These are considered elsewhere in relation to their associated neonatal abnormalities. However, an extensive tabulation in this chapter (Table 2-1) lists a majority of maternal disorders and the fetal or neonatal effects they are known or presumed to produce.

MECHANICS OF NORMAL LABOR

A review of normal labor is essential for an understanding of the abnormalities that play a role in fetal or neonatal difficulties. The classic division of labor into three stages is as follows:

First stage. Cervical dilatation is initiated with the first contraction and ends when the cervix is completely dilated.
Second stage. Fetal expulsion begins when the cervix is completely dilated and ends with birth of the infant.
Third stage. Placental expulsion starts after birth of the baby and terminates with delivery of the placenta.

Before considering each stage of labor, a discussion of uterine contractions is appropriate.

Characteristics of uterine contractions

Contractions provide the force necessary for descent of the fetus; they accentuate differentiation of the uterine wall into upper and lower segments, and they bring about dilatation and effacement of the cervix (see later). During the first stage, intrauterine pressure ranges from 20 to 50 mm Hg. At these pressures the cervix seems to dilate easily. During the second stage, with the addition of conscious maternal expulsive efforts (bearing down), pressures may rise to 70 mm Hg. At the onset of the first stage of labor, contractions appear every 10 minutes, increasing in frequency to every 1 or 2 minutes during the second stage. They normally last for 30 to 90 seconds. Alternation of contraction and relaxation is indispensable to fetal well-being because the flow of blood through the intervillous space is greatly impeded during a contraction, returning to normal during relaxation. The significance to the fetus of abnormally long and vigorous contractions is thus apparent; that is, sustained reduction of placental blood flow impairs maternofetal gas exchange, and fetal hypoxia may ensue.

As labor proceeds, increasing differentiation of the uterine wall into a thick muscular superior segment and a thin inferior one (Fig. 2-1) assures that most of the force produced by contractions emanates from the upper segment. The lower one remains relatively passive and distensible. This arrangement is essential if fetal descent is to be accom-

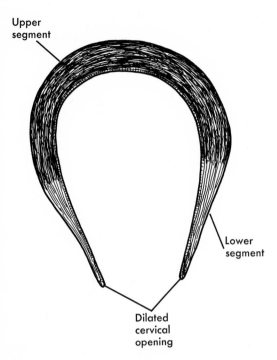

Upper
segment

Lower
segment

Dilated
cervical
opening

Fig. 2-1. Upper (dark shading) and lower uterine segments are shown delineated from each other. Most of the force that propels the fetus originates from the thick muscular upper segment. (Modified from Hellman, L. M., and Pritchard, J. A.: Williams obstetrics, ed. 14, New York, 1971, Appleton-Century-Crofts.)

plished. If the entire uterine wall were as thick and muscular as the upper segment, the force of each contraction would be applied to the fetus equally from all sides rather than from above. The fetus would get nowhere. Furthermore, as will be seen in the description of the first stage, the cervix would neither efface nor dilate.

First stage of labor. As the upper and lower segments become more sharply differentiated with each contraction, cervical effacement (thinning) and dilatation progresses gradually. At the onset of labor the cervical wall is approximately 2 cm in thickness, surrounding a thin canal of equal depth. Fully effaced at the end of the first stage, the wall of the cervix is only a few millimeters thick. It becomes incorporated into and indistinguishable from the uterine wall of the lower segment. Fully dilated, the cervical canal becomes a shallow, wide orifice that is 10 cm in diameter (Fig. 2-2). The canal becomes wider and thinner as the wall of the cervix retracts to become part of the uterine wall. Thinning and widening of the cervix occurs in response to downward pressure on the fetus that is provided by repeated contractions. Most of the effacement is accomplished during the early part of the first stage, when dilatation is minimal. Later, with effacement almost complete, dilatation progresses more rapidly to completion, marking the onset of the second stage (Fig. 2-3).

A

B

Fig. 2-2. Effacement and dilatation of the cervix. **A**, Appearance of the cervix before onset of labor. The cervical canal is only a few millimeters wide. **B**, Appearance of the cervix late in labor. The cervix is effaced and dilated, having been drawn upward and incorporated into the wall of the lower uterine segment. The cervical canal has widened to approximately 10 cm. (Modified from Hellman, L. M., and Pritchard, J. A.: Williams obstetrics, ed. 14, New York, 1971, Appleton-Century-Crofts.)

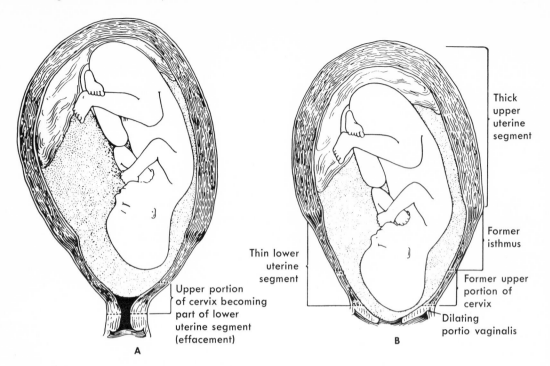

Fig. 2-3. Pregnant uterus. **A,** Late pregnancy. Bracket marks part of cervix that is incorporated into lower uterine segment during effacement. **B,** During labor. Effacement is complete, and dilatation is in progress. Upper segment is thicker, whereas lower segment is longer and thinner. (From Reid, D. E., Ryan, K. J., and Benirschke, K.: Principles and management of human reproduction, Philadelphia, 1972, W. B. Saunders Co.)

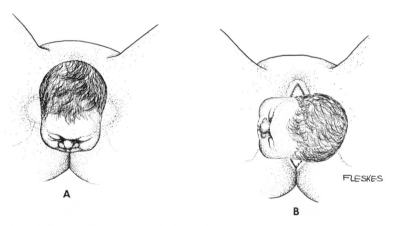

Fig. 2-4. Rotation of the shoulders prior to delivery. **A,** The head has just been delivered. The shoulders are in a horizontal direction. **B,** Ninety-degree rotation of the entire body has now placed the shoulders in a vertical (anteroposterior) direction while the face has turned to one side. (Modified from Hellman, L. M., and Pritchard, J. A.: Williams obstetrics, ed. 14, New York, 1971, Appleton-Century-Crofts.)

Second stage of labor. Although variations are numerous, significant descent of the fetus usually does not occur until the cervix is completely dilated. During the second stage, fetal descent is brought about not only by uterine contractions but also by periodic increases of intra-abdominal pressure. The latter is accomplished by the mother during voluntary contraction of abdominal muscles and fixation of the diaphragm. Maternal oversedation may reduce or eliminate voluntary cooperation.

As fetal descent proceeds, the head rotates to accommodate to the contour of the bony pelvis and thus is normally delivered face downward. Delivery of the shoulders is accomplished when the unextruded body rotates 90 degrees in order to change their internal position from a horizontal to an anteroposterior one. The face is now turned to one side (Fig. 2-4). The anterior (upper) shoulder is delivered first, then the posterior (lower) shoulder, and rapidly thereafter, the rest of the body. The cord is cut by the operator after extrusion of the body, the proximal end remaining attached to the undelivered placenta while the distal segment is attached to the infant.

Third stage of labor. After birth of the baby, the placenta separates and is extruded by continued contractions that pry it loose from its attachment to the uterine wall. There is thus a smooth transition from intrauterine placental respiration in a liquid environment to extrauterine pulmonary respiration in a gaseous one. If extensive separation of the placenta occurs during the first or second stage, the reduction of surface area available for gas exchange produces hypoxia, which cannot be relieved until the head is delivered.

DYSTOCIA (DIFFICULT LABOR)

Prolongation of labor due to mechanical factors is called dystocia. Precise time limits for the normal duration of labor are difficult to fix. However, it is generally agreed that the combined length of the first and second stages should not exceed approximately 20 hours and that the second stage itself is abnormal if it surpasses 2 hours in primiparas and 1 hour in multiparas. If labor is prolonged, perinatal mortality and morbidity increase because (1) separation of the placenta during the second stage is more likely, and severe fetal hypoxia may ensue; (2) compression of the cord is more likely, and it causes profound fetal hypoxia because blood flow in the umbilical vessels is obstructed; and (3) the incidence of intrauterine bacterial infection rises sharply as labor becomes more protracted, especially if the amniotic membranes have ruptured early (Chapter 12).

Dystocia may be caused by one or more of the following factors: (1) uterine dysfunction (inertia), which involves abnormal contractions of uterine muscle; (2) abnormal presentation, excessive fetal size, or congenital anomalies (such as hydrocephalus), which obstruct fetal descent during the birth process; or (3) abnormal size or shape of the birth canal, which impedes fetal passage. A contracted pelvis is the commonest manifestation of this abnormality.

Uterine dysfunction

Uterine dysfunction may be hypotonic (weak contractions) or hypertonic (excessive contractions and muscle tone). The former, which is by far the commonest variety, is usually due to impairment of normal fetal descent (contracted pelvis or abnormal fetal presentation). In some labors hypotonic dysfunction is due to overdosage of anesthetic and analgesic agents. This type of dysfunction generally appears during the latter part of the first stage. Progressive dilatation of the cervix is retarded or halted, and contractions weaken or cease altogether. Dangers of prolonged labor to the fetus were described earlier.

The hypertonic variety of dysfunction is infrequent. It appears early in the first stage of labor. Contractions are inordinately painful and sustained. Progress of labor is either slowed or nonexistent. In these circumstances fetal hypoxia is due to impaired placental

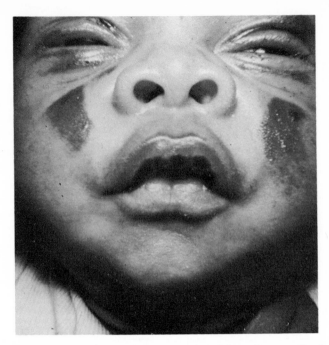

Fig. 2-5. Typical facial appearance after a face presentation. There is generalized swelling, most pronounced in the upper lip. Ecchymoses and abrasions are the result of birth trauma.

blood flow from continuously increased intrauterine pressure. The effects of diminished placental blood flow on maternofetal gas exchange are discussed on p. 36.

Contracted pelvis as a cause of dystocia

An abnormal contour of the bony pelvis often involves a constricted birth passage that impedes normal descent of the fetus; complete obstruction is a rare phenomenon. Pelvic contraction occurs in approximately 5% of white women and in about 15% of black women. Pelvic size may be diminished in the anteroposterior diameter, the transverse diameter, or both. The slowed fetal descent caused by a narrow birth canal causes hypotonic uterine dysfunction and prolonged labor. The fetal dangers of protracted labor have already been enumerated, but in addition, trauma often occurs as a consequence of pressure exerted by the bony pelvis on a tightly fitting fetal part. For instance, cephalopelvic disproportion may cause molding of the fetal head, which is characterized by a misshapen skull, usually in the anteroposterior dimension. Occasionally pressure marks on the scalp are also seen at the point of contact with the maternal sacrum. In the extreme, a depressed fracture that is grossly visible as an indentation in the surface of the skull may result from excessive pressure against the bony pelvis.

Abnormal fetal presentation as a cause of dystocia

The normal vertex presentation (head first) occurs in 95% of all deliveries. Abnormal presentations include breech, face, brow, and shoulder. Breech deliveries comprise approximately 4%, whereas the others comprise 1% of all births.

Face and shoulder presentations can in themselves prolong labor by impeding fetal passage, even if the pelvis is normally constituted. Breech presentations do not in themselves prolong labor unless pelvic narrowing is also present.

Face presentations are not common. Characteristically the head is drawn back so that

Fig. 2-6. Breech presentations. **A,** Complete breech: the legs, feet, and buttocks present simultaneously. **B,** Frank breech: only the buttocks are born first because the hips are maximally flexed, placing the thighs against the abdomen. **C,** Footling breech: one or both feet appear first.

the occiput almost touches the upper spine. The resultant misfit of the head in the birth canal usually precludes normal passage, and delivery may be considerably delayed. At birth, facial edema and ecchymosis impart a characteristically grotesque appearance, which disappears in about a week (Fig. 2-5). Just as it was in utero, the head is held backward as the infant lies in his crib. Fetal and neonatal mortality are increased severalfold, primarily because of the hypoxic effects of prolonged labor and trauma.

A shoulder presentation occurs when the fetus lies transversely across the pelvis (transverse lie). In this position the long axis of the body is perpendicular to the axis of the birth canal; the head is on one side of the pelvis and the buttocks on the other, with one shoulder up and the lower one protruding through the cervical orifice (shoulder presentation). Prolongation of labor is inevitable because fetal passage is obstructed. A considerable degree of obstetric skill is required for correction of a transverse lie; if correction fails, the only alternative is delivery by cesarean section.

BREECH PRESENTATION

The breech position does not in itself impede progress of labor unless pelvic size is diminished. Depending on the part of the body that presents at delivery, breech presentations may occur in one of three varieties. In *frank breech* the buttocks are the presenting part, the lower extremities being flexed upward against the body. In a *com-*

plete breech the buttocks and lower extremities present simultaneously, since the latter are not flexed upward but are approximately on the same plane as the buttocks. *Footling (incomplete) breech* refers to presentation of the feet and legs first, the buttocks later (Fig. 2-6).

The fetal and neonatal hazards of breech delivery are trauma, asphyxia, and prematurity. As a consequence, perinatal mortality is increased three or four times over vertex deliveries. The most serious traumatic event, and one that is twice as frequent as in vertex deliveries, is intracranial hemorrhage resulting from excessive and sustained pressure on the head during delivery. In vertex deliveries, the oncoming head may be slowed because of cephalopelvic disproportion. Since labor is still in an early stage, a decision to perform a cesarean section is timely, as well as effective in avoiding head trauma. In breech deliveries, however, difficulty in descent of the head cannot be appreciated early in labor—at least not until the hips and shoulders have already been delivered. It is then too late for a cesarean section, and sustained compression of the head during attempts to extract it often causes trauma and hemorrhage due to torn cerebral veins. The outcome is either lethal or permanently crippling. Spinal cord injury is also more common than in vertex presentations because stretching of the vertebral column occurs as traction is applied to the body during the anxious moments that precede delivery of the head. Hemorrhage into the abdominal

Fig. 2-7. Placenta previa. **A,** Total: the cervical outlet is completely occluded by the placenta,
B, Partial: the placenta does not completely block the cervical outlet. **C,** Low implantation: the cervical outlet is not obstructed. (Modified from Netter: In Oppenheim, E., editor: Ciba collection of medical illustrations, vol. 2, Reproductive system, 1965.)

viscera may occur, particularly in the adrenals and kidneys, and occasionally in the spleen. It may be due to pressure exerted by the hands of the obstetrician while grasping the flanks of the infant's exteriorized body and in an attempt to extract the head under difficult circumstances. Other injuries include brachial plexus palsy (p. 48) and fractures of the humerus and femur (p. 46).

Compression of a prolapsed cord (p. 36) may cause severe asphyxia. This is more common in complete and footling (incomplete) breech than in vertex deliveries. It is infrequent in frank breech presentations because the buttocks effectively occlude the cervical orifice, and the cord is thus prevented from advancing. Placenta previa is an important cause of breech presentation, and in itself often leads to asphyxia. Separation of the placenta well before delivery of the head deprives the fetus of its only source of oxygen.

Persistent hyperextension of the neck in utero is an infrequent association of breech presentation. This unusual position may be detected by abdominal palpation, which reveals the fetal head to be drawn backward, as in opisthotonos. Ultrasound or x-ray examination confirms the suspicion. If hyperextension persists into the onset of labor, and vaginal delivery is attempted, 25% of such fetuses will suffer transection of the spinal cord at the cervical level, which results in severe permanent disability or in death. Delivery by cesarean section consistently avoids the spinal cord injury.

ABNORMAL PLACENTAL IMPLANTATION AND SEPARATION
Placenta previa

Placenta previa is the result of abnormal implantation of the fertilized egg. Normally implantation is in the thick muscular wall of the upper uterine segment; in placenta previa it is misplaced in the lower uterine segment. Depending on the proximity of the placenta to the cervical os, three types are recognized (Fig. 2-7). Total placenta previa completely covers the cervical orifice. Partial placenta previa occludes the cervical orifice incompletely. In the third type, called low implantation of the placenta, the placental edge barely encroaches on the margin of the cervical aperture. Although these placental positions may impede or totally block fetal passage, the most frequent causes of fetal and neonatal jeopardy are early placental separation and premature onset of labor. In early placental separation, fetal asphyxia occurs because the surface area available for maternofetal gas exchange is dangerously reduced. Even when fetal asphyxia is averted by expert management, perinatal mortality remains high because of the increased incidence of prematurity.

The hemorrhage that follows early placental separation may cause maternal shock. Occasionally cleavage also occurs through the fetal side of the placenta, and acute hemorrhage causes fetal shock that is clearly recognizable at birth (p. 187).

The placenta separates early because it is tenuously attached to the thin lower uterine wall. As pregnancy and labor proceed, the wall of the lower segment becomes progressively thinner. The placental attachment is thus easily disrupted before its time; hemorrhage and premature onset of labor are the result.

Abruptio placentae

Premature separation of a normally implanted placenta is called abruptio placentae. If the placenta separates at its margin, blood drains toward the cervix between the uterine wall and the amniotic membrane, ultimately becoming visible as vaginal bleeding. Approximately 80% of abruptions are of this marginal variety. If separation of the placenta is limited to its central portion while the margin remains intact, a more sinister situation exists because a considerable amount of blood loss may occur before it is recognized. In both instances the major fetal hazards are asphyxia (because of reduced gas exchange surface) and prematurity (because abruptio placentae stimulates early onset of labor). As in placenta previa, separation may cause hemorrhage from the fetal side of the placenta to produce neonatal shock at birth or soon thereafter (p. 187).

IMPAIRED BLOOD FLOW THROUGH THE UMBILICAL CORD

The umbilical vessels may be partially or completely occluded by compression of the cord. Prolapse of the cord involves visible protrusion through the cervical opening in advance of the presenting fetal part. Compression occurs when the cord is trapped between a fetal part and the bony pelvis or the dilated cervix. The same mechanism is operative in occult prolapse, which involves compression by a presenting fetal part but without visible protrusion of the cord through the cervix. Transient compression in utero without prolapse occurs frequently throughout pregnancy and is usually, but not always, innocuous. If fetal heart rate is monitored, these evanescent episodes of compression are marked by periods of deceleration that are unrelated to uterine contractions (variable deceleration). If these episodes are frequent and protracted, the fetus is in danger of severe asphyxia.

Prolapse of the cord, occult or obvious, is a dangerous complication that may cause complete depletion of fetal oxygen within $2\frac{1}{2}$ minutes if the compression is not relieved. Prolapse is most common in breech delivery, multiple gestation, premature rupture of membranes, and transverse lie.

A cord wrapped around the fetal neck or body is generally, but not always, harmless because occlusion of umbilical circulation may occur if the cord is stretched in the extreme.

FETAL ASPHYXIA: RELATIONSHIP TO OBSTETRIC ABNORMALITIES

Fetal distress is often due to diminution in the flow of oxygen from mother to fetus. The factors that inhibit oxygen transfer from mother to fetus simultaneously reduce the transfer of carbon dioxide from fetus to mother. These factors include maternal hypoxia, disrupted uteroplacental circulation, placen-tal dysfunction, impaired blood flow through the umbilical cord, or an intrinsic fetal disorder.

Biochemical characteristics of asphyxia

Fetal asphyxia implies reduction in P_{O_2} (hypoxia), elevation of P_{CO_2} (hypercapnia), and lowering of blood pH (acidosis). The acidosis is termed *mixed* because it is comprised of respiratory and metabolic components (Chapter 7). Respiratory acidosis is characterized by an accumulation of carbon dioxide in the blood that renders it more acid than normal (low pH). Metabolic acidosis refers to a low pH that follows accumulation of organic acids (Chapter 7). In the presence of asphyxia these acids (principally lactic acid) are the end products of an abnormal process that must produce glucose at low levels of oxygen. This process is called anaerobic glycolysis because the breakdown of glycogen (principal source of glucose) transpires in the presence of hypoxia. Hypoxia thus causes metabolic acidosis because it forces anaerobic glycolysis. If the asphyxiated fetus were properly oxygenated by removing the cause of impaired gas exchange, P_{CO_2} would also diminish (eliminating respiratory acidosis), and the production of lactic acid would decline because glycogen breakdown could then proceed aerobically. Thus the concern with suboptimal oxygenation of the fetus is directed not only to the cellular damage caused by lack of oxygen but also to the difficulties of the resultant acidosis.

Signs of fetal asphyxia

Fetal asphyxia is suggested by the presence of meconium in amniotic fluid. It is demonstrable in changes of cardiac rate and by sampling fetal scalp blood. Meconium-stained fluid is observable only when membranes rupture or when amniocentesis is performed. Alterations in heart rate are detectable by fetal heart rate monitoring. Asphyxial blood gas and pH changes are demonstrated by determinations on fetal scalp blood.

Text continued on p. 43.

Table 2-1. Maternal abnormalities and associated fetal and neonatal disorders

Maternal factors	*Fetal, neonatal disorders*
	Antepartum
Metabolic	
Diabetes mellitus	Prematurity*
	Hyaline membrane disease
	Hyperbilirubinemia
	Hypoglycemia
	Macrosomatia
	Hypocalcemia
	Renal vein thrombosis
	Polyhydramnios
	Congenital anomalies
	Intrauterine growth retardation
Gout	Hyperuricemia (transient, asymptomatic)
Malnutrition	Intrauterine growth retardation
Porphyria	Porphyrinuria (transient, asymptomatic)
Endocrine	
Addison's disease	Prematurity
	Intrauterine growth retardation
Chronic hypoparathyroidism	Hyperparathyroidism (intrauterine and postnatal)
Primary hyperparathyroidism	Neonatal tetany (hypocalcemia)
	Hypomagnesemia
Thyroid	
Goiter (nontoxic)	Goiter
Hyperthyroidism (untreated)	Hyperthyroidism (goitrous or nongoitrous)
Hyperthyroidism (treated)	Goiter (nontoxic)
	Hyperthyroidism (goitrous or nongoitrous)
	Hypothyroidism (goitrous or nongoitrous)
Hypothyroidism	CNS defects
	Hypothyroidism
Cardiac	
Congestive failure	Prematurity
	Asphyxia†
Hypertensive cardiovascular disease	Asphyxia
	Intrauterine growth retardation
Pulmonary	
Asthma (intractable) or any disorder associated with hypoxemia and hypercapnia	Asphyxia
	Prematurity
	Intrauterine growth retardation
Gastrointestinal	
Regional ileitis	Prematurity
Renal	
Polycystic kidney disease	Polycystic kidney disease
Chronic glomerulonephritis	Prematurity
	Intrauterine growth retardation
	Asphyxia
Neurologic	
Myasthenia gravis	Myasthenia gravis
Status epilepticus	Asphyxia
Hematologic	
Blood incompatibility (Rh, ABO, other)	Erythroblastosis fetalis
Idiopathic thrombocytopenic purpura	Idiopathic thrombocytopenia purpura (transient)
Leukemia (acute)	Prematurity

*Prematurity = gestational age less than 37 completed weeks.   *Continued.*
†Asphyxia = hypoxemia, hypercapnia, low pH.

Table 2-1. Maternal abnormalities and associated fetal and neonatal disorders—cont'd

Maternal factors	Fetal, neonatal disorders
	Antepartum—cont'd
Hematologic—cont'd	
Megaloblastic anemia	Hazards of abruptio placentae
Sickle cell anemia	Low birth weight
	Intrauterine growth retardation
Anemia (iron deficiency)	Low birth weight, prematurity
Skin	
Pemphigus	Bullae (transient)
Neoplastic	
Hodgkin's disease	Hodgkin's disease
Ovarian tumors (complicated)	Prematurity
Collagen disease	
Lupus erythematosus (acute)	Systemic lupus erythematosus
Lupus erythematosus (subacute)	Syndrome of congenital heart block, fibroelastosis, fibrosis of liver, spleen, kidney, adrenals
Infection (antepartum or intrapartum)	
Viral	
Coxsackie	Coxsackie infection (encephalomyocarditis)
Cytomegalic inclusion disease	Cytomegalic inclusion disease
Hepatitis (SH)	Neonatal hepatitis
Herpesvirus infection	Herpesvirus infection
Measles	Measles
Mumps	?Congenital anomalies
Poliomyelitis	Poliomyelitis
Rubella	Congenital rubella syndrome
Smallpox	Smallpox
TRIC agent (cervicitis)	Inclusion blennorrhea
Vaccinia (primary vaccination)	Generalized vaccinia
Varicella	Varicella
Western equine encephalomyelitis	Western equine encephalomyelitis
Protozoan	
Candidiasis (vaginal)	Thrush
Malaria	Malaria
Toxoplasmosis	Toxoplasmosis
Trypanosomiasis	Trypanosomiasis
Bacterial	
Acute pyelonephritis	Prematurity
	Bacterial infections
Enteropathogenic *E. coli* (carrier)	Diarrhea (enteropathogenic *E. coli*)
Gonorrhea	Gonorrheal infection (usually ophthalmia)
Listeriosis	Listeriosis
Pneumococcal meningitis	Pneumococcal meningitis
Salmonellosis	Salmonellosis
Septicemia (any organism)	Septicemia (any organism)
Shigellosis	Shigellosis
Syphilis	Congenital syphilis
Tuberculosis	Tuberculosis
Typhoid fever	Typhoid fever
Obstetric and gynecologic	
Amputated cervix	Prematurity
Incompetent cervix	Prematurity

Prematurity = gestational age less than 37 completed weeks.
Asphyxia = hypoxemia, hypercapnia, low pH.

Table 2-1. Maternal abnormalities and associated fetal and neonatal disorders—cont'd

Maternal factors	Fetal, neonatal disorders
	Antepartum—cont'd
Obstetric and gynecologic—cont'd	
Toxemia	Prematurity
	Intrauterine growth retardation
	Hypoglycemia
	Hypocalcemia
	Aspiration syndrome
	Polycythemia
	Asphyxia
Pharmacologic	
Alcohol (chronic alcoholism)	Low birth weight
	Developmental delay
	Microcephaly
	Small palpebral fissures
	Maxillary hypoplasia
	Cardiac anomaly (ventricular septal defect, patent ductus arteriosus)
	Abnormal palm creases
Aminopterin and amethopterin	Multiple anomalies
	Abortion
	Intrauterine growth retardation
Ammonium chloride	Acidosis
Androgen (methyl testosterone)	Masculinization of females
	Advanced bone age
Barbiturates	Withdrawal syndrome
	Diminished sucking
	Diminished serum bilirubin
Cephalothin	Direct Coombs' positive test
Chlorambucil	?Renal agenesis
Chlorothiazide	Thrombocytopenia
	Salt and water depletion
Chloroquine	?Retinal damage
	Death
	Mental retardation
Chlorpromazine	Depression
	Lethargy
Chlorpropamide	Hypoglycemia
	Increased fetal wastage
Cigarette smoking	Intrauterine growth retardation
	Increased neonatal hematocrit
Diazepam (Valium)	Hypothermia
Dicumarol	Fetal hemorrhage and death
Diphenylhydantoin (Dilantin)	Hypoplastic phalanges
	Diaphragmatic hernia
	Cleft lip
	Coloboma
	Pulmonary atresia
	Patent ductus arteriosus
Estrogen	Masculinization of females
	Carcinoma of vagina and cervix (years later)
	Advanced bone age
Ethchlorvynol (Placidyl)	Irritability, jitteriness (withdrawal symptoms)

Continued.

Table 2-1. Maternal abnormalities and associated fetal and neonatal disorders—cont'd

Maternal factors	*Fetal, neonatal disorders*
	Antepartum—cont'd
Hexamethonium bromide	Paralytic ileus
Insulin shock	Death
Intravenous fluid (copious, hypotonic)	Hyponatremia
	Convulsions
	Edema
Lithium	Lithium toxicity (cyanosis, hypotonia)
Lysergic acid diethylamide	Chromosome damage
Magnesium sulfate	Hypermagnesemia
	CNS depression
	Peripheral neuromuscular blockage
Meperidine (Demerol)	Placental vasoconstriction
	CNS and respiratory depression
Mepivacaine	Bradycardia
	Convulsions
	Apnea
	Death
	Depression
	Tachycardia
	Flaccidity
	Metabolic acidois
	Hypoxemia
Methimazole	Goiter
Morphine, heroin, methadone	Withdrawal symptoms (tremors, dyspnea, cyanosis, convulsions, death)
	Intrauterine growth retardation
	Lower serum bilirubin
Naphthalene (mothballs)	Hemolytic anemia (in G-6-PD deficiency)
Nitrofurantoin	Hemolytic anemia (in G-6-PD deficiency)
Nortriptyline	Urinary retention (bladder)
Potassium iodide	Goiter
Primaquine	Hemolytic anemia (in G-6-PD deficiency)
Progestins	Masculinization of female infants
	Advanced bone age
Propanolol	Low Apgar scores
Propoxyphene (Darvon)	Hyperactivity
	Sweating
	Convulsions
	Withdrawal symptoms
Propylthiouracil	Goiter
Quinine	Thrombocytopenia
	Abortion
Radioactive iodine	Hypothyroidism
	Thyroid destruction
Reserpine	Obstructed respiration due to nasal congestion
	Lethargy
	Bradycardia
	Hypothermia
Salicylates	Neonatal hemorrhage due to platelet dysfunction
Sedatives (excessive during labor)	CNS depression and respiratory distress
Steroids (adrenocortical)	Increased incidence of fetal death
	Adrenal suppression
	Accelerated fetal lung maturation (betamethasone)
	?Cleft palate

Prematurity = gestational age less than 37 completed weeks.
Asphyxia = hypoxemia, hypercapnia, low pH.

Table 2-1. Maternal abnormalities and associated fetal and neonatal disorders—cont'd

Maternal factors	Fetal, neonatal disorders
Antepartum—cont'd	
Streptomycin	Deafness, eighth nerve damage
Stilbestrol	Adenocarcinoma of vagina in adolescents
Sulfonamides (long-acting)	Kernicterus at low bilirubin levels
Tetracyclines (after first trimester)	Tooth stain, enamel hypoplasia (primary teeth)
	Temporarily inhibiteod linear growth (premature infants)
Thalidomide	Phocomelia and other anomalies
	Death
Tolbutamide (Orinase)	Thrombocytopenia, bilirubin displaceemnt from albumin
Vitamin D (excessive)	?Hypercalcemia (supravalvular aortic stenosis, mental retardation, osteosclerosis)
Vitamin K (excessive)	Hyperbilirubinemia
Intrapartum	
Cord pathology	
Inflammation	Bacterial infection
	Umbilical vein thrombosis (asphyxia)
Meconium staining	Asphyxia
Prolapsed cord	Asphyxia
Single umbilical artery	Congenital anomalies
	Intrauterine growth retardation
True knot	Asphyxia
Velamentous insertion, vasa previa	Intrauterine blood loss
Rupture of normal cord (precipitous delivery), varices, aneurysm	Intrauterine blood loss
Fetal membrane, amniotic fluid	
Amnion nodosum	Renal agenesis
	Severe obstructive uropathy (bilateral)
	Intrauterine parabiotic syndrome (small twin)
Amnionitis	Infection, usually bacterial
Early membrane rupture	Bacterial infection
	Prematurity
	Prolapsed cord
Meconium stain (fluid or membranes)	Asphyxia
	Aspiration syndrome
	Pneumonia
Oligohydramnios	Postmaturity
	Renal agenesis and dysplasia
	Polycystic kidney
	Urethral obstruction
	Intrauterine parabiotic syndrome (small twin)
	Fetal death
Polyhydramnios	High gastrointestinal obstruction
	Spina bifida
	Hydrocephalus
	Anencephaly
	Achondroplasia
	Hydrops fetalis
	Intrauterine parabiotic syndrome (large twin)

Continued.

Maternal factors	Fetal, neonatal disorders
	Intrapartum—cont'd

Placenta

Maternal factors	Fetal, neonatal disorders
Placenta previa	Prematurity
	Asphyxia
	Prolapsed cord
	Intrauterine blood loss
Abruptio placentae	Prematurity
	Asphyxia
	Intrauterine blood loss
Fetomaternal transfusion	Intrauterine blood loss (chronic or acute)
	Asphyxia
Incision during cesarean section	Intrauterine blood loss (acute)
Placental insufficiency	Asphyxia
	Intrauterine malnutrition
Multilobed placenta (rupture of communicating vessels)	Intrauterine blood loss (acute)

Complications of labor

Maternal factors	Fetal, neonatal disorders
Breech delivery	Asphyxia
	Intracranial hemorrhage
	Visceral hemorrhage (adrenal, kidney, spleen)
	Spinal cord trauma
	Brachial plexus injury
	Bone fracture (clavicle, humerus, femur)
	Epiphyseal injury (proximal femur or humerus)
	Characteristic posture
	Edema, ecchymosis of buttocks, genitalia, and lower extremities
Face and brow presentation	Edema, ecchymosis of face
	Asphyxia
	Characteristic posture (head retraction)
Transverse presentation	Asphyxia, trauma
Precipitate delivery	Asphyxia, trauma
	Intracranial hemorrhage
Prolonged labor	Asphyxia, trauma
	Bacterial infection
Uterine inertia	Hazard of prolonged labor
Uterine rupture	Asphyxia
Uterine tetany	Asphyxia
Shoulder dystocia	Asphyxia
	Brachial plexus injury
	Fractured clavicle
	Fractured humerus
Manual version, extraction	Asphyxia
	Bone fractures
	Brachial plexus injury, spinal cord trauma
Forceps (high or mid)	Asphyxia
	Cephalhematoma
	Intracranial hemorrhage
Multiple gestation	Asphyxia (usually second twin)
	Prematurity
	Intrauterine growth retardation
	Intrauterine parabiotic syndrome (fetofetal transfusion)
	Hypoglycemia (smaller twin)
	Congenital anomalies
	Bacterial infection (first or both twins)

Prematurity = gestational age less than 37 completed weeks.
Asphyxia = hypoxemia, hypercapnia, low pH.

Specific maternal abnormalities associated with fetal asphyxia

A number of maternal disorders produce fetal vulnerability to asphyxial episodes. The detection of this vulnerability and the hypoxia that results from it have been discussed in Chapter 1. Maternal disorders that jeopardize the fetus are, with few exceptions, easily identified. The significance of the important ones, and the mechanisms by which they endanger the fetus must be understood by all who care for sick neonates. The future of optimal perinatal care will largely depend on the obstetrician's (or perinatologist's) capacity to identify fetal compromise as early in its course as possible. Alertness to fetal hazard will usually depend on identification of maternal difficulty.

Maternal hypoxia deprives the fetus of oxygen by reducing oxygen tension in the blood that perfuses the placenta. The maternofetal P_{O_2} gradient is thus reduced or eliminated, and fetal oxygen deprivation follows. Specific conditions that produce maternal hypoxia are (1) acute asthma; (2) severe pneumonia; (3) low environmental oxygen tension at high altitudes; (4) apnea associated with convulsive episodes of idiopathic epilepsy or eclampsia; (5) depressed ventilation caused by oversedation; (6) disturbed oxygen-carrying ability of hemoglobin resulting from carbon monoxide poisoning or hemolytic anemia; (7) the diminished blood flow to all maternal organs (including the placenta) that characterizes congestive heart failure; and (8) maternal hypotension from any cause, such as septic shock, traumatic hemorrhage, or the inferior vena cava syndrome (supine hypotension syndrome). The inferior vena cava syndrome results from pressure exerted on the inferior vena cava by the uterus when the mother is supine for long intervals. Venous return to the heart thus is impeded. A change in maternal position removes the obstruction to blood flow. The result of vascular occlusion is diminished perfusion of the intervillous space and reduced fetal oxygen supply. Low maternal blood pressure may also be associated with improperly managed conduction anesthesia (spinal, epidural, caudal, or saddle). Systolic blood pressures below 80 mm Hg impair perfusion of the intervillous space.

As described previously, placenta previa and abruptio placentae reduce placental gas exchange in quite another way. A considerable reduction in the surface area available for oxygen diffusion results from the placental separation that characterizes both of these conditions. Furthermore, considerable maternal blood loss may cause hypotension and impair perfusion of the intact portion of the placenta.

The disorders mentioned above originate on the maternal side of the placenta. On the fetal side, and often unrelated to maternal status, the most frequent cause of fetal oxygen deprivation is compression of the cord, which reduces blood flow to vessels in the chorionic villi. In the extreme the arteries and the vein may be compressed. When less pressure is applied to the cord, the vein may be more occluded than the arteries because venous walls are thinner and more easily collapsed, whereas the thicker walls of the arteries are more resistant to external pressure.

TRAUMA OF LABOR AND DELIVERY

Although trauma to the fetus may be inevitable in certain abnormalities of labor and delivery, skillful obstetric manipulation may often avoid or minimize it. Traumatic lesions of the neonate are listed below. Most of them are mild and transient. Occasionally they cause permanent disability; rarely they cause death.

MECHANICAL INJURIES TO THE FETUS

A. *Skin, subcutaneous tissue*
  1. Caput succedaneum
  2. Cyanosis and edema of buttocks, upper or lower extremities
  3. Diffuse scalp hemorrhage
  4. Subcutaneous fat necrosis (pressure necrosis)
  5. Abrasion of the skin
  6. Petechiae and ecchymoses of the skin

B. *Skull*
   1. Molding
   2. Fracture (linear or depressed)
   3. Cephalhematoma
C. *Long bone fractures*
   1. Clavicle
   2. Humerus
   3. Femur
D. *Central nervous system*
   1. Hemorrhage into brain substance
   2. Subdural hematoma
   3. Spinal cord injury
E. *Ocular*
   1. Subconjunctival (scleral) hemorrhage
   2. Retinal hemorrhage
   3. Abrasion of the cornea
F. *Peripheral nerves*
   1. Brachial plexus injury
   2. Diaphragmatic paralysis (phrenic nerve injury)
   3. Facial paralysis
G. *Hemorrhage into abdominal organs*
   1. Liver
   2. Spleen
   3. Kidney
   4. Adrenals
H. *Rib fracture*

Physical signs of trauma

Caput succedaneum is a localized edematous swelling of the scalp caused by sustained pressure of the dilating cervix against the presenting part. Venous return from the affected area is thus obstructed, and edema results. The swelling is most pronounced in prolonged labor. It disappears in several days and is of no pathologic significance.

Edema and cyanosis of the buttocks and extremities are produced by obstructed venous return from pressure of the presenting part against the dilating cervix in abnormal presentations. Swelling of the buttocks and genitalia may thus be quite severe in frank breech deliveries. In footling breech the lower extremities are involved (Fig. 2-8); in complete breech the buttocks and lower extremities are simultaneously affected. The upper extremity is involved in shoulder presentation from a transverse lie.

Cephalhematoma is a collection of blood from ruptured blood vessels situated between

Fig. 2-8. Double footling breech, with edema and cyanosis of legs and feet, considerably more on left than on right. Note frog leg position and absence of molding of head.

the surface of the parietal bone and its tough, overlying periosteal membrane. It is usually unilateral, but occasionally bilateral (Fig. 2-9). Within 24 to 48 hours an obvious swelling develops beneath the scalp over one or both parietal bones. A cephalhematoma is delineated by definite margins. It does not cross suture lines, being limited to an area overlying a single bone. In contrast, the margins of caput succedaneum are indistinct, and the swelling usually crosses suture lines. Cephalhematoma disappears gradually in 2 to 3 weeks, sometimes sooner. In a number of instances x-ray examinations reveals a linear skull fracture beneath it. There are no known abnormal sequelae, whether or not a linear fracture is present. Occasionally, however, and particularly if the lesion is bilateral, hyperbilirubinemia may result from breakdown of the accumulated blood (p. 196).

Diffuse scalp hemorrhage is an infrequent occurrence that involves bleeding into the entire scalp or a major portion of it. Loss of blood may be life threatening if a coagulation defect is present. The most severe

Fig. 2-9. Bilateral cephalhematoma over the parietal bones.

bleeding is associated with failure to administer vitamin K at birth or with other abnormalities of the clotting process that are unrelated to vitamin K deficiency, such as hemophilia. Hemoglobin levels may fall as low as 3 or 4 grams/100 ml. Immediate simple transfusion is lifesaving. Scalp hemorrhage is cumulative over the first 24 to 48 hours. Tremendous swelling of the scalp extends over the forehead and behind the ears, and a characteristic blue discoloration is seen through the overlying skin. The scalp swelling is not limited by suture lines as in cephalhematoma. The life-threatening nature of this condition requires its early recognition. Swelling of part of the scalp and blue discoloration of the skin are the earliest signs that indicate a need for immediate attention.

Subcutaneous fat necrosis is a localized lesion produced by pressure against the bony pelvis or by forceps. It may also occur if the infant is slapped vigorously in attempts to stimulate the onset of respiration. The area of pressure necrosis varies in size, is sharply limited by distinct margins, and is always firm. The overlying skin remains intact and is occasionally blue or red. The lesion resolves in a few days and is of no pathologic significance. It occurs most often in the face.

Abrasion of the skin may be caused by application of forceps, by pressure of an involved part against the bony pelvis, or by careless handling of the infant after birth. The abraded area may serve as a portal of entry for infection.

Petechiae and ecchymoses of the skin are purple discolorations caused by hemorrhage into the superficial skin layers. By definition, petechiae are pinpoint in size, and ecchymoses are larger areas that resemble the common bruise. These skin lesions may be due to severe systemic infection, but more commonly they are the result of direct injury or of pressure that obstructs the venous return from a presenting part. The resultant increase in back pressure ruptures capillaries, and skin hemorrhage ensues. Hemorrhage into the skin thus may indicate difficult labor and delivery, severe infection, or a clotting defect. It is also common in small premature infants in whom extensive bruising is evident, presumably as a function of capillary fragility. These small infants regularly develop hyperbilirubinemia from breakdown of extravasated blood.

Molding of the head is usually present to some degree in almost all vertex presentations. The contour of the head may be minimally distorted or grotesquely misshapen. Molding is caused by gradual shaping of the head as it accommodates to the contours of the bony and soft parts of the birth canal during labor. It is more severe in dystocia due to contracted pelvis and in primiparous women. Usually the distortion is characterized by flattening of the anterior half of the head, with gradual rise to an apex at the posterior half, and an abrupt drop at the occiput (Fig. 2-10). Schaffer has described the severely molded head as reminiscent of the drawings

Fig. 2-10. Commonest type of molding, characteristic of vertex presentation.

Fig. 2-11. X-ray film of fractured humerus, after difficult breech delivery.

of Egyptian queens. The normal spherical shape of the cranium is gradually restored in 2 or 3 days. There is no valid evidence to suggest that subsequent brain dysfunction is associated with molding, but in the most severe cases the suspicion is inescapable.

Skull fractures may be linear or depressed. Linear fractures are asymptomatic unless the force that produces them also ruptures underlying blood vessels to produce a subdural hematoma. Depressed fractures are often self-correcting, but they may require surgical elevation if the depressed bone compresses underlying brain tissues. These fractures may result from high forceps or midforceps application or from severe contraction of the pelvis associated with prolonged labor.

Fractures of the clavicle and humerus (Fig. 2-11) are the commonest long bone fractures. The clavicle is affected far more frequently than the humerus. Each of these injuries is produced during difficult delivery of a shoulder or upper extremity in vertex or in breech deliveries. The incidence of trauma increases with birth weight. They are thus more frequent among infants who weigh over 4000 grams. Clavicular fracture is usually detectable during movement of the shoulder when a snapping sensation is palpable over the involved bone. Spontaneous movement of

the upper extremity may not be restricted, and the Moro response may be normal. Fracture of the humerus is suspected by diminished motion of the extremity, by pain on passive movement, and often by a grossly visible deformity. Attempts to elicit a snap are contraindicated. Spontaneous motion of the involved extremity is diminished, and forced movement is painful. Reduced motion and pain are especially prominent in fractures of the humerus.

Fracture of the femur is an infrequent injury generally associated with breech deliveries. Swelling of the thigh and severely restricted spontaneous motion of the extremity are characteristic findings. Occasionally the involved thigh is blue because of associated hemorrhage into muscle and subcutaneous tissue.

Intracranial hemorrhage is a relatively common event in the sick newborn. It may be caused by trauma or hypoxia. Traumatic hemorrhage occurs into the brain substance or into the subdural space (subdural hematoma). Hemorrhage due to hypoxia occurs in the ventricles of the brain and in the subarachnoid space. Hypoxic hemorrhage is relatively frequent in premature infants and is apparently not associated with trauma. Symptoms are variable. Apneic episodes and other forms of respiratory distress are common. Hypotonia, a tense bulging anterior fontanelle, diminished spontaneous movement, convulsions, coma, and lethargy are the commonest neurologic signs.

Subdural hematoma is a life-threatening collection of blood in the subdural space that results from laceration of the dura. The dura is the toughest and most external of the three membranes that envelop the brain (the other two are the arachnoid and the pia mater). Most subdural hematomas are produced by stretching and tearing of large veins in the dural membrane that separates the cerebral hemispheres from the cerebellum (tentorium cerebelli). The resultant collection of blood is usually inaccessible to aspiration by subdural taps. This type of subdural hematoma is caused by compression of the head in the anteroposterior diameter with expansion in the transverse diameter and consequent stretching of the dura. This response can best be visualized by compressing an air-filled balloon on two opposed surfaces and noting the expansion that occurs in the surfaces that are free. The dural membrane that runs parallel to the expanded diameter must also stretch during this broadening process. The danger of compression of the skull is greatest when it is relatively abrupt. Abrupt compression is precisely what occurs during precipitate labor and delivery (less than 3 hours' duration). Occasionally the same type of stress is imposed when high forceps or midforceps are applied inaccurately. Less frequently, subdural hematoma occurs over the surface of the cerebral hemispheres when veins in the subdural space are torn. In this location the collection of blood can be evacuated by subdural taps through the coronal suture. Subdural hematoma increases intracranial pressure, and the resultant telltale

signs are separation of the sutures and tense bulging of the anterior fontanelle. Convulsions, coma, and repeated vomiting are frequently noted. Death is not uncommon.

Spinal cord injury is a rare event that is virtually restricted to breech deliveries. It is inflicted by forcible traction applied to the legs during the last phase of breech extraction when the head remains to be delivered. The spinal cord itself is relatively inelastic and does not comply to stretching, whereas the vertebral column is quite compliant. Since the spinal cord is fixed to the vertebral column, stretching of the latter results in tears of the cord or rupture of vessels within it. The type of paralysis that results is dependent on the level at which the cord is injured. Trauma to the lumbar area is most common, producing paralysis of the lower extremities, bladder, and anal sphincter. Laceration in the cervical region may cause total paralysis below the neck. When injury to the phrenic nerve is included, paralysis of the diaphragm follows, and normal establishment and maintenance of extrauterine respiration is impossible.

Cervical spinal cord injuries present three types of clinical signs. In one, there is stillbirth or death immediately after delivery. In another, survival is only for a short period of time. These infants are in spinal shock; they have respiratory depression, and the pathologic picture of their lungs simulates hyaline membrane disease. The third type is characterized by long-term survival with transient or permanent paralysis, usually of the lower limbs.

Subconjunctival (scleral) and *retinal hemorrhages* are due to rupture of capillaries from increased intracranial pressure during the birth process. Ophthalmoscopy reveals flame-shaped and round hemorrhages in the retina. Retinal hemorrhage has been noted in as many as 20% of apparently normal full-term infants. Subconjunctival hemorrhage (into the sclera) imparts a striking external appearance to the eyes, which in the extreme are bright red except for the iris and pupil (Fig. 2-12). Abnormal sequelae to these le-

Fig. 2-12. Scleral (subconjunctival) hemorrhage. There were no sequelae.

Fig. 2-13. Brachial plexus palsy (Erb's paralysis), left. Diagnosis can be suspected at a glance. See text for complete description.

sions have not been documented. They clear within several days after birth.

Brachial plexus palsy is the result of injury to the brachial plexus, a network of major nerve trunks situated at the base of the neck just above the clavicle. The brachial plexuses are formed by nerves from the fifth cervical through the first thoracic spinal roots (C-5 through T-1). Peripheral nerves that supply the muscles of the upper extremities emanate from the brachial plexuses. Injury thus causes some degree of paralysis of the upper extremity on that side. This rather common occurrence is related to a traumatic delivery. Paralysis of an upper extremity is usually partial, rarely complete. In vertex deliveries it results from stretch injury to the brachial plexus when the operator laterally flexes the head excessively toward one of the shoulders, thus damaging the brachial plexus on the opposite side. It also occurs during breech deliveries when the extruded body is flexed laterally just prior to delivery of the head. Usually the involved nerve trunks become edematous; this condition resolves within days or weeks, and the paralysis clears. Occasionally paralysis is permanent.

Brachial plexus injury can be suspected at a glance. It occurs in two forms. One type *(Erb's paralysis)* involves the nerve trunks

of the brachial plexus that emanate from its *upper spinal roots* (C-5, C-6). It is by far the commonest variety, primarily producing variable degrees of paralysis of the shoulder and arm muscles. Spontaneous activity of that extremity is reduced. The arm is held close to the body, and the elbow is straightened, in contrast to that of the opposite, unaffected arm. When the baby is lifted and held in the supine position, the affected extremity is limp, whereas the normal one is held in a flexed position. In eliciting of the Moro reflex, the paralyzed arm responds little or none at all, but the fingers extend almost normally. Involvement is primarily at the shoulder and arm and not in the hand muscles. In Fig. 2-13 is shown a baby at rest who has Erb's paralysis. The diagnosis can be sus-

Fig. 2-14. Response to Moro reflex of infant with left brachial plexus palsy. **A,** Baby held supine, with left arm dangling. **B,** When head is dropped, left arm responds weakly, right arm completely. Note the position of fingers before Moro reflex and later.

pected at a glance. The involved extremity is straight; the opposite one is flexed. Both fists are closed. If the hand muscles of the paralyzed extremity were affected, the fingers would not be fisted. The Moro reflex of such an infant is illustrated in Fig. 2-14. Held supine, the involved left upper extremity is limp; it dangles (Fig. 2-14, *A*). The Moro reflex is characterized by partial movement of the paralyzed extremity; the baby raises it partially from the original position. The

opposite member responds with full motion (Fig. 2-14, *B*). Furthermore, the fingers of the left hand are partially extended. An infant with the second type of brachial plexus injury, *Klumpke's paralysis,* is shown in Fig. 2-15. This variety involves the nerve trunks that originate from the *lower spinal roots* that supply the brachial plexus (C-7, T-1). Principal clinical involvement is therefore in the hands and forearms. Fig. 2-15 shows an unusually affected infant, with

Fig. 2-15. Brachial plexus palsy (Klumpke's paralysis). Note bilateral wrist drop, relaxed fingers.

Fig. 2-16. X-ray film of chest showing right diaphragmatic paralysis associated with brachial plexus palsy on same side. Note inordinate height of right diaphragm and partial atelectasis of the upper lobe of the right lung.

bilateral wrist drop. The fingers are relaxed, not fisted as is normal. This baby's Moro reflex was characterized by active motion of the shoulder and arm; the upper extremities extended and abducted normally. However, the wrists and fingers remained flaccid.

Facial paralysis occurs as frequently in normal deliveries as in traumatic ones. It results from pressure on the facial nerve at a point just posterior to the lower part of the ear lobe, where it lies close to the surface. This pressure is exerted against the maternal bony pelvis during labor or by forceps that are applied inaccurately. Facial paralysis is easily detected when the infant cries. The paralyzed side of the face is immobile, and the palpebral fissure remains open. The muscles on the functional side of the face contract, the eye closes, and the lips deviate toward the normal side. Facial paralysis usually disappears spontaneously in a few days.

Paralysis of the diaphragm (phrenic nerve palsy) usually occurs in association with brachial plexus injury, rarely by itself. It is caused by the same forces that are implicated in brachial plexus palsy, but with additional involvement of the phrenic nerve at its origin from the cervical portion of the spinal cord.

The phrenic nerve receives fibers from the third, fourth, and fifth cervical nerves (C-3 through C-5). Because the phrenic nerve is the only one that innervates the diaphragm, respiratory distress may be severe. The lung on the affected side fails to expand completely, and pneumonia often ensues. In one report, death occurred in 20% of affected infants by the third month of life. We have not seen death of any of these infants. The diagnosis of diaphragmatic paralysis is strongly suggested in an infant who has respiratory distress and a paralyzed upper extremity. It is confirmed by x-ray films of the chest, in which the paralyzed diaphragm is abnormally high (Fig. 2-16).

Hemorrhage into abdominal viscera is usually associated with breech extractions. The adrenals and kidneys are most commonly involved. The liver and spleen are affected occasionally. Injury to the latter two organs poses a threat to survival because blood loss is extensive. The kidney may seem enlarged to palpation in the presence of adrenal hemorrhage because blood seeps downward and surrounds it. In these circumstances the urine does not contain blood. If the kidney itself is traumatized, hematuria is the rule.

MULTIPLE BIRTHS

Perinatal mortality among twins is two or three times greater than among singletons. Therefore the presence of multiple gestation should be detected as early as possible, and the remainder of the pregnancy should be managed with the high risk in mind. The overriding cause of neonatal mortality in twins is prematurity. A number of other complications of pregnancy, labor, and delivery occur with increased frequency (Table 2-1). They include placenta previa, premature separation of the placenta, prolapsed cord, and abnormal presentations (especially breech). The increased incidence of fetal and neonatal abnormalities is also attributable to congenital malformations, intrauterine growth retardation, fetofetal (twin) transfusion syndrome (p. 186), hypoglycemia (p. 204), and intrauterine bacterial infection.

Approximately one third of all twins who are born in the United States are identical; the remainder are fraternal. Identical twins originate from a single ovum (monovular, or monozygous), they are thus of the same sex, and they resemble each other very closely. Fraternal twins are derived from the separate fertilization of two ova (biovular, or dizygous). They may not be of the same sex, and they do not necessarily resemble each other. In approximately half the cases fraternal twins are of like sex. Perinatal mortality is higher among identical twins.

Twinning is more frequent in blacks (approximately one in 70 births) than in whites (one in 80 births). It is least frequent in Orientals. The widely held belief that twin pregnancies are familial applies only to biovular (fraternal) twins. Genetic and ethnic factors do not influence the incidence of identical twins. Multiple gestation appears to increase in frequency as maternal age and parity advance.

References

Adamsons, K., and Joelsson, I.: The effects of pharmacologic agents upon the fetus and newborn, Am. J. Obstet. Gynecol. **96:**437, 1966.

Alstalt, L. B.: Transplacental hyponatremia in the newborn infant, J. Pediatr. **66:**985, 1965.

Benirschke, K.: Origin and clinical significance of twinning, Clin. Obstet. Gynecol. **15:**220, 1972.

Bhagwanani, S. G., Price, H. V., Laurence, K. M., and Ginz, B.: Risks and prevention of cervical cord injury in the management of breech presentation with hyperextension of the fetal head, Am. J. Obstet. Gynecol. **115:**1159, 1973.

Bresnan, M. J., and Abroms, I. F.: Neonatal spinal cord transection secondary to intrauterine hyperextension of the neck in breech presentation, J. Pediatr. **84:**734, 1974.

Bronsky, D., Kiamko, R. T., Moncado, R., et al.: Intrauterine hyperparathyroidism secondary to maternal hypoparathyroidism, Pediatrics **42:**606, 1968.

Cannell, D., and Veron, C. P.: Congenital heart disease in pregnancy, Am. J. Obstet. Gynecol. **85:**744, 1969.

Desmond, M. M., et al.: The relation of maternal disease to fetal and neonatal disorders, Pediatr. Clin. North Am. **8:**421, 1961.

Ertel, N. H., Reiss, J. S., and Spergel, G.: Hypomagnesium in neonatal tetany associated with maternal hypoparathyroidism, N. Engl. J. Med. **280:**260, 1969.

Guillozet, N.: The risks of paracervical anesthesia: intoxication and neurological injury of the newborn, Pediatrics **55:**533, 1975.

Hellman, L.: The birth process. In Cooke, R. E., editor: Biologic basis of pediatrics practice, New York, 1968, McGraw-Hill Book Co.

Hellman, L., and Pritchard, J. A.: Williams obstetrics, ed. 14, New York, 1971, Appleton-Century-Crofts.

Hutchen, P., and Kessner, D. M.: Neonatal tetany: diagnostic lead to hyperparathyroidism in the mother, Ann. Intern. Med. **61:**1109, 1964.

Jones, K. L., Smith, D. W., Ulleland, C. N., and Streissguth, A. P.: Pattern of malformation in offspring of chronic alcoholic mothers, Lancet **1:**1267, 1973.

Jones, W. S., and Martin, E. B.: Thyroid function in pregnancy, Am. J. Obstet. Gynecol. **101:** 898, 1968.

Kincaid-Smith, P.: Bacteriuria and urinary infection in the kidney in pregnancy, Clin. Obstet. Gynecol. **11:**533, 1968.

Klein, R. B., Blatman, S., and Little, G. A.: Probable neonatal propoxyphene withdrawal: a case report, Pediatrics **55:**882, 1975.

McKay, R. J., and Lucey, J. F.: Medical progress: neonatology, N. Engl. J. Med. **270:**1231, 1964.

Mizrahi, A., and Gold, A. P.: Neonatal tetany secondary to maternal hyperparathyroidism, J.A.M.A. **190:**155, 1964.

Morgan, J.: Placenta praevia: report on a series of 538 cases, J. Obstet. Gynecol. Br. Commonw. **72:**700, 1965.

Morrison, J. E.: Foetal and neonatal pathology, ed. 2, London, 1963, Butterworth & Co. (Publishers), Ltd.

Moya, F., and Thorndike, V.: The effects of drugs used in labor on the fetus and newborn, Clin. Pharmacol. Ther. **4:**628, 1963.

Nathenson, G., Cohen, M. I., Litt, I. F., and McNamara, H.: The effect of maternal heroin addiction on neonatal jaundice, J. Pediatr. **81:** 899, 1972.

Niswander, K. R., and Berendes, H.: Effect of maternal cardiac disease on the infant, Clin. Obstet. Gynecol. **11:**1026, 1968.

Palmer, R. H., Quellette, E. M., Warner, L., and Leichtman, S. R.: Congenital malformations in offspring of a chronic alcoholic mother, Pediatrics **53:**490, 1974.

Pomerance, J. J., and Yaffe, S. J.: Maternal medication and its effect on the fetus. In Gluck, L., Cone, T. E., et al., editors: Current problems in pediatrics, Chicago, 1973, Year Book Medical Publishers, Inc.

Potter, E. L.: Pathology of the fetus and infant, ed. 2, Chicago, 1961, Year Book Medical Publishers, Inc.

Reid, D. E., Ryan, K. J., and Benirschke, K.: Principles and management of human reproduction, Philadelphia, 1972, W. B. Saunders Co.

Rumack, B. H., and Walravens, P. A.: Neonatal withdrawal following maternal ingestion of ethchlorvynol (Placidyl), Pediatrics **52:**714, 1973.

Russell, C. S., Taylor, R., and Maddison, R. N.: Some effects of smoking in pregnancy, J. Obstet. Gynaecol. Br. Commonw. **73:**742, 1966.

Schaffer, A.: Disorders related to the birth process. In Cooke, R. E., editor: Biologic basis of pediatric practice, New York, 1968, McGraw-Hill Book Co.

Seeds, E. A.: Adverse effects of the fetus of acute events in labor, Pediatr. Clin. North Am. **17:**811, 1970.

Sever, J., and White, L. R.: Intrauterine viral infections, Ann. Rev. Med. **19:**471, 1968.

Shearer, W. T., Schreiner, R. L., and Marshall, R. E.: Urinary retention in a neonate secondary to maternal ingestion of nortriptyline, J. Pediatr. **81:**570, 1972.

Soyka, L. F.: Prenatal exposure to stilbestrol and adenocarcinoma of the female genital tract: the pediatrician's responsibility, Pediatrics **55:** 455, 1975.

Sutherland, J. M., and Light, I. J.: The effect of drugs on the developing fetus, Pediatr. Clin. North Am. **12:**781, 1965.

Towell, M. E.: The influence of labor on the fetus and the newborn, Pediatr. Clin. North Am. **13:**575, 1966.

Webster, A.: Management of premature rupture of the fetal membranes, Obstet. Gynecol. Survey **24:**485, 1969.

Zelson, C., Lee, S. J., and Pearl, M.: The incidence of skull fractures underlying cephalhematomas in newborn infants, J. Pediatr. **85:** 371, 1974.

Chapter 3

Evaluation and management of the infant immediately after birth

I HAVE LONG BEEN CONVINCED that primary evaluation and care of infants at birth should be delegated to an appropriately trained neonatal nurse who can consult a qualified physician when the need arises. Contemporary therapeutic regimens evolved over the past decade have created a need for skilled personnel to care for infants in the delivery room during the first minutes after birth and in the nursery thereafter. Salvage of increasing numbers of jeopardized infants occurs in hospitals that utilize these regimens properly. However, their application has not been sufficiently widespread due to a lack of skilled personnel. The physician performing a delivery is preoccupied with the mother and yet must turn from her to help the distressed baby; or a pediatrician must be summoned, perhaps from some distance, only to arrive after the issue has been resolved unhappily. Obviously, the continuous presence of someone who is adept and knowledgeable is essential for the care of all infants, especially the sick ones; wasted minutes are crucial to survival and to the preservation of intact central nervous system function. The trained

neonatal nurse should play a vital role in solving these problems.

EVALUATION: THE APGAR SCORE

In 1952 Dr. Virginia Apgar introduced a simple straightforward scoring system for the clinical evaluation of infants at birth. A total score ranging from 0 to 10 is assigned; the more vigorous the infant, the higher the score. The procedure is best performed by an impartial nurse who is not directly involved with delivery of the infant and is primarily concerned with the postnatal status. This method of evaluation provides a grossly quantitative expression of the infant's condition that is well correlated with prenatal events and the postnatal course.

Procedure for scoring

Table 3-1 presents the components of the Apgar scoring system. A score of 0 to 2 is assigned to each item. The total of the five individual assessments is the Apgar score. A total score of 0 to 2 represents severe distress, 3 to 6 signifies moderate difficulty, and 7 to 10 indicates absence of stress or only the

Table 3-1. Apgar scoring chart

Sign	Score 0	Score 1	Score 2
Heart rate	Absent	Slow (below 100)	Over 100
Respiratory effort	Absent	Slow, irregular, hypoventilation	Good Crying lustily
Muscle tone	Flaccid	Some flexion of extremities	Active motion, well flexed
Reflex irritability	No response	Cry Some motion	Vigorous cry
Color	Blue, pale	Body pink Hands and feet blue	Completely pink

mildest difficulty. Evaluations are ordinarily conducted at 1 and 5 minutes after delivery of the entire body. One minute was chosen as the optimal time for the first score because experience had indicated that maximal depression occurred at that time. The 5-minute score correlates more closely with neurologic status at 1 year of age than does the score at 60 seconds. Most babies score 6 or 7 at 1 minute and 8 to 10 at 5 minutes after birth. If a score of 7 or less is assigned at 5 minutes, assessment should be repeated at 10 minutes. The individual components are evaluated as follows.

The *heart rate* is just as sensitive an indication of hypoxia after birth as it is in utero. A rate below 100 beats per minute is associated with severe asphyxia. The heart rate should be counted for at least 30 seconds. If a stethoscope is not available at the moment, palpation of the umbilical cord at its junction with the skin of the abdomen is also reliable for counting. In fact, pulsations of the cord are normally visible at this location. The heart rate is the most important of the five evaluated items. A score of 2 is assigned if the heart rate exceeds 100, a value of 1 is given if it is below 100, and if no heartbeat is detected, the score is 0. If it is less than 100 beats per minute, an urgent need for resuscitation exists.

Respiratory effort is next in importance to heart rate. Regular respirations and a vigorous cry merit a score of 2. If respirations are irregular, shallow, or gasping, a score of 1 is appropriate, whereas 0 indicates complete absence of any respiratory effort (apnea).

Muscle tone refers to the degree of flexion and the resistance offered to straightening the extremities. The normal infant's elbows are flexed, and his thighs and knees are drawn up toward the abdomen (flexed hips). In addition, some degree of resistance is encountered when one attempts to extend the extremities. This normal muscle tone is assigned a score of 2. At the other extreme, an asphyxiated infant is limp. There is no resistance to straightening of the extremities, nor is there any semblance of flexion at rest. This

state of muscle tone is scored 0. Muscle tone that is intermediate between the normal and limp asphyxiated states is given 1 point.

Reflex irritability is judged by the infant's response to flicking the sole of the foot. If he cries, a score of 2 is given. If he only grimaces or cries feebly, a score of 1 is given. If there is no response, the score is 0.

Color evaluation is directed to the presence or absence of pallor and cyanosis. Only a few infants are completely pink; they are assigned 2 points. Most babies are given a score of 1 because normally their hands and feet are blue, whereas the rest of the body is pink (acrocyanosis). Only 15% of all infants score 10 at 1 minute because of the high incidence of acrocyanosis. Pallor and cyanosis over the entire body is scored 0.

Relationship of Apgar scores to arterial pH and clinical depression

Table 3-2 demonstrates the close relationship of the Apgar score to arterial blood pH. As the score declines, pH diminishes; acidosis is thus more profound, and clinical depression of the infant is increasingly severe. Acid-base status of the infant can be remarkably well estimated from the simple observations of the Apgar evaluation. The scores provide a sound basis for the management of neonates immediately after birth, and the resuscitative procedures that are described later are based on them. There are, however, two notable exceptions to the close relationship between the Apgar score and blood pH: (1) A low score may be associated with a normal or slightly diminished

Table 3-2. Relationship of Apgar score to arterial blood pH*

Apgar score	Arterial pH
9 or 10	7.30 to 7.40 (normal)
7 or 8	7.20 to 7.29 (slight acidosis)
5 or 6	7.10 to 7.19 (moderate acidosis)
3 or 4	7.00 to 7.09 (marked acidosis)
0 to 2	Below 7.00 (severe acidosis)

*Modified from Saling, E.: Int. J. Gynecol. Obstet. **10:**211, 1972.

pH if the infant is depressed as a consequence of maternal anesthesia; and (2) a relatively high score may be associated with a low pH in small-for-dates infants who have suffered chronic marginal intrauterine hypoxia.

Relationship of Apgar scores to birth weight and neonatal mortality

Systematic observations on thousands of infants have clearly demonstrated a relationship between Apgar scores and birth weight, time of scoring, neonatal mortality, and neurologic status at 1 year of age.

The increased prevalence of stress among low birth weight infants is indicated by the incidence of low scores. In 57% of infants who weigh 1500 grams or less, the 1-minute scores are 0 to 3, whereas these low scores occur in only 5% of infants over 3000 grams. Vigor at birth is far more common among larger babies; scores of 9 and 10 occur in 52% of them, whereas in small infants only 4% score similarly.

The status of most infants improves between the 1- and 5-minute scores. Fewer babies are in a precarious state at 5 minutes than at 1 minute. In the *Collaborative Perinatal Study,* observations on 17,000 infants revealed that at 1 minute 7% scored 0 to 3, and at 5 minutes 2% scored similarly. The same trend toward improvement is indicated by the incidence of higher scores. At 1 minute 79% scored 9 or 10, and at 5 minutes 95% achieved the same scores. Because improvement between 1 and 5 minutes occurs in a substantial number of infants, the later scores are generally more reliable for the prediction of death during the first 28 days of life (neonatal mortality), and of abnormal neurologic status at 1 year.

The risk of death is increased if the 5-minute Apgar score is low. In the absence of an intensive care program, death can be expected during the neonatal period in 50% of all infants with a 5-minute score of 0 or 1, and the vast majority of these babies expire within the first 48 hours of life. Low birth weight enhances this risk considerably. For instance, among babies under 2000 grams who score 0 to 3 at 5 minutes, approximately 80% die during the neonatal period, but among infants over 2500 grams with the same scores the mortality is 15%. The vast majority of these deaths occur during the first 2 postnatal days.

These data were compiled in the era that immediately preceded contemporary intensive care of the neonate. Although mortality and morbidity have improved, the relative predictive value of lower scores for more ominous outcomes is probably unchanged. Death of low-scored infants may be up to fifteen times more frequent than in those whose scores are high.

Relationship of Apgar scores to neurologic status at 1 year of age

The link between later brain dysfunction and perinatal distress is also convincingly demonstrated in data from the *Collaborative Perinatal Study.* A close relationship was evident between low birth weight, low Apgar scores at 5 minutes, and an increased incidence of neurologic abnormalities at 1 year of age. That hypoxia around the time of birth may well be lethal can be appreciated from the correlation of low scores with increased neonatal mortality. A low 5-minute score indicates persistence of asphyxia. Thus, if a distressed infant with a low score survives, his chances of brain damage are considerably greater than they would have been if he had scored normally. This is reflected in statistical data that relate birth weight and Apgar scores to 1-year outcomes. Birth weight exerts the same sort of influence on 1-year outcome as on neonatal mortality. Table 3-3 is taken from data compiled by the *Collaborative Perinatal Study.* With identical scores, the frequency of neurologic abnormalities at 1 year increases as birth weight diminishes. At identical birth weights, the frequency of abnormalities increases as the Apgar score declines. Together the effects of weight and score reinforce each other. Thus, of all the groups in the table the smallest infants with the lowest scores are most likely

Table 3-3. Percentage of neurologic abnormality at 1 year according to 5-minute Apgar score and birth weight*

Birth weight	5-minute Apgar scores		
(in grams)	0-3	4-6	7-10
1001 to 2000	18.8%	14.3%	8.8%
2001 to 2500	12.5%	4.6%	4.0%
Over 2500	4.3%	4.2%	1.4%

*Modified from Drage, J. S., and Berendes, H.: Pediatr. Clin. North Am. 13:635, 1966.

to have brain damage (18.8%), whereas the largest babies with the highest scores are least likely to be affected (1.4%).

The diminished incidence of neurologic deficit among surviving infants that has occurred since the advent of intensive care is well documented. The results described above have thus undoubtedly improved, but the influence of low scores and low birth weight on poor outcome is probably unchanged.

Value of Apgar scores

The quality of neonatal care has improved as a result of the Apgar score. Perhaps the most important contribution of the procedure is that it requires scrutiny of the baby immediately after birth. Thorough evaluation of heart rate, respiration, muscle tone, reflex response, and color was not performed systematically prior to the introduction of scoring. The value of the procedure is so well established that it is unquestionably negligent to omit it. Aside from its predictive value, the score identifies high-risk infants who urgently require resuscitation. It also provides a universally understood quantitative expression of the infant's condition. It further enables statistical assessment of a hospital's perinatal practices and the level of risk in the population it serves. The procedure is simple, but it requires conscientiousness and skill if its purposes are to be fulfilled. The most accurate results are obtained when a knowledgeable nurse executes the scoring.

MANAGEMENT: ROUTINE CARE AND RESUSCITATION OF DISTRESSED INFANTS

Information regarding resuscitative procedures is presented with full awareness that too few nurses have been taught to use them, and with the distinct conviction that many infants would be salvaged if more nurses could do so. The procedures cannot be learned from a printed page. These descriptions are like a map; real familiarity with the terrain is gained only after traveling the road, but the itinerary must be known beforehand. Resuscitation and its rationale must first be read about and then performed with proper supervision.

Care of normal infants (Apgar score 7 to 10)

There is often a moment of suspense, sometimes tension, when birth is imminent as the top of the baby's head first becomes visible. The events that follow birth have their origins in those that preceded it. If the history is known in detail, and if labor and delivery have been followed closely, many of the infant's potential difficulties can be anticipated, and they have already been discussed in some detail. Although most babies are normal and have no difficulties, they nevertheless must be supported by a few simple procedures.

After delivery of the entire body, the operator holds the head downward as suction is applied to the nostrils and oropharynx with a bulb syringe. The cord is cut and clamped, and the nurse takes the baby in charge. The infant is placed in a 15-degree Trendelenburg position on a table supplied with radiant heat emanating from above. The importance of providing environmental warmth to minimize loss of body heat cannot be overemphasized. Control of body temperature (thermoregulation) is discussed in detail in Chapter 4. At birth, a major cause of heat loss is the evaporation of amniotic fluid that covers the infant's skin. The infant must therefore be dried rapidly, preferably by another individual, while the neonatal nurse removes oropharyngeal secretions with a bulb syringe if they have reaccumulated.

The 1-minute Apgar score should now be performed, and if the result is 7 to 10, resuscitative therapy is unnecessary. The infant should be observed on a warmed table until the 5-minute Apgar score is assigned, and for at least an additional 5 minutes thereafter. During the interval after the 5-minute Apgar score, the nurse should examine the infant. Auscultation of the chest will ascertain proper position of the heart and normal air exchange. The head and body surfaces are scrutinized for trauma and for obvious congenital anomalies. Spontaneous movement of the extremities is observed for indications of weakness or paralysis. The abdomen is palpated for masses and for enlargement of the liver, spleen, or kidneys. The genitalia are examined for normal sexuality. Each of the shoulders is moved while a finger is placed over the clavicle. A crunching sensation (crepitus) betrays a fracture. Normal findings of the physical examination and their variants are presented in detail in Chapter 6.

At some time prior to transfer of the infant to the nursery, the cord is cut again, leaving a stump approximately 1 inch in length to which a clamp is applied. Before the clamp is applied, the cut surface should be examined closely for the normal number of vessels (two arteries and one vein). The presence of only one artery suggests one or more major congenital malformations. The cut edges of the arteries are seen as two white papular structures, which usually stand out slightly from the surface. The vein is larger, often gaping so that the lumen and thin wall are readily discernible (Fig. 1-4). A drop of silver nitrate is now placed in each eye for prophylaxis against gonorrheal infection. The eyes should not be irrigated thereafter. In some communities antibiotic drops are preferred for this purpose, but silver nitrate is the preparation of choice.

A complete record of labor, delivery, and postnatal events must accompany the infant on transfer to the nursery. The condition should be reported verbally to the physician in charge before the nurse leaves the delivery room with the baby. The nursery should have already been notified of the infant's anticipated arrival.

Care of moderately depressed infants (Apgar score 3 to 6)

Moderately depressed infants are limp, cyanotic or dusky, and dyspneic. Respirations may be shallow, irregular, or gasping. The heart rate is normal, however, and there is at least a fair response to flicking of the sole. Management entails the same regimen described for normal infants during the first minute after birth, but if effective spontaneous respiration is not established thereafter, ventilatory support is essential. The urgency for this support is indicated by continued cyanosis and flaccidity. Initially a laryngoscope is inserted. The larynx is visualized, and suction is applied through a catheter attached to a De Lee trap. The De Lee trap is operated by suction from the operator's mouth. This procedure, under direct visualization of the larynx, assures removal of blood clot, particles of meconium and vernix, and thick mucus. The suction catheter is withdrawn, and a curved plastic airway is inserted between the tongue and palate to prevent the base of the tongue from falling backward over the glottic opening of the larynx. Oxygen is then administered through a tightly fitting face mask attached to a hand-operated bag that receives 100% oxygen and delivers it to the infant in high concentrations. At our hospital we have used the Penlon mask-and-bag apparatus with satisfaction. The chest rises with each squeeze of the bag if oxygen is delivered adequately. Further ascertainment is obtainable if an assistant listens to each lung with a stethoscope for the presence of breath sounds. If color and respirations have not improved after 1 minute or the heart rate falls below 100 beats per minute at any time, endotracheal intubation is urgently indicated (see following discussion). If the mask-and-bag procedure is effective, spontaneous respiration begins within 1 minute; cyanosis and hypotonicity should disappear. When the baby begins to breathe, free-flowing oxygen should be supplied.

Care of severely depressed infants (Apgar score 0 to 2)

Gentle swiftness is the essence of resuscitation of profoundly depressed infants. Their woeful state is instantly recognizable. They are blue and limp, and they make little or no attempt to breathe. The heart rate is less than 100 beats per minute, if it is at all present; preliminary suction of the upper airway and a vigorous flick of the sole are of no avail. The Apgar score is 0 to 2. This evaluation should consume no more than a few seconds. The experienced observer recognizes the gravity of the situation without consciously scoring the infant's status. Suction and endotracheal intubation under direct visualization with a laryngoscope are the only procedures that can save an infant in such straits. Generally, once oxygen is delivered to the lungs, the response is gratifying. Improvement may be noted in seconds, although frequently intubation must be maintained for 10 minutes or longer. The heartbeat returns; or if it is present initially, the rate quickens and the sounds are louder and sharper. With the return of more effective cardiac function the baby becomes pink, and some spontaneous muscle activity may appear. If heart activity is absent after 3 or 4 insufflations, external cardiac massage is mandatory. After cardiac activity is restored, and only then, intravenous administration of sodium bicarbonate and dextrose is essential because hypoxia causes metabolic acidosis and may produce hypoglycemia as a result of rapid depletion of glycogen stores. The details of resuscitation follow.

Equipment

1. *Laryngoscope* (pencil handle with attached Miller size 0 premature or size 1 infant blade). The adequacy of the light source must be ascertained during periodic routine checks of all equipment when not in use.

2. *Endotracheal tubes.* Some operators prefer Cole endotracheal tubes with metal stylet to prevent kinking. These tubes are tapered at the distal end (sizes 10, 12, or 14). We prefer untapered Portex tubes in sizes ranging from 2.5 to 4 mm. We avoid metal stylets because of the trauma they may cause during intubation.

3. *De Lee trap.* With a Rausch catheter attached (two holes at the tip), the De Lee trap is preferred for suction. Wall suction in delivery rooms is traumatic to neonates because it is too forceful. If wall suction is used, it must be modulated by a regulator to a level no greater than 120 mm Hg.

4. *Bag resuscitator.* This bag is attached to the inserted endotracheal tube. It receives 100% oxygen from a wall source or from a tank. Infant masks are usually supplied with this apparatus but are of no value in resuscitation of severely depressed infants (as noted previously).

Procedure for ventilation by tracheal intubation

1. The infant should be supine, with a flattened, rolled towel to support the upper back at the level of the shoulders.

2. The baby's head is held with the right hand; the face looks upward. The laryngoscope is held in the left hand with the blade attachment downward.

3. The blade is slipped past the right corner of the mouth for a distance of approximately 2 cm along the right side of the oral cavity. In so doing, the blade is moved toward the midline, thus displacing the tongue to the left side of the oral cavity.

4. The tip of the blade is advanced slightly so that it comes to rest in a wedge-like space (the vallecula), which is situated between the epiglottis and the base of the tongue (Fig. 3-1). A slight upward tilt of the tip of the blade now exposes the opening of the larynx (glottis). The glottis is more easily seen if slight downward pressure is applied externally to the larynx by the hand that holds the laryngoscope, or by an assistant. As now viewed, the following structures are identifiable from above downward (an-

Fig. 3-1. A, Position of laryngoscope blade prior to insertion into the vallecula. **B,** Blade tip resting in vallecula directly above the epiglottis. **C,** Misplaced blade inserted into the esophagus. (Modified from film "Resuscitation of the Newborn," Special Committee on Infant Mortality of the Medical Society of New York, produced by Smith, Kline & French Medical Film Center, Philadelphia.)

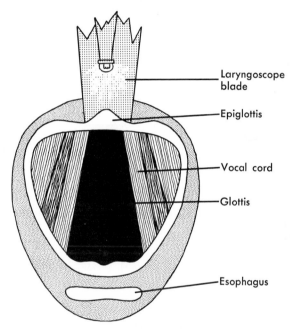

Fig. 3-2. Direct view of the glottis and surrounding structures after the blade tip is inserted into the vallecula.

terior to posterior): the base of the tongue, the blade placed in the vallecula, the epiglottis, the glottis, the esophageal opening, and the posterior hypopharyngeal wall (Fig. 3-2). The epiglottis is a valuable landmark because it is sometimes visible when the glottis is not. The epiglottis appears as an arched rim of pink tissue, which often tapers to a rounded point so that it resembles a diminutive tongue. If it is visible and the glottis is not, you need only tilt the laryngoscope slightly so that the tip of the blade moves upward. The glottic opening is thus revealed as a black vertical slit. If obstructed by fluid and particulate matter, the slit is discerned with difficulty. Suction is necessary to clear the area and to evacuate unseen material that may fill the trachea as well. The suction catheter should be advanced through the glottis to clear the trachea prior to insertion of an endotracheal tube.

5. If spontaneous respirations do not im-

mediately follow the removal of fluid and particulate matter, an endotracheal tube is introduced through the glottis. If the Cole tube is used, it is advanced until the widened flange of the tube no longer permits passage. If a straight tube such as the Portex is used, insertion past the glottis should not exceed 1 to 1.5 cm. Remove the laryngoscope cautiously while holding the tube in place. Oxygen may now be delivered through a bag (Penlon) attached to the endotracheal tube. The bag is abruptly squeezed and released at a rate approximating 50 times per minute. If the bag is grasped in the palm of the hand and is squeezed with all five fingers, pressures in excess of 60 to 70 cm H_2O are delivered, and pneumothorax may ensue. By squeezing with the thumb, index, and middle fingers only, safer and usually effective pressures of 25 to 40 cm H_2O are delivered. Sometimes higher pressures are required initially for adequate lung expansion, necessitating use of the entire hand for bag compression. If the endotracheal tube has been inserted too deeply, it will pass directly into the right main stem bronchus. Delivery of oxygen is therefore confined to the right lung, and insufflation causes expansion in the right chest, with little or no visible excursion on the left. This discrepancy can be determined more accurately by an assistant who listens with a stethoscope. Breath sounds are absent on the left, whereas on the right they are loud and clear. This being the case, the endotracheal tube should be withdrawn slightly until breath sounds are equal on each side of the chest.

External cardiac massage

1. If the heartbeat has not returned after three or four insufflations, external cardiac massage must be instituted immediately. It should be performed by an assistant, leaving the primary operator free to manage ventilation. When downward pressure is applied at the left margin of the lower sternum, the heart is compressed (systole); when the pressure is released, the heart is dilated (diastole).

2. The index and middle fingers are placed at the appropriate spot and abruptly pressed downward and released. The total downward displacement of the chest wall should not exceed 1 inch. Excessive vigor may cause a laceration of the liver with severe blood loss.

3. It is imperative to maintain cardiac massage and ventilation. This is accomplished by alternating the two maneuvers. The heart is compressed two or three times (at a rate approximating 120 times per minute), after which a breath of oxygen is supplied. The two procedures should never be performed simultaneously, since the pressure applied during cardiac massage may rupture a lung that is simultaneously inflated by artificial ventilation. Pneumothorax and pneumomediastinum may ensue.

4. If cardiac massage is effective, the femoral or temporal artery pulses are palpable in synchrony with depression of the sternum. Cardiac compression should be discontinued every 30 to 60 seconds to detect the presence of spontaneous cardiac activity.

5. When a regular heartbeat is discerned, cardiac massage may be discontinued. Assisted ventilation may be discontinued when spontaneous respiration appears.

Correction of metabolic acidosis. The association of metabolic acidosis with prolonged hypoxia has been discussed previously. Resuscitative measures should therefore include the administration of alkali intravenously after cardiac activity is established, even though manual ventilation is still in progress. If heart action is depressed or absent, the infusion of sodium bicarbonate is of little avail because much of it remains where it was injected.

If intravenous medication is an urgent need, rapid access is accomplished by inserting a catheter into the umbilical vein. The catheter is passed into the umbilical vein for distances varying from 5 to 9 cm, depending on the size of the baby. The distal end of the catheter should never be open to room atmosphere because a deep gasp may cause the entry of a significant quantity of air into the heart. A three-way stopcock thus should be attached at the distal end of the fluid-filled catheter for administration of sodium bicarbonate by syringe and for slow infusion of 10% dextrose solution afterward. Sodium bicarbonate is available as a 7.5% solution containing 0.88 mEq/ml. For ease of calculation one may assume that each milliliter contains 1 mEq of sodium bicarbonate. In severely depressed infants, the physician should order at least 3 ml/kg of body weight of this solution, which must be diluted in equal amounts of 10% dextrose water or water for infection. Undiluted, 7.5% sodium bicarbonate is very hypertonic (osmolality of 1400) and alkaline (pH 7.80). This mixture is administered at a rate not in excess of 2 ml/min through the three-way stopcock that was placed at the end of the catheter. After alkali infusion, 10% dextrose is given by continuous drip at a rate of 65 ml/kg of body weight per 24 hours. The infusion rate is adjusted subsequently in the nursery. The umbilical vein should be abandoned as soon as possible in favor of a peripheral vein if continued intravenous administration of fluid is necessary. An infusion pump must be used to maintain the appropriate flow rate.

Maintenance of body heat. Provision of external heat is indispensable if optimal results are to be derived from the resuscitative procedures just described. The implications of low body temperature are discussed in Chapter 4. Evaluation and management of all infants must be performed on a table that is supplied by an overhead source of radiant heat. Without it, the response to resuscitation is delayed, diminished, or absent. The prevention of heat loss is also crucial during transfer of the baby to the nursery. The severely depressed infant should be moved in an incubator that is equipped with a battery-operated heat source and an independent oxygen supply. If this equipment is not available, double-layered plastic bags that are designed to minimize heat loss may be used. These transparent bags fit snugly over the infant. The two layers are separated by large, multiple, self-contained

air bubbles. If these bags are unavailable, the baby should be wrapped in a warmed blanket and transferred rapidly.

Errors commonly committed during resuscitation

With so many procedures to be performed, and with so little time in which to accomplish them, it is no wonder that errors are sometimes committed even by experienced personnel, not to mention the blunders of the uninitiated and untrained. Perhaps the most fundamental of all errors is the attempt to resuscitate with little knowledge of rationale and with ignorance of the physiologic processes that have gone awry. The quality of performance increases directly with an understanding of rationale.

Specific errors in technique should be recognized if they are to be avoided or quickly corrected. The most frequent error during laryngoscopy is passage of the blade beyond the epiglottis into the esophageal opening, which is round or oval rather than slitlike and vertical (Fig. 3-2). At this point one is peering into the esophagus while the glottic slit is concealed above the blade and is closer to the operator by several centimeters or millimeters. The blade should be withdrawn slowly while pointing the tip slightly upward. The glottis and the epiglottis soon fall into full view. If, on the other hand, the blade tip is placed short of its goal, very slight advancement will position it in the vallecula.

Often an operator extends the baby's head in the erroneous assumption that intubation is facilitated, when in fact such positioning virtually precludes success. One frequently observes an operator with one hand on the chin, pulling it backward to extend the head while the laryngoscope is being inserted. The resultant stretching of the neck projects the larynx upward (anteriorly) so that it is hidden by the base of the tongue. It also tends to close the glottis. In these circumstances the tip of the blade is invariably directed into the esophagus, and even when it is withdrawn gingerly, the larynx will not drop into view while the head is maintained in extension. Rather than pull the chin backward, one should place the head in a neutral position.

Trauma is always a hazard when a metallic instrument is swiftly introduced into soft tissues. Lacerations and bruises of pharyngeal and laryngeal structures may result from rough insertion of the laryngoscope. Injury to the larynx is particularly serious because the airway may be occluded by edema or hemorrhage.

Another frequently committed error, previously mentioned, is insertion of the endotracheal tube too deeply into the trachea. The bifurcation of the trachea into two main stem bronchi is such that the right bronchus is almost a direct continuation of the trachea, whereas the left one branches from it at a sharper angle. Thus, overinsertion of the tube almost invariably places it in the right main stem bronchus; ventilation is restricted to the right lung, whereas the left lung remains unventilated. Detection and correction of this error have already been described.

In the anxiety of the moment, the operator often insufflates at a needlessly rapid rate, sometimes over 100 times per minute. The optimal rate is 50 times per minute. Also, if a bag-and-tube arrangement is used, the operator should be certain that the bag is connected to a source of oxygen; otherwise only room air (20% oxygen) will be delivered, and although it may sometimes be effective, higher oxygen concentrations are usually an urgent requirement.

Several additional factors require mention. Secretions may accumulate in the pharynx while endotracheal ventilation is in progress. Before removing the tube, suction should be applied to evacuate the secretions. Failure to provide ambient (surrounding) heat is a gross error. Every delivery room must be equipped with a heating apparatus.

The use of central nervous system stimulants such as caffeine, nikethamide (Coramine), and pentylenetetrazol (Metrazol) has no place in modern resuscitative procedures. The latter two drugs are particularly danger-

ous. The most effective stimulator of respiration is oxygen. Initial efforts to resuscitate the newborn must therefore be concerned exclusively with delivery of oxygen to the lungs. Certain pharmacologic agents are sometimes indicated, but only for purposes other than central nervous excitation. Thus the use of narcotic antagonists is essential in drug-induced respiratory depression due to maternal narcotic overdosage. Nalorphine (Nalline) and levallorphan (Lorfan) are given if fetal depression from maternal narcosis is due to morphine, meperidine (Demerol), dihydromorphone (Dilaudid), and methadone (Dolophine). If used for respiratory depression due to other causes, the antidotes themselves may be depressant. This is especially true if they are used to counteract the effects of barbiturates.

Summation

The extent of resuscitative procedures varies from the simple provision of free-flowing oxygen by mask to insufflation through an endotracheal tube, depending on the severity of depression. The Apgar score is an excellent indication of the infant's status and the type of resuscitation required. All babies need a clear airway and warmth. The establishment of spontaneous respiration is the most important and immediate goal of resuscitation; failure to prevent loss of body heat and to correct acidosis may prolong the time to complete recovery, or preclude it. The ultimate goal of resuscitation is not only immediate survival of the baby but also the prevention of central nervous system dysfunction during the years after birth.

References

Apgar, V.: The newborn (Apgar) scoring system, Pediatr. Clin. North Am. **13**:645, 1966.

Apgar, V., and James, L. S.: The first sixty seconds of life. In Abramson, H., editor: Resuscitation of the newborn infant, ed. 3, St. Louis, 1973, The C. V. Mosby Co.

Berendes, H., and Drage, J. S.: Apgar scores and outcome of the newborn, Pediatr. Clin. North Am. **13**:635, 1966.

Desmond, M. M., Rudolph, A. J., and Phitaksphraiwan, P.: The transitional care nursery, Pediatr. Clin. North Am. **13:**651, 1966.

James, L. S., and Adamsons, K., Jr.: Intrapartum period. In Barnett, H. L., editor: Pediatrics, New York, 1968, Appleton-Century-Crofts.

James, L. S., and Apgar, V.: Resuscitation procedures in the delivery room. In Abramson, H., editor: Resuscitation of the newborn infant, ed. 3, St. Louis, 1973, The C. V. Mosby Co.

Moya, F., James, L. S., Burnard, E. D., and Hanks, E. C.: Cardiac massage in the newborn infant through the intact chest, Am. J. Obstet. Gynecol. **84:**798, 1962.

Shanklin, D. R.: The influence of placental lesions on the newborn infant, Pediatr. Clin. North Am. **17:**25, 1970.

Chapter 4

Thermoregulation

THERMOREGULATION IN THE NEONATE: IMPORTANCE OF HEAT BALANCE

MAINTENANCE of an optimal thermal environment is one of the most important aspects of effective neonatal care, and without knowledge of the basic principles of thermoregulation, it cannot be provided consistently. However, with the facts at hand, cold stress can be prevented, and many of the riddles that arise daily can be solved. For example, why did a premature infant in our nursery continue to lose body heat even though the air temperature in his incubator constantly registered at 92° F on two thermometers? Why did this same infant fail to gain weight optimally in spite of an adequate caloric intake? The answers: Heat loss occurred because the incubator walls were chilled by a continuous blast of cold air from a window air conditioner that was only inches away. Weight gain was poor because the energy of metabolism was partially diverted to the compensatory production of body heat in preference to the laying down of new tissue. To one of our informed nurses the solution was simple: the baby must be moved across the room in his incubator, away from the air conditioner. The basis for that decision and other aspects of heat balance are discussed in some detail in the pages that follow.

The association of low body temperature with lower survival rates was observed in 1900 by the French neonatologist Pierre-Constant Budin, who was probably the first such physician on record. In his observation, only 10% of neonates survived if body temperatures were 90.5° to 92.3° F; 77% survived at temperatures between 96.8° and 98.6° F. The significance of this early obser-

vation was not appreciated until about 40 years later, when modern inquiries began. A voluminous literature continues to accumulate. Although the complex problem of maintaining an appropriate environment for small, sick neonates is not yet completely solved, sufficient data are on hand to permit provision of a thermal environment to minimize the morbidity and mortality that is directly or indirectly due to cold stress.

The human being is homeothermic (Greek: *homoios* = similar, *thermē* = heat); that is, the organism can maintain its body temperature within narrow limits in spite of gross variations in environmental temperatures. In contrast, animals such as the turtle are poikilothermic (Greek: *poikilos* = variable, *thermē* = heat). Their body temperatures vary widely in response to environmental changes. In man, normal deep-body (core) temperature is maintained within very narrow limits; it does not vary more than 0.3%. This is contrasted to the more variable limits of blood sugar, which may fluctuate 50% normally, and to hydrogen ion concentrations (pH), which vary from 10% to 20% within normal limits.

Thermal balance is maintained by regulation of heat loss and heat production. Perhaps the most frequently encountered example of heat imbalance at any age is fever, in which heat is produced in excess of the capacity to dissipate it. Core (rectal) temperature thus rises. In neonates, particularly the smaller ones, heat loss is excessive by adult standards in spite of a capacity for reasonably effective heat production. Hypothermia is therefore the principal problem of heat balance in the newborn infant. The tendency to lose heat rapidly at ordinary room temperatures is often a threat to survival, particularly for small babies who are ill.

MODALITIES OF THERMAL TRANSFER

Exchange of heat between the body and the environment occurs by 4 modalities: convection, radiation, evaporation, and conduction. Although they are discussed in the context of body heat losses, thermal gains from external sources occur in a like manner.

Convective loss. Convection involves a flow of heat from the body surface to cooler surrounding air. The rate of loss by convection depends on ambient (surrounding) temperature, the velocity of airflow, and relative humidity. A rapid flow of air enhances heat loss. Ideal ambient temperature in the incubator reduces convective heat loss only, having no significant effect on the loss of heat by radiation or evaporation.

Radiant loss. Radiant loss involves transfer of body heat to cooler *solid* objects in the environment that are *not in contact* with the baby (incubator walls). Thermal dissipation increases as these solid objects become colder or closer to the body. *Radiant heat loss is independent of ambient temperature in the incubator.* It was by this mechanism that inordinate heat loss occurred in the premature infant mentioned earlier. The incubator wall that was closest to the air conditioner was cold, and as a result the baby continuously lost heat to the wall by radiation in spite of the high temperature of incubator air, which minimized only convective heat loss. Thus, even if the temperature of ambient air is high, significant loss may occur by radiation if the incubator walls are inordinately cool. This loss is a common phenomenon at ordinary room temperature, and especially during the winter in inadequately insulated nurseries where babies are placed close to windows. It is also frequent in air-conditioned nurseries when the vents release concentrated drafts of cool air directly onto incubators.

Evaporative loss. Evaporative heat loss occurs during conversion of a liquid to a vapor because thermal energy is utilized in the process. Thus the evaporation of sweat promotes thermal dissipation by virtue of the body heat that is consumed. Evaporation, and thus the rate of heat loss, is increased when humidity is low. At birth, a considerable amount of thermal dissipation occurs, especially in air-conditioned delivery rooms with low humidity. Because the infant is covered with amniotic fluid, he loses a considerable amount of heat as the fluid evaporates. This mode of heat loss is readily eliminated when the baby is dried immediately with a warm towel. Another practical consideration in respect to evaporative heat loss is the timing of the first bath after arrival in the nursery. Whether full term or premature, neonates should not be bathed until the body temperature is stable at normal levels.

Conductive loss. Conductive loss of body heat occurs during *direct contact* of the skin with a cooler *solid* object. Placement of a naked infant on a cold table would thus promote conductive heat loss.

Anatomic peculiarities

The neonate's anatomy predisposes him to the loss of heat by convection, radiation, evaporation, and conduction. Thermal balance is more precarious in newborns than in older individuals, particularly in infants weighing less than 2000 grams. The newborn's normal capacity for heat production in itself presents no problems. The crucial issue is heat loss, which is largely a function of the ratio of body surface to body weight. The larger the surface in relation to body mass, the greater the opportunity to dissipate heat to the environment. At birth the full-term infant is only 5% of adult body weight; yet his body surface is 15% of the adult's. The discrepancy between weight and body surface is even greater for low birth weight infants. A larger surface area provides more extensive exposure to the environment, thus promoting more heat loss (external gradient). Loss of heat per unit of body weight is four times greater in the full-term newborn, and five times greater in a 1500-gram premature infant, than in the adult. This loss of heat is the principal source of the neonate's difficulty with maintaining thermal balance.

Another important anatomic handicap to conservation of body heat is the thin layer of subcutaneous fat, especially in infants who weigh less than 2000 grams. Heat is thus more readily transferred from the core of the body to the skin (internal gradient). Deep body temperature is generally somewhat higher than surface (skin) temperature. Since a gradient exists between the core and the surface (internal gradient), constant transfer of heat occurs in that direction. This transfer is normally impeded by a substantial layer of subcutaneous fat; it is accelerated if the fat layer is minimal. Therefore, because small infants are poorly insulated, they lose their core body heat to the skin more readily than full-term infants.

An infant's posture influences the rate of heat loss. Flexion of the extremities reduces the area exposed to the environment. Normal posture at rest varies with gestational age; the tendency for flexion of the extremities increases as gestational age advances. Where thermal balance is concerned, the premature infant is thus at a functional neuromuscular disadvantage as well as an anatomic one.

In summary, the loss of heat from the skin to the environment is increased in low birth weight babies because the skin surface is relatively large; loss of heat from deep body layers to the skin is greater because the insulating layer of fat is thin. Therefore the smaller the infant, the greater are the thermal losses to the environment. The well-trained nurse is constantly aware of these factors because they affect survival and the rapidity of recovery from asphyxia; they influence the effectiveness of therapy for respiratory distress, and they may alter the rate of weight gain.

THERMOGENESIS (HEAT PRODUCTION)

In a heat-losing environment, newborn infants increase the rate of heat production by increasing metabolic rate. This phenomenon is operative in both full-term and premature infants, although heat production is augmented somewhat less in the latter. The full-term infant who is exposed to cold can increase the thermogenic rate two and one-half times over the resting state, to a level that almost equals the adult's.

Heat production in the adult who is exposed to cold stress involves involuntary muscle activity (shivering) and increased metabolic rate (nonshivering thermogenesis). In contrast, the nondepressed neonate becomes restless and hyperactive when first exposed to cold, but this form of voluntary muscle activity is not a significant source of heat. This has been shown by the administration of curare (which paralyzes skeletal muscle); the metabolic response to cold stress is not diminished in spite of the resultant absence of muscle activity. The neonate does not shiver when chilled, but in the adult these involuntary tremors are a significant source of heat. Thus nonshivering thermogenesis appears to be the only mechanism available for increasing heat production in the cold-stressed newborn infant.

Nonshivering thermogenesis refers to the heat that is produced by a metabolic rate (and therefore a rate of oxygen consumption) that is minimal in an ideal thermal environment or increased in a cold one. In the neonate, enhancement of heat production must involve a hypermetabolic state that requires increased oxygen consumption. Obviously a severely depressed hypoxic infant can ill afford the oxygen cost of cold stress. Heat is produced as a by-product of the accelerated chemical reactions that occur at a cellular level when metabolic rate increases. The neonate's brain, liver, and perhaps skeletal muscle are important thermogenic organs. Augmented rates of metabolism at these sites probably contribute in some measure to increased heat production, but the major source of heat that is produced by *nonshivering thermogenesis* seems to be brown fat. Direct evidence for the significant role of this tissue has been derived from animal experiments, but there is also considerable evidence to support its role in human neonates.

Brown fat comprises 2% to 6% of the neonate's body weight. It is located subcutaneously as a thin, diamond-shaped mass between the scapulae, in smaller deposits around the muscles and blood vessels of the neck, and in larger masses at the axillae. Somewhat deeper deposits are located in the anterior mediastinum, and still deeper masses are found along the vertebral column, and around the kidneys and adrenals. The color of brown fat is easily distinguished from white fat distributed throughout the body. The brown color is imparted by a copious blood supply, a dense cellular content, and a profusion of nerve endings. Brown fat is densely innervated by sympathetic nerves, which seem to furnish the stimulus for its enhanced metabolism during cold stress by releasing norepinephrine.

Primitive brown fat cells first appear at 26 to 30 weeks of gestation. The tissue mass continues to enlarge as late as the third to the fifth postnatal week, unless significant cold stress intervenes and depletes it. It ordinarily disappears some weeks after birth. Exposure to cold, acutely or over protracted periods, tends to deplete the stores. Tissue from autopsied babies who were clothed and kept in room air at only 70° to 80° F is considerably depleted in comparison to tissue of infants who were managed in incubators as warm as 93° to 95° F.

Norepinephrine is released from sympathetic nerve endings. It is currently thought to be the principal mediator of *nonshivering thermogenesis*. When norepinephrine is infused intravenously into the neonate, oxygen consumption increases by 60%, indicating induced hypermetabolism. That enhanced production of norepinephrine occurs in response to cold stress is indicated by its increased excretion in urine at these times. Norepinephrine stimulates fat metabolism in brown adipose tissue. The by-product of this increased chemical activity is a relatively bountiful amount of heat, which is then applied directly to blood that perfuses the tissue mass. Warmer skin temperatures have been recorded over subcutaneous deposits of brown fat during periods of cold stress, suggesting the tissue's thermogenic role in such circumstances.

Impairment of thermogenesis

The neonate's capacity to respond to cold stress may be impaired by several factors. Hypoxia is among the most important of these. In babies who suffer from hyaline membrane disease, the metabolic response to cold is somewhat limited when arterial P_{O_2} is 45 to 55 mm Hg, and it is abolished at 30 mm Hg. In normal infants these arterial oxygen tensions are produced by breathing gas mixtures that contain 12% and 8% oxygen, respectively.

Other factors that impair the response to cold include intracranial hemorrhage, severe cerebral malformations, and symptomatic hypoglycemia. Infants in deep sleep, when exposed to cold, at first respond suboptimally until they awaken several minutes later. This observation, and the limitation of response that is associated with severe central nervous system abnormalities, suggest that the stimulus to heat production depends on intact brain function. Anencephalic infants, for example, do not increase heat production in lowered environmental temperatures; yet their brown fat stores are completely normal. Interference with the response to cold by symptomatic hypoglycemia may thus be rooted in disrupted function of the central nervous system.

Protracted cold stress seems to deplete brown fat stores, and when this depletion is severe, it is hypothesized that effective thermogenic capacity is eliminated. Infants who have died of "neonatal cold injury" were noted to be virtually devoid of brown fat.

METABOLIC CONSEQUENCES OF COLD STRESS

The principal metabolic difficulties that beset a cold-stressed baby are hypoxemia, metabolic acidosis, rapid depletion of glycogen stores, and reduction of blood glucose levels. The newborn responds to chilling by increasing his metabolic rate, which inherently entails augmented oxygen consumption. If there is no change in the oxygen concentration of inspired air, arterial P_{O_2} may fall. Lowered oxygen tension is apparently related to diminished effectiveness of ventilation, which is a consequence of pulmonary vasoconstriction caused by norepinephrine, which in turn is released in response to cold stress. Breakdown of glycogen to glucose now proceeds under hypoxic circumstances, and the alternate chemical pathway (anaerobic glycolysis) that must be utilized dissipates glycogen at approximately twenty times the normal aerobic rate. Hypoglycemia ensues. Furthermore, anaerobic glycolysis generates extra lactic acid, and now metabolic acidosis appears. In babies with intrauterine malnutrition, hypoglycemia is more likely in the presence of cold stress because glycogen stores are already diminished at birth (p. 206). These phenomena are also more pronounced in babies who are inadequately oxygenated because of ventilatory difficulty or as a result of some other disorder. The critical significance of an optimal thermal environment for such infants is therefore obvious. Relentless monitoring is required if normothermia is to be maintained or restored.

Oxygen deprivation itself impairs or abolishes the metabolic response to chilling, thus depriving the infant of the principal source of heat. It may contribute to the abrupt drop in body temperature that occurs in normal infants at birth; since low oxygen saturation is the rule. There is evidence to indicate that thermogenesis is impaired at an arterial P_{O_2} of 45 mm Hg or less. The infant with severe hyaline membrane disease may thus require higher environmental temperatures to maintain body heat, presumably because thermogenesis is handicapped by oxygen deprivation.

During the nursery stay, failure to provide an optimal thermal environment may impair weight gain. This was described in the example cited earlier in this chapter. Experiments with human infants indicate, however, that in most instances increased caloric intake can compensate for energy diverted from the growth process to the production of heat.

THERMAL MANAGEMENT IN THE DELIVERY ROOM

All babies lose body heat to some extent during the moments immediately after birth. Vigorous, full-sized babies usually experience little adversity as a result, but low birth weight infants, depressed or not, are in noteworthy danger. Metabolic acidosis, hypoxemia, and hypoglycemia can be expected in the most severely cold-stressed infants.

The fall in core (rectal) and skin temperatures is most rapid immediately after birth. In the usual air-conditioned delivery room, if no countermeasures are applied, deep body temperature of the normal full-term infant falls 0.1° C (0.2° F) per minute; skin temperature declines 0.3° C (0.5° F) per minute. The total drop in deep body temperature may be as great as 2° to 3° C (3.6° to 5.4° F).This high rate of thermal dissipation is largely attributable to the anatomic factors that have been previously described in this chapter. An inappropriately cold environment accentuates the difficulty. The resultant rapid rate of heat loss cannot be fully compensated, even if the infant's metabolic response was unimpaired by some disorder in oxygenation. In normal infants the response to cold has been observed to be somewhat limited during the first few minutes of life because of low arterial oxygen tensions that often persist for 10 or 15 minutes after birth. The observed hypoxemia is comparable to that of an infant who breathes only 15% oxygen. Thermal loss is more accentuated as birth weight declines and as respiratory distress increases. Contemporary standards thus require rational measures to minimize heat loss in normal full-term babies and especially in those who are small and depressed.

The modalities by which heat is lost in the delivery room, and their relative significance,

Table 4-1. Equivalent centigrade and Fahrenheit temperature reading*

Centigrade degrees	Fahrenheit degrees	Centigrade degrees	Fahrenheit degrees
0	32.0	31	87.8
21	69.8	32	89.6
22	71.6	33	91.4
23	73.4	34	93.2
24	75.2	35	95.0
25	77.0	36	96.8
26	78.8	37	98.6
27	80.6	38	100.4
28	82.4	39	102.2
29	84.2	40	104.0
30	86.0	41	105.8

*For values between centigrade degrees listed, add 0.18° F for each 0.10° C.

Example: 30.5° C = 86.0 plus 5 × 0.18 = 0.9 = 86.90° F.

35.7° C = 95.0 plus 7 × 0.18 = 1.26 = 96.26° F.

must be known to all who care for infants during the moments that follow birth. The baby is drenched in amniotic fluid when delivery occurs into a cool room with moderately low humidity. Skin and core temperatures in utero and at birth are slightly higher than the mother's. A substantial amount of heat is immediately lost to the cold environment by evaporation. This loss can be eliminated by drying the baby with a warm towel or blanket. After drying is done, loss by convection and radiation must be minimized. During the first 30 minutes of life, twice as much heat is dissipated by convection and radiation together than by the evaporation alone. Several alternative measures may be taken, and some are better than others. The baby may be dried and then wrapped in a warm blanket and kept in room air; he may be dried and placed in an incubator, or he may be dried and placed on an open table that is warmed by an overhead radiant heater. If resuscitation is required, the open table is mandatory for adequate accessibility to the infant. There should be one such table in every active delivery room.

In one study, infants who were neglected remained wet in room air. Within 30 minutes, they experienced a mean fall in rectal temperature of 2.1° C (3.8° F), and a mean fall in skin temperature of 4.6° C (8.3° F). In contrast, those who were dried and placed nude under a radiant heater experienced a fall in core temperature of only 0.7° C (1.3° F), and a fall in skin temperature of 0.8° C (1.5° F). Wet babies who were not wrapped but were placed under radiant heat suffered a 60% greater drop in core temperature than did those who were dried before being placed under radiant heat. Simply drying and wrapping infants in warm blankets diminished their heat loss considerably. Thermal losses were as much as 65% lower in such babies than in those who were not dried and were left nude in room air. Also, heat loss in infants who were dried and wrapped was 40% less than in babies who were dried but not wrapped.

In essence, optimal thermal management requires immediate drying and placement under a radiant heater. Drying and placement in an incubator that is warmed at 32° to 35° C (90° to 95° F) is satisfactory. Simply drying and wrapping in a warm blanket is helpful but not nearly so protective as the additional subsequent warming. *Under any circumstances, failure to dry is negligent; allowing a wet, nude baby to remain in room air for any length of time is callous.*

A certain amount of heat loss is physiologic. Indeed, cold stimuli are probably essential to the initiation of extrauterine respiratory function. Stimuli from thermal skin sensors are transmitted to the reticular formation (respiratory center) in the medulla oblongata, and thence down the phrenic nerve to stimulate contraction of the diaphragm. Experiments with lambs have demonstrated convincingly that delivery into warm fluid, simulating intrauterine conditions, impairs or precludes the onset of respiration. Furthermore, alternate gradual cooling and warming of a water bath in which full-term newborn lambs are immersed results in stimulation of respiratory activity at the cool temperatures and cessation of respiratory activity at the warm ones. Human infants who are delivered by cesarean section into a warm bath cease to breathe. Some cold is therefore necessary, but too much is hazardous. Purposeful exaggeration of physiologic cold stimuli cannot be justified by available evidence, nor can delivery into a warmwater bath.

THERMAL MANAGEMENT IN THE NURSERY

By adult standards the neonate's *thermal stability* is restricted, not so much by his inability to produce heat, as by his propensity for losing it. Thermal management in the nursery attempts to provide conditions that are as close as possible to the baby's *neutral thermal environment*. At the very least, the *control range* of environmental temperature must be maintained. Definitions of these terms follow in subsequent paragraphs.

Thermal stability is the capacity to oppose changes in body heat content caused by the loss or gain of heat that results from exchange with the environment. Heat production and heat conservation effected by constriction of surface blood vessels tend to prevent the diminution of core temperature due to dissipation of body heat to the environment. The functions of production and conservation are critical for maintenance of thermal stability in any patient at any age. Thermal stability also requires effective dissipation of heat by vasodilatation, by sweating, and by rapid breathing to prevent elevation of core temperature due to heat gain from the environment. The net effect of activities that bring about the production and conservation of heat on one hand, and dissipation on the other, is the maintenance of a normal core temperature that is maintained within narrow limits. This is *thermal stability.*

A *neutral thermal environment* provides conditions that permit maintenance of normal core temperature when oxygen consumption in a resting subject is minimal. In the nursery, determination of the components of each infant's neutral thermal environment is not particularly practical; at

least four factors are involved: the temperature of surrounding air, the temperature of surrounding radiant surfaces, the velocity of ambient air flow, and relative humidity.

The *control range of environmental temperature* defines the upper and lower limits of environmental temperatures in which the body can effectively regulate heat loss or gain. The lower limit of the control range for nude adults is 0° C (32° F); for the full-term infant the lower limit is 20° to 23° C (68° to 73° F). The smaller the infant and the more meager the subcutaneous fat insulation, the narrower is the range of environmental temperature (control range) in which heat balance can be maintained.

Provision of a warm microenvironment

Intensive care of neonates almost always requires nudity of the patient. Historically, when the baby was stripped of diapers, shirts, and blankets, monitoring and therapy became feasible as never before. The problems of thermoregulation that resulted, however, have since preoccupied the neonatologist as have few other facets of total infant care.

Since demonstration of the close relationship between abdominal skin temperature and oxygen consumption, it has been the usual practice of intensive care units in this country to automatically adjust the thermal environment in response to changes in skin temperatures as they are registered over the epigastrium. Oxygen consumption (and therefore metabolic rate) is minimal at an abdominal skin temperature of 36.5° C (97.7° F). When skin temperature increases to 37.2° C (98.9° F), oxygen consumption increases by 6%; when skin temperature declines to 35.9° C (96.6° F), oxygen consumption also increases but by 10%. Thus the temperature of the skin signals the presence of a metabolic response. It reflects a change in the environment that requires increased metabolic activity to preserve normal core temperature. A drop in skin temperature indicates a heat-losing environment that requires warming. This servocontrol practice is based on data derived from infants in incubators. Similar information is not available for the radiant-heated open beds that are so widely used in special care units.

Normal full-term infants can generally maintain heat balance in an open bassinet when the room temperature is approximately 75° F, if they are clothed with diaper and shirt, covered with some sort of cotton blanket, and have not been placed in a high velocity of airflow. Sick infants of any size, and low birth weight infants in any state of health, especially those below 2000 grams, require a controlled microenvironment for maintenance of normal core temperature. The full-term infant acquires maximal thermal stability for age several hours after delivery, although the baby's ability to increase metabolic rate in response to cold stress has been demonstrated as early as 15 minutes after birth. Small infants require variable lengths of time for development of a maximal metabolic response, sometimes as long as several weeks. Infants who weigh less than 1500 grams are particularly handicapped because of minimal insulation and a large ratio of body surface to weight.

Incubators. Controlled microenvironments are commonly provided by incubators in which the temperature of circulating air is either manually adjusted or automatically controlled (servocontrolled) in response to signals from a thermal sensor attached to the abdominal skin. Incubators currently available provide heat by convection only. Humidification is provided by passing the heated air over a reservoir of water situated beneath the deck on which the infant lies.

Incubators suffer from a number of shortcomings. They are constructed of a single-layered plastic wall, which is a major inadequacy. The temperature of these walls is midway between the temperature of room air and that of air within the incubator. The cool walls induce radiant heat loss from the infant. The cooler the walls, the greater is the rate of loss. *Heat loss by radiation is independent of the temperature of circulating air in the incubator.* A significant disadvantage of contemporary incubators is their inability to control radiant heat loss, and most of the thermal loss in small babies is by radiation. This deficiency is critical to microenvironmental control for small infants, particularly those below 1250 grams. One solution is to provide an inner plastic heat shield that minimizes radiant losses. The baby is surrounded by an inner removable second wall that serves as the closest (primary) surface to which heat can be lost by radiation. If this surface is warmed by circulating incubator air, radiant losses are far less than to the cool outer wall. The heat shield is shaped like a cylinder that has been cut in half longitudinally. The warmed plastic cylinder is virtually the same temperature as incubator air. Surrounding the baby with a warm primary surface eliminates radiant loss to the cool outer wall.

Another deficiency of incubator design is dependence on a reservoir of water for humidity. Stagnant water is a suitable medium for the growth of "water bugs," most notable of which is *Pseudomonas aeruginosa* (Chapter 12). With a few exceptions involving very small infants, weighing less than 1250 grams, humidification of incubator air is not essential; the water reservoir can be eliminated.

Readings from a thermometer located in a corner of the incubator are lower than air temperature that immediately surrounds the infant. The thermometer should therefore be located closer to the baby.

Incubator temperature is controlled either by an on-and-off (all-or-none) output of heat or by a gradual (partial) increase or decrease in the output of heat, depending on skin temperature. The set point for activation of the heater is adjustable. A skin temperature of 97.5° F is usually chosen. In the partial response device, heat output diminishes gradually as skin temperature rises farther above the set point; it increases gradually as skin temperature falls below it. The gradual response eliminates fluctuations in incubator temperature that are characteristic of the all-or-none response mechanism. The partial response mechanism was introduced after abrupt rises and falls in ambient incubator temperature were observed to be associated with an increased incidence of apneic episodes in premature infants. Most of the apneic episodes occurred in relation to sudden rises in incubator temperature.

Cold drafts from air-conditioning vents should not strike directly on incubator walls, nor should incubators be near cold windows. Recurrent or relentless cold stress due to large radiant heat losses can thus be avoided.

Water in reservoirs is required for only a small number of infants, and if the reservoir is utilized, water should be changed frequently, preferably every 8 hours.

With a heat-sensing probe on the abdomen, the infant should never be prone, since the resultant false registration of high skin temperature diminishes or eliminates activation of the heater. The result may be a very cold baby.

Heat gain is possible from protracted exposure of the incubator to sunlight from a window. Serious elevation of core temperature may ensue. Oxygen consumption increases in response to hyperthermia. The metabolic penalties are similar to those of hypothermia, and they are often even more dangerous.

Radiant-heated open tables. The open table provides indispensable accessibility for resuscitation during acute emergencies and for sustained treatment of gravely ill infants. Heat emanates from an overhead radiant source that is servocontrolled to abdominal skin temperatures in a like manner as incubators. Heat loss by convection may pose a serious problem for babies on such open tables. Airflow in the nursery often makes it difficult or impossible to maintain normal rectal temperatures, especially in the smallest babies. The skin probe must be covered with a foam plastic pad to prevent spurious registration of high temperatures that are in fact due to the direct effect of radiant heat on the sensor itself. The baby remains hypothermic because the sensor, having been warmed directly by radiant heat, rather than

by abdominal skin, discontinues the output of heat. In these circumstances, the sensor is heated, but the baby remains cold. We have tried a plastic disc covered with aluminum foil to shield the sensor from the heat source, and it is apparently more effective than the foam rubber pad.

Clinical assessment and management of the infant's thermal status

Traditional recordings of rectal and axillary temperatures for thermal monitoring of sick babies leave much to be desired. *Normal core temperature does not indicate thermal balance in a cold environment.* Axillary temperatures are often falsely high because of subjacent deposits of heated brown fat and because artifactual warmth is created by apposing skin of the inner arm and the upper chest wall.

The major concern in the assessment and management of body temperature is maintenance of normal heat balance at the lowest level of oxygen consumption. Metabolic rate increases rapidly in response to cold stress that is sensed by thermal receptors in the skin, particularly those over the face. The response does not await a drop in core temperature to become activated. Rather, to support core temperature, it is triggered early and rapidly by a change in the environment that is sensed by the skin. Rectal temperature may therefore be normal in the cold-stressed baby because metabolic hyperactivity compensates successfully for thermal losses. The increased metabolic rate is triggered by environmental changes that are perceived by thermal receptors in the skin. When rectal temperature becomes subnormal, the thermal battle is lost; the baby cannot generate enough heat to maintain normal core temperature.

As previously described, skin temperatures can indicate the state of oxygen consumption. Deviations sufficiently above (hyperthermia) or below (hypothermia) the normal range generally mean that oxygen consumption at the cellular level has increased.

Skin temperature also indicates the appropriateness of environmental temperature. If skin temperature drops, cold stress is present; if it rises, hyperthermia exists. Small babies must be managed with abdominal skin temperature readings for variable lengths of time after birth (for over 2 months in the smallest).

Available data unequivocally demonstrate that thermal sensors of the face are more influential in activating increased metabolism than other nerve endings in the skin elsewhere over the body. When the environment is well heated below the neck, a baby whose facial environment is cool will react as if cold stressed. The practical importance of this observation relates to oxygen administration. *It is mandatory that oxygen supplied to a head hood be warmed.* Ambient temperature within the hood should be monitored and maintained at levels equal to the incubator. Furthermore, under no circumstances should oxygen be blasted onto an infant's face through a face mask or tube. The mask is appropriate only for tight application during resuscitation with a manually operated bag.

A significant quantity of heat is lost from the respiratory tract, particularly in infants who are tachypneic. Oxygen must be warmed and humidified, particularly for intubated babies. Dry oxygen causes significant evaporation from the extensive mucosal surface that lines the respiratory tract, and heat loss by this modality can be significant. Furthermore, evaporation may incur significant fluid losses from the respiratory tract.

Whether they are nurses, physicians, or attendants in any capacity, the neonate's best caretakers are his most protective ones. Unflagging attention to the environmental requirements of optimal heat balance is the essence of such protectiveness. In respect to temperament, training, continuous presence, and sphere of activity, no one is better equipped to perform this function than the neonatal nurse. Furthermore, if the nurse fails to perform it, quite likely no one else will.

References

Adamsons, K., Jr.: The role of thermal factors in fetal and neonatal life, Pediatr. Clin. North Am. **13:**599, 1966.

Adamsons, K., Jr., Gandy, G. M., and James, L. S.: The influence of thermal factors upon oxygen consumption of the newborn human infant, J. Pediatr. **66:**495, 1965.

Adamsons, K., Jr., and Towell, M. E.: Thermal homeostasis in the fetus and newborn, Anesthesiology **26:**531, 1965.

Anagnostakis, D., Economou-Mavrou, C., Agathopoulas, A., and Matsaniotis, N.: Neonatal cold injury: evidence of defective thermogenesis due to impaired norepinephrine release, Pediatrics **53:**24, 1974.

Anonymous by request: Comment: speed of rewarming after postnatal chilling, J. Pediatr. **85:**551, 1974.

Aynsley-Green, A., Robertson, N. R. C., and Rolfe, P.: Air temperature recordings in infant incubators, Arch. Dis. Child. **50:**215, 1975.

Bruck, K.: Temperature regulation in the newborn infant, Biol. Neonate **3:**65, 1965.

Cross, K. W., and Stratton, D.: Aural temperature of the newborn infant, Lancet **2:**1179, 1974.

Dahm, L. S., and James, L. S.: Newborn temperature and calculated heat loss in the delivery room, Pediatrics **49:**504, 1972.

Day, R., Curtis, J., and Kelly, M.: Respiratory metabolism in infancy and in childhood, Am. J. Dis. Child. **65:**376, 1943.

Day, R. L., Caliguiri, L., Kamenski, C., et al.: Body temperature and survival of premature infants, Pediatrics **34:**171, 1964.

Glass, L., Silverman, W. A., and Sinclair, J. C.: Effect of the thermal environment on cold resistance and growth of small infants after the first week of life, Pediatrics **41:**1033, 1968.

Harned, H. S., Jr., and Ferreiro, J.: Initiation of breathing by cold stimulation: effects of change in ambient temperature on respiratory activity of the full-term fetal lamb, J. Pediatr. **83:**663, 1973.

Hey, E. N.: The relation between environmental temperature and oxygen consumption in the newborn baby, J. Physiol. **200:**589, 1969.

Hey, E. N., and Mount, L.: Temperature control in incubators, Lancet **2:**202, 1966.

Hey, E. N., and Mount, L. E.: Heat losses from babies in incubators, Arch. Dis. Child. **42:**75, 1967.

James, L. S., and Adamsons, K., Jr.: Intrapartum period. In Barnett, H. L., editor: Pediatrics, New York, 1968, Appleton-Century-Crofts.

Levison, H., Linsao, L., and Swyer, P. R.: A comparison of infra-red and convective heating for newborn infants, Lancet 2:1346, 1966.

McCance, R. A.: The maintenance of stability in the newly born. 2. Thermal balance, Arch. Dis. Child. 34:459, 1959.

Mestyan, J., Jarai, I., Bata, G., and Fekete, M.: The significance of facial skin temperature in the chemical heat regulation of premature infants, Biol. Neonate 7:243, 1964.

Motil, K. J., Blackburn, M. G., and Pleasure, J. R.: The effects of four different radiant warmer temperature set-points used for rewarming neonates, J. Pediatr. 85:546, 1974.

Oliver, T. K., Jr.: Temperature regulation and heat production in the newborn, Pediatr. Clin. North Am. 12:765, 1965.

Perlstein, P. H., et al.: Apnea in premature infants and incubator-air-temperature changes, N. Engl. J. Med. 282:461, 1970.

Perlstein, P. H., Hersh, C., Glueck, C. J., and Sutherland, J. M.: Adaptation to cold in the first three days of life, Pediatrics 54:411, 1974.

Scopes, J. W.: Metabolic rate and temperature control in the human baby, Br. Med. Bull. 22:88, 1966.

Scopes, J. W., and Ahmed, I.: Range of critical temperatures in sick and premature newborn babies, Am. J. Dis. Child. 41:417, 1966.

Silverman, W. A.: Diagnosis and treatment; use and misuse of temperature and humidity in care of the newborn infant, Pediatrics 33:276, 1974.

Silverman, W. A., et al.: The oxygen cost of minor changes in heat balance of small newborn infants, Acta Paediatr. Scand. 55:294, 1966.

Silverman, W. A., and Sinclair, J. C.: Temperature regulation in the newborn infant, N. Engl. J. Med. 274:146, 1966.

Silverman, W. A., Zamelis, A., Sinclair, J. C., and Agate, F. J.: Warm nape of the newborn, Pediatrics 33:984, 1964.

Sinclair, J. C.: Heat production and thermoregulation in the small-for-date infant, Pediatr. Clin. North Am. 17:147, 1970.

Stephenson, J. M., Du, J. N., and Oliver, T. K., Jr.: The effect of cooling on blood gas tensions in newborn infants, J. Pediatr. 76:848, 1970.

Yashiro, K., Adams, F. H., Emmanouilides, G. C., and Mickey, M. R.: Preliminary studies on the thermal environment of low-birth-weight infants, J. Pediatr. 82:991, 1973.

Chapter 5

Significance of the relationship of birth weight to gestational age

UNTIL 15 YEARS AGO, birth weight was considered the most reliable index of an infant's maturity. If an infant weighed less than 2500 grams, he was assumed to be prematurely born; if his weight exceeded 2500 grams, he was considered mature. This approach implied that intrauterine growth rates were similar for all fetuses and that birth weight could thus be utilized as an accurate expression of gestational age. However, a considerable amount of data have accumulated to demonstrate the inaccuracy of this assumption. Regardless of birth weight, an infant is in fact premature if he is born before term. Birth weight less than 2500 grams simply indicates that growth was incomplete, whether due to a short gestational age, impairment of intrauterine growth, or both. These separate considerations of weight (for assessment of growth) and gestational age (for assessment of maturity) have resulted in a more meaningful classification in which important biologic correlates are identifiable.

CLASSIFICATION OF INFANTS BY BIRTH WEIGHT AND GESTATIONAL AGE
Terminology

In 1961 the World Health Organization recommended that babies who weigh less than 2500 grams be designated as "low birth weight" (LBW) infants. This definition eliminated all implications of prematurity. It disregards gestational age. Definitions of gestational age correspondingly disregard any consideration of birth weight. A *premature (preterm)* infant is born before the end of the thirty-seventh week. A *term* infant is born between the beginning of the thirty-eighth week and the completion of the forty-first week. A *postmature (post-term)* baby is born at the onset of the forty-second week or anytime thereafter. Gestational weeks are calculated from the first day of the last menstrual period (LMP). These definitions of fetal age have nothing to do with weight, length, head circumference, or other measurements of fetal size. However, the relationship of these physical attributes to calculated age is of great importance.

The various types of low birth weight infants (under 2500 grams) are as follows:

1. Infants whose rate of intrauterine growth was normal at the moment of birth. They are small only because labor began before the end of 37 weeks. *These premature infants are appropriately grown for gestational age (AGA).*

2. Infants whose rate of intrauterine growth was slowed and who were delivered at or later than term (end of 37 weeks). These term or post-term (postmature) infants are undergrown for gestational age. *They are small-for-dates or small for gestational age (SGA).*

3. Infants whose in utero growth was retarded and who, in addition, were delivered prematurely. These premature infants are small by virtue of both early delivery and impaired intrauterine growth. *They are small-for-dates, premature infants.*

The corollary of 2500 grams for low birth weight is 4000 grams for high birth weight. Optimum weight for the lowest perinatal mortality is between 3500 and 4000 grams. Above the latter level, mortality begins to increase, and on that basis the weight of 4000 grams serves to delineate high birth weight infants. *Babies are considered large for gestational age (LGA), at any weight, when they fall above the ninetieth percentile on the intrauterine growth curves.*

Intrauterine growth curves

The intrauterine growth chart offers a simple and effective way of assessing growth and maturity of newborn infants. It was derived by plotting birth weights of a large neonatal population against the weeks of gestation to show the range of expected weights for each week. The graph lists birth weights vertically and weeks of gestation horizontally. Data from the Colorado intrauterine growth chart are most widely used for this purpose (Fig. 5-1). They plot birth weights from 400 to 4000 grams against gestational ages from 24 to 43 weeks or more. Five curves are drawn across the charts, dividing the population into tenth, twenty-fifth, fiftieth, seventy-fifth, and ninetieth percentiles. Weights below the tenth percentile curve

are observed in only 10% of the population for any given gestational age. These infants are considered undergrown (small-for-dates). Weights above the ninetieth percentile curve are higher than the remaining 90% of the population, and these infants are overgrown (large-for-dates). Babies who are categorized between the tenth and ninetieth percentiles are appropriately grown for their gestational age. All infants below 2500 grams, as well as any high-risk baby, regardless of weight, should be evaluated with these or similar graphs soon after admission to the nursery. Consider a neonate you have admitted who weighs 2000 grams at 40 weeks. According to the growth chart this mature infant is well below the tenth percentile, presumably as a consequence of intrauterine growth retardation. He is thus at risk for several disorders that require special measures.

Fig. 5-2 simplifies and extends the graph that is shown in Fig. 5-1 and is generally used instead. It delineates only the tenth and ninetieth percentiles, thereby dividing infants

Fig. 5-1. Distribution of birth weights according to gestational age among neonates studied in Denver, Colorado. (From Lubchenco, L. O., Hansman, C., Dressler, M., and Boyd, E.: Pediatrics **32**:793, 1963.)

into small, appropriate, or large for gestational age. At the bottom of the chart the weeks of gestation are divided into categories of preterm (through the thirty-seventh week), term (38 through 41 weeks), and postterm (above 42 weeks). Plotting an infant's weight and gestational age on this chart demonstrates that growth is appropriate, excessive, or diminished for age and that the baby is either premature, term, or postmature.

Fig. 5-2. Intrauterine growth status for gestational ages, according to appropriateness of growth. Points *A, B,* and *C* (added to original diagram by author) correspond to babies shown in Fig. 5-3. See text for explanation. (From Battaglia, F. C., and Lubchenco, L. O.: J. Pediatr. **71:**159, 1967.)

Fig. 5-3. Three babies, same gestational age, weigh 600, 1400, and 2750 grams, respectively, from left to right. They are plotted on Fig. 5-2 at points *A, B,* and *C*.

Interpretation of growth curve data

An infant whose weight is appropriate for gestational age has presumably grown at a normal rate in utero, whether the birth was premature, at term, or postmature. Preterm babies whose weights are between the tenth and ninetieth percentiles are appropriately grown but small because normal intrauterine growth was interrupted by early onset of labor. If these same premature infants are below the tenth percentile for birth weight, they are small for gestational age as well. Consider, for instance, a 1500-gram infant whose gestational age is 36 weeks. According to the intrauterine growth charts, this infant is below the tenth percentile for birth weight at that age and is thus clearly undergrown. Demeanor, appearance, and course in the nursery will differ considerably from those of an appropriately grown infant of the same size who is born at 31 weeks.

An infant who is small for gestational age (small-for-dates) has presumably grown at a retarded rate in utero, regardless of age at birth. Although this phenomenon may occur at any gestational age, most small-for-dates infants are born at or close to term. Inspection of the intrauterine growth chart reveals that at term most infants who are small for gestational age weigh less than 2500 grams. At first glance these babies may appear prematurely born. At our institution 40% of all low birth weight infants are born at or near term. They are thus mature small-for-dates babies; yet according to the old concept, which interpreted weight and age interchangeably, they would have been considered premature infants. The unique attributes of small-for-dates infants are discussed in more detail later in this chapter.

Infants who are large for gestational age have presumably grown at an accelerated rate during intrauterine life. Less is known about them than the small-for-dates babies. Infants of diabetic mothers are characteristically large for gestational age (p. 97), but they constitute a minority of all oversized babies. Inaccurately short estimates of gestational age are probably responsible for mis-taken classification of many of these infants, although the frequency of these errors has not been documented (p. 97).

Fig. 5-3 shows three infants of different sizes who were born at 32 gestational weeks. From left to right, their birth weights were 600, 1400, and 2750 grams, respectively. The largest baby is the infant of a diabetic mother, and the two small babies are twins delivered of a toxemic mother. On the growth curves in Fig. 5-2, points *A, B,* and *C* represent each of the infants on the 32-week line at their respective weights. At the same age, they are, respectively, small *(A),* appropriate *(B),* and large *(C)* for gestational age. Their clinical problems vary because their intrauterine growth problems were produced by diverse etiologies. The smallest baby is grossly malnourished, probably by virtue of impaired placental circulation. The middle baby is small only because of premature delivery. Her growth, which was progressing at a normal rate, was interrupted by her birth. The largest baby was growing more rapidly than normal in utero, as is characteristic of most diabetic pregnancies. These problems in management, as well as the mechanisms by which babies of different size emerge at the same gestational age, and by which babies of equal size emerge at different gestational ages, are discussed later in this chapter.

PRENATAL ESTIMATION OF GESTATIONAL AGE
History of pregnancy; maternal examinations

Estimation of gestational age has traditionally involved counting the weeks that have elapsed since the first day of the last menstrual period (LMP); in the majority of instances this procedure is still reasonably reliable. Accuracy of historic data is thus totally dependent on the mother's recall. A valid history is best obtained early in pregnancy, when recall of the LMP is more likely to be accurate. The mother's history should not be underestimated; properly taken, it is valid in at least 75% to 85% of patients.

For some women, accurate dating of LMP is virtually impossible. Irregular menses in the nonpregnant state frequently complicate the calculations, or the interval between pregnancies is so short that a normal menstrual pattern has yet to be reestablished. In nursing mothers, menstruation may not resume for months after the end of pregnancy. Another cause of miscalculation is the occurrence of postconceptional bleeding, which is often misinterpreted as a menstrual period, thereby erroneously shortening the calculated gestational age.

The obstetrician utilizes certain physical milestones in pregnancy to estimate fetal age. The height of the uterine fundus above the symphysis pubis provides a good indication of the length of pregnancy. It varies from 25 cm above the symphysis at 26 gestational weeks to approximately 33 cm in the thirty-eighth week. Other useful indications are the first maternal perception of fetal movement at approximately 16 weeks, and the perception of fetal heartbeats at approximately 20 weeks. If weekly prenatal visits were scheduled between 18 and 22 weeks (contrary to current practice), the initial appearance of fetal heart tones could be dated more precisely, possibly increasing the accuracy of fetal age calculations.

Prenatal tests for maturity

Estimation of fetal maturity in utero by analysis of amniotic fluid and by other means is important in troubled pregnancies that may require a rapid decision regarding cesarean section. This is particularly true of pregnancies complicated by diabetes and other chronic illnesses in which fetal distress may be indicated by falling maternal levels of urinary estriol (p. 13). In these circumstances the pregnancy must be terminated if fetal survival is in doubt, but on the other hand, the more premature the fetus, the less are his chances of extrauterine survival. Assessment of fetal age is therefore important. Discussion of prenatal evaluation is presented in Chapter 1. It should be reviewed for a better understanding of the application of

prenatal data to the postnatal problems discussed in this chapter. In amniotic fluid a creatinine level over 1.8/100 ml generally correlates well with a gestational age of 36 weeks or more (p. 9), assuming that maternal creatinine is normal. High levels in the mother may elevate those of amniotic fluid. A low level or absence of bilirubin probably indicates maturity, although it is less reliable than creatinine concentration. Lecithin-sphingomyelin ratios are valuable for the estimation of pulmonary maturity and for prediction of subsequent development of hyaline membrane disease (p. 10). At 35 or 36 weeks this ratio rises as lecithin concentration increases. If the lecithin-sphingomyelin ratio is 2.0 or more, hyaline membrane disease is unlikely to occur after delivery; the fetus is probably more than 35 or 36 weeks of age.

POSTNATAL ESTIMATION OF GESTATIONAL AGE

In the nursery, examination for certain external characteristics and neuromuscular signs is extremely valuable for assessment of maturity. Once learned, these observations can be made in a few minutes. The neonatal nurse should be familiar with these physical characteristics and neuromuscular responses. The system used in our nursery was reported by Dubowitz and co-workers. Their study utilized confirmatory observations by three nurses who had no previous experience with these examinations. Once instructed in the procedure, the nurses' appraisals were reliable, correlating well with those of the principal investigator.

Utilizing this system, an estimate of gestational age is usually accurate within 2 weeks. The accuracy of the method has been confirmed in studies primarily concerned with term infants. Another study has confirmed accuracy in babies of very low birth weight (less than 1500 grams). Measurements can be made any time up to 5 days after birth, but because the information is so important in management of sick infants, the examination is best performed within 24

SOME NOTES ON TECHNIQUES OF ASSESSMENT OF NEUROLOGIC CRITERIA
(for use in conjunction with Fig. 5-4 on p. 83)*

POSTURE: Observed with infant quiet and in supine position. Score 0: Arms and legs extended; 1: beginning of flexion of hips and knees, arms extended; 2: stronger flexion of legs, arms extended; 3: arms slightly flexed, legs flexed and abducted; 4: full flexion of arms and legs.

SQUARE WINDOW: The hand is flexed on the forearm between the thumb and index finger of the examiner. Enough pressure is applied to get as full a flexion as possible, and the angle between the hypothenar eminence and the ventral aspect of the forearm is measured and graded according to diagrams [Fig. 5-4]. (Care is taken not to rotate the infant's wrist while doing this maneuver.)

ANKLE DORSIFLEXION: The foot is dorsiflexed onto the anterior aspect of the leg, with the examiner's thumb on the sole of the foot and other fingers behind the leg. Enough pressure is applied to get as full a flexion as possible, and the angle between the dorsum of the foot and the anterior aspect of the leg is measured.

ARM RECOIL: With the infant in the supine position the forearms are first flexed for 5 seconds, then fully extended by pulling on the hands, and then released. The sign is fully positive if the arms return briskly to full flexion (Score 2). If the arms return to incomplete flexion or the response is sluggish, it is graded as Score 1. If they remain extended or are only followed by random movements, the score is 0.

LEG RECOIL: With the infant supine, the hips and knees are fully flexed for 5 seconds, then extended by traction on the feet, and released. A maximal response is one of full flexion of the hips and knees (Score 2). A partial flexion scores 1, and minimal or no movement scores 0.

POPLITEAL ANGLE: With the infant supine and his pelvis flat on the examining couch, the thigh is held in the knee-chest position by the examiner's left index finger and thumb supporting the knee. The leg is then extended by gentle pressure from the examiner's right index finger behind the ankle and the popliteal angle is measured.

HEEL TO EAR MANEUVER: With the baby supine, draw the baby's foot as near to the head as it will go without forcing it. Observe the distance between the foot and the head as well as the degree of extension at the knee. Grade according to diagram. Note that the knee is left free and may draw down alongside the abdomen.

SCARF SIGN: With the baby supine, take the infant's hand and try to put it around the neck and as far posteriorly as possible around the opposite shoulder. Assist this maneuver by lifting the elbow across the body. See how far the elbow will go across and grade according to illustrations. Score 0: Elbow reaches opposite axillary line; 1: Elbow between midline and opposite axillary line; 2: Elbow reaches midline; 3: Elbow will not reach midline.

*From Dubowitz, L. M., Dubowitz, V., and Goldberg, C.: Clinical assessment of gestational age in the newborn infant, J. Pediatr. **77:**1, 1970.

SOME NOTES ON TECHNIQUES OF ASSESSMENT OF
NEUROLOGIC CRITERIA—cont'd

HEAD LAG: With the baby lying supine, grasp the hands (or the arms if a very small infant) and pull him slowly toward the sitting position. Observe the position of the head in relation to the trunk and grade accordingly. In a small infant the head may initially be supported by one hand. Score 0: Complete lag; 1: Partial head control; 2: Able to maintain head in line with body; 3: Brings head anterior to body.

VENTRAL SUSPENSION: The infant is suspended in the prone position, with examiner's hand under the infant's chest (one hand in a small infant, two in a large infant): Observe the degree of extension of the back and the amount of flexion of the arms and legs. Also note the relation of the head to the trunk. Grade according to diagrams [Fig. 5-4].

If score differs on the two sides, take the mean.

Table 5-1. Scoring system for external criteria*

External sign	Score†				
	0	1	2	3	4
Edema	Obvious edema of hands and feet; pitting over tibia	No obvious edema of hands and feet; pitting over tibia	No edema		
Skin texture	Very thin, gelatinous	Thin and smooth	Smooth; medium thickness. Rash or superficial peeling	Slight thickening. Superficial cracking and peeling especially of hands and feet	Thick and parchment-like; superficial or deep cracking
Skin color	Dark red	Uniformly pink	Pale pink; variable over body	Pale; only pink over ears, lips, palms, or soles	
Skin opacity (trunk)	Numerous veins and venules clearly seen, especially over abdomen	Veins and tributaries seen	A few large vessels clearly seen over abdomen	A few large vessels seen indistinctly over abdomen	No blood vessels seen
Lanugo (over back)	No lanugo	Abundant; long and thick over whole back	Hair thinning especially over lower back	Small amount of lanugo and bald areas	At least ½ of back devoid of lanugo

*From Dubowitz, L. M. S., Dubowitz, V., and Goldberg, C.: Clinical assessment of gestational age in the newborn infant, J. Pediatr. **77:**1, 1970; modified from Farr, V., et al.: Dev. Med. Child. Neurol. **8:** 507, 1966.

†If score differs on two sides, take the mean.

Continued.

Table 5-1. Scoring system for external criteria—cont'd

External sign	Score				
	0	*1*	*2*	*3*	*4*
Plantar creases	No skin creases	Faint red marks over anterior half of sole	Definite red marks over > anterior ½; indentations over < anterior ⅓	Indentations over > anterior ⅓	Definite deep indentations over > anterior ⅓
Nipple formation	Nipple barely visible; no areola	Nipple well defined; areola smooth and flat, diameter < 0.75 cm	Areola stippled, edge not raised, diameter < 0.75 cm	Areola stippled, edge raised, diameter > 0.75 cm	
Breast size	No breast tissue palpable	Breast tissue on one or both sides, < 0.5 cm diameter	Breast tissue both sides; one or both 0.5 to 1.0 cm	Breast tissue both sides; one or both > 1 cm	
Ear form	Pinna flat and shapeless, little or no incurving of edge	Incurving of part of edge of pinna	Partial incurving whole of upper pinna	Well-defined incurving whole of upper pinna	
Ear firmness	Pinna soft, easily folded, no recoil	Pinna soft, easily folded, slow recoil	Cartilage to edge of pinna, but soft in places, ready recoil	Pinna firm, cartilage to edge; instant recoil	
Genitals Male	Neither testis in scrotum	At least one testis high in scrotum	At least one testis right down		
Female (with hips ½ abducted)	Labia majora widely separated, labia minora protruding	Labia majora almost cover labia minora	Labia majora completely cover labia minora		

hours after delivery. The accompanying notes on techniques describe the procedures for evaluating postures and primitive reflexes; Fig. 5-4 illustrates responses elicited and the scores assigned to each, and Table 5-1 describes external features and their scores. The scores from all the neuromuscular findings and from all the external characteristics comprise a maximum total of 70. Gestational age may be read from the corresponding score given in Table 5-2. A score of 50 thus corresponds to 37 gestational weeks, and a score of 20 corresponds to 29 weeks. The gestational age and birth weight may now be plotted on the intrauterine growth chart for the classification of an infant according to his growth characteristics and age at birth, as previously described. Proficiency depends on repeated careful performance of this entire procedure. With experience, a nurse can perform it accurately in no more than 10 minutes, and usually in less.

Having estimated gestational age, the nurse can now plot this information against birth

Fig. 5-4. Scoring system of neurologic signs for assessment of gestational age. (From Dubowitz, L. M. S., Dubowitz, V., and Goldberg, C.: J. Pediatr. **77:**1, 1970.)

Table 5-2. Dubowitz score/gestational age

Score	Weeks of gestation	Score	Weeks of gestation
0-9	26	40-43	35
10-12	27	44-46	36
13-16	28	47-50	37
17-20	29	51-54	38
21-24	30	55-58	39
25-27	31	59-62	40
28-31	32	63-65	41
32-35	33	66-69	42
36-39	34		

weight on the intrauterine growth chart for assessment of the infant's status as it relates to his age. The causes and clinical significance of deviations from normal weights at various gestational ages are discussed in the remainder of this chapter.

INTRAUTERINE GROWTH RETARDATION
Terminology

Intrauterine growth retardation is also referred to as dysmaturity, small-for-dates, small for gestational age, pseudoprematurity, and fetal or intrauterine malnutrition. We prefer to use the terms small-for-dates, small for gestational age, and intrauterine growth retardation interchangeably to indicate fetal undergrowth of any etiology. Although the word dysmaturity is used frequently in reference to a small but mature baby, it is not completely accurate; according to its word derivation, it denotes any abnormality of maturity, therefore implying that the baby may be either small or large for his age. The word pseudoprematurity is also unacceptable because it suggests that these small infants appear deceptively premature, which is not the case if they are born at or near term. Fetal, or intrauterine, malnutrition should be reserved for reference to growth retardation due to a deficient supply of nutrient from the mother to her fetus, thus excluding diminished growth that is caused by intrauterine infections such as rubella or that is associated with other congenital malformations (p. ??).

Cellular characteristics of growth-retarded infants

Normal cellular growth. Normal cellular growth progresses through three stages that blend into each other. Overall, growth is characterized by the initial production of nuclei by mitosis, followed by the laying down of cytoplasm. Stated differently, nuclei, and therefore DNA, are first produced, and they are responsible for the early growth of any organ. Organ enlargement that results from cell multiplciation is called *hyperplasia.* As growth proceeds, each cell enlarges by the addition of cytoplasm. Organ growth due to cytoplasmic enlargement of existing cells is called *hypertrophy.*

DNA content of any organ can be measured accurately. The amount of DNA in a single nucleus for any given species is uniform. The total number of *cells* in any organ can be calculated by dividing the amount of DNA in a single nucleus into the total DNA determined for that organ. To determine the *average weight per cell,* one need only divide the total weight of the organ by the determined number of cells. The weight/DNA ratio varies from one normal stage of growth to the next, as hyperplasia evolves into hypertrophy. It indicates the amount of cytoplasm relative to DNA for each cell, and it also varies according to the type of growth retardation.

Data from experiments on rats demonstrate a good correlation between weight/DNA ratios and the normal growth stages. Presumably, these same phenomena are applicable to the human growth process. During the first stage of growth, nuclei proliferate; cytoplasmic mass is minimal, being laid down at approximately the same rate as DNA. During this stage of pure hyperplasia, the weight/DNA ratio is unchanged.

The second stage of growth entails increased production of cytoplasm while the rate of nuclear proliferation (DNA) declines. Existing cells enlarge by addition of cytoplasm, and the rate of cell multiplication declines. Hypertrophy and hyperplasia coexist, but the rate of hypertrophy is greater. Therefore, the weight/DNA ratio increases, indicating an increase in cell size.

The third stage of growth entails increasing hypertrophy and virtual cessation of hyperplasia. Existing cells continue to enlarge, but new cells are no longer produced. Weight/DNA ratio now increases further, indicating that cell size is further increased.

The type of growth impairment suffered by the embryo or the fetus depends on the stage of growth that is disrupted.

Impaired cellular growth. Mention has already been made of two different types of growth retardation, which may occur separately or simultaneously. The hypoplastic type of impairment involves insult to the embryo early in pregnancy, during the initial stage of growth. Because mitosis is impaired, fewer new cells are formed, organs are small, and organ weight is subnormal. The individual cells usually, but not always, have a normal amount of cytoplasm. In contrast, growth failure that begins later in pregnancy is associated with cellular characteristics that are quite different. The total number of cells in affected organs is normal or nearly so, but their size is diminished by virtue of reduced amounts of cytoplasm. Abnormally small organ size, in this instance, is thus largely the result of decreased cytoplasmic mass, rather than a diminished number of cells as in hypoplasia. Organ weight/DNA ratios correlate well with these anatomic observations. When the weight of an organ is subnormal only because it contains fewer cells (hypoplasia), the ratio of total organ weight to DNA content is similar to that of normally grown tissue if the number of nuclei and the amount of cytoplasm are diminished approximately to the same extent. On the other hand, if an abnormally small organ contains about the same quantity of nuclei (DNA) as a normally grown one, but the cytoplasmic mass is reduced, the ratio of total organ weight to DNA content is lower than normal. Cytoplasm is decreased, whereas the number of cell nuclei (DNA) is not.

Insult during the first stage of growth (hyperplasia) retards the rate of cell division, which results in fewer than normal cells in an organ that is smaller than normal. This type of impairment is not reversible, regardless of attempts to provide optimal nutrition later on. However, if the insult occurs during the hypertrophic stage of growth, individual enlargement of existing cells is impaired. The result is a smaller organ with a normal number of diminutive cells. This impairment is reversible to some extent. With proper nutrition, the cytoplasmic mass becomes normal, and the resultant cellular enlargement ultimately imparts normal size to the involved organ.

In animals (rats, monkeys, dogs, pigs), two types of malnutrition have been produced that are correlated with the distribution of organ involvement rather than with their cellular characteristics. Their significance is in the differing effects they exert on the brain. In one type, ligation of placental blood vessels during the latter third of pregnancy produced an asymmetric type of undergrowth. The overall weight of the rats was reduced by 20%; liver weight was reduced by as much as 50%; brain weight was unaffected. Furthermore, liver cells were devoid of glycogen. The ratio of brain weight to liver weight was inordinately large. *This brain-sparing pattern is characteristic of growth retardation that occurs in fetuses of toxemic women.* In them, uteroplacental vascular insufficiency is thought to contribute fundamentally to fetal undergrowth. The relationship of a relatively large brain to a small, glycogen-deprived liver is thought to be responsible for the high incidence of hypoglycemia in this type of growth retardation. Glucose demands are greater in the brain than in any other organ; glucose supply is principally from the liver. The demand for glucose by a relatively normal-sized brain on a diminutive liver is probably significant in the pathogenesis of hypoglycemia in babies of toxemic mothers.

A second type of malnutrition was produced in these animals. It entailed maternal protein deprivation throughout pregnancy, rather than interference with uteroplacental blood supply late in pregnancy. The resultant pattern of fetal undergrowth involved all organs to an equal extent. The growth failure was symmetric. Weight and DNA content were both reduced. The liver was not affected any more than any other organ and the brain was not spared.

Two types of fetal undergrowth were thus demonstrated in these animals; the one associated with vascular insufficiency during the last third of pregnancy was asymmetric, sparing the brain but profoundly affecting the liver and the rest of the body. The other, associated with maternal malnutrition throughout gestation, was symmetric, affecting all organs similarly, including the brain.

The available data demonstrate heterogeneity in the types of fetal undergrowth. These varying types of undergrowth may be responsible for the different outcomes that have been noted in human infants whose growth was retarded in utero. There seem to be two broad categories of intrauterine growth retardation: intrinsic and extrinsic. The intrinsic variety involves reduction of growth caused by factors that are operative within the fetus itself, such as severe chromosomal or genetic disorders, intrauterine infection due to rubella virus or cytomegalovirus, or normal hereditary small stature. The extrinsic variety entails diminution of maternal support to a fetus that otherwise would have been normal. Clinically, diminished maternal support is seen in uteroplacental vascular insufficiency including toxemia, essential hypertension, severe far-advanced diabetes mellitus, chronic renal disease, multiple pregnancy, recurrent bleeding late in pregnancy from a normally implanted placenta, and probably chronic severe maternal malnutrition throughout gestation.

Data relating malnutrition to general body growth have stimulated an intense interest in the effects of this phenomenon on growth of the brain. Although the issue is far from resolved, evidence from observations in animals, as described previously, indicates that malnutrition during the period of most rapid brain growth is associated with permanent reduction in the total number of cells. In humans this critical period probably begins at about (15) gestational weeks. Estimates of the time of cessation of hyperplasia vary from 8 to 15 months after term. If this critical period does exist in humans, continuous malnutrition from prenatal into postnatal life may reduce cellular quantity irrevocably and thus permanently impair intellectual capacity. Suggestive evidence in support of this assumption was noted in a severely deprived population of low birth weight infants who died of undernutrition during the first few months of life. There was a 60% reduction in the expected number of brain cells. Among infants who were not of low birth weight, but whose lethal malnutrition was apparently confined to the postnatal period, there was only a 15% to 20% reduction in the number of brain cells. In the first group of infants, the combined effects of prenatal and postnatal deprivation may have resulted in a greater reduction of brain cells than in the second group, which suffered only from postnatal malnutrition. That malnutrition sustained in utero and into early infancy can affect brain structure permanently has indeed been well documented in animals. In humans the similarities are suggestive. The public health and socioeconomic implications of these data are awesome to contemplate if one accepts the hypothesis that malnutrition is a pervasive cause of subnormal mentality on the one hand and that it is socially remediable on the other.

Factors associated with intrauterine growth retardation

Intrauterine growth is associated with a variety of disorders in the mother, the fetus, and the placenta. Most of these known factors are listed:

    I. *Maternal factors*
        A. Low socioeconomic status
        B. Toxemia
        C. Hypertensive cardiovascular disease
        D. Chronic renal disease
        E. Diabetes (advanced)
        F. Malnutrition
        G. Cigarette smoking
        H. Heroin addiction
        I. High-altitude residence
   II. *Fetal factors*
        A. Multiple gestation
        B. Congenital malformation
        C. Chromosomal abnormality
        D. Chronic intrauterine infection
            1. Rubella
            2. Cytomegalovirus
  III. *Placental factors*
        A. "Placental insufficiency"

B. Vascular anastomoses (twin to twin)
C. Single umbilical artery
D. Abnormal cord insertion
E. Separation
F. Massive infarction
G. ? Vascular anomalies and tumors
H. ? Site of implantation

Maternal factors

Low socioeconomic status. Infant losses, like low birth weight itself, are profoundly influenced by maternal social class, parity, age, and, in particular, maternal height. These factors are interrelated and additive when statistical analysis is undertaken. At the happy end of the spectrum is the well-nourished white woman in her twenties, married to a business or professional man, who is having her second baby. She is more likely than anyone else to have a well-grown, normal infant who weathers labor, delivery, and the immediate neonatal period with no difficulty. At the unhappiest extreme of the spectrum is a malnourished, short, black, adolescent mother who is unmarried, or perhaps a somewhat older woman who is a grand multipara (more than five previous pregnancies) married to an unskilled, often unemployed laborer. Women from these and similar backgrounds are more likely than anyone else to have low birth weight infants who cannot weather the perinatal experience alive or unscathed.

The association of small stature and poor fetal outcome is undoubtedly an indirect one. Aside from genetically determined short stature in any social class, the repeatedly observed association between height and social class suggests that short stature is in part the result of poor nutrition during the growth period in childhood. It thus follows that short stature merely signifies the many unfavorable circumstances that characterize poverty.

Toxemia. Toxemia of pregnancy (eclampsia, preeclampsia) is a maternal disorder that is frequently cited as a cause of fetal growth retardation. Its clinical attributes include hypertension, proteinuria, and edema. The cause of toxemia and the mechanisms by which the fetus is affected are unknown.

There is agreement, however, that toxemia is a generalized vascular disorder in which diminution of uterine and placental blood flow impairs the function of the latter organ. Some evidence suggests that maternal malnutrition predisposes to toxemia. Among infants of toxemic mothers, mortality is increased. The principal abnormality in most babies who die is undergrowth for gestational age. Otherwise, a distinctive pattern of morphologic abnormalities has not been identified. Growth retardation is presumably a function of fetal malnutrition in which cellular abnormalities are characterized by diminished cytoplasmic mass in most organs, particularly the liver and adrenals. The brain is usually less affected than are other organs. The gross and microscopic appearance of tissues in these infants closely resembles that of infants who died during the first year of life from postnatally acquired malnutrition.

Hypertension and chronic renal disease. Hypertension and chronic renal disease exert influences on fetal growth that are similar to those of toxemia.

Diabetes (advanced). Most diabetic women (class A or B; see classification on p. 207) deliver large-for-dates babies who may nevertheless be prematurely born. However, advanced maternal diabetes involves generalized vascular damage that impairs normal placental blood flow. The woman with advanced (early onset) diabetes is more likely to give birth to a small-for-dates infant rather than a large one, particularly if the diabetes has significantly affected her kidneys.

Maternal malnutrition. Although evidence for the adverse fetal effects of maternal malnutrition is very suggestive, there are also some data to indicate that birth weight may be relatively unchanged from normal. However, severe undernutrition in the human female does result in an increased incidence of early abortions or in failure to conceive. The acute shortage of food in Holland during World War II was studied for its effects on birth weight. The average maternal weight gain during pregnancy fell from approximately 25 pounds in normal times to 5 pounds during the period of famine, but the mean birth weight of offspring was reduced by only 7%. In a similar vein, there was less than 10% increment in birth weight at the end of 20 postwar years in Japan, during which severe poverty was replaced by relative affluence. The studies in Holland and Japan showed only small changes in mean birth weights, as related to severe changes in economic conditions, but weight is a crude end point compared to sophisticated methodology in which cell quantity and protein/DNA ratios are determined. These and other sensitive procedures may produce more precise data in the future for better definition of the fetal effects of maternal malnutrition. The nature of the consistently positive association between poverty and low birth weight has not been satisfactorily explained. That long-standing maternal malnutrition is the predominant cause of fetal undergrowth in low socioeconomic populations is still presumptive. Results of animal experiments strongly suggest a significant role of maternal malnutrition in faulty fetal growth. Some epidemiologic data in humans are also strongly suggestive.

Cigarette smoking. Among moderate smokers, the incidence of small-for-dates babies is twice that of nonsmokers; among heavy consumers it is three times as great. The end result is related to the number of cigarettes smoked and the duration of the insult. Birth weight tends to be reduced more than gestational age, and body length is also reduced. At 7 years of age, children of smoking gravidas are shorter than controls and have a higher incidence of educational retardation, regardless of social class, maternal age, or parity. The statistical association of maternal smoking and the incidence of intrauterine undergrowth is among the most direct and unequivocal of all the maternal factors thus far scrutinized for this purpose.

Heroin addiction. In some urban hospitals the incidence of addicted babies from maternal addiction is as high as one in fifty deliveries. The threats to survival of the fetus and neonate are multiple, particularly when one considers the daily life most addicts must resort to if their drug need is to be met. Generally, about half the babies born of maternal addicts are low birth weight infants; over 40% are small-for-dates. Intrauterine undergrowth is therefore a greater problem than prematurity itself.

High altitude. Residence at high altitudes may be related to lower birth weight of offspring, presumably as a function of lower oxygen tension. There is some reason to doubt this relationship, since adults adjust satisfactorily to high altitudes by increasing the oxygen-carrying capacity of blood. Furthermore, large changes in maternal arterial P_{O_2} cause only small ones in the fetus. Nevertheless, at least a superficial association between altitude and birth weight at term has been demonstrated. The median birth weight at term in Lake County, Colorado (altitude 10,000 feet), was 3.07 kg. Approximately 30% of babies in this community were 2500 grams or less at birth, whereas the national average for low birth weight was 10%. In Denver, at 5000 feet, the median birth weight was 3.29 kg, and in Baltimore, virtually at sea level, it was 3.32 kg. These figures suggest a relationship between high altitude and retarded fetal growth.

Fetal factors

Multiple gestation. Most twins have a subnormal rate of growth late in gestation. This pattern is not unlike the decelerated growth rate in normal singletons, which begins at 36 to 38 weeks and is sustained for several days after birth. This effect is more pronounced in twins, and it begins earlier, at approximately 30 weeks. In either case the slowed rate of growth has been attributed to progressive diminution in the effective transfer of nutrient substances across the placenta, perhaps as a function of placental aging. Tissue abnormalities in twins seem to correlate with the prevalent impression that nutritional deficiency late in pregnancy is responsible for their small size. Subnormal organ weights are primarily a function of diminished cytoplasmic mass.

Congenital malformations and chromoso-

mal abnormalities. Anencephalic babies, infants with congenital heart disease, and infants with chromosomal abnormalities are small-for-dates as a result of hypoplasia. This variety of growth retardation originates early in pregnancy, when cell multiplication (hyperplasia) is the predominant factor in the growth process. Mitotic activity is impaired, and the number of cells is reduced. The incidence of a variety of major congenital anomalies is increased severalfold in small-for-dates infants compared to those who are appropriately grown for their age.

Chronic intrauterine infections. Impairment of growth is virtually a hallmark of fetal infections that begin early in pregnancy, particularly during the first trimester. Rubella is the best known example of this phenomenon; infections due to cytomegalovirus are similarly implicated. Hypoplastic growth retardation is identical to that described for congenital malformations. The details of these and other infections are discussed in Chapter 12.

Placental factors

General considerations. A great deal of mystery surrounds the role of placental pathology as an original cause of fetal undergrowth. When a placental lesion is identified, the question arises whether it is a manifestation of intrauterine growth retardation or whether it is the original source of fetal difficulty. Vascular anomalies, tumors, infarctions, and abnormal implantation sites have all been observed in association with isolated instances of fetal malnutrition, but apparently they are not responsible for a significant number of growth-retarded babies.

Placental insufficiency. Placental insufficiency is a conceptual term that is frequently invoked to explain the occurrence of fetal malnutrition. It implies impaired exchange between mother and fetus, particularly suboptimal delivery of nutrient material and hormones to the fetus. A number of well-defined pathologic lesions in the placenta seem to be associated with placental insufficiency, but these lesions occur in only a few cases. They include extensive fibrosis, occlu-sion of fetal vessels in the villi, large hemangiomas, and early separation. Clinical entities such as advanced diabetes and toxemia are apparently associated with insufficiency of placental function. However, in most instances dysfunction is not associated with morphologic abnormalities, and quite often there are no apparent maternal disorders. In any case, retarded fetal growth seems to be the end result of placental insufficiency, which is a concept that requires better definition than is presently available.

Intrauterine parabiotic syndrome (twin transfusion). The intrauterine parabiotic syndrome occurs in a small percentage of identical twins. It is a direct result of placental arteriovenous anastomoses that connect the circulations of both fetuses. Blood is transferred from artery to vein (twin to twin) when there is a connection between the arteries of one fetus and veins of the other. The discrepancy in blood volume between the two infants at birth may or may not be associated with weight differences in other body organs, depending on the duration and extent of fetofetal blood transfer. At birth the twin who received the blood (the "venous" twin) is intensely red because of polycythemia, whereas the donor twin (the "arterial" twin) is pale as a consequence of anemia. Increased blood volume in the polycythemic twin may cause congestive heart failure due to cardiac overload, and hyperbilirubinemia often occurs because there are more red cells available for breakdown (p. 191). The anemic twin may be in shock at birth if blood loss to his sibling was acute. A dramatic discrepancy in birth weight is usually but not always noted. Weight of the recipient twin may exceed that of the donor by as much as 50%, but in many instances a difference in size is less obvious. Polyhydramnios is often present in the recipient baby, whereas oligohydramnios is observed in the donor. The most important initial observation that the nurse can make is the difference in color between the twins. This is sometimes an urgent situation that requires immediate withdrawal of blood from the overloaded baby and a transfusion for shock in the anemic one.

Single umbilical artery. Presence of only one umbilical artery is often associated with a variety of major congenital anomalies, most commonly in the urinary tract. A number of investigators have reported single umbilical artery in 0.2% to 2% of all births. Among such infants, 20% to 65% have congenital anomalies. In the delivery room or in the nursery, the nurse should inspect the cut surface of the umbilical cord to ascertain the presence of two arteries and one vein. Observation of a single artery may lead to the early identification of major congenital malformations.

Physical findings of intrauterine growth retardation

On first inspection of many small-for-dates infants, several obvious physical characteristics immediately suggest the presence of impaired intrauterine growth. One is struck by the seemingly large head, but head circumference is actually normal or nearly so; it is the chest and abdominal circumferences that are reduced. The head merely appears large for the body. Apparently the brain was spared or less affected by the intrauterine insult, which probably had its inception relatively late in pregnancy. Since the ratio of brain mass to liver mass is large, hypoglycemia is likely to be present in such infants. It was largely the hypertrophic (third stage) of growth that was impaired; one would expect a normal number of cells (nuclei) and diminished cytoplasm in most organs. The weight/DNA ratio would be smaller than normal. Diminution of subcutaneous fat and loose, dry skin are prominent (Fig. 5-5). Even though the skin appears pale, half of these babies are polycythemic; their venous hematocrit may be greater than 60 vol %. In the extreme, muscle mass over the buttocks, thighs, and cheeks is also wanting. Since body length is not as diminished as subcutaneous fat, these infants often appear thin and long.

Fraternal twins are shown in Fig. 5-6; the longer is minimally undergrown, and the

Fig. 5-5. Severe intrauterine malnutrition in a postterm baby. Diminished subcutaneous fat is in dramatic evidence at lower extremities. Cord is stained, thin, and dull. Body is thin and appears long, although length was normal.

smaller is poorly grown. The paucity of subcutaneous fat in the small baby imparts a relatively long and thin appearance, whereas the head gives the illusion of being large. Longitudinal skin creases in the thighs indicate severe subcutaneous fat depletion, in contrast to the horizontal thigh creases of the larger baby, whose nutritional state is far better. Note the sparse hair of the small twin and the normal hair in the large one. The smaller baby is wide-eyed, presumably as a result of chronic hypoxia in utero. He appears alert compared to his sleepy sibling. The abdomen is sunken (scaphoid), rather than rounded as in the better-nourished baby. At birth the umbilical cord is thin, slightly yellow, dull, and dry in contrast to the normal cord, which is rotund, gray, glistening, and moist. Because all cords wither progres-

Fig. 5-6. Fraternal twins. The smaller infant is typically malnourished. Thin body gives a large appearance to head, longitudinal skin creases in thighs are characteristic of diminished subcutaneous fat, and hair is sparse. Alert appearance is in contrast to sleepy sibling; the wide-eyed look indicates chronic intrauterine hypoxia.

sively after birth, their condition after 24 hours of age is of little diagnostic significance. The cords of small-for-dates babies wither more rapidly. Scalp hair is typically sparse; heavy hair growth is exceptional in growth-retarded babies, except in those who are postmature (p. 97). Skull sutures are frequently wide as a result of impaired bone growth. The anterior fontanelle, although large, is soft or sunken, thereby ruling out increased intracranial pressure as a cause of the widened sutures. Ossification centers at the distal femur and proximal tibia are frequently absent in term babies who are undergrown (Fig. 1-9). Most of these infants are more active than expected for their low weight. The vigor of their cry may be particularly impressive. Often, an alert, wide-eyed facial expression is combined with repetitive tongue thrusts that simulate a sucking motion. The overall impression of vigor and well-being is misguided, for these are signs of chronic marginal hypoxia in utero. Many of these babies convulse 6 to 18 hours later, particularly those whose anterior fontanelle is firm due to cerebral edema from intrauterine hypoxia. On the other hand, when perinatal asphyxia is severe, the baby is depressed, appearing flaccid and lethargic. Hypoglycemia produces similar symptoms.

Another type of growth retardation is seen in small-for-dates infants whose appearance is quite different from that just described. These babies, whose insult probably began early and was sustained throughout gestation, do not appear wasted. They are diminutive, but body members are of proportionate size. The head does not appear large for the trunk. The skin is not redundant, but it is thicker (the subcutaneous vascular pattern is obscure or absent) than expected for infants of the same size who are appropriately grown for their gestational age. They are generally quite vigorous and are much less likely to be hypoglycemic or polycythemic. These are hypoplastic babies in whom major malformations are present or in whom an early intrauterine infection occurred (rubella or cytomegalic inclusion disease). Their weight/DNA ratio is probably normal, although absolute weight is subnormal.

Two general types of fetal undergrowth are thus identifiable by body measurement and by reference to intrauterine growth curves. In one type, the most common one, the insult seems to begin during the last trimester. These babies have a head circumference and body length within the normal percentiles, generally between the twenty-fifth and fiftieth, but their body weight is below the tenth percentile. Associated maternal factors most frequently include toxemia, chronic hypertension, and chronic renal disease. The second type probably begins early in pregnancy. It is characterized by equally distributed reduction in head circumference, body length, and weight. All these measurements fall below the tenth percentile. Associated factors include intrauterine virus infection, chromosomal disorders, major congenital malformations, genetically small but otherwise well infants, and probably maternal malnutrition.

Predisposition to neonatal illness in small-for-dates babies

Thus far this chapter has been concerned with the fundamental characteristics, classification, and causes of fetal growth retardation. The diagnosis and treatment of certain neonatal illnesses are greatly facilitated by early identification of abnormal growth status. Clinical application of the concepts that have been discussed should reduce neonatal morbidity and mortality significantly, particularly when one considers that in low socioeconomic groups as many as 7% of all term infants are growth retarded. The incidence of undergrowth in premature infants is not known. At our facility this percentage represents more than 500 babies annually, who must be identified to ensure proper management. The illnesses to which small-for-dates infants are vulnerable are discussed in the ensuing paragraphs.

Perinatal asphyxia. Growth-retarded fetuses are often chronically hypoxic for variable periods of time prior to the onset of labor. Whereas healthy fetuses can withstand the asphyxia of normal birth and are well equipped to compensate for it after delivery, those who are chronically distressed can ill afford the insult. They are thus severely disturbed by normal labor, and at birth recovery is difficult or impossible without proper therapy. Apgar scores at 1 and 5 minutes reflect their depressed state. Appropriate management of these infants in the delivery room is often crucial to their survival. The details of resuscitation at birth are described in Chapter 3. Evaluation before the onset of labor with the oxytocin challenge test predicts the inability of the fetus to withstand labor. Later, fetal heart monitoring during labor demonstrates the presence of stress. Even if this information is not available, identification of high-risk historic factors are

a valuable aid in identifying these infants in advance of their birth. From the maternal history the neonatal nurse can often anticipate the arrival of babies at risk even before the onset of labor. The commonest antecedent conditions are toxemia, cigarette smoking, low socioeconomic status, multiple gestation, previously diagnosed infections during pregnancy (such as rubella), and advanced diabetes.

Aspiration syndrome. Aspiration of particulate matter may occur in utero before the onset of labor or during the birth process. Small-for-dates infants are more likely to be affected than others because intrauterine hypoxia occurs so frequently among them. The aspiration of meconium is apparently mediated by the fetal response to hypoxia—the release of meconium into amniotic fluid by increased intestinal peristalsis and reflex relaxation of the anal sphincter plus reflex gasping movements that suck the released meconium particles into the bronchial tree. Much of the material in the respiratory tract is aspirated more deeply into terminal bronchioles and alveoli after birth. Respiratory distress thus occurs at birth, and a normal rapid recovery from intrauterine asphyxia is precluded. The extrauterine asphyxial state should be viewed as a continuation of events that have transpired in utero. The aspiration syndrome can be clearly distinguished from hyaline membrane disease by the distinctive radiologic appearance of the lungs in each of these disorders. Diagnosis is also aided by accurate estimation of gestational age; hyaline membrane disease is unlikely to occur in infants born at term. The prognosis for the baby with syndromes due to aspiration or fluid retention is generally better than for the infant with hyaline membrane disease. These disorders and their complications are discussed in Chapter 8.

Hypoglycemia. Hypoglycemia is characterized by an abnormally low concentration of blood glucose. In full-sized infants at term, blood glucose levels below 30 mg/100 ml are considered abnormal during the first 72 hours of life, whereas levels below 40 mg/100 ml are abnormal thereafter. In low birth weight infants, concentrations below 20 mg/100 ml are thought to indicate hypoglycemia. Hypoglycemia is frequent among small-for-dates infants, whether they are born at term or before. The incidence may be as high as 40% among the most severely underweight and wasted infants. Babies of toxemic mothers and the smaller of twins are particularly vulnerable if birth weight is below 2000 grams. Untreated symptomatic babies with low blood sugar have a higher incidence of neurologic abnormality and a lower mean IQ level later in childhood than normal controls. Because of this suboptimal outcome in later life and because survival may be endangered during the early neonatal period, hypoglycemia must be identified and treated at the earliest possible moment. Infants who are below the tenth percentile on the intrauterine growth chart must be monitored periodically for blood glucose concentrations during the first 3 or 4 days of life. Most small-for-dates infants first become hypoglycemic after 12 to 24 hours of age, but we have encountered this disorder much earlier in severely undernourished premature infants. Although a central laboratory can perform blood sugar determinations several times daily, nurses should screen frequently for low blood sugar with Dextrostix. *Optimal management requires that they do so according to their own judgment, without need for physicians' orders.* The details of hypoglycemic syndromes—their pathogenesis, symptoms, and treatment—are presented in Chapter 11.

Heat loss. Compared to their full-sized contemporaries, small-for-dates infants are ill equipped to conserve body heat because of their disproportionately large surface area. The problems of thermoregulation in the neonate are discussed in Chapter 4. Chilling must be avoided in the delivery room and nursery because it delays recovery from birth asphyxia; depletes the stores of glycogen, which are already sparse in undernourished babies; and increases the risk of hypoglycemia.

Cerebral edema. Cerebral edema is an infrequent complication in malnourished infants. It may be noted within 24 hours after delivery, at which time convulsions often occur. The skull sutures are abnormally wide; the increased intracranial pressure caused by cerebral edema is indicated by tightness and bulging of the anterior fontanelle. Anticonvulsant drugs are administered for control of seizures, and intravenous mannitol is utilized in an attempt to diminish edema of the brain by promoting diuresis.

Polycythemia. Abnormally high hematocrit values (greater than 60 vol %) have been reported in as many as 50% of small-for-dates infants. Symptomatic babies whose difficulties were attributed to polycythemia have regularly had capillary or venous hematocrits in excess of 60 vol %. *However, the hematocrit in capilliary blood is generally higher than that of venous or arterial blood.* We therefore insist on central blood samples, since capillary samples yield misleadingly high results. Contrary to reported experiences, we have not encountered symptoms attributable to polycythemia in babies whose hematocrits were less than 70 vol %. In fact, most infants with these high values do not have detectable clinical abnormalities.

The symptoms associated with polycythemia are most commonly those of respiratory distress (tachypnea, retractions, grunting). They are probably the result of diminished lung compliance in polycythemic babies. Hyperbilirubinemia due to the breakdown of erythrocytes is also common. Less frequently, convulsions appear. Cardiac failure, pleural effusion, edema of the scrotum, and priapism have also been reported. A more detailed discussion of symptomatic polycythemia may be found in Chapter 9.

Outcome of small-for-dates infants

Neonatal mortality is a crude but critical measure of the risk imposed by intrauterine growth retardation. The consequences to central nervous system function later in childhood are equally sensitive.

Neonatal mortality. The differing rates of mortality and their relation to birth weight and gestational age have been clearly but

Table 5-3. Relationship of percentage of neonatal mortality to birth weight and gestational age*

Group	Weight (grams)	Gestational age (weeks)	Weight for age	Percentage of mortality	Increase over group I
I	Over 2500	37 or over	Appropriate term	0.5	—
II	Over 2500	Less than 37	Large-for-dates, preterm	1.4	×2.8
III	1501 to 2500	37 or over	Small-for-dates, term	3.2	×6.4
IV	1501 to 2500	Less than 37	Appropriate, preterm	10.5	×21.0
V	1500 or less	All	Preterm	70.7	×141.0

*Modified from Yerushalmy, J.: Classification of newborn infants by weight and gestational age, J. Pediatr. **71:**164, 1967.

crudely demonstrated by designating five general categories: infants over 2500 grams who are above and below 37 gestational weeks, respectively; infants between 1500 and 2500 grams who are similarly divided according to gestational age; and a fifth category that includes infants under 1500 grams regardless of their age at birth. Table 5-3 lists these groups and the percentage of neonatal mortality for each from records of single live births in New York City over a period of 3 years. The increased risks are indicated in the last column as a multiple of the mortality percentage in group I, which is the lowest-risk category. The column entitled "weight for age" characterizes the majority of infants in each group. Most growth-retarded infants are in group III. In comparison to the appropriately grown term infants in group I, neonatal mortality is increased sevenfold. Additional perspective is gained by comparing the mortality of small-for-dates term babies in group III to premature infants in group IV. Although the outlook for undergrown infants is considerably worse than for those who are normal and at term, it is not as grim as in premature infants of group IV. The gravest prognosis prevails among group V babies who weigh less than 1500 grams, over 90% of whom are preterm. Their mortality rate is 141 times greater than that of normal term infants in group I. Little is known about the babies in group II who are large for gestational age, but increased neonatal mortality rates have been noted by a number of investigators. Infants of diabetic mothers, who are at comparatively great risk, usually fall into this category, but they comprise only a minority of the babies in group II.

Assessment of neonatal mortality must be considered in finer detail than by means of the statistical associations just described. The variations and disagreements between numbers of published inquiries are no doubt largely due to the heterogeneous nature of infants who are categorically labeled "small-for-dates." Immediate outcomes vary among infants with major malformations, those whose insult began early in pregnancy, and those whose insult began later on; yet in all three categories, the babies are simply labeled small-for-dates. Heterogeneity is even more significant when one attempts to analyze long-term status in regard to stature and central nervous system function.

Postneonatal outcome. Any analysis that seeks to relate stature, weight, and IQ in later childhood to fetal growth must consider the heterogeneity of small-for-dates babies—that is, the magnitude and type of in utero insult, and the time of its inception. Most studies have been unable to accomplish this delineation because data are not complete. Furthermore, the postnatal environmental influences exerted by socioeconomic level must also be assessed in the light of the long-term outcome. Intrauterine growth retardation is commonest among poor families, and the socioeconomic factors that influence impaired growth in utero are likely to be operative after birth as well. Thus an abnormal outcome may not be due solely to intrauterine events. The IQ is a case in point. A study in Scotland has revealed that infants who were undergrown at birth had lower IQ scores at 10 to 12 years of age than those who were appropriately grown at the same gestational age, but this phenomenon was noted only in poor homes. On the other hand, in superior homes, IQ scores were virtually identical in both groups. According to these data, fetal malnutrition exerts an influence on intellectual status, but primarily in low socioeconomic families. Apparently the low IQ of children in poor homes cannot be attributed solely to intrauterine growth retardation, unless there exists one type of undergrowth among the poor and yet another among the more favored socioeconomic groups.

There seems little doubt that fetal undergrowth plays a significant role in later subnormal central nervous system function. What remains in doubt are the specific variety or varieties of fetal insult that are implicated and the extent of that implication. It is obvious from years of published studies that not all undergrown neonates fare poorly. Babies who are small by virtue of intrauterine virus infection (rubella, cytomegalovirus) are profoundly affected from direct invasion of the brain by the offending virus, and babies who are small-for-dates by virtue of a chromosomal disorder or some major anomaly are similarly affected. The data are straightforward and uncontested. However, infants who are small for no other reason than that their well-nourished parents are small, are not afflicted later in life. The data on these infants are also unequivocal. Between these categories is a heterogeneous group of babies whose fetal growth was impeded by an adverse social environment, such as maternal malnutrition, as well as by disorders of pregnancy itself regardless of social class. Any inquiry that does not limit its data and conclusions to specific etiologic categories of fetal undergrowth, insofar as these categories can be determined, will produce invalid results. This failure to establish specific categories is

probably the fundamental reason for the differing literature on this subject. An attempt to assess the severity of in utero insult was made in a recently published, well-controlled study of approximately 500 babies. It indicates that low birth weight babies (1500 to 2500 grams) whose gestational age is at term (40 weeks) are most likely to be smallest in weight and height at 10 years of age compared to babies of similar birth weight but shorter gestational age (34 to 38 weeks). Stated differently, infants of equal weight in whom intrauterine growth was slowest (born after the longest gestations, 40 weeks) were the most deeply insulted group and experienced the worst outcome at 10 years of age. Similar assessment of IQ was not made.

It now appears that if one excludes intrauterine infections, chromosomal disorders, and major congenital malformations, small-for-dates infants have a low incidence of severe mental and neurologic handicaps. However, less profound impairments that cause learning difficulties and behavior problems are probably quite common. From various studies, these impairments include minimal cerebral dysfunction characterized by hyperactivity, short attention span, and poor fine coordination. Neurologic abnormalities of a mild, diffuse nature are common. Speech defects featuring immature reception and expression are also rather frequent. Furthermore, the stimulating postnatal environment and optimal nutrition in preschool years that are so essential for all children are probably more urgently required for those who were poorly grown in utero.

The incidence of severe central nervous system handicaps such as mental retardation and cerebral palsy seems to be more clearly a function of gestational age. Premature low birth weight infants have a higher incidence of these unfortunate results, and the more premature the birth, the higher is the incidence of abnormality. In terms of central nervous system function, growth impairment in babies born at or near term may result only in some diminution of intellectual capacity, rather than in the severe disabilities that characterize cerebral palsy. Generally the immediate prognosis for survival and the long-term outlook for normal function seem to be better in small-for-dates infants than in those who are premature and normally grown for gestational age; yet neither group fares as well as the normal-sized term infant. In most categories of abnormality, the application of contemporary intensive care techniques has substantially reduced the incidence of neonatal mortality and brain damage among survivors.

PREMATURITY

As discussed at the beginning of this chapter, premature births occur before the end of the thirty-seventh gestational week, regardless of birth weight. The majority of babies who weigh less than 2500 grams and almost all infants below 1500 grams are prematurely born. Most of them are appropriately grown; some are small-for-dates. On the other hand, many premature infants of diabetic mothers weigh over 2500 grams at birth.

Prenatal factors

In the past, most studies of the maternal factors associated with prematurity were based on birth weight as the sole criterion of premature birth. Among the so-called premature babies who were studied, a substantial number of low birth weight infants were actually born at term. In spite of this difficulty, a number of factors have been shown to be clearly associated with prematurity, although definitive causes are demonstrable in only a minority of affected mothers. The obstetric conditions that play a role in the initiation of premature labor include chronic hypertensive disease, toxemia, placenta previa, abruptio placentae, and cervical incompetence. Other factors that have been implicated are low socioeconomic status, short maternal stature, absence of prenatal care, malnutrition, and a history of previous premature delivery. The difficulty in evaluating any of the latter group of conditions singly is that they usually occur in some sort of combination with each other. Thus mothers of

short stature are often malnourished, do not receive prenatal care, and are the same women who deliver premature infants repeatedly. Furthermore, these particular factors are inseparable from poverty, of which they are the essence. In spite of remarkable advances in perinatal medicine, our persistent ignorance of the causes of prematurity remains a major disappointment.

Mortality and morbidity

Mortality rates are highest among premature infants, and these rates increase as birth weight decreases. Premature infants are poorly equipped to withstand the stresses of extrauterine life. The lungs may not be ready for air exchange; the digestive tract fails to absorb 20% to 40% of the fat contained in milk feedings. Defenses against infections are relatively ineffective, and an increased rate of heat loss creates serious thermoregulatory problems. The capillaries are relatively sparse so that perfusion of tissues is at best marginal. Increased capillary fragility predisposes to hemorrhage, especially in the ventricles of the brain. The commonest disorders to which premature babies are predisposed are hyaline membrane disease, intracranial hemorrhage, infections, and fetal asphyxia. Retrolental fibroplasia (p. 153), which often culminates in blindness, occurs almost exclusively in preterm infants in response to inappropriately high concentrations of ambient oxygen. Anemia of prematurity occurs at 4 to 8 weeks, when hemoglobin levels may be as low as 6 or 7 grams/100 ml.

Postneonatal outcome

Premature infants have a relatively high incidence of mental retardation and abnormal neurologic signs. Microcephaly, spastic diplegia, convulsive disorders, and abnormal electroencephalograms are the most frequently encountered signs of brain disorder. The incidence of neurologic abnormality has diminished substantially since the advent of intensive care techniques. Approximately 70% to 90% of very low birth weight infants who survive are neurologically intact. (See

Chapter 14.) Blindness due to retrolental fibroplasia was quite common between 1940 and 1955, and it was shown to be caused by excessive ambient oxygen concentrations. It was particularly frequent among infants whose birth weights were less than 1500 grams. Restriction of oxygen administration resulted in a significantly decreased incidence of the disease. Sophisticated therapeutic regimens requiring the use of oxygen in high concentrations have diminished mortality rates impressively, but there has also been a resurgence in the incidence of retrolental fibroplasia.

POSTMATURITY

Prolonged gestation is dated from the beginning of the forty-second week; infants born afterward are said to be postmature. By this definition approximately 12% of all pregnancies are prolonged. Postmature infants may be appropriately sized for gestational age; yet quite often they are small-for-dates by virtue of a progressive increase in placental dysfunction. In such circumstances the infant may be considerably wasted. The physical appearance of a wasted postmature baby differs in several respects from the appearance of his earlier born counterpart of equal size. Changes in the skin, nails, hair, subcutaneous tissue, and body contour are the obvious differences. Vernix caseosa is characteristically absent in postmature babies, except in the deepest skin folds at the axillae and groin, whereas at term the skin of malnourished infants is well covered with this cheeselike material. In postmature babies the skin becomes dry and cracked quite soon after birth, imparting a parchmentlike texture to it. The nails are often lengthened. Scalp hair is profuse, in contrast to earlier born malnourished infants, whose hair is quite sparse. Wasting involves depletion of previously deposited subcutaneous tissue; as a consequence, skin is loose, and fat layers are almost nonexistent (Fig. 5-4). The body appears thin and long. Meconium staining occurs frequently, coloring the skin, nails, and cord in shades ranging from green to golden yellow.

Release of meconium in response to intrauterine hypoxic stress may occur just before delivery or about 10 to 14 days before. Typically, these infants appear alert and wide-eyed, an attractive but misleading feature that is ominous because it may indicate chronic intrauterine hypoxia.

Perinatal mortality is higher in postmature infants than in those born at term, particularly in pregnancies that progress into the forty-third week and beyond. In these infants, mortality is two or three times greater than in babies born at term. Approximately 75% to 85% of all deaths among postmature babies occur during labor. This is not particularly surprising when one considers that fetal oxygenation is marginal or depressed for days prior to the onset of labor. The subsequent stresses of labor are poorly tolerated, and intrauterine demise or severe depression at birth ensues.

INTRAUTERINE GROWTH ACCELERATION (BABIES LARGE FOR GESTATIONAL AGE; MACROSOMIA)

The highest birth weight recorded in medical literature is 11,350 grams (25 pounds), a stillborn infant who was delivered in 1916. The *Guinness Book of World Records* (1975) reports the heaviest normal neonate, born in 1961, weighed 11,200 grams (24 pounds 4 ounces); a baby weighing 13,381 grams (29 pounds 8 ounces), who lived only 2 hours, was born in 1939. Five percent of infants weigh over 4000 grams at birth, and from 0.4% to 0.9% weigh over 4500 grams. Whereas low birth weight is delineated below 2500 grams for any gestational age, high birth weight is above 4000 grams. The same variations in weight for age at birth that were described for small infants are applicable to large ones. An infant who is plotted above the ninetieth percentile on the intrauterine growth curve (at any week of gestation) is large for gestational age (LGA).

Large babies are characteristic of diabetic mothers, except for those mothers with advanced disease. However, only a minority of all large infants are born of diabetic mothers.

Excessive birth weight (over 4000 grams) often reflects the genetic predisposition of the fetus. It has been found to be proportional to prepregnancy weight and to weight gain during pregnancy. Large infants are born to multiparous mothers three times as often as to primiparous ones; male infants have long been known to be heavier at birth than females. The small number of infants who have transposition of the great vessels are usually overgrown.

Categorization of babies as large for gestational age has been found, in the majority of instances, to be due to miscalculation of dates. The source of error, difficult to avert, appears to be postconceptional bleeding, a spurious menstrual episode after fertilization.

In diabetic pregnancies, birth weight over 4000 grams is four times more frequent than in nondiabetic pregnancies. The discrepancy is of greater magnitude for babies over 4500 grams: they are fourteen to twenty-eight times more frequent among diabetic women than in the general population.

The mortality rate for large babies born at or near term is higher than for average-sized neonates. The obvious mechanical difficulties posed by delivery of an oversized baby are significant. The need for midforceps and cesarean section is considerably increased. Cesarean section is usually necessary because of cephalopelvic (fetopelvic) disproportion. Shoulder dystocia has been noted in 10% of large babies delivered per vaginam. Fractured clavicle, depressed skull fracture, brachial plexus palsy, and facial paralysis are all increased in frequency, together occurring in 15% of oversized infants. Low Apgar scores occur more frequently in overgrown infants.

Large babies have received relatively scanty attention compared to those who are undergrown. Prenatal identification of overgrown fetuses would seem to be as necessary as the identification of those who are undergrown. Abnormal and traumatic labor and delivery could thus often be averted.

SUMMATION

A nurse's expertise in the care of newborn patients requires, among other things, an understanding of the abnormalities of intrauterine growth patterns as they relate to gestational age. An infant's course in the nursery is in large measure determined by these factors, and the illnesses that develop postnatally are often peculiar to a particular type of aberrant intrauterine growth pattern. Thus hyaline membrane disease, for all practical purposes, is confined to preterm babies, whereas hypoglycemia is a frequent hazard in small-for-dates infants. With knowledge of maternal factors and with the ability to categorize babies in terms of growth status, the nurse can readily recognize a large number of high-risk infants and plan their management accordingly.

References

Battaglia, F. C., and Lubchenco, L. O.: A practical classification of newborn infants by weight and gestational age, J. Pediatr. **71:**159, 1967.

Beck, G. J., and van den Berg, B. J.: The relationship of the rate of intrauterine growth of low-birth-weight infants to later growth, J. Pediatr. **86:**504, 1975.

Benirschke, K.: Multiple births. In Barnett, H., editor: Pediatrics, New York, 1968, Appleton-Century-Crofts.

Campbell, S.: Fetal growth, Clin. Obstet. Gynecol. **1:**41, 1974.

Clifford, S. H.: Postmaturity with placental dysfunction: clinical syndrome and pathologic findings, J. Pediatr. **44:**1, 1954.

Cornblath, M., and Swartz, R.: Disorders of carbohydrate metabolism in infancy, Philadelphia, 1966, W. B. Saunders Co.

Drillien, C. M.: Prenatal and perinatal factors in etiology and outcome of low birth weight, Clin. Perinatol. **1:**197, 1974.

Dubowitz, L. M. S., Dubowitz, V., and Goldberg, C.: Clinical assessment of gestational age in the newborn infant, J. Pediatr. **77:**1, 1970.

Fitzhardinge, P. M., and Steven, E. M.: The small-for-date infant. II. Neurological and intellectual sequelae, Pediatrics **50:**50, 1972.

Gluck, L., Kulovich, M. V., Borer, R. C., Jr., and others: The diagnosis of the respiratory distress syndrome (RDS) by amniocentesis, Am. J. Obstet. Gynecol. **109:**440, 1971.

Gruenwald, P.: The fetus in prolonged pregnancy, Am. J. Obstet. Gynecol. **89:**503, 1964.

Gruenwald, P.: Growth of the human fetus. I.

Normal growth and its variation, Am. J. Obstet. Gynecol. **94**:1112, 1966.

Hellman, L. M., and Pritchard, J. A.: Williams' obstetrics, ed. 14, 1971, New York, Appleton-Century-Crofts.

Horger, E. O., III, Miller, C., III, and Conner, E. D.: Relation of large birthweight to maternal diabetes mellitus, Obstet. Gynecol. **45**:150, 1975.

Humbert, J. R., Abelson, H., Hathaway, W. E., and Battaglia, F. C.: Polycythemia in small for gestational age infants, J. Pediatr. **75**:812, 1969.

Iffy, L., Chatterton, R. T., and Jakobovits, A.: The "high weight for dates" fetus, Am. J. Obstet. Gynecol. **115**:238, 1973.

Koenigsberger, M. R.: Judgment of fetal age. I. Neurologic evaluation, Pediatr. Clin. North Am. **13**:823, 1966.

Low, J. A., and Galbraith, R. S.: Pregnancy characteristics of intrauterine growth retardation, Obstet. Gynecol. **44**:122, 1974.

Lubchenco, L. O., Hansman, C., and Boyd, E.: Intrauterine growth in length and head circumference as estimated from live births at gestational ages from 26 to 42 weeks, Pediatrics **37**:403, 1966.

Lubchenco, L. O., Hansman, C., Dressler, M., and Boyd, E.: Intrauterine growth as estimated from liveborn birth-weight data at 24 to 42 weeks of gestation, Pediatrics **32**:793, 1963.

Lubchenco, L. O., Searls, D. T., and Brazie, J. V.: Neonatal mortality rate: relationship to birthweight and gestational age, J. Pediatr. **81**:814, 1972.

Malan, A. F., and Higgs, S. C.: Gestational age assessment in infants of very low birth-weight, Arch. Dis. Child. **50**:322, 1975.

Naeye, R. L.: Human intrauterine parabiotic syndrome and its complications, N. Engl. J. Med. **268**:804, 1963.

Naeye, R. L.: Unsuspected organ abnormalities associated with congenital heart disease, Am. J. Pathol. **47**:905, 1965.

Naeye, R. L.: Abnormalities in infants of mothers with toxemia of pregnancy, Am. J. Obstet. Gynecol. **95**:276, 1966.

Naeye, R. L., Bernirschke, K., Hagstrom, J. W. C., and Marcus, C. C.: Intrauterine growth of twins as estimated from liveborn birth-weight data, Pediatrics **37**:409, 1966.

Schlesinger, E. R., and Allaway, N. C.: The combined effect of birthweight and length of gestation on neonatal mortality among single premature births, Pediatrics **15**:698, 1955.

Scott, K. E., and Usher, R.: Epiphyseal development in fetal malnutrition syndrome, N. Engl. J. Med. **270**:822, 1964.

Shanklin, D. R.: The influence of placental lesions on the newborn infant, Pediatr. Clin. North Am. **17**:25, 1970.

Silverman, W. A.: Dunham's premature infants, New York, 1961, Paul B. Hoeber, Medical Division, Harper & Row, Publishers.

Silverman, W. A., and Sinclair, J. C.: Infants of low birth weight, N. Engl. J. Med. **274**:448, 1966.

Sinclair, J. C.: Heat production and thermoregulation in the small-for-date infant, Pediatr. Clin. North Am. **17**:147, 1970.

Smith, C. A.: Effects of maternal undernutrition upon the newborn infant in Holland, J. Pediatr. **71**:390, 1967.

Winick, M.: Cellular growth of human placenta. III. Intrauterine growth failure, J. Pediatr. **71**:390, 1967.

Winick, M.: Cellular growth in intrauterine malnutrition, Pediatr. Clin. North Am. **17**:69, 1970.

Winick, M., Brasel, J. A., and Velasco, E. G.: Effects of prenatal nutrition upon pregnancy risk, Clin. Obstet. Gynecol. **16**:184, 1973.

Yerushalmy, J.: The classification of newborn infants by birth weight and gestational age, J. Pediatr. **71**:164, 1967.

Chapter 6

Physical examination of the newborn infant

The physical findings associated with birth trauma are described in Chapter 3.

The nurse who learns to evaluate physical signs in the neonate can contribute substantially to his proper management. Contemporary expansion of nursing skills involves many new functions, one of which is the competent performance of a physical examination. Physical findings in the newborn will thus be presented in considerable detail, with emphasis on normal characteristics and their variations, most of which require no therapy. *Some pathologic findings will be described, but they are usually discussed more completely in chapters devoted to the specific diseases in which they occur.*

The initial physical examination should be performed as soon as possible after arrival in the nursery. Its purpose is to identify existing abnormalities and to provide a basis on which future changes can be assessed. After the admission examination a number of observations must be made during the nursery stay. The first passage of stool and the first urination should be noted. Sucking behavior and performance during feedings are extremely important observations. The appearance of jaundice, cyanosis, pallor, excessive salivation, abdominal distention, abnormal stools, respiratory distress, and a number of other events must all be sought in a systematic fashion.

The purpose of the neonatal physical examination is to identify and record evidence of stress, trauma, malformations, and disease during the first days of life. Physical assessment is only one component of the total evaluation. A well-considered chronologic account of antecedent events must be known prior to examination. Laboratory and other procedural data are usually acquired afterward.

SEQUENCE OF EXAMINATION

The sequence in which the various features of the examination are assessed is a matter of personal preference. All examiners eventually develop their own individual approach. Regardless of the system used, it is best to order observations in reference to the amount of disturbance they produce. I prefer to first make assessments that cause the least disturbance, particularly those that require a quiet baby. It seems advisable to then proceed to the more disturbing maneuvers that are not so dependent on the resting state for accurate interpretation.

Inspection without contact. A tremendous amount of information is available by simply looking at a baby, without touching him. The examiner should not, when first confronting an infant, abruptly thrust a stethoscope to the chest before doing anything else. This maneuver betrays a sad lack of sensitivity to the neonate's reactions and a total lack of perspective regarding the relative importance of the individual observations that comprise the physical examination.

The infant's overall size and contour are immediately apparent, as is the relative size of the head, extremities, and trunk. Microcephaly or cranial enlargement are obvious. If hydrocephalus is present, the forehead is often prominently protrusive (bossing). The cranial vault is always large in relation to the face (Fig. 6-1). The amount of subcutaneous fat is assessable at a glance. A thin trunk often causes a normal head to appear enlarged. The abdomen is either distended, flat, or sunken (scaphoid), or it may bulge

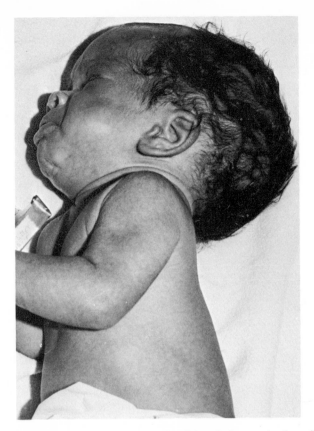

Fig. 6-1. Hydrocephalus. Note the large size of the head in relation to the face. The occiput is prominent, the forehead less than usual. This infant also had severe chorioretinitis. The diagnosis was toxoplasmosis.

Fig. 6-2. Abdominal distention due to unilateral hydronephrosis. Bulging of the right side is immediately apparent.

Fig. 6-3. Upper extremities are flaccid, as seen in the relaxed fingers and elbows. Lower extremities are spastic, and their flexed posture is exaggerated. Note the congenitally amputated finger on the left hand.

on one side because of a massively enlarged kidney (hydronephrosis, Fig. 6-2).

The baby's *posture* is informative. Normal flexion of the extremities indicates good muscle tone. Lack of flexion is associated with hypotonicity (flaccidity), whereas excessive flexion usually suggests hypertonicity (spasticity). Both these findings are evident in the baby in Fig. 6-3, who had flaccid upper extremities and spastic lower ones. If only one arm is straight instead of flexed, it is probably paralyzed to some extent. This paralysis suggests brachial plexus palsy, which is described on p. 48 and is illustrated in Figs. 2-13 and 2-14. Breech presentations can be identified by the characteristic positions of the lower extremities. These positions are described later in this chapter. The absence of molding plus the position of the lower extremities should suggest a breech

delivery. Retraction of the head with relatively normal vertebral posture indicates a face presentation.

A number of features of the *skin* are immediately obvious. If cyanosis is present, its distribution is of great importance because distribution relates to the significance of cyanosis (generalized cyanosis) or lack of it (acrocyanosis). Jaundice, pallor, rash, and evidence of trauma are all there to be discerned by those who will look.

The *face* is informative. Abnormal facies must be appreciated. The alert, wide-eyed baby who appears to be sucking is really agitated as a result of intrauterine hypoxic insult to the brain (Fig. 5-6). Facial paralysis may be evident at rest, or it may not be apparent until the baby cries (p. 50).

Spontaneous movements can be evaluated only if the infant is not disturbed. At rest, sporadic, well-coordinated movements are the rule. If no movement is noted, significant depression is probably the cause, whether from hypoxia in utero, maternal anesthesia, hypoglycemia, or any other of a large number of etiologies. The baby who moves little or not at all is usually flaccid as well. Repetitive, rhythmic motions of one or more extremities are convulsive movements. Facial and eyelid twitches are also convulsive phenomena. Absent or diminished movement of one extremity (or two), while the others are used normally, is indicative of paresis or paralysis.

Much information is obtainable for the evaluation of *respiration* by simple inspection. Retractions are obvious (Fig. 6-4); grunting and stridor are audible. Increased anteroposterior diameter of the chest (barrel chest) usually indicates overexpanded lungs (massive aspiration, respiratory distress syndrome type 2). If one side of the chest appears larger than the other, pneumothorax, chylothorax, or diaphragmatic hernia are possible causes. If the left chest is larger, cardiomegaly associated with congenital heart disease is an additional possibility.

Several *scattered observations* by inspection are also of value. The undergrown term or preterm infant's hair is sparse (Fig. 5-5),

Fig. 6-4. Severe retraction during inspiration. The lower end of the sternum and the subcostal margins are severely indrawn. The upper anterior thorax is somewhat expanded. Electrodes to the chest are connected to apnea and heart rate monitors.

whereas the postmature baby's hair is dense. The cord is thin in mature infants who are small-for-dates, and it may be the only part of the body that is meconium stained, if meconium release occurs immediately before delivery. Fingernails are long in postmature infants.

These diverse signs are described here to emphasize the value of purposeful inspection without touching. This inspection accomplished, one may then proceed to the more manipulative aspects of the physical examination.

Auscultation, palpation, and other manipulations. With the baby supine, I prefer to palpate the abdomen immediately after the initial inspection. If the infant is disturbed by manipulations beforehand, an adequate evaluation of the abdomen is difficult or temporarily impossible. The fingertips must be gently placed on the abdomen while not exerting any downward pressure. Deep palpation should then proceed gradually. Sudden plunging of the examining hand into the abdomen is thoughtless; it produces discomfort and precludes a successful examination. The neonate is easily agitated by abrupt manipulations. Auscultation of the anterior chest should follow abdominal palpations.

In conjunction with cardiac evaluation, gently palpate the femoral and brachial pulses. Now palpate the extremities by enveloping them with your hands, and then move the joints gingerly. This maneuver completed, take the wrists and pull the infant into the sitting position to evaluate head lag. The baby may now be turned to the prone position. Crying caused by the disturbance is of little concern because the resultant deep inspirations and the noise of crying are helpful in auscultation of the lungs. Now move the index finger over the vertebrae down to the sacrum in order to ascertain the absence of gross anomalies such as agenesis of the sacrum. Separate the buttocks and look at the anus for position and presence. The infant, who is probably crying now, is then returned to the supine position. Manipulate the hip joints to rule out congenital dislocation. The head, neck, and face are next to be examined. With one hand holding a flashlight, gently separate the eyelids with the index finger and thumb. Shine the light tangentially into the eyes to rule out corneal lesions and large cataracts. Now proceed to the neurologic evaluation (p. 118). Examination of the mouth and throat is performed as the last maneuver of the physical evaluation. It is the most agitating. The physical examination completed, now hold the baby in your arms for a few moments. Both of you will feel better.

PHYSICAL FINDINGS
Contour, proportions, and postures

The body of a normal newborn is essentially cylindric; the head circumference slightly exceeds that of the chest. For the term baby, average circumference of the head is 33 to 35 cm (13 to 14 inches), whereas for the chest it is 30 to 33 cm (12 to 13 inches). Sitting height may be measured from crown to rump, and it is approximately equal to head circumference. These values may vary somewhat, but their relationship to each other is normally constant. For example, if the head circumference is significantly smaller than the chest, microcephaly is suspect; if it is larger than expected, hydrocephalus must be considered. During the first 24 hours, because of molding, the head may be equal to or slightly smaller than the chest. On the second and third days a normal contour replaces the molded one, and the head circumference increases by 1 or 2 cm as a result. If the head is over 4 cm larger than the chest, and this has been verified by repeated measurements on several successive days, abnormal enlargement due to increased intracranial pressure is suspect. In these circumstances, additional signs of increased intracranial pressure are ordinarily detectable. These signs are described later in this chapter. A word of caution is in order regarding the relative sizes of head and chest when one is considering abnormal enlargement of the cranial vault. A discrepancy between the two measurements may be exaggerated in a malnourished baby if the chest circumference is diminished by virtue of depleted subcutaneous tissue. If this is the case, other signs of malnutrition are evident, and the head size itself is in the range of normal, even though the chest size is not.

During the first few days of life, posture is largely the result of position in utero. Placed on the side, the normal infant who was delivered from a vertex presentation tends to keep the head flexed, with the chin close to the chest. The arms are close to the trunk, the elbows are flexed so that the forearms rest on the chest to some degree, and the hands are held in a fisted position. The back is somewhat bent, and the hips are flexed so that the thighs are drawn on the abdomen. Flexion is also maintained at the knees, and the feet are dorsiflexed onto the anterior aspects of the legs. This fetal position is often assumed to some extent by adults and older children while they sleep. During the first days of life, it is the position of comfort for the baby. Frequently he may be quieted during crying episodes by taking him up from the crib and gently curling him into this described position.

Other postures are associated with more unusual fetal positions. After a footling breech presentation the thighs are abducted in the so-called frog-leg position (Fig. 2-8). Some babies born in the frank breech position tend to keep their knees straightened. After a brow or face delivery the head is extended and the neck appears elongated.

These postures depend on normal muscle tone, which is strikingly diminished in hypoxic babies. Thus affected, they make no attempt to assume previous intrauterine postures but remain in almost any position imposed on them by the examiner. The extremities lie flat on the table surface, and the head turns to one side, depending on the position in which it is placed (Fig. 6-5).

Skin and subcutaneous tissue

At birth the skin is covered extensively with *vernix caseosa,* a gray-white substance with a cheeselike consistency. If not removed, it dries and disappears within 24 hours. For the first day of life the skin is blush red and smooth; toward the second or third days it becomes dry, somewhat flaky, and pink.

In approximately half of all normal newborn infants *jaundice* is visible during the second or third days of life and disappears between the fifth and seventh days. This is physiologic jaundice; the mechanism of its

Fig. 6-6. Traumatic cyanosis, with bruising of forehead and scalp. Vertex delivery of a premature infant.

Fig. 6-5. A depressed, flaccid baby delivered in breech position. Extremities lie flat on table, and head remains turned to one side. Note traumatic cyanosis of lower half of body, a result of breech delivery.

development is described in Chapter 10. Jaundice in the first 24 hours is abnormal, and this requires extensive diagnostic evaluation. Icteric skin may be difficult to detect when redness is prominent, but blanching readily demonstrates the underlying yellow discoloration. Blanching is described in later paragraphs devoted to petechiae and ecchymoses.

The subcutaneous tissue may be moderately *edematous* for several days. Edema is most noticeable about the eyes, the legs, and the dorsal aspects of the hands and feet.

Peripheral cyanosis (acrocyanosis) involves the hands, feet, and circumoral area (around the lips). It is evident in most infants at birth and for a short time thereafter. If limited to the extremities in an otherwise normal infant, it is due to venous stasis and is innocuous. Localized cyanosis may occur in presenting parts, particularly in association with abnor-

mal presentations. In breech presentations the buttocks or the feet and legs are blue as a result of venous stasis and are edematous (Fig. 2-8); in a transverse lie a prolapsed arm may be similarly discolored because of obstructed venous return. Occasionally a circular area of edema and cyanosis in the scalp is present at the top of the head as a result of pressure against a dilated cervix (caput succedaneum). Sometimes the forehead and scalp (or even the entire head above the neck) are cyanotic (Fig. 6-6).

Ecchymoses appear as bruises of varying size anywhere over the body, sometimes involving extensive areas. They are most frequently due to trauma during difficult labor or to brisk handling of the infant during or after delivery. Occasionally they indicate serious infection or a bleeding diathesis. When the extravasated blood in an ecchymosis is broken down, the resultant elevated serum bilirubin levels may occasionally reach dangerous heights. The pathogenesis of hyperbilirubinemia and the role of extraneous blood are discussed in Chapter 10.

Petechiae are pinpoint hemorrhagic areas that occur in a number of disease states involving infection and thrombocytopenia. Occasionally, however, scattered petechiae are noted over the upper trunk or the face as a result of increased intravascular pressure, which causes capillaries to rupture during delivery. These petechiae fade within 24 to 48 hours, and fresh lesions do not appear subsequently. Identification of petechiae may be verified by blanching the skin. Both index fingers are held next to each other, and while maintaining pressure, they are separated to reveal the area in question. Petechiae and ecchymoses do not disappear when the skin is blanched, since blood is fixed in the tissue. Red rashes involving local vascular engorgement disappear completely when the skin is blanched, since blood is emptied from the engorged vessels. The same maneuver reveals underlying jaundice that would otherwise be masked by flushed skin that is suffused with blood.

Mongolian spots are irregular areas of pale blue pigmentation over the sacrum and buttocks, but they may be so extensive as to cover the back and sometimes the extensor surfaces of the extremities as well. They are common in black infants and in babies of Asian and southern European lineage. These harmless discolorations are caused by pigmented cells in the deep layer of the skin. They disappear by 4 years of age, and often much sooner.

Telangiectatic nevi (stork bites) are flat, red localized areas of capillary dilatation seen in almost all neonates. They can be eradicated by blanching the skin. They are most commonly situated at the back of the neck, the lower occiput, the upper eyelids, and the nasal bridge. They disappear by 2 years of age, but in many children they often reappear during crying episodes.

Strawberry hemangiomas are not seen in normal term infants during the nursery stay because they generally appear in the second or third week of life. As a result, they are seen in premature infants who are hospitalized for protracted periods of time and in term babies after discharge. They are first evident as bright red, flat spots, 1 to 3 mm in diameter, which blanch easily. Subsequently they grow in all directions, protruding prominently from the skin surface. Their texture and color are very much like that of the strawberry. They may not reach their fullest size for 1 to 3 months or more. There is a great temptation to remove these lesions, but it should be resisted because they invariably resolve spontaneously several weeks or months after reaching peak growth. *The cosmetic effect is best when they are allowed to resolve.* Resolution is heralded by a pale purple or gray spot on the surface of the lesion, which grows as the hemangioma shrinks. Appearance of the pale spot indicates spontaneous sclerosis, and thus obliteration, of the capillaries that comprise the lesion.

Subcutaneous fat necrosis (p. 45) is due to trauma. These lesions are sharply demarcated, firm masses of varying size that are located in subcutaneous tissue and are fixed to overlying skin. Occasionally a pale purple discoloration is in evidence at the surface of these lesions.

Harlequin color change is a rare, peculiar discrepancy in color between the two longitudinal halves of the body, extending from the forehead to the symphysis pubis. A curiosity of no known pathologic significance, it is elicited by placing the baby on his side for several minutes. The dependent half of the body turns pink while the upper half remains pale. The colors are reversed when the infant is turned onto the opposite side. The same phenomenon may occur in the supine position.

Lanugo is fine hair, sometimes barely visible, that is characteristic of the newborn period. It is more noticeable in premature infants and is most easily seen over the shoulders, back, forehead, and cheeks.

Milia are minute, white papules on the chin, nose, cheeks, and forehead. They represent distended sebaceous glands that disappear spontaneously in several days or weeks. *Sudamina* are tiny vesicles over the face and neck that are formed by distention of sweat glands (Fig. 6-7).

Erythema toxicum is a pink papular rash on which vesicles are often superimposed (Fig. 6-8). The vesicles frequently appear purulent and are sometimes confused with the lesions characteristic of staphylococcal pyoderma. They appear anywhere over the body within 24 to 48 hours after birth and resolve spontaneously after several days. The vesicles contain eosinophils that are demonstrable on a smear prepared with Wright's stain. The rash is innocuous, and its etiology is unknown.

Sclerema is hardening of the skin and subcutaneous tissue associated with life-threatening disorders such as septicemia, shock, and severe cold stress. As a rule, the cheeks and the buttocks are first involved, then the calves and thighs, and eventually perhaps the entire body. The skin is so hard it feels wooden. Sclerema should not be confused with subcutaneous fat necrosis, which is confined to small areas and is usually present in babies who are otherwise well.

Head

After vaginal deliveries from the vertex position, *molding* of the head is apparent to some degree in virtually all neonates as a

Fig. 6-7. Sudamina (distended sweat glands) appear vesicular. They disappear spontaneously.

Fig. 6-8. Erythema toxicum. Patches of swollen redness with superimposed vesicles, often mistaken for staphylococcal lesions. Lesions in this instance are distributed over the abdomen and thorax.

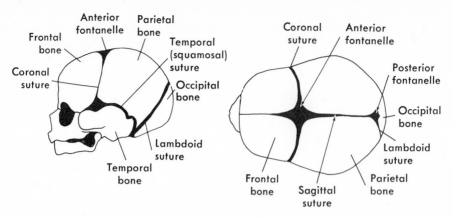

Fig. 6-9. Neonatal cranial bones, sutures, and fontanelles from lateral view and from above. (Modified from Crelin, E. S.: Anatomy of the newborn, an atlas, Philadelphia, 1969, Lea & Febiger.)

result of pressures exerted during the birth process. The change in shape is more pronounced in first-born infants and in those whose heads are engaged for prolonged periods of time. Pressure during the usual vertex delivery causes flattening of the forehead with a gradual rise to an apex posteriorly and an abrupt drop at the occiput (Fig. 2-10). In brow presentations the forehead may be unusually prominent, rather than flattened as in vertex deliveries. When the forces of the birth process are not exerted on the cranium, its spherical contour is undisturbed. Thus the head is characteristically spherical in an infant born from the breech position or delivered by cesarean section. These modes of delivery can be presumed from inspection of the cranial contour. Molding generally disappears by the end of the first or second day of life.

The *cranium* comprises six bones (Fig. 6-9): the frontal, occipital, two parietals, and two temporals. The *frontal bone* runs the width of the cranium at its anterior third. The *occipital bone* occupies the width of the cranium at its posterior third, whereas the two *parietal bones* are situated in the middle third between the frontal and occipital bones. The *temporal bones* are the most lateral and inferior of the cranial bones. They are adjacent to the parietals.

The *sutures* and *fontanelles* of the cranium are extremely important landmarks (Fig. 6-9). They are bands of connective tissue that separate the six major cranial bones. Sutures are palpable as cracks; fontanelles are broader "soft spots" at specific locations. The *coronal suture* runs from one side of the cranium to the other, separating the frontal bone (the forehead) from the two parietal bones posterior to it. The *lambdoid suture,* situated toward the posterior third of the skull, runs from one side to the other, separating the occipital bone from the two parietal bones anterior to it. The *sagittal suture* runs in an anteroposterior direction in the midline, terminating anteriorly at the coronal suture and posteriorly at the lambdoid suture. It separates the two parietal bones. The *squamosal (temporal) sutures* also run in an anteroposterior direction, but they are situated just at the level of the earlobes. They, like the sagittal suture, terminate at the coronal and lambdoid sutures.

The *fontanelles* are relatively wide, soft areas at the junctions of each of the sutures. The *anterior fontanelle* is at the junction of the sagittal and coronal sutures. It is diamond shaped and variable in size. It may be small as a result of molding, but it enlarges as the molding disappears. At its widest point it may measure up to 5 cm. The *posterior fontanelle* is triangular; it measures 1 cm or less in width and is situated at the junc-

Fig. 6-10. Overlapped cranial bones producing visible ridge in a small premature infant. Easily visible overlapping does not often occur in term infants.

tion of the sagittal and lambdoid sutures. Four other fontanelles are of less clinical significance. They are at the junctions formed by the squamosal sutures with the coronal and lambdoid sutures.

Appraisal of the head by external examination depends on an appreciation of the contours that are expected as a result of various presentations and on the status of sutures and fontanelles, particularly the anterior fontanelle. At birth and for a day or two afterward, as a result of molding, the edges of the cranial bones may overlap, obliterating the sutures. The lines of overlap seem to be ridges when palpated, and the fontanelles are small (Fig. 6-10). Later, as the shape of the cranium becomes more normal, the bones separate and the sutures can be felt as cracks several millimeters in width. The anterior fontanelle now expands to its full size. In premature infants the overlapping is often easily seen (Fig. 6-10). It may persist for weeks in the smallest infants. In malnourished infants the sutures may be wide at birth, perhaps over 1 cm, because of

impaired growth of the cranial bones. The anterior fontanelle is large for the same reason, but it is also flat and soft. On the other hand, an abnormal increase in intracranial pressure actually separates the cranial bones, expanding suture lines and fontanelles. Rather than being flat and soft, the anterior fontanelle is firm and bulging as a function of high intracranial pressure. These signs, especially those in the anterior fontanelle, are present in babies with hydrocephalus (Fig. 6-1), meningitis, subdural hematoma, and cerebral edema.

Eyes

Eyelids are frequently edematous during the first 2 days after delivery, and the infant rarely opens them. Separation of lids must be accomplished gently because forceful traction easily everts them, thus precluding an adequate view of the eyes.

Instillation of silver nitrate drops into the eyes at birth may cause *chemical conjunctivitis* to appear within an hour or soon thereafter. The resultant purulent discharge disappears without treatment in 1 or 2 days with no residual difficulty.

Purulent conjunctival exudate is also a sign of *conjunctivitis* due to infection (p. 223). Most commonly, these infections are caused by staphylococci and by a variety of gram-negative rods. Gonorrheal infection, which may also involve the eye itself, occasionally occurs in spite of the application of silver nitrate drops that are ordinarily effective in preventing it.

Subconjunctival hemorrhages are frequent. They result from pressure on the fetal head during delivery, with resultant impairment of venous return and rupture of capillaries in the sclera. They can be seen in the sclerae and are of no pathologic significance, even when the entire sclera is reddened by extravasated blood (Fig. 2-12). *Retinal hemorrhages* are produced by the same mechanism, and they may occur in as many as 10% of normal neonates. They are flame shaped or round and are thought to be harmless. However, extensive hemorrhage over a large seg-

Fig. 6-11. Bilateral cataracts. Note white pupils. Entire lenses were involved. Infant had congenital rubella.

Fig. 6-12. Corneal opacity, unilateral. Cornea is white, its surface rough; overall appearance is that of ground glass. This baby had congenital glaucoma due to intrauterine rubella infection. The cornea is thus abnormally large.

ment of the retina usually indicates the presence of a subdural hematoma.

Cataracts, if present, must be identified at the time of the first examination. Cataracts are opacities of the lens that can vary from pinpoint size to involvement of the entire lens. Occasionally they develop several days or weeks after birth. If the entire lens is affected, they are usually seen easily by shining a light into each eye, with the light source held to one side. If the opacity is small, it can be identified only with an ophthalmoscope. Bilateral cataracts involving the entire lens are illustrated in Fig. 6-11. In this picture the pupils are white because the opacified lens behind them reflects the light, which is applied close to the eyes from the side of the face. White pupils may also be seen in the presence of lesions deeper in the eye, such as retinoblastoma. Normally the pupils appear black to the bare eye of the examiner when light is directed at them. Cataracts are usually bilateral, but they are sometimes unilateral. They are a major manifestation of intrauterine rubella infection (p. 225) and are occasionally seen in cytomegalovirus infection (p. 226). They may be hereditary, being transmitted as a dominant trait from an affected parent. In congenital

galactosemia, cataracts sometimes appear several weeks after birth.

Corneal opacities are also discerned by directing light to the eyes (Fig. 6-12). They occur after trauma, in association with congenital glaucoma, and as a result of infection such as herpesvirus. Compare the illustrations of the cataracts (Fig. 6-11) and the corneal opacity (Fig. 6-12). The two lesions are clearly distinguishable from each other. In the presence of a cataract, the iris can be seen because the affected structure (the lens) is behind it. The cornea is smooth and clear. The corneal opacity involves the eye's outside window (the cornea), and the underlying iris is thus obscure. Furthermore, the surface of the involved cornea is rough, much like ground glass.

Nose

Neonates must breathe through the nose; they cannot ordinarily breathe through the mouth. Any obstruction to the nasal passages thus causes some degree of respiratory distress. Partial or complete occlusion may be caused by mucus secretion that has not been removed or by choanal atresia or stenosis. The latter are congenital anomalies of the

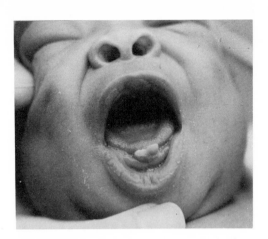

Fig. 6-13. Precocious teeth in the usual location. Teeth were sufficiently loose to threaten spontaneous detachment and aspiration, and they were removed.

Fig. 6-14. Rib fractures, healing. Round opacities in the ribs to the left of cardiac apex are sites of callus formation during healing process. They were palpated as round, bony masses.

posterior nares, which may be life threatening (p. 171).

Mouth and throat

Complete visualization of the mouth and pharynx is difficult when the tongue is depressed; such attempts are usually met with strong reflex protrusion of the depressed tongue. However, an excellent view is obtained by stimulating a cry before gently depressing the tongue. Examination of the mouth is extremely important for the identification of a cleft palate, which often occurs in the absence of a cleft lip. Cleft palate may involve either the hard or soft palates or both. Occasionally only the uvula is cleft.

Precocious teeth occur infrequently. They are most often situated at the lower central incisor positions (Fig. 6-13). When covered with membranous tissue, they are pink rather than white. If detachment is imminent, they should be removed to prevent aspiration.

Epstein's pearls are small, white papular structures, one on each side of the midline of the hard palate. They are insignificant and usually disappear within a few weeks after birth.

The *frenulum* of the tongue is a sharp, thin ridge of tissue that arises in the midline from the base of the tongue and attaches to its undersurface for varying distances toward the tip. When the attachment extends far forward, a concavity (or a groove) is evident at the tip of the tongue on its upper surface. This condition is referred to as tongue-tie. It rarely if ever interferes with feeding, nor does it produce a speech impediment in childhood. "Clipping of the tongue" by incising the frenulum is therefore rarely indicated, especially since there is some danger of severing a rather large vein in the area of the frenulum. Furthermore, the procedure creates a portal of entry for infection.

Thorax

The ribs are flexible; slight sternal retraction is sometimes evident during normal respiration. The *xiphoid cartilage* is at the lower end of the sternum. It may curve anteriorly to produce a prominent pointed protrusion beneath the skin that disappears in several weeks.

Rib fracture may be present in the neonate. Fig. 6-14 depicts the fracture of two ribs that were palpable as rounded, bony masses. They are seen as two opaque, white nodules

Fig. 6-15. Supernumerary nipple, unusually well developed. The upper nipple is the supernumerary one. Above and lateral to it, near the axilla, is a small spot that is another rudimentary extra nipple.

Fig. 6-16. Breast hypertrophy.

in the lower left chest that are not present in the lower right chest. Resuscitation was attempted by the ineffective and dangerous method of squeezing the thoracic cage. Vigorous application of this useless procedure resulted in fracture of the anterior portion of the fourth and fifth ribs.

Supernumerary nipples (Fig. 6-15) are occasionally noted inferior and medial to the normal ones, less often they occur superior and lateral to the normal nipples. They are harmless pink or pigmented spots that vary from a few millimeters in diameter to the size of normal nipples, but they do not contain glandular tissue.

Breast enlargement may occur in some infants (Fig. 6-16). It appears on the third day, and toward the end of the first week a milklike substance ("witch's milk") may be evident. Massaging such breasts with various preparations is a common lay practice that often produces breast abscess. Breast hypertrophy should not be confused with *breast abscess* (Fig. 6-17), which involves asym-

Fig. 6-17. Breast abscess. Note purulent drainage just superior to nipple.

metric swelling around the areola and severe erythema of the skin. Pus, usually yellow or blood tinged, may exude from the nipple or through inflamed skin; it should not be confused with "witch's milk," which is blank white.

Lungs

Physical examination of the lungs is only a first step, but an indispensable one, in the identification of respiratory disorders. Radiologic and blood gas studies should follow if the suspicion of a respiratory disorder is aroused by positive physical findings. The respiratory pattern should be observed before the infant is disturbed. Normal neonates breathe at rates varying between 40 and 60 respirations per minute. Rapid rates are likely to be present for the first few hours after birth. Fluctuations of respiratory rates are the rule, and for this reason several assessments may be necessary before one can conclude that an abnormality exists. *Periodic breathing,* a frequent normal finding in premature infants that requires no therapy, is characterized by sporadic episodes in which respirations cease for up to 10 seconds. Periodic breathing is not associated with cyanosis or bradycardia, and it is rare during the first 24 hours of life. It should not be confused with apneic episodes, which are of longer duration, often cause generalized cyanosis, and may occur at any time.

In the normal neonate, respiratory movements are predominantly diaphragmatic. The thoracic cage remains relatively immobile while the abdomen rises and falls with inspiration and expiration. Occasionally the immobile chest gives the false appearance of being drawn inward as the abdomen protrudes with each inspiration. This should not be confused with the retractions that characterize abnormal respiration.

Respiratory difficulties can be identified by simply observing the infant. A number of abnormal signs are clearly indicative of distress, generalized cyanosis being the most obvious and serious. A sustained rate in excess of 60 respirations per minute *(tachypnea)*

after 3 or 4 hours of age is abnormal, but this condition should be ascertained by obtaining several counts of no less than 30 seconds' duration. Irregular respirations associated with repeated *apneic episodes* are often the result of depressed central nervous system function caused by severe hypoxia or intracranial hemorrhage. *Retractions* indicate obstruction to airflow at any level of the respiratory tract from the nose to the alveoli. They are visible with each inspiration and are characterized by indrawing of the thoracic wall at the sternum between the ribs, above the clavicles, and below the inferior costal margins (Fig. 6-4). The *respiratory grunt* is an unequivocal sign of difficulty. It is a fascinating compensatory mechanism by which an infant attempts to retain air in order to increase arterial P_{O_2} (p. 143). An audible sigh during each expiration is a variant of the respiratory grunt that serves the same purpose. Air hunger is commonly associated with *flaring of the nostrils* (alae nasi) during each inspiration. As a rule, an infant in respiratory distress has more than one of the abnormal signs just described.

No matter how accurate and well phrased they may be, descriptions of *auscultatory findings* cannot replace experience with the stethoscope. Nevertheless, several introductory remarks may serve to properly orient the examiner. Auscultatory signs in the lungs are of less value in the neonate than in any other pediatric age group. The chest is so small that localization of findings is often impossible. The diminutive lung effectively transmits breath sounds from one region to another. The absence of breath sounds in one part of the lung may not be appreciated because the sounds from the unaffected areas are transmitted from a distance. With experience, diminution of air exchange can be confidently detected, particularly when there is a discrepancy between the two lungs. Diminished breath sounds occur in hyaline membrane disease, atelectasis, emphysema, pneumothorax, and as a function of shallow respirations from any cause. Fine *rales* are produced in terminal bronchioles and alveoli by the rush of air through fluid within them. These rales are classically described as crackling in character. They can be reproduced with some degree of accuracy by rubbing your own hair between two fingers as close to your ear as possible. Rales are heard in some infants with hyaline membrane disease, pneumonia, and pulmonary edema, and occasionally in normal babies immediately after birth. They are sometimes audible only after deep inspiration, which must be induced by stimulating a cry. *Rhonchi* are coarse sounds that resemble snoring. They emanate from large bronchi as air rushes through fluid contained within them. Rhonchi are most frequently present after aspiration of oral secretions or feedings.

Heart

Inspection occasionally reveals a localized pulsation on the chest wall at about the fifth intercostal space in the midclavicular line, toward the lateral half of the left hemithorax. The pulsations are more evident in small babies with thin chest walls. If pulsations are prominent in the epigastrium, the heart is probably enlarged considerably.

By *palpation* the normal apical impulse can be identified at the fifth intercostal space. Ascertainment of cardiac position is particularly important in dyspneic infants. Detection of an abnormal position early in the examination is an important initial step in establishing a correct diagnosis. A shift in the mediastinum caused by pneumothorax, for example, moves the apical impulse away from the affected side of the chest (p. 165). Pneumothorax in the right chest thus causes a shift of the mediastinum to the left; the apical impulse can be felt farther toward the left lateral chest wall than is normal. On the other hand, if the left chest is affected, the apical beat is palpable closer to the midline of the chest or sometimes to the right of it. Such cardiac displacements also occur in diaphragmatic hernia, which usually affects the left chest (p. 173). In the rare occurrence of bilateral pneumothorax, the point of maximal cardiac impulse is displaced downward toward the epigastrium. Abnormal apical

location also occurs in dextrocardia, which is a mirror image reversal of cardiac position; the apex is in the right chest. If abdominal organs are also reversed, the anomalous position of the heart may or may not be significant in terms of abnormal cardiovascular function. However, if the abdominal viscera are normally placed and the position of the heart is reversed, cardiac anomalies are more likely. The normal locations of abdominal organs are described on p. 115.

Auscultation is the most informative component of the physical examination of the heart. The ability to perceive abnormalities by evaluating heart sounds depends on continuous, thoughtful practice. The first and second heart sounds are normally clear and well defined. In the neonate they acoustically resemble the syllables toc-tic. The second sound is somewhat higher in pitch and sharper than the first. Heart rates normally fluctuate between 120 and 160 beats/min. In agitated states a rate of 200 beats/min may occur transiently. The heart rate of premature infants is usually between 130 and 170 beats/min, and during occasional episodes of bradycardia it may slow to 70 beats/min or less. *Murmurs* are erroneously considered to be regularly indicative of congenital cardiac malformations, when in fact over 90% of those detected during the neonatal period are not associated with anomalies. Many murmurs are transient. Conversely, murmurs are sometimes absent in seriously malformed hearts. Most murmurs are systolic; they occur after the first sound and end at or before the second sound. Continuous murmurs extend beyond the second sound into diastole.

Abdomen

Inspection. The contour of the abdomen should be noted before it is palpated. It is ordinarily cylindric, sometimes protruding slightly in normal full-term infants. Several gross abnormalities are apparent on inspection. *Distention* in its most severe form is characterized by tightly drawn skin through which engorged subcutaneous vessels are easily seen. *Localized bulging* at one or both

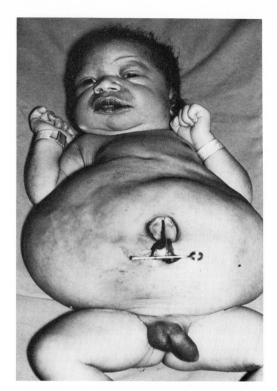

Fig. 6-18. Congenital absence of abdominal muscle ("prune belly" syndrome). Massive bilateral hydronephrosis and hydroureter were present.

flanks suggests enlarged kidneys, usually hydronephrosis (Fig. 6-2). A grotesque abnormality of contour characterizes the rare malformation known as congenital absence of abdominal musculature ("prune belly" syndrome), in which severe renal anomalies are also present. The anterior aspect of the abdomen is sunken, or perhaps slightly protuberant, whereas the intestines, which are covered only by skin and a thin layer of subcutaneous tissue, bulge pendulously from the flanks (Fig. 6-18).

Palpation. With rare exceptions the edge of the *liver* is normally palpable below the right costal margin, often as far as 3 cm inferior to it. The tip of the spleen can sometimes be felt in normal infants. Examination of the abdomen must include palpation of each *kidney,* and this is most easily accomplished immediately after birth, when the intestines are not yet distended with air. With the infant supine, a finger is placed at the posterior flank (costovertebral angle) in order to maintain upward pressure while the other hand presses downward toward the posteriorly placed finger. The kidney can be felt as an oval structure between the finger and hand. The lower poles of each kidney are normally situated approximately 1 or 2 cm above the level of the umbilicus. If enlargement is present, they are below this level. By simple palpation, the astute examiner can identify approximately 90% of gross renal anomalies. *Bladder distention* should be sought in the suprapubic region. If present, a firm globular mass is palpable. If it persists to any degree after voiding, the bladder is incompletely emptied, and an obstruction may be present at the outlet. *Masses* that are perceptible elsewhere in the abdomen are usually of intestinal origin.

The normal *umbilical cord* is blue-white and moist at birth. Within 24 hours it begins to dry and becomes dull and yellow-brown. Later it turns black-brown and shrivels considerably. In this gangrenous state it sloughs from its attachment at approximately 1 week of age.

If meconium has not been passed by the end of the first day of life, *patency of the anus* should be ascertained by inserting the tip of a thermometer or a plastic feeding tube for a distance not in excess of 1 cm.

Male genitalia

The *prepuce* covers the entire *glans penis* so that the external meatus is not visible. The prepuce is not retractable in the neonate and sometimes cannot be displaced until 4 to 6 months of age. It thus should never be forcibly retracted. This condition is not phimosis, and it is not an indication for circumcision. The trauma of forceful retraction is thought by some to be responsible for phimosis later on. According to a statement by the American Academy of Pediatrics, *"there is no absolute medical indication for routine circumcision of the newborn. It is not an essential component of adequate total health care."*

Good penile hygiene accomplishes as much. If the ventral surface of the glans is not covered by preputial tissue, *hypospadias* is present. Hypospadias is characterized by an anomalous position of the urethral meatus on the ventral portion of the glans penis, rather than at its center. It may also be situated on the ventral surface of the penile shaft anywhere along its length.

In term infants the *testes* are in the *scrotum*. In premature infants the testes are in the inguinal canal, or they may not be palpable. The scrotum varies in size in relation to maturity. In premature infants it is small and close to the perineum. In term babies the scrotum is large, hanging loosely at a greater distance from the perineum.

Female genitalia

In full-term babies the *labia minora* are sometimes more prominent than the *labia majora;* in premature infants this is almost the rule. The *clitoris* varies in size. It may be so large as to confound determination of the baby's sex. The diagnosis of adrenogenital syndrome, an endocrine disorder that involves excessive secretions of androgenic and other hormones from the adrenal gland, may then be made. In the affected neonate, life-threatening electrolyte disturbances and dehydration may occur rapidly within a few days after birth.

The *hymenal tag* is a normal redundant segment of the hymen that protrudes from the floor of the vagina and disappears in several weeks. During the first week of life, a milk-white mucoid discharge, which is sometimes blood tinged, may be evident in the vagina. This is a physiologic manifestation of maternal hormonal influences that disappears within 2 weeks.

Extremities

The extremities should be examined for malformations and trauma. Malformations frequently involve the fingers. *Polydactyly* is an excessive number of digits on the hands or feet. In its commonest form it consists of a rudimentary digit (digitus postminimus)

Fig. 6-19. Digitus postminimus (see text). Hypotrophic finger hangs by a thin pedicle from lateral aspect of fifth finger.

Fig. 6-20. Syndactyly (see text).

attached to the lateral aspect of the little finger by a thin pedicle (Fig. 6-19). It is treated by firmly tying a silk suture around the pedicle, close to the surface of the normal finger. Gangrene of the anomalous digit ensues in a few days, and it falls away. Less commonly an extra, fully formed digit is present. *Syndactyly* is the fusion of two digits into one structure (Fig. 6-20), and it most commonly involves the toes.

Fractures have been discussed in Chapter 2. The clavicle, humerus, and femur are respectively involved in descending order of frequency. Fractures should be suspected in any baby who fails to move one extremity as extensively as the others. Malposition and a visible local deformity at the fracture site are often helpful signs.

Clavicles must be palpated to ascertain their presence as well as to detect fractures. Absence of the clavicles, either total or segmental, is characteristic of *cleidocranial dysostosis* (Fig. 6-21), an inherited disorder of bone formation in the skull, the clavicles, and occasionally the pubic bone. Absence of the clavicles permits innocuous anterior displacement of the shoulders so that they almost meet in the midline (Fig. 6-21).

Congenital ring constrictions (annular or amniotic bands) are poorly understood malformations that occur infrequently. They affect the extremities, which are thought to become entangled in a local early rupture of the amniotic membrane. Subsequent growth occurs in the presence of constricting amniotic bands. In the extreme, amputation occurs, either of an extremity somewhere along its length or of one or more digits. Milder expressions of this disorder are seen as banded depressions of the skin that are much like a tight rubber band around the extremity (Fig. 6-22). The most common sites of involvement in order of frequency

Fig. 6-21. Cleidocranial dysostosis (congenital absence of clavicles). If clavicles were not examined as a routine part of examination, this major syndrome would not have been identified in the neonate, when it should be. Shoulders are drawn anteriorly, and when compressed, they meet in midline.

Fig. 6-22. Congenital amniotic bands above the ankle.

are the fingers, toes, ankle, leg, forearm, and arm. Amniotic bands and the amputations with which they are sometimes associated may involve more than one extremity but are usually unilateral.

Neurologic evaluation

Abnormal neurologic signs may be transient or persistent. They may disappear by the time the infant is discharged from the nursery, or they may be present throughout the nursery stay. Predictions of later brain dysfunction cannot be made with consistent accuracy on the basis of neurologic abnormalities during the newborn period.

Observations should be made with as little disturbance to the baby as possible. Reflexes that require the greatest degree of disturbance should be elicited toward the end of the examination. Thus *spontaneous movements* should be studied first. Infants who are generally depressed will move very little or not at all. They are hypotonic as well. Intrauterine asphyxia, or hypoxia at any time, is the commonest cause of this neuromuscular abnormality. Drugs administered to the mother are also frequent causes of depression. These drugs include analgesics (Demerol), hypnotics (barbiturates, magnesium sulfate, alcohol), and local anesthetics (lidocaine). Central nervous system infections, bacterial or nonbacterial, and metabolic disturbances (hypoglycemia, hypothyroidism) also cause depression. Trauma to the central nervous system, most often in the form of cerebral contusion or subdural hematoma, is an additional cause of diminished or absent spontaneous activity.

Spontaneous hyperirritability and exaggerated responses to ordinary tactile or acoustic stimuli are abnormal. These responses may range from severe agitation or jitteriness to frank convulsions. They may thus be manifested as localized twitches, gross rhythmic repetitive jerks of one or more muscle groups (myoclonus), or generalized clonic convulsions. There is little to be gained in attempting to localize central nervous system lesions based on these localized convulsive phenomena, since in the neonate there is generally no such correlation. There is also little use in attempting to differentiate between a severely agitated state characterized by ceaseless movement and a frank convulsion. Usually they are of equal significance. These irritative phenomena are most common during recovery from asphyxia, after a period of depression. They also occur in babies of narcotic-addicted mothers (heroin or morphine withdrawal) and among infants of mothers who are habituated to barbiturates (phenobarbital withdrawal). Hypocalcemia, hypomagnesemia, and hypoglycemia may cause irritative phenomena. Neonatal hyperthyroidism and pyridoxine dependency are rare causes. Maternal administration of local anesthetics such as lidocaine may produce depression at first, but this is followed by convulsions. Intracranial hemorrhage and, occasionally, central nervous system infection may also produce irritative responses early in their courses.

Asymmetry in movement of the extremities indicates weakness, paralysis, or bone fracture. In brachial plexus palsy, for example, the affected upper extremity is hypoactive or immobile. Failure to move the lower extremities suggests a spinal cord injury. Asymmetry of movement or tone is always abnormal.

Muscle tone is extremely important in the neurologic evaluation of neonates. The normal infant maintains some degree of flexion in all the extremities, and extension by the examiner of any one of them is followed by at least a partial return to the previous position of flexion. Flexion posture is less pronounced in premature infants. Infants who experience intrauterine hypoxia are hypotonic; they may not be flexed at rest. Furthermore, straightening of the extremities is not followed by return to flexion. Poor head control, described later, is additional evidence of abnormally diminished muscle tone.

The elicitation of certain reflex responses is essential for assessment of the infant's neurologic status. The *grasp reflex* is normally strong in full-term infants. It is elicited by placing a finger across the palm at the base of the fingers. In response, the examiner's finger may be grasped so firmly that, using both hands, the infant can often be raised off the surface of the crib. This response is considerably more feeble in premature babies or in depressed infants. It is asymmetric in some cases of brachial plexus palsy (Klumpke type), being absent or weak on the affected side.

The *rooting reflex* is activated by lightly stroking the angle of the lips. The baby turns his head to the stroked side. Recently fed infants and those who are lethargic or depressed merely purse the lips or do not respond at all. Vigorous infants turn the head briskly and instantly, pursuing the finger as long as contact with the lips is maintained.

The *suck* is evaluated by inserting a sterile nipple into the mouth. In normal infants, particularly those who are hungry, the response is immediate, coordinated, and forceful. Recently fed infants, premature babies, and those who are depressed respond with varying degrees of feebleness.

The *knee jerk* is normally brisk. It is weak in depressed infants, exaggerated to the point of clonus (repetitive jerks) in irritated ones, and asymmetric in babies who have spinal cord lesions, fractures of the femur, or bone and joint infection of the examined extremity.

Ankle clonus is elicited by placing two fingers against the anterior sole of the foot and abruptly, with a short, brisk movement, dorsiflexing it. The response will usually consist of several repetitive jerks (beats) of the foot or none at all. If more than eight to ten beats occur, the baby is probably in an irritated state.

Head control in the normal neonate is more effective than is generally realized. With the infant supine the examiner takes the wrists and lifts him slowly to a sitting position. The normal term infant reinforces the maneuver by contracting the shoulder and arm muscles, followed by flexion of the neck. As the sitting position is reached, the infant controls his head by action of neck muscles and thus prevents it from falling forward onto the chest. In many babies the head falls forward but is soon righted to the erect position. Hypotonic infants, such as those with Down's syndrome or those who are hypoxic, have little or no head control, and they do not respond to traction by activating the muscles of the arms and shoulders. The neck is extremely lax, and the head bobbles in any direction dictated by the combined effects of body position and gravity. There is no attempt to assume an erect posture once the head has fallen to either side or onto the chest.

The *Moro reflex* is demonstrable in all normal neonates (Fig. 6-23). It is often erroneously elicited by slapping the bassinet or jerking it. Some examiners abruptly pull a blanket from under the baby. Others lift him slightly off the crib surface by the wrists and allow him to fall back. The most consistent responses are obtained by holding the baby in a supine position with both hands, one palm beneath the sacrum and buttocks and the other beneath the occiput and upper back. By suddenly slipping the hand down from the occiput onto the back, the head is allowed to fall through an angle of approximately 30 degrees, thus activating the Moro reflex. The normal response is characterized by straightening of the arms and elbows away from the body and by extension of the wrists and fingers. This is followed by return of the upper extremities onto the chest in a position of passive flexion. A cry often accompanies the baby's startled response. Reflex movement of the hips and knees occurs quickly and is of short duration. If an extremity does not respond fully, a localized neurologic defect or fracture is suspect. Suboptimal vigor of the overall response occurs in depressed infants, whereas in premature infants the response is disorganized and incomplete to varying degrees.

Transillumination of the skull is a useful procedure if neurologic disorder is suspected. It is performed with a strong light source from a flashlight fitted with a rubber collar that fits snugly to the skull. In a dark room devoid of light leaks, the examiner must first become dark-adapted. As a rule, dark adaptation is present when the light, placed into

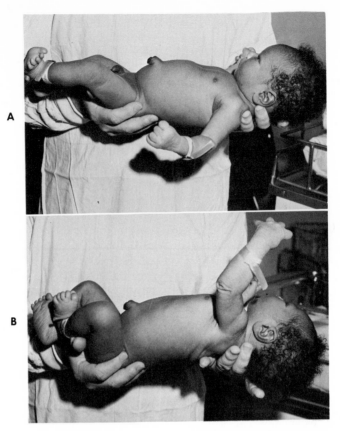

Fig. 6-23. Moro reflex. **A,** The baby is supported beneath the sacrum and upper back, including the occiput. The head is level with the body. **B,** The head is allowed to fall backward. In response, the upper extremities are abruptly thrust upward and outward while the knees and hips are rapidly flexed. Compare changes in position of the head and upper and lower extremities. Compare also this normal response to that in brachial plexus palsy (Fig. 2-14).

the examiner's palm, is transmitted through the hand so that shadows of the distal metacarpal bones are clearly visible as light penetrates the soft tissue between them. The flashlight is then applied to the scalp tightly, and while the snug fit is maintained to avoid light leak, it is moved over the surface of the head. We use a two-battery flashlight. With it, a flare of light greater than 1.5 to 2 cm beyond the rim of the rubber fitting is considered abnormal. The entire cranium lights up like a red electric bulb in babies who have congenital absence of the cerebral hemispheres (hydranencephaly). In this instance the cranial vault is filled with fluid instead of brain tissue. These infants may

behave normally during the newborn period. Severe hydrocephalus produces the same phenomenon. Abnormal light flare is seen locally over subdural hematomas or porencephalic cysts (local absence of cerebral tissue).

A number of conditions cause abnormal light transmission that is not indicative of a brain disorder. Most understandable and common is edema of the scalp, which may occur in infiltration of intravenous fluids being given into a scalp vein or in caput succedaneum. The water-logged scalp transmits more light over a greater area. In the region of the anterior fontanelle, abnormal light transmission is also misleading. The flare of light increases and may extend beyond 2 cm because of the absence of bone. Infants who weighed less than 1250 grams at birth, have grown rapidly, and are approximately 1 month of age may often manifest generalized abnormal light transmission. This does not indicate developing hydrocephalus nor cerebral malformation. It is apparently the result of normal enlargement of the subarachnoid space, which seems to occur during this period of rapid growth. Serial measurements of *both head and chest circumferences* will reveal that the apparent rapid growth of the head is actually a component of growth of the entire body. Misinterpretation of this normally increased transillumination, combined with failure to assess head enlargement as a normal component of overall body growth, has resulted in numerous needless pneumoencephalograms, ventriculograms, and other extensive neurologic inquiries.

Final impression of the infant's neurologic status must be formed with great caution. The neurologic examination is not in itself inadequate, but the nature of the neonate's neurologic disorders makes it difficult to localize the disorder or, in marginal situations, to be certain there is any disorder at all. Certainly one cannot take the sum of abnormal findings and arrive at a conclusion in a manner more appropriate for a bookkeeper than a clinician. The incidence of false-positive and false-negative signs is high. Furthermore, repeated observations are absolutely indispensable because abnormal signs are often transient, disappearing in a matter of hours. Extremes are seldom a puzzle; the gross abnormalities and the unequivocal normal state cause little difficulty for the clinician. The in-between phenomena are notoriously troublesome in the total physical examination generally, and in the neurologic evaluation particularly.

References

Behrman, R. E.: The fetus and newborn infant. In Vaughan, V. C., and McKay, R. J., editors: Nelson's textbook of pediatrics, Philadelphia, 1975, W. B. Saunders Co.

Grossman, M.: Physical examination of the newborn. In Barnett, H. L., editor: Pediatrics, New York, 1968, Appleton-Century-Crofts.

Korones, S. B.: The newborn: perinatal pediatrics. In Hughes, J. G., editor: Synopsis of pediatrics, ed. 4, St. Louis, 1975, The C. V. Mosby Co.

Lucey, J. F.: Examination of the newborn. In Reed, D. E., Ryan, K. J., and Benirschke, K., editors: Principles and management of human reproduction, Philadelphia, 1972, W. B. Saunders Co.

Paine, R. S.: Neurologic examination of infants and children, Pediatr. Clin. North Am. 7:471, 1960.

Parmelee, A. H.: Management of the newborn, Chicago, 1959, Year Book Medical Publishers, Inc.

Speck, W. T.: Special orthopedic problems. In Behrman, R. E., editor: Neonatology: diseases of the fetus and infant, St. Louis, 1973, The C. V. Mosby Co.

Chapter 7

Basic principles and clinical significance of acid-base disturbances

IN NEWBORN BABIES almost all serious illnesses eventually involve an acid-base imbalance that in itself may be more hazardous to the baby's survival than the primary disease process. The infant often can be sustained by partial or complete correction of the acid-base disturbance while the primary pathophysiology runs its course. In hyaline membrane disease, for example, there is no effective therapy for eradication of the basic pulmonary pathology (atelectasis), but with spontaneous appearance of adequate quantities of a phospholipid substance known as surfactant, the atelectasis tends to resolve spontaneously in a few days (p. 135). In the meantime, if no attempt is made to correct biochemical abnormalities that arise from the primary pulmonary disorder, death is inexorable in severely affected infants. Diarrhea is another case in point. Whether or not antibiotics are ultimately effective in eliminating the etiologic agent (and most often they are not), fluid therapy must be instituted early to rectify the life-threatening acidosis and dehydration that develop so rapidly. Although the diarrhea usually subsides in several days, acid-base balance and optimal hydration must be maintained during its course if the baby is to survive.

An understanding of acid-base disturbances is essential if the nurse is to correlate laboratory data with the clinical course of the disease process and thus assess an infant's progress accurately. Appreciation of the rationale of appropriate therapy is indispensable if the nurse is to participate intelligently in its administration. The discussion that follows will summarize pertinent acid-base fac-

tors that are operative in the production of life-threatening illness. Emphasis on terminology is appropriate because understanding of terms and mastery of concepts are inseparable.

pH, ACIDS, AND BASES
pH

At any given moment acid-base status is determined by the concentration of hydrogen ion (H^+) present in body fluids as a result of the production, neutralization, and elimination of various acids. The higher the concentration of hydrogen ion, the more acid the fluid, and conversely the lower the concentration of hydrogen ion, the more alkaline the fluid. The acidity of a fluid, whether blood, plasma, or urine, is expressed as its pH. The mathematic derivation of pH is such that a rise or fall indicates a change of hydrogen ion concentration in the opposite direction. The pH of a solution is therefore inversely proportional to the concentration of hydrogen ion within it. A pH of 4.0 is more acid than a pH of 5.0, but not simply one fifth more acid as is superficially apparent from the difference between the two values. Rather, there is a tenfold difference between the two figures because, being negative and logarithmic, each figure represents a multiple of minus 10, or the number of places to the right of a decimal point. Thus a pH of 4.0 represents 0.0001 gram of hydrogen ion per liter of solution. This representation is ten times greater than a pH of 5.0, which indicates 0.00001 gram of hydrogen ion per liter. Other translations of pH values are listed here to emphasize the large differences in acidity that are indicated by various pH units:

pH 1.0 indicates 0.1 gram of hydrogen ion per liter

pH 2.0 indicates 0.01 gram of hydrogen ion per liter

pH 3.0 indicates 0.001 gram of hydrogen ion per liter

pH 4.0 indicates 0.0001 gram of hydrogen ion per liter

A solution with a pH of 1.0 thus contains a hydrogen ion concentration 100 times greater than a solution with a pH of 3.0, or 1000 times greater than at pH 4.0. The reader should again note that the greater the pH value, the less is the concentration of hydrogen ion. The accepted normal values for the pH of arterial blood in newborn infants at 24 hours of age is 7.35 to 7.44. The range of pH values compatible with life is 6.8 to 7.8. Most clinically important deviations occur between 7.00 and 7.25. These values represent enormous increases in hydrogen ion concentrations compared to the seemingly small differences between the numbers themselves. Compared to 7.35, a pH of 7.20 represents an increase of 40% in hydrogen ion concentration; a pH of 7.10 represents an increase of approximately 80%, and at pH 7.00 the blood is over twice normal acidity (actually an increase of 124%).

Acids

Acids are substances capable of surrendering hydrogen ion (H^+) when in solution. The strength of their acidity depends on the extent to which the hydrogen ion is dissociated from its molecule when in solution, and this varies from one acid to another. Hydrochloric acid (HCl) is powerful because it is dissociated almost completely when in solution, thereby surrendering greater amounts of hydrogen ion than most other acids. The resultant high concentration of hydrogen ion in solution renders a lower pH than other, less-soluble acids in similar concentration. Carbonic acid (H_2CO_3), for example, does not dissociate as readily as hydrochloric acid;

it surrenders fewer hydrogen ions in solution and is therefore a considerably weaker acid.

Bases

Bases are alkaline molecules capable of accepting hydrogen ions. When an acid is added to a base in solution, the dissociated hydrogen ion becomes bound to the base, with the resultant formation of a weaker acid. The base thus acts as a buffer by diminishing the potential acidity of a solution. Buffering is indispensable to the continuous maintenance of acid-base balance. In the neonate it is often overwhelmed by pathophysiologic events such as asphyxia, pulmonary dysfunction, or diarrhea. Therapeutic measures to enhance the buffering capacity of blood are therefore applied without delay.

PHYSIOLOGIC MAINTENANCE OF ACID-BASE EQUILIBRIUM

Normal metabolism entails a relentless production of acids, principally carbonic acid, which must be neutralized and ultimately eliminated from the body. These acids are categorized as volatile and nonvolatile (or fixed) acids. Carbonic acid (H_2CO_3) is volatile because it is constantly converted to carbon dioxide (CO_2) in the blood and eliminated in the gaseous state through the lungs. The nonvolatile, or fixed, acids are principally lactic, sulfuric, and phosphoric acids. They are buffered in blood and excreted through the kidneys. The three principal mechanisms by which acid products of normal metabolism are neutralized or eliminated are buffering activity in blood, elimination of carbon dioxide (volatile acid) through the lungs, and excretion of fixed acid through the kidneys. The respiratory apparatus directly controls blood levels of carbonic acid; the kidneys directly regulate the concentrations of bicarbonate buffer and hydrogen ion in the blood.

Buffers and buffer pairs

A buffer is a substance that, by its presence in a solution, is capable of minimizing changes in pH caused by the addition of acids or bases. Thus when a strong acid or base is added to a solution that contains a buffer, a weaker acid or base is formed and the change in pH is thus minimized. Buffers exist in pairs that are normally in sufficiently high concentration to stabilize changes in pH. These pairs are comprised of a weak acid and its salt. The principal buffer pairs in blood are sodium bicarbonate/carbonic acid (Na-HCO$_3$/H$_2$CO$_3$) and sodium proteinate/acid protein. The protein buffer system resides predominantly in hemoglobin. The first member of each pair is a salt; the second member is a weak acid. The hydrogen ion concentration in blood, and therefore the pH, is determined by a *ratio of the constituents that comprise each buffer pair;* the proportion of bicarbonate to carbonic acid (normally 20:1) is the most important determinant. The ratio may be altered by a decrease in bicarbonate or an increase in carbonic acid, thus elevating hydrogen ion concentration and lowering pH.

Buffering of nonvolatile acids. Normally the changes in pH of body fluids caused by the addition of lactic and other nonvolatile acids are minimized and held within physiologic limits principally by the buffering activity of the bicarbonate/carbonic acid system. In this reaction lactic acid is buffered by sodium bicarbonate and converted to sodium lactate plus carbonic acid. Sodium lactate is excreted through the kidneys, and carbonic acid is excreted in the gaseous state (CO$_2$) through the lungs. These events are represented in the following formulas:

(1) HL (lactic acid) + NaHCO$_3$
$$\rightarrow \text{Na lactate} + \text{H}_2\text{CO}_3$$
(2) H$_2$CO$_3$ $\rightarrow$ H$_2$O + CO$_2$

Other nonvolatile acids also combine with sodium bicarbonate to form salts and carbonic acid.

Buffering of volatile acid (H$_2$CO$_3$). Carbonic acid is produced in greater quantity than any other acid during the course of normal tissue metabolism. It is buffered in the erythrocyte by hemoglobin. From tissue fluid it crosses capillary walls to enter the plasma and thence into erythrocytes. By a series of reactions within erythocytes it is converted to bicarbonate, which is released into plasma as sodium bicarbonate. Thus the carbon dioxide that originates in tissues is largely carried in plasma as sodium bicarbonate. The acid change in pH that would have occurred is held within normal limits by the production of bicarbonate in the red blood cells.

Stabilizing influence of the respiratory apparatus

The concentration of carbonic acid in plasma is determined by the amount of carbon dioxide that is present (P$_{CO_2}$), which in turn is largely dependent on the capacity of the respiratory apparatus to ventilate normally. In the fetus this process depends on normal placental function. The quantity of carbon dioxide excreted through the lungs increases with the depth and the rate of respiration. The depth and rate of respiration are subject to neural control of the respiratory center in the medulla of the brain, which is exquisitely sensitive to changes in blood pH. The respiratory center directs an increase in rate in order to eliminate more carbon dioxide when blood pH declines; it directs a decrease in rate in order to conserve carbon dioxide when the pH is elevated. If the ratio of bicarbonate to carbonic acid falls below normal as a result of an elevated carbonic acid concentration, pH declines. The respiratory rate is then accelerated in response to stimulation of the medullary respiratory center. An increased amount of carbon dioxide is blown off, the ratio of bicarbonate to carbonic acid is restored toward normal, and the pH of blood now rises. On the other hand, if blood pH rises abnormally, as it may when excessive doses of intravenous sodium bicarbonate are administered, the ventilatory rate is slowed. Carbon dioxide is retained, and the level of carbonic acid rises. Although the absolute quantities of carbonic acid and bicarbonate are now increased, their ratio is closer to normal and the pH declines. Ultimately excess bicarbonate is excreted by the kidneys, whereas temporarily retained carbon dioxide is eventually eliminated through the lungs.

Stabilizing influence of the kidneys

Whereas the respiratory apparatus directly regulates the concentration of volatile acid, the kidneys control the blood content of non-volatile acid. This is primarily accomplished by the excretion of hydrogen ion plus the simultaneous conservation of bicarbonate. In contrast to the rapidly activated compensatory efforts of the lungs, the kidneys respond more slowly, but they tend to carry compensatory mechanisms closer to completion.

CLASSIFICATION OF ACID-BASE DISTURBANCES

Disturbances in acid-base equilibrium may culminate in a diminished pH (acidosis) or an increased pH (alkalosis). Changes in either of these directions are caused by primary disorders of ventilation (respiratory acidosis and alkalosis) or primary disorders of general metabolism, renal function, or both (metabolic or nonrespiratory acidosis and alkalosis). The distinctions and variations of these disturbances are defined here,

having been distilled from a broad literature. When appropriate, the biochemical deviation is described in association with the pathophysiologic event that gives rise to it. Over the years biochemists and physiologists who are concerned with the problems of acid-base balance have been at odds regarding proper definitions of various disturbances. There is frequent mention, in a voluminous literature, of the advantages and pitfalls of a "physiologic language" or a "laboratory language." For us the definitions presented here have facilitated the teaching and clinical applications of the concepts they describe. Table 7-1 summarizes the attributes of the various types of acid-base disturbance and their degrees of compensation.

Uncompensated disturbance

The uncompensated abnormalities defined here are characterized in each instance by the presence of an abnormal pH. The same underlying abnormalities also exist in compensated forms. They are described later in this chapter.

Acidosis is a condition that causes an inordinate accumulation of acid (nonvolatile

Table 7-1. Attributes of acid-base disturbances according to type and degree of compensation

Disturbance	Blood pH	Blood P_{CO_2} (mm Hg)	Blood HCO_3^- (mEq/L)
Normal	7.35 to 7.44	30 to 35	20 to 24
Metabolic acidosis			
Uncompensated	Lowest	Normal	Low
Partially compensated	Low	Low	Low
Fully compensated	Normal	Lowest	Low
Metabolic alkalosis			
Uncompensated	Highest	Normal	High
Partially compensated	High	High	High
Fully compensated	Normal	Highest	High
Respiratory acidosis			
Uncompensated	Lowest	High	Normal
Partially compensated	Low	High	High
Fully compensated	Normal	High	Highest
Respiratory alkalosis			
Uncompensated	Highest	Low	Normal
Partially compensated	High	Low	Low
Fully compensated	Normal	Low	Lowest

or volatile) or loss of base. The net result is an increase in hydrogen ion concentration and thus a diminution of blood pH to levels below normal.

Alkalosis is a condition that causes an excessive accumulation of base or a loss of acid (nonvolatile or volatile). The net result is a decrease in hydrogen ion concentration and thus an increase in blood pH to levels that are above normal.

Metabolic (nonrespiratory) acidosis occurs with an increase in the concentration of non-volatile acids as a result of (1) deranged metabolism in which there is overproduction of acids; (2) disrupted renal function with impaired excretion of nonvolatile acids; and (3) excessive loss of base through the gastro-intestinal tract (diarrhea) and rarely through the kidneys (renal tubular acidosis).

Metabolic (nonrespiratory) alkalosis is characterized by an increased concentration of base (bicarbonate). In the neonate it is most frequently caused by inappropriately large therapeutic doses of sodium bicarbonate. Repeated vomiting due to pyloric stenosis is occasionally encountered, causing metabolic alkalosis because a significant quantity of hydrochloric acid is lost in vomited gastric secretions. Rarely metabolic alkalosis results from an excessive renal loss of hydrogen ion or from renal retention of bicarbonate.

Respiratory acidosis follows decreased pulmonary gas exchange with resultant retention of carbon dioxide (increased P_{CO_2}). Perinatal asphyxia and hyaline membrane disease are the commonest neonatal clinical entities in which respiratory acidosis occurs.

Respiratory alkalosis, caused by respiratory dysfunction, is characterized by an abnormally low P_{CO_2} resulting from excessive elimination of carbon dioxide during hyperventilation. It is most frequently encountered in therapy with mechanical ventilators that are incorrectly set to deliver respiratory rates and tidal volumes in excess of physiologic needs.

Compensated disturbances

Although definitions in the preceding paragraphs are based on an abnormal pH, acid-base disturbance can be also operative in the presence of a normal or nearly normal pH, provided certain compensatory mechanisms are effective. A description of the data in Table 7-1 is presented in the paragraphs that follow.

Compensation is a physiologic process that occurs in response to an antecedent (primary) derangement of acid-base balance. It tends to restore the ratio of buffer pairs toward normal. If compensation is complete, a normal ratio is reestablished and the pH is normal even though concentrations of the individual members of a buffer pair are abnormal. However, the original source of acid-base disturbance may still exist. The importance of recognizing these compensated disorders cannot be overestimated, since their corrective effects are often only temporary. The underlying disturbance, masked by these compensatory responses, requires cautious therapy.

Compensated metabolic (nonrespiratory) acidosis is characterized chiefly by hyperventilation for the reduction of P_{CO_2} to levels below normal. Hyperventilation is the compensatory process activated by accumulation of nonvolatile acid that consumes available base (bicarbonate). The excretion of volatile acid (CO_2) through the lungs must be increased in order to lower carbonic acid concentration to match the lowered level of bicarbonate, and thus to restore the sodium bicarbonate/carbonic acid ratio in that buffer pair. In this compensated state the pH is normal or almost normal, but both the P_{CO_2} and the serum bicarbonate concentrations are low.

Compensated metabolic (nonrespiratory) alkalosis involves hypoventilation that is activated for the purpose of diminishing the elimination of carbon dioxide. Since the primary disturbance is accumulation of bicarbonate, retention of volatile acid (CO_2) tends to restore the ratio between sodium bicarbonate and carbonic acid. In this compensated state the pH is virtually normal, but the P_{CO_2} and serum bicarbonate concentrations are elevated.

Compensated respiratory acidosis involves retention of bicarbonate as a result of adjustment in renal function. Since the primary disturbance is accumulation of carbon dioxide, and thus an increase in carbonic acid, the rise in bicarbonate tends to restore the bicarbonate/carbonic acid ratio toward normal. In a fully compensated state the pH is normal, but P_{CO_2} and serum bicarbonate are increased. Whereas the renal mechanism seeks to restore pH by conserving bicarbonate, the respiratory apparatus attempts to eliminate the accumulated carbon dioxide. The clinically evident result of this activity is tachypnea.

Compensated respiratory alkalosis also involves adjustment of renal function. The primary disturbance is caused by hyperventilation with excessive elimination of carbon dioxide and resultant decline of P_{CO_2}. The kidney thus acts to increase excretion of bicarbonate in order to restore the bicarbonate/carbonic acid ratio to normal. In the fully compensated state pH is normal, but P_{CO_2} and serum bicarbonate are individually diminished although in normal ratio.

Mixed disturbances of acid-base balance

Some clinical disorders simultaneously give rise to disturbances of the respiratory and metabolic components of acid-base balance. These are called mixed disturbances, and they are characterized by a concurrence of respiratory and metabolic acidosis or alkalosis. In neonates the most commonly encountered variety is mixed acidosis associated with severe perinatal asphyxia and hyaline membrane disease. In mixed respiratory and metabolic acidosis the combination of retained carbon dioxide and diminished bicarbonate causes a considerable decrease in pH.

LABORATORY PROCEDURES FOR MEASURING ACID-BASE STATUS

The advent of microtechniques for the direct measurement of blood gases and pH has been a boon to the management of sick neonates. Rational therapy to rectify acid-base disorders is currently based on these procedures. Serial determinations are indispensable during the entire course of an illness because blood gas content and pH may change rapidly and repeatedly. Infants on mechanical respirators, for instance, must be monitored repeatedly and at frequent intervals for blood gas and acid-base status.

The collection of samples should be accomplished with precision and with a minimum quantity of blood. The blood P_{CO_2}, P_{O_2}, and pH can be measured from as little as 0.1 ml. Indwelling umbilical artery catheters are commonly utilized as a source of arterial blood samples. If this route is unavailable, capillary blood obtained by heel prick may be used for P_{CO_2} and pH determinations. Capillary blood P_{O_2} is not accurate. This method of collection requires warming of the heel with a moist pack for a minimum of 5 minutes in order to dilate capillaries and arterioles. The sample thus obtained is arterialized capillary blood.

An inordinate delay in performing determinations after collection of samples usually causes inaccurate results if the blood is kept at room temperature. The pH drops and the P_{CO_2} rises because continued glycolysis in the red blood cells produces lactic acid in the sample. The average pH error in normal blood that is analyzed 20 minutes after collection is only minus 0.01 unit. Errors are minimal and clinically insignificant if the blood is stored in ice. Determinations can then be made up to 2 hours later with only a slight fall in pH (less than 0.015 unit). Exposure to room air is another pitfall to be avoided. In these circumstances the P_{CO_2} falls considerably because it escapes to lower carbon dioxide tensions in the atmosphere, and this causes the pH to rise. When blood is exposed to the atmosphere, P_{O_2} is also altered, since it tends to equilibrate with the oxygen tension of room air, which is approximately 140 mm Hg.

Heparin is the only acceptable anticoagulant for collection of blood samples. Other anticoagulants, such as citrate, oxalate, and EDTA, have significant effects on blood pH. Tubes utilized for capillary samples are commercially prepared with proper amounts of heparin to prevent clotting.

Capillary blood samples are useless for P_{O_2} determinations because they do not correlate with arterial blood levels. Oxygen tension must be monitored from blood taken directly from an artery. This is especially important for premature infants who are given supplemental oxygen; hyperoxia may cause retrolental fibroplasia (p. 153). Arterial samples are obtainable from an umbilical artery catheter or from punctures of the radial, brachial, or temporal arteries. Determinations of pH and P_{CO_2} in capillary blood are valid, however, because they are well correlated with arterial values if the sample is properly collected. However, difficulty arises when the extremities are poorly perfused for any reason. Venous stasis is evident in distressed infants whose extremities are cyanotic. Stasis of capillary blood lowers pH and augments P_{CO_2}; both of these values may thus differ considerably from those of arterial blood, therefore precluding reliable reference to such data for therapy.

Most neonatal special care units utilize blood gas and pH measurements for the characterization of acid-base status. Ideally personnel and laboratory should be close at hand so that results are available within minutes after they are ordered. The parameters pertinent to acid-base evaluation are as follows:

pH is a measure of hydrogen ion concentration. It expresses the end result of buffer activity and *in itself does not indicate whether an abnormality originates in respiratory or nonrespiratory dysfunction.* Normal values range from pH 7.35 to 7.44.

P_{CO_2} expresses the partial pressure of carbon dioxide dissolved in plasma. *Deviations from normal are indicative of disorders in the respiratory apparatus.* Normal neonatal values range from 30 to 37 mm Hg.

Plasma bicarbonate measures total bicarbonate concentration. Normal values are between 20 and 25 mEq/L.

Base excess (B.E.) or deficit is a value that is calculated rather than directly measured by the laboratory (see later). It is expressed as a positive or negative value. The negative value is sometimes referred to as a base deficit. Base excess indicates, in milliequivalents per liter, the quantity of blood buffer base remaining after hydrogen ion is buffered. It thus expresses the combined buffering capacity of plasma bicarbonate and hemoglobin. Normal neonatal values range from +4 to −4 mEq/L.

Alignment nomogram

Base excess is calculated from the alignment nomogram reproduced on p. 129. The computation of base excess is possible when hemoglobin concentration and any two of the following parameters are known: blood pH, P_{CO_2} plasma bicarbonate, or total carbon dioxide content of plasma. The variables most commonly utilized in newborn laboratories are pH and P_{CO_2}.

Assume that an infant in rather severe respiratory distress is admitted to your facility. Blood samples are collected soon after admission, and the following information is forwarded to you:

pH = 7.10 (normal = 7.35 to 7.44)
P_{CO_2} = 75 mm Hg (normal = 30 to 37 mm Hg)
Hemoglobin = 20 grams/100 ml

The values for pH and P_{CO_2} are plotted on their appropriate scales at points *A* and *B,* as shown on the nomogram. A line is drawn through points *A* and *B* across all four scales. The base excess is read at minus 10 mEq/L at point *C,* where the drawn line intersects a grid line representing hemoglobin concentration of 20 grams/100 ml. The plasma bicarbonate concentration can now also be read at 23 mEq/L. If only the pH and bicarbonate are known (as well as the hemoglobin concentration), base excess and P_{CO_2} can be derived by drawing a line through points corresponding to the known values.

Basis of therapy

Intravenous sodium bicarbonate is utilized to correct a negative base excess (base deficit). Sodium bicarbonate is available in am-

**NEWBORN SERVICE
LABORATORY**

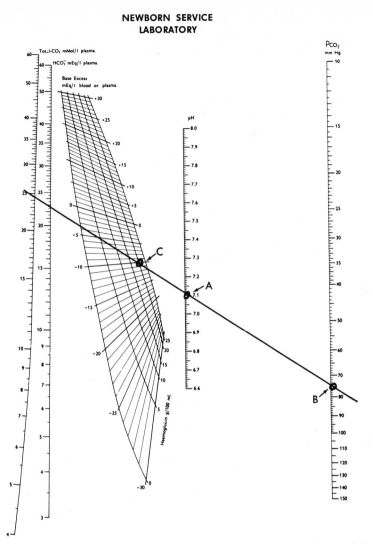

Fig. 7-1. Acid-base nomogram (from Siggaard-Andersen) with an example of plotted data from a sick infant. (See text for explanation.) (Modified from Winters, R. W., Engel, K., and Dell, R. B.: Acid-base physiology in medicine, a self-instruction program, Cleveland, 1967, The London Co.)

pules of a 7.5% solution containing 0.88 mEq/ml. For ease of calculation it is satisfactory in clinical situations to consider the concentration as 1.0 mEq/ml. The dose of sodium bicarbonate is computed from the following formula:

mEq of NaHCO₃ to be given = base deficit ×
0.3 × body weight in kilograms

The factor 0.3 represents the approximate portion of body weight composed of extra-cellular fluid. If the infant whose base deficit was 10 mEq/L weighs 2500 grams, calculation of the dose of sodium bicarbonate is as follows:

$$\begin{aligned} \text{mEq of NaHCO}_3 &= 10 \text{ mEq} \times 0.3 \times 2.5 \text{ kg} \\ &= 10 \times 0.75 \\ &= 7.5 \end{aligned}$$

Thus 7.5 ml of the 7.5% solution of sodium bicarbonate will be required. It must always be diluted because the extremely alkaline pH may damage blood vessels near the site of infusion. The required dose should be mixed with at least an equal quantity of water for injection or with 10% glucose water. Generally one fourth to one half of the calculated dose is injected (after dilution) over a period of 2 to 5 minutes, and the remainder is added to intravenous fluid already dripping. In some centers the entire dose is infused, particularly if the infant is profoundly ill.

SUMMATION

Principles of acid-base relationships apply to the management of all neonates admitted to the intensive care nursery. Mechanisms by which these normal relationships are disrupted and restored are operative in every sick baby. Acid-base imbalance is a by-product of the entire spectrum of primary neonatal disorders. It occurs in response to cold stress, during respiratory embarrassment, in gastrointestinal disturbances, as a result of all types of infectious disease, in disorders of the central nervous system, during postoperative periods, and even during the normal birth process. Preoccupation with the obvious symptomatology of these primary disorders often diverts attention from the subtle and perhaps more sinister effects produced by acid-base imbalance. These effects can be identified with certainty only by recourse to laboratory data. It is thus imperative for the neonatal nurse to comprehend the significance of these data.

References

Behrman, R. E.: The use of acid-base measurements in the clinical evaluation and treatment of the sick neonate, J. Pediatr. **74:**632, 1969.

Current concepts of acid-base measurements, Report of Ad-hoc Committee On Acid-Base Terminology, Ann. N.Y. Acad. Sci. **133:**251, 1966.

Kildeberg, P.: Clinical acid-base physiology; studies in neonates, infants and young children, Baltimore, 1968, The Williams & Wilkins Co.

White, A., Handler, P., and Smith, E.: Principles of biochemistry, New York, 1968, McGraw-Hill Book Co.

Winters, R. W.: Terminology of acid-base disorders, Ann. N.Y. Acad. Sci. **133:**211, 1965.

Winters, R. W., Engel, K., and Dell, R. B.: Acid-base physiology in medicine, a self-instruction program, Cleveland, 1967, The London Co.

Chapter 8
Respiration

ALTHOUGH REPORTS on the incidence of pulmonary disorders may vary from one source to another, there is universal agreement that these diseases are the most frequent causes of neonatal mobidity and mortality. Broadly categorized, they are due to perinatal misadventures that impair adaptation to extrauterine life, to prenatal and postnatal infections, to congenital anomalies, and to extrapulmonary disorders such as cardiac failure, which secondarily give rise to respiratory dysfunction. This chapter describes the adaptive mechanisms responsible for adjustment to extrauterine respiration and the major clinical entities that are associated with respiratory distress.

FETAL CARDIOPULMONARY APPARATUS
Pulmonary circulation

The fetal circulation is described in Chapter 1. However, allusion to its pulmonary component is pertinent to the present discussion, particularly in reference to the changes that accompany the first breath (see later). The fetal lung is perfused by only 3% to 7% of cardiac output as a result of the high vascular resistance created by constricted pulmonary arterioles and collapsed alveolar capillaries. Most of the blood emanating from the right ventricle is thus shunted from the main pulmonary artery into the ductus arteriosus, bypassing the lungs. In the mature circulation, all blood from the right ventricle enters the pulmonary circulation directly. Blood supply to the fetal lung is further minimized by diversion of a major portion of inferior vena caval blood into the left atrium by way of the foramen ovale, thus constituting another pulmonary bypass. Establishment of normal extrauterine respiration requires that these fetal pathways be converted to the mature pattern very soon after birth. Further discussion of these changes may be found on p. 137.

Development of the fetal lungs

At 24 days the *primitive lung bud* appears as a localized pouch from the ventral surface of the *embryonic gut* (endoderm). This segment of gut will ultimately develop into the esophagus; the lung bud will be the trachea (Figs. 8-1 and 8-2). Persistence of a connection between the two structures is the basis for one of several possible types of tracheoesophageal fistulas (p. 171). At 26 to 28 days the lung bud divides into two structures that will become the two major bronchi. Subsequent growth progresses into surrounding mesenchyme (mesoderm), which becomes incorporated into pulmonary structures as differentiation proceeds: branching of each terminal structure continues as it grows laterally and downward into the pleural space, carrying with it the surrounding mesenchyme. The right and left branches of the original single bud thus give rise to successive generations of bronchi, bronchioles of diminishing size, alveolar ducts, and alveoli. The mesenchyme that surrounds these developing airway structures ultimately differentiates into blood vessels, muscle, connective tissue, cartilaginous plates in the bronchi, and the connective tissue that supports and separates alveolar and other structures in the lung.

By 6 weeks the *segmental bronchi* are formed, and at 12 weeks the *major lobes* are delineated. *Respiratory bronchioles* are differentiated at approximately 16 weeks; from them, at about 24 weeks, alveolar sacs are formed. At birth, they are considerably

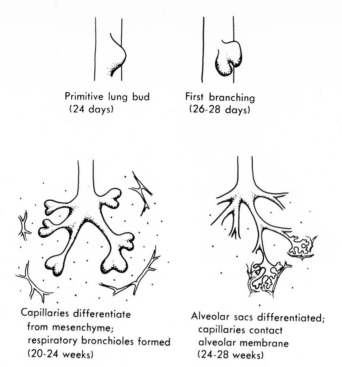

Primitive lung bud
(24 days)

First branching
(26-28 days)

Capillaries differentiate
from mesenchyme;
respiratory bronchioles formed
(20-24 weeks)

Alveolar sacs differentiated;
capillaries contact
alveolar membrane
(24-28 weeks)

Fig. 8-1. Development of primitive lung bud and subsequent branching into surrounding mesenchyme. (Modified from Avery, M. E., and Fletcher, B. D.: The lung and its disorders in the newborn infant, Philadelphia, 1974, W. B. Saunders Co.)

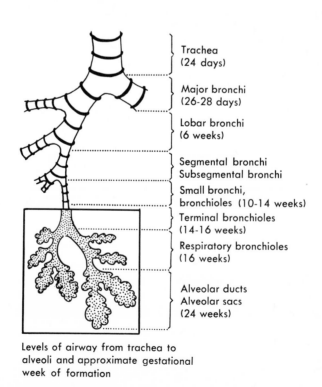

Trachea
(24 days)

Major bronchi
(26-28 days)

Lobar bronchi
(6 weeks)

Segmental bronchi
Subsegmental bronchi

Small bronchi,
bronchioles (10-14 weeks)

Terminal bronchioles
(14-16 weeks)

Respiratory bronchioles
(16 weeks)

Alveolar ducts
Alveolar sacs
(24 weeks)

Levels of airway from trachea to
alveoli and approximate gestational
week of formation

Fig. 8-2. Branching pattern of respiratory tract. The mature structures are indicated, with approximate gestational age of formation.

smaller and more shallow than at 1 and 2 months of age. Meanwhile, capillaries have been differentiating from the surrounding mesenchyme since the twentieth week. At 26 to 28 weeks the capillaries are in direct contact with the walls of *alveolar sacs* (alveolar membranes), but the intervening tissue poses a thicker barrier to air passage from alveolus to blood vessel than later on in postnatal life. Alveolar membranes are comprised of *type I* and *type II cells.* Function of the former is unknown; the latter cell produces surfactant. At 26 to 28 weeks, with the proximity of capillaries and alveolar walls established, extrauterine gas exchange is possible, assuming there is sufficient total alveolar surface area.

Congenital malformations can be better understood with some knowledge of pulmonary development. Agenesis of the lung and tracheal stenosis are the result of maldevelopment in the earliest differentiation of the primitive lung bud. Tracheoesophageal fistulas of various types probably originate during the earlier branching of the lung bud. Defective deposition of bronchial cartilage from embryonic mesenchyme results in the syndrome of deficient cartilaginous rings. The bronchi collapse during inspiration for lack of supporting tissue. Congenital lung cysts probably result from detachment of respiratory bronchioles, alveolar ducts, and sacs from the proximal airways with which they should normally be continuous. They may enlarge because trapped fluid, secreted by cells in respiratory bronchioles and alveoli, accumulates continuously.

The fetal lungs are metabolically active structures, even though they have no real function until the advent of extrauterine respiration. The blood vessels are narrow, and the alveoli are filled with fluid. Lung fluid differs in origin and composition from amniotic fluid. Lung fluid is derived from cells in the respiratory tract. It is less viscous, and it contains a lower protein concentration than amniotic fluid. Lung liquid must be evacuated soon after birth during the establishment of normal respiration. Its diminished viscosity presumably facilitates postnatal evacuation.

Postnatal lung growth is a vigorous, active process. The chest diameter increases rapidly in early infancy, mostly because of increased numbers of alveoli and respiratory bronchioles. The term baby is born with 24 million alveoli. At 3 months there are 77 million, and in the adult, 296 million. The alveolar sacs are considerably more shallow in the neonate, being 50 μm in diameter, compared to 100 to 200 μm in older children and 200 to 300 μm in the adult. The surface area available for gas exchange in the adult is about twenty times greater than in the neonate, which is close to the average increase of adult over neonatal body weight.

Intrauterine fetal breathing movements

It has only been in recent years that human fetal breathing movements have been identified unequivocally as such. A considerable amount of investigation in lambs preceded work on the human fetus. As in the lamb, human intrauterine breathing movements are episodic, being present in a normal pregnancy 70% of the time. They have been recorded as early as 13 weeks of gestation. The rate varies from 30 to 70 respirations per minute. The movements are identifiable by ultrasound techniques, but occasionally the mother can perceive them as localized movements of her abdomen, particularly near term. Since research on the subject has just begun, knowledge is limited. The incidence of breathing episodes is diminished in some high-risk pregnancies, such as those in which diabetes, hypertension, or toxemia is present. Apparently a fall in breathing incidence, accompanied by gasps, is a sinister sign that seems to be associated with subsequent death of small-for-dates babies. Fetal breathing is a new parameter for monitoring, and it may become valuable in the detection of fetal distress. Whether there is validity in the speculation that without previous practice the respiratory muscles would be weak at birth, remains to be seen.

FIRST BREATH

Insight into the changes involved in the baby's first breath provides a sound basis for the understanding of pulmonary disturbances of the neonatal period, particularly hyaline membrane disease. During intrauterine life, exchange of oxygen and carbon dioxide occurs across the placental membrane from one liquid medium to another. After birth this exchange occurs across the alveolar membrane between a gaseous medium (air in the alveolus) and a liquid one (blood in alveolar capillaries). Among the many changes the infant undergoes at birth, the most abrupt and crucial ones are concerned with adaptation of respiratory function to a gaseous environment. Several requirements must be satisfied before the lungs can assume and maintain these functions:

1. *Respiratory movements must be initiated.*

2. *Entry of air must overcome opposing forces if the lungs are to expand.*

3. *Some air must remain in the alveoli at the end of expiration so that the lungs do not collapse (establishment of functional residual capacity).*

4. *Pulmonary blood flow must be increased, and cardiac output must be redistributed.*

Although these events transpire simultaneously, they lend themselves well to sequential description.

Initiation of respiratory movements

The precise roles of the various stimuli that bombard the infant to initiate his respiratory movements after birth have not been clarified. Their separate effects are difficult to delineate. The identification of intrauterine respiratory movements has given rise to the idea that extrauterine breathing is a continuation of fetal respiratory movements. The neonate may therefore be well practiced by virtue of his fetal experience. If this experience explains the ease with which regular respirations are established after birth, additional explanation is required for the greatly enhanced vigor with which the first extrauterine breaths are executed.

Asphyxia is a significant stimulator of the first breath. Low arterial P_{O_2}, low pH, and high P_{CO_2} are each known to stimulate respiratory movement under certain conditions. They initiate impulses from the carotid and aortic chemoreceptors that are transmitted to the respiratory control center in the medulla. These asphyxial changes are present to some extent at birth in most normal newborn infants, and they are considered potent stimulators of the first breath. Before the onset of respiration, oxygen saturation of umbilical venous blood (from the placenta to the fetus) varies from 9% to 96%, whereas in umbilical artery blood (returning to the placenta) it ranges from 0% to 67%; yet many of these transiently hypoxemic infants are vigorous. In a substantial number of them, oxygen saturations are below 10%. Some have no measurable oxygen at all, and yet most of them breathe spontaneously within seconds after delivery. The average P_{CO_2} at birth is elevated to 58 mm Hg, and the mean pH is depressed to 7.28. These asphyxial chemical changes also activate chemoreceptor nerve endings in the carotid arteries and the aortic arch. These short periods of asphyxia are presumably components of the normal birth process. They are characterized by absence of metabolic acidosis (normal buffer base), although respiratory acidosis (high P_{CO_2} and diminished pH) is present. On the other hand, protracted asphyxial episodes are obviously not normal. They are characterized biochemically by metabolic acidosis (diminished buffer base) in addition to respiratory acidosis (hypercapnia) and hypoxemia. Short asphyxial episodes are thought to be powerful stimuli to the first breath; prolonged asphyxial episodes depress it.

Another important stimulus to the onset of respiratory movement is the abrupt drop that occurs in the infant's ambient temperature on arrival in room air. The baby leaves a fluid intrauterine environment of 98.6° F and is thrust into a dry ambient temperature of 70° to 75° F in an air-conditioned delivery room. This sudden change in environmental temperature stimulates nerve endings in the skin, with subsequent transmission of impulses to the medullary respiratory control center. This is probably an intense stimulus, and the response is instantaneous. The rapid onset of breathing requires an instantaneous response. The drop in body temperature that follows birth (Chapter 4) is probably a further stimulus to breathing. Lambs fail to breathe when delivered into a normal saline bath that is at normal body temperature. The same phenomenon has been noted in human infants. During the first few minutes after delivery, core temperature falls at a rate of approximately 0.2° F (0.1° C) per minute, whereas the decline in skin temperature is three times as great. These temperature changes are apparently within physiologic limits. Purposeful excessive cooling of depressed infants is contraindicated. It causes profound depression due to an abnormal fall in body temperature, which produces the penalties of severe cold stress, including hypoxia (p. 67).

The tactile stimulation provided during ordinary handling of infants at birth is probably of only minor significance in the initiation of respiratory movement. Although the traditional slaps to the heels or buttocks may have some influence in stimulating respiratory movement in normal babies, the time so expended on depressed infants is better utilized for more effective resuscitative measures.

The net result of the initial extrauterine activity of respiratory muscles is the creation of lower pressure within the lungs than in the atmosphere. This negative intrathoracic pressure "invites entry" of air into the lungs. The negative pressure created by expansion of the thorax is largely accomplished by descent of the diaphragm, by contraction of its muscle fibers. The contribution of intercostal muscles to thoracic expansion is relatively minor. The air that is "sucked in" as a result of the normal activity of the diaphragm must now reach the alveoli by overcoming forces that obstruct its free flow.

Entry of air into the lungs and expansion of alveoli

The forces most important in opposing the entry of air into the lungs are exerted by surface tension in the alveoli and by the viscosity of lung fluid in the entire respiratory tract. Surface tension forces are minimized by *surfactant* in the alveoli. Lung fluid is evacuated into lymphatic vessels and blood capillaries if the lungs expand normally. Initial negative intrathoracic pressures may reach 60 to 80 cm H_2O. The volume of inspired air has been measured as high as 80 cc. At end expiration much of it remains in the lungs as residual air.

Surface tension and surfactant. Surface tension forces are produced by an imbalance in the attraction of one molecule for an adjacent one. Consider a cup of liquid. Below the surface its molecules are attracted to and repelled from each other with equal force from all directions because they are completely surrounded by other molecules. However, the situation is different in the surface layer of molecules because the molecular forces of attraction cannot be equal from all directions. The air above the surface layer exerts little upward pull, and the balance of forces thus favors downward and horizontal directions. The force exerted by this imbalance in intermolecular attraction at the uppermost level of molecules is called surface tension. It produces a constant tendency for contraction of a surface area. Now apply this concept of surface area contraction to the spherical inner surface of alveolar walls. In the absence of a counteracting influence (surfactant) and in the presence of an interface with air, surface tension tends to contract alveolar surfaces, thus promoting alveolar collapse.

Alveoli of the lung are similar to a conglomerate of bubbles. Alveolar walls are largely liquid; they envelope air within them. Since an air-liquid interface is present (much like that just described for the uppermost molecular layer of water in a cup), surface-active forces are operative. Intermolecular attraction contracts the surface area of the liquid wall of the bubble (alveolus). Furthermore, in accordance with a law of physics (La-Place), the smaller the bubble, the stronger the forces of surface tension. Therefore the smaller the bubble, the greater its tendency to collapse as a result of unopposed surface forces. Ultimately the bubble (alveolus) collapses completely (atelectasis).

In man, surfactant is generated through two enzymatic pathways, methyl transferase and phosphocholine transferase. The earliest-appearing pathway (methyl transferase) produces surfactant that is first detectable at 22 to 24 weeks of gestation. Presence of this pathway permits the human fetus to be born prematurely and yet survive. Its activity increases as gestation progresses, so that at birth and throughout life it contributes half of the surface-active lecithin. The other system that produces surface-active lecithin is the phosphocholine transferase pathway, which ordinarily matures at 35 gestational weeks. At this time the human lung is biochemically mature; it is equipped for normal unassisted extrauterine breathing. This pathway matures at the time the L/S ratio assumes a value of 2.0.

In the normal lung, surface tension is minimized or eliminated by surfactant, a complex substance principally composed of lipoprotein that is elaborated by type II cells in the alveolar wall. It appears in the fetal lung at approximately 22 to 24 weeks of gestation. Without surfactant, unopposed surface tension forces increase directly with shrinkage of alveoli during expiration, ultimately resulting in alveolar collapse (atelectasis). However, in the presence of surfactant the effects of surface tension forces are eliminated or minimized. As alveoli shrink in the presence of surfactant during normal breathing, surface tension forces diminish rather than increase in magnitude because the surfactant layer, by becoming compressed, is made thicker; in this state surfactant counteracts surface forces most effectively. Conversely, the surfactant layer is thinned as alveoli expand during normal inspiration, and in this attenuated state the lining layer is less effective in diminishing surface tension. The influence of surfactant is therefore least at peak inspiration, when alveolar expansion is greatest. At this point, recoil of the ex-

panded lung is relatively unopposed, and the deflation required for expiration is facilitated. The alveolar lining layer (surfactant) functions principally to maintain alveolar stability (residual expansion at end-expiration) once air has entered the alveolus.

Lung fluid. Since 1948 it has been realized that the lungs secrete fluid that ultimately is added to amniotic fluid. A number of animal experiments in which fetal tracheas were ligated in utero have confirmed this original suggestion. In these circumstances, lungs at term were found to be overdistended with returned fluid and considerably heavier than lungs that were not ligated at the trachea. Even at an earlier date (1941), accumulation of pulmonary fluid was noted in a human fetus whose anomalous lung was not connected to the trachea. Fetal lung fluid presents a major opposing force to entry of air during the first breath. As the chest emerges from the birth canal, 30 to 40 ml of fluid are squeezed from the lung through the nose and mouth. With complete delivery of the chest, brisk recoil of the rib cage occurs, at which time 7 to 42 cc of air are "sucked" into the upper airway to replace the expressed fluid.

The expulsion of fluid may sometimes be observed as the head is exteriorized, before delivery of the trunk. Most lung fluid is evacuated across alveolar membranes through the lymphatic vessels and blood capillaries. The rate of fluid evacuation by each of these routes has not been clearly defined, but data from rabbits and lambs indicate increased lymph flow during the first breath and for several hours thereafter. Protein content (300 mg/ 100 ml) of lung fluid approximates amniotic fluid, and it has been suggested that this protein concentration would require evacuation by way of the lymphatics during the first breaths. Disappearance of lung fluid is far more rapid in rabbits delivered vaginally (several hours) than by cesarean section (several days). The mechanical effect of vaginal delivery is apparently an important factor in fluid evacuation. Absorption by lung capillaries and removal through lymphatics are also significant. Presumably these observations hold true for the human fetus, but to an unknown extent.

Establishment of functional residual capacity (FRC)

If normal respiration is to follow the first breath, some air must remain in the alveoli at the end of expiration to maintain them in a partially expanded state. The volume of this retained air is the lung's *functional residual capacity*. The ability to retain the air is called *alveolar stability*.

In normal term human lungs, the first expansion may require an opening pressure as high as 60 to 80 cm H_2O. At the end of expiration the pressure is again zero, but if all is well, the lungs retain about 40% of their fully expanded volume, since some air remains in the alveoli; functional residual capacity is thus established. It reaches its neonatal maximum by the end of 3 hours. From this partially expanded state the second inspiration is accomplished with minimal effort because now small pressure changes can produce relatively extensive inflation. During the second inspiration a high opening pressure is not necessary, since the lungs are already partially expanded at rest. The lung thus is approximately 40% inflated at zero intrathoracic pressure. Failure to retain air, together with the resultant collapse of alveoli, is precluded by the presence of surfactant. Expansion of the immature lung is quite different, presumably because surfactant activity is diminished. At the end of expiration, at zero pressure, the alveoli collapse in response to unopposed surface tension forces (absence of surfactant). The difference between normal and abnormal expansion is graphically depicted in Fig. 8-3. Thus, with failure to establish functional residual capacity, each succeeding inflation requires the same amount of opening pressure as the first breath. The work of respiration is considerably increased, and continuity of alveolar gas exchange is not established. This phenomenon is of fundamental significance in the pathogenesis of hyaline membrane disease.

Fig. 8-3. Pressure-volume curves for normal lungs (solid lines) and surfactant-deficient lungs (broken lines). Normal lung expands maximally at 40 cm H_2O. Note that descending limb does not return to 0 level, indicating partial expansion at end-expiration (alveolar stability). The hyaline membrane disease curve peaks at a low expansion for 40 cm H_2O because lung compliance is poor. The curve returns to 0, indicating alveolar collapse at end-expiration (no alveolar stability). (From Klaus, M. In Barnett, H., editor: Pediatrics, ed. 15, New York, 1972, Appleton-Century-Crofts, Publishing Division of Prentice-Hall, Inc.)

Increased pulmonary blood flow and redistribution of cardiac output

Cardiovascular adaptation to extrauterine life proceeds simultaneously with pulmonary adaptation. Five attributes of the fetal circulation must be altered if the mature cardiovascular pattern is to evolve. These fetal characteristics fall into two broad categories:

1. *Pulmonary-systemic pressure relationships*
   High pulmonary artery pressure due to increased pulmonary vascular resistance
   Low aortic systemic pressure (placental circuit)
2. *Sites of venous admixture (right-to-left shunts)*
   Foramen ovale
   Ductus arteriosus
   Ductus venosus

Pulmonary-systemic pressure relationships

Fetal aortic blood pressure is lower than pulmonary artery pressure. The placenta receives 40% to 50% of the fetal cardiac output. The fetal placental vessels are apparently not supplied with nerve endings; they are generally relaxed. Therefore they offer little resistance to the flow of blood. The placenta therefore constitutes a low-resistance circuit. The blood that perfuses it comes from the fetal aorta and returns to the fetal inferior vena cava, thus making it a prominent low-resistance component of the *systemic circulation*. Clamping of the cord eliminates the placental vascular bed, thus reducing considerably total intravascular space in the systemic circuit; in consequence, at birth the aortic blood pressure is raised. Simultaneously, return flow to the inferior vena cava is reduced by severance of the placenta, and a small drop in pressure occurs in the venous side of the circulation.

Pulmonary artery pressure is higher than aortic pressure because of the extremely high pulmonary vascular resistance in the fetus. Resistance to blood flow through the lungs is so high as to permit only 3% to 7% of cardiac output to perfuse them, in contrast to the low-resistance placental circuit, which accommodates 40% to 50% of cardiac output. If the lungs expand sufficiently, vasodilatation produces a precipitous fall in pulmonary vascular resistance within the first few minutes after birth. Resistance has been calculated to fall by 80% from fetal levels. A more gradual reduction in resistance transpires over the next 6 to 8 weeks. With the abrupt diminution of resistance comes an equally abrupt increase in pulmonary blood flow. Within minutes after the establishment of adequate ventilation, pulmonary perfusion has increased approximately fivefold. Relaxation of the pulmonary arterioles is principally in the precapillary segments. An overwhelming stimulus to this vasodilatation is the increase in blood P_{O_2} that follows the first few breaths. Of secondary significance is the dilatation of capillaries that results from elimination of their compression by alveolar fluid as air enters the alveoli.

High fetal pulmonary arteriolar resistance is not solely a function of constriction. The relative thickness of the muscle layer of these arterioles is considerably greater than it will be later in postnatal life. Thus the gradual diminution of vascular resistance that occurs over the first 6 to 8 weeks is related to thinning out of the muscle layer, rather than to ongoing relaxation of existing muscle. In summary, initial lung expansion and adequate oxygenation diminish blood pressure in the pulmonary circuit by forcefully stimulating pulmonary arteriolar relaxation. At the same time, blood pressure in the systemic circuit increases because of greater resistance brought about by severance of the placenta. With this reversal of relative blood pressures in the pulmonary and systemic circuits, the stage is now set for elimination of the fetal sites at which venous admixture occurs (right-to-left shunt).

Fetal sites of venous admixture (right-to-left shunts)

Closure of the foramen ovale. The foramen ovale is an aperture in the interatrial septum. It is covered by a thin flap of tissue that can open like a swinging door in only one direction—into the left atrium. Since, in the fetus, pressure in the right atrium is higher than that in the left (because pulmonary circuit pressure is high), the flap remains open, permitting most of the well-oxygenated blood from the inferior vena cava to flow from the right atrium into the left atrium. The position of the flap is thus a function of the pressure relationship between both atria. If pressure in the right atrium is *higher* than that in the left, the flap is open and blood flows from the right to left atrium. This is normal for the fetus. When pressure in the right atrium is *lower* than that of the left, the flap closes. This is normal for the neonate. Lung expansion during the first breath causes an abrupt decline in pulmonary vascular resistance and a marked increase in pulmonary blood flow. The amount of blood that flows into the left atrium is therefore increased (pulmonary venous return), causing the left atrial pressure to rise slightly. Right atrial pressure falls because of lowered pulmonary vascular resistance. The pressure relationship between the atria is now reversed. When the left atrial pressure increases over that of the right, the swinging flap of tissue abuts against the margins of the foramen ovale. The foramen is now *functionally* closed, and one site of right-to-left shunting is eliminated. The tissue flap does not become immovably adherent to the atrial septum for several months. It is held in the closed position by the higher left atrial pressure. If right atrial pressure again becomes higher than that on the left (the baby is suddenly asphyxiated), the foramen will reopen.

Closure of the ductus arteriosus. The fetal ductus arteriosus is a large vessel, almost equal in diameter to the pulmonary artery. When it constricts, its substantial muscle layer has the capacity of obliterating the lumen. Constriction of the ductus arteriosus occurs in response to the increased blood P_{O_2} that occurs during the first few breaths. Vasoconstrictive response of the ductus to oxygen is in contrast to the vasodilating response of pulmonary arterioles. If the lungs do not expand normally, failure of P_{O_2} to rise causes sustained ductus patency. Normally, functional closure (constriction) is complete by 15 hours after birth in term infants. Anatomic closure (fibrosis) is usually complete by 3 weeks of age. In premature infants the ductus remains patent for much longer, and variable, periods because the capacity to constrict in response to augmented oxygen tension is not yet developed. Prior to completion of anatomic closure in term or premature babies, the ductus may reopen in response to lowered blood oxygen tension. The older the infant, the less likely is the ductus to reopen. With ductal closure, another fetal right-to-left shunt is eliminated.

Closure of the ductus venosus. The ductus venosus is a channel that, in the fetus, connects the portal (hepatic and intestinal) venous circulation with the inferior vena cava. In the fetus, umbilical vein blood passes through the liver, into the ductus venosus, to the inferior vena cava, and thence to the heart. The mechanism of closure of the ductus venosus is unknown. After birth, very

little blood flows through it. Anatomical closure (fibrosis) is completed in 3 to 7 days.

In summary, changing pressure relationships are responsible for elimination of the fetal sites of right-to-left shunting. With adequate lung expansion, an increase in pulmonary blood flow occurs. This is brought about by the diminished vascular resistance that results from dilatation of pulmonary vessels. Almost all subsequent changes in circulation are a consequence of decreased pulmonary vascular resistance associated with normal lung expansion. Increased blood flow through the lungs leads to a larger flow into the left atrium, thereby raising left atrial pressure above that in the right atrium. When this occurs, the foramen ovale closes, thus eliminating the fetal right-to-left shunt at this site. The ductus arteriosus begins gradual closure by constriction of its wall as a result of a rising arterial P_{O_2}. Earlier, diminished ductus blood flow is a function of changes in pressure relationships between the pulmonary and the systemic circulations. As pulmonary blood pressure declines with lung expansion, pressures in the pulmonary and systemic circuits are almost equalized. There is thus gradual elimination of the pressure gradient that directed fetal blood from the pulmonary artery through the ductus into the aorta. Constriction of the ductus in response to increased oxygenation plus the change in pressure relationships between the pulmonary and systemic circulations therefore combine to obliterate another fetal site of right-to-left shunting.

What causes the pulmonary vascular bed to dilate and thus receive a greater flow of blood? Perhaps the most powerful influence is an increase in arterial P_{O_2}. Conversely, hypoxia constricts pulmonary vasculature. Most of this activity occurs in the precapillary arterioles. With the establishment of extrauterine respiration, the increase of arterial P_{O_2} exerts very different effects on pulmonary arterioles and the ductus arteriosus. The former relax as P_{O_2} rises; the latter constricts. The aveolar capillaries dilate as the lung expands and alveolar fluid is replaced by air during the first few breaths.

HYALINE MEMBRANE DISEASE

Hyaline membrane disease (HMD) is also known as the idiopathic respiratory distress syndrome (IRDS), or simply as the respiratory distress syndrome (RDS). It is an acute disorder that is symptomatic at birth or soon thereafter. Primarily characterized by respiratory distress, it occurs almost exclusively in premature infants. Its natural course is 3 to 5 days in duration. The case fatality rate is high. Estimates of deaths in the United States due to hyaline membrane disease varied from 25,000 to 40,000 infants annually but this rate has diminished significantly since the introduction of various types of respiratory support.

Incidence and prognosis

Hyaline membrane disease occurs in 1% to 2% of total live births in all races and in all socioeconomic groups. Reports of incidence are quite variable, but a common trend has been noted in all parts of the world. It is almost exclusively a disease of premature infants, rarely occurring in babies born at term. Furthermore, the incidence varies from one birth-weight group to another. It is commonest among infants who weigh between 1000 and 1500 grams, next most frequent in those between 1500 and 2000 grams, and it is least common between 2000 and 2500 grams. In general, 25% to 35% of all premature infants are affected. In the 1000- to 1500-gram group, the one of highest incidence, hyaline membrane disease has been reported to affect as many as 57% of babies. Severe respiratory distress is even more frequent in babies below 1000 grams. In them the clinical picture differs from classic hyaline membrane disease, but the pathogenesis is probably similar. This disorder occurs in 65% of infants in this lowest birth weight category.

Case fatality rates are too variable to quote precisely, but as one might expect, the lower the birth weight, the less likely is survival. Although recent advances in therapy have diminished the percentage of mortality impressively, it remains high nevertheless.

Pathophysiology

Comprehension of the pathophysiology of hyaline membrane disease requires familiarity with the events of the first breath. In essence, hyaline membrane disease is a partial persistence of, or reversion to, the fetal cardiopulmonary state. Whatever other factors may influence the course of events, the central difficulty seems to be a deficiency in surfactant activity. Hyaline membrane disease is fundamentally a developmental disorder. The maturation of surfactant synthesis has been amply demonstrated by extensive studies. They have thus far confirmed the validity of L/S ratio measurements, which indicate that, with a few exceptions, the lungs are capable of normal extrauterine function at approximately 35 gestational weeks. The central significance of a developmental concept seems plausible because the disease preponderantly affects premature infants; term infants are rarely affected. A well-defined sequence of biochemical events must transpire in utero before maturation of the lungs is established. If birth occurs prior to completion of this sequence, the neonate with premature lungs is incapable of normally coping with a gaseous environment.

The principal factors that are operative in the evolution of hyaline membrane disease are depicted in Fig. 8-4. The narrative that follows will refer to the numbered squares in the diagram. The *persistent fetal state (1)* implies *surfactant deficiency* and increased *pulmonary vascular resistance* as well. The latter would ordinarily disappear in the presence of normal lung expansion, but this disappearance is precluded in the premature lung because of surfactant deficiency. In most instances there is probably enough functional surfactant present at birth to accommodate reasonably effective breathing, since the methyl transferase system appears very early (22 to 24 gestational weeks). However, it seems to fail soon after birth because it is so sensitive to hypoxia and acidosis. The choline transferase system is not so sensitive, but it has not yet matured. Thus, at birth, and for a short time thereafter, most infants

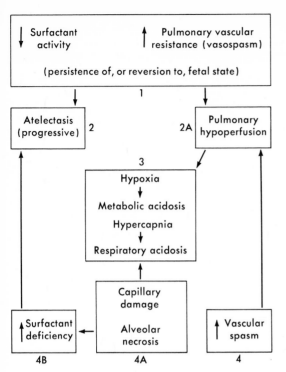

Fig. 8-4. Principal intrapulmonary factors in pathogenesis of hyaline membrane disease. (See text.)

breathe with little or with moderate difficulty. Soon respiration becomes more labored as surfactant from the methyl transferase system is dissipated but not replaced. Consequently, normal functional residual capacity (alveolar stability) is not possible. Alveoli that are inflated during inspiration are again collapsed at end expiration. Each breath is like the first; collapsed alveoli require reinflation. The work of respiration is thus relatively tremendous; an effort similar to that expended for the first breath must be mounted for each one that follows. As the infant becomes more feeble, he fails to open more alveoli. *Atelectasis (2),* already present at birth to some extent, now becomes more widespread. Pulmonary hypoperfusion from vasospasm has been present from the beginning *(2A).* These two factors *(2, 2A)* produce *hypoxia* and *hypercapnia (3).* As hypoxia becomes prolonged, anaerobic glycolysis

is activated for the production of glucose from glycogen. The unfortunate by-product of this process is an increased quantity of lactic acid, which causes *metabolic acidosis (3).* Furthermore, carbon dioxide cannot be blown off due to atelectasis and the paucity of blood that delivers it to the lungs. The resultant retention of CO_2 (hypercapnia) causes *respiratory acidosis (3);* blood pH is therefore diminished considerably.

Hypoxia and acidosis accentuate preexisting *vascular spasm (4),* which in turn increases *pulmonary hypoperfusion (2A).* Hypoxia and acidosis also inflict *capillary damage* and *alveolar necrosis (4A),* both of which aggravate *surfactant deficiency (4B)* by impairing its production. As a consequence, *progressive atelectasis (2)* is unabated.

Failure of lung expansion and persistence of high vascular resistance result in increased blood pressure in the pulmonary circuit. Venous admixture (right-to-left shunt) through the foramen ovale, as it existed in utero, is maintained after birth. If pressure in the pulmonary circuit is sufficiently high in relation to aortic pressure, a right-to-left shunt (pulmonary artery to aorta) is also present at the ductus arteriosus. The effect of these extrapulmonary shunts is to divert blood from the lungs and thus add to their hypoperfusion. To a variable extent, the fetal cardiopulmonary circulation persists in each patient.

This entire sequence of events can be ascribed to failure of lung expansion and inability to establish alveolar stability as a result of a primary surfactant deficiency. There are those who hold that surfactant deficiency is secondary to intrauterine asphyxia, rather than simply a developmental phenomenon. Asphyxia would then cause pulmonary vasoconstriction in utero. The resultant ischemia damages alveolar walls and impairs surfactant production.

The incidence of intrauterine asphyxia in premature infants is indeed higher than in term babies, but the majority of infants who have hyaline membrane disease give no evidence of antecedent stress. Acute asphyxia probably accentuates the maturational inadequacy. At present, the concept of primary surfactant deficiency related to incomplete maturation is the most attractive hypothesis.

Lung compliance is diminished in hyaline membrane disease. Compliance is a function of the elasticity of lung tissue. It expresses the capacity of the lung to increase in volume in response to a given amount of applied pressure during inspiration. The lungs in hyaline membrane disease require far more pressure than normal lungs for equal amounts of expansion. Pressures of 35 cm H_2O, which usually expand normal lungs, cause little inflation of lungs with hyaline membrane disease. The abnormal lung tissue is thus said to be "stiffer," or less distensible. Compliance is expressed in milliliters (volume change) per centimeter of water (pressure change), or ml/cm H_2O. Compliance of normal newborn lungs is 4 to 6 ml/cm H_2O; in hyaline membrane disease it is one fourth to one fifth as much. The stiffness of affected lungs, and thus their limited distensibility, contributes significantly to the work of breathing in these sick babies. It also permits therapy with end-expiratory positive pressure (discussed later).

The role of the hyaline membranes in disruption of pulmonary function has not been delineated. In years past they were believed to arise solely from aspiration of vernix and other particulate matter in amniotic fluid. It has become evident, however, that they are principally the product of cellular necrosis in the alveoli and terminal respiratory bronchioles. Hyaline membranes do not in themselves cause atelectasis. They probably contribute to diminution of compliance.

Predisposing factors

Prematurity is virtually a constant predisposing factor; complications of pregnancy and labor play an additional major role. Maternal bleeding and other causes of fetal asphyxia are associated with the disease but not in the majority of babies. Maternal diabetes is an important predisposing factor in itself; it also predisposes to the disease be-

cause of the high incidence of prematurity among infants of diabetic mothers (p. 206). The role of cesarean section is still debated. The current consensus is that in itself it does not play a role in the pathogenesis. The causes of fetal distress that urgently necessitate cesarean section seem to be the decisive factors. Most studies indicate that elective cesarean sections (performed in the absence of detectable fetal difficulty) are not associated with an increased incidence of the disease. On the other hand, there is impressive evidence for a contributory role by cesarean section itself. A recent study from the Boston Hospital for Women revealed a higher incidence of hyaline membrane disease in babies delivered by cesarean section, both from diabetic and nondiabetic mothers.

Morphologic pathology

At autopsy the lungs are purple red, resembling the consistency of liver. They contain little or no air in contrast to normal lungs, which are salmon pink and spongy by virtue of their air content. The microscopic appearance is characterized by widespread atelectasis and hyaline membranes. These membranes are present only in previously aerated portions of the lung, and with usual staining techniques in microscopic sections they may vary in color from pale pink to red (eosinophilic). Generally they have a homogeneous, waxen appearance. They line the surfaces of alveoli and terminal respiratory bronchioles. Epithelial cells are necrotic or absent in areas occupied by membranes and in collapsed alveoli.

Clinical manifestations

Infants with hyaline membrane disease were previously believed to be free of abnormalities for the first few hours of life, but as more careful observations were made, it became obvious that the majority of affected babies had some sort of respiratory difficulty at birth or within 2 hours thereafter. If there is truly no respiratory distress within 6 hours after delivery, the diagnosis of hyaline membrane disease is not tenable. In the past, errors were due to infrequent observation, failure to appreciate the more subtle signs of respiratory difficulty, and failure to perform Apgar scoring at birth.

Increased respiratory rate (over 60 respirations per minute) is the commonest sign of abnormal ventilation. Occasionally an expiratory grunt or sigh is the only perceptible sign. The expiratory grunt is a fascinating phenomenon. It is an effort to obstruct exhalation of air temporarily and thus, by increasing "back pressure," to maintain some degree of alveolar expansion in order to increase functional residual capacity. The epiglottis is held so that the glottis is closed. Pressure mounts within the respiratory tract as the outflow of air is obstructed. When the epiglottis is abruptly released, the sudden rush of air over the vocal cords produces a grunt. Infants who grunt can raise their arterial P_{O_2} by 10 to 20 mm Hg. Since the exhalation of air must be obstructed by closure of the glottis, passage of an endotracheal tube eliminates the grunt. However, this should not be interpreted as a contraindication to intubation of severely affected infants who require such therapy.

Retraction of the chest wall during inspiration is a classic sign of respiratory distress or, more specifically, diminished lung compliance. Retractions indicate a failure to fill the lungs with air during efforts exerted by respiratory muscles, especially the diaphragm. They thus indicate inadequate distention of the lungs during inspiration. Retractions are not always a sign of intrinsic lung disease, although this is their most frequent cause. They may also result from obstruction of airflow in the nose, larynx, trachea, or major bronchi. In hyaline membrane disease, airflow is diminished by incomplete expansion of the lungs, which is due to diminished compliance. The lungs are stiffer than normal, and they fail to inflate fully as the diaphragm descends to enlarge the thorax. Negative pressure persists in the pleural space between the chest wall and the unexpanded lungs, and since the lungs do not expand to fill this space, the flexible chest wall is pulled inward. The net result is retraction of the chest wall.

In addition to *tachypnea, grunting,* and *retractions, flaring of the external nares* is also a frequent sign of respiratory distress. Auscultation of the chest reveals generalized *diminution of breath sounds* and, occasionally, *crepitant rales. Apneic episodes* occur in severely affected babies. They are an ominous sign, particularly when observed during the first 24 hours of life. *Cyanosis* in room air is the rule.

Cardiac signs are not ordinarily prominent. The heart rate is usually quite variable, but it becomes fixed as the disease increases in severity. Bradycardia (less than 100 beats/min) occurs when hypoxemia is severe. Cardiac failure is rare.

Pallor is the result of peripheral vasoconstriction, rather than anemia. *Edema,* which is common in normal premature babies, is more frequent and severe in those with hyaline membrane disease. *Pitting edema* of the hands and feet appears within the first 24 hours and resolves by the end of the fifth day.

Decreased body temperature is frequently observed. In mildly or moderately involved infants it is correctable in an optimal thermal environment, but in severely affected infants it often defies remedial measures. Ambient incubator temperatures of 95° F or more may be required to raise the body temperature.

Specific central nervous system signs are few. The muscles are universally *flaccid,* and the infant is *hypoactive* or *motionless.* Severely ill infants assume a frog-leg position, with the mouth open and the head fallen to one side.

Several clinical signs may portend a fatal outcome. For instance, the mortality rate is high among infants with severe retractions during the first 6 hours; the situation is grim if air exchange has not improved after 24 hours, or if cyanosis persists despite oxygen administration. A falling respiratory rate in profoundly affected infants is an ominous sign. Severe flaccidity and hypoactivity as early as 6 hours also indicate a troublesome course.

Retractions continue for approximately 72 hours, and then they diminish. Tachypnea often persists for several days afterward. Improvement is signaled by diminution of retractions, increased muscle tone and spontaneous activity, and frequent voiding accompanied by resolution of edema. Death is unlikely after 72 hours except for infants with complications such as intracranial hemorrhage, pneumonia, or pulmonary hemorrhage.

Laboratory data

Except for the recently described foam stability test on gastric aspirate, there are no specific laboratory tests for the diagnosis of hyaline membrane disease. The characteristic biochemical abnormalities (hypoxemia, hypercapnia, and acidosis) are identical to those of perinatal asphyxia and postnatal respiratory failure from any cause. In severely ill infants in room air the arterial P_{O_2} is below 40 mm Hg (normal lower limit: 50 mm Hg), the arterial P_{CO_2} is over 65 mm Hg (normal upper limit: 45 mm Hg), and the pH is below 7.15 (normal: 7.35 to 7.45).

Hypoxemia. Inadequate ventilation plus poor perfusion of tissues combine to cause low arterial oxygen tensions. Restoration of normal levels is the primary aim of therapy. Hypoxemia induces metabolic acidosis because lactic acid production increases. It also causes pulmonary arteriolar constriction with intrapulmonary right-to-left shunting because alveoli are bypassed. Other deleterious effects of hypoxemia include damage to capillary endothelium all over the body, impaired metabolic response to cold stress, and ultimately a low systemic blood pressure from diminished cardiac output.

Hypercapnia. Accumulation of carbon dioxide in the blood is due to inadequate ventilation caused by atelectasis and hypoperfusion. A rising arterial P_{CO_2} signifies deterioration of pulmonary function. Although initially an increase of arterial P_{CO_2} is a respiratory stimulant, excessive accumulation is depressant. In the extreme, arterial P_{CO_2} may exceed 100 mm Hg.

Acidosis. Mixed respiratory and metabolic acidosis is the rule in hyaline membrane disease. Early in the course of the disease respiratory acidosis may predominate, but soon a metabolic component also appears. The arterial pH may approach 6.8 terminally. The deleterious effects of acidosis include pulmonary vasoconstriction, irregular heartbeat, depression of myocardial function, dilatation of cerebral vessels that imposes a hazard of cerebral hemorrhage, further impairment of surfactant activity, and detachment of bilirubin from albumin to cause kernicterus at unexpectedly low serum bilirubin concentrations (p. 198).

Other blood chemical values. Serum electrolyte values may remain relatively unaltered, except for potassium, which increases as a result of hypoxic cellular injury in untreated or unsuccessfully treated babies. Lactic acid levels rise in conjunction with hypoxemia. Serum bilirubin levels are generally higher in babies with hyaline membrane disease; this is apparently related to depressed liver function (p. 196).

Foam stability test (shake test) on gastric aspirate. The foam stability test was first described for amniotic fluid (p. 12), for which it is generally used as a screening procedure preliminary to L/S ratio determination. The presence of surfactant causes the formation of stable bubbles (foam) in a test tube of amniotic fluid that is shaken for 15 seconds after the addition of 95% ethanol. If surfactant is absent, bubbles are not formed. The test is negative.

The same procedure on gastric aspirate taken from the baby within an hour after birth is useful in distinguishing hyaline membrane disease from other causes of respiratory distress. One-half milliliter gastric aspirate is mixed with an equal quantity of normal saline. The resultant 1 ml mixture is added to 1 ml of 95% ethanol, and this is shaken briskly for 15 seconds. The test tube is left standing in room air, and the result is read after 15 minutes. The test tube must be viewed from above against a black background in good light. The test is positive if a complete ring of bubbles is present in the meniscus. A positive shake test indicates that surfactant is present and that, with rare exception, hyaline membrane disease will not ensue. A negative test is indicated by complete absence of bubbles. It predicts almost certainly that hyaline membrane disease will follow. An intermediate result is comprised of bubble patterns that form a ring around one third of the circumference of the meniscus or less. Most of these babies will have hyaline membrane disease. Properly executed, this procedure could aid substantially in determining the need for transfer of an infant to a regional center.

The reader is urged to refer to the original description of this test in the article by Cowett and associates. Their procedure utilizes four different dilutions of gastric aspirate and saline. The procedure described here utilizes only one of these dilutions, which we have found quite satisfactory.

Fig. 8-5. Radiologic appearance of severe hyaline membrane disease. The lungs are dense. The cardiac shadow is barely discernible in left chest. Prominent black streaks emanating from both hilar areas are air bronchograms.

Radiologic findings

The typical x-ray appearance of the lungs is well correlated with the morphologic pathology of the disease. Almost every author who writes about it describes a reticulogranular pattern that is diffuse over both lung fields, occasionally involving one lung more than the other. The general impression one receives on viewing such a film is that the lungs appear clouded or similar to ground glass. White density is particularly prominent and homogeneous at the hilar areas. Close inspection peripheral to the hilar regions reveals tiny, closely spaced, comma-like densities that sometimes suggest a heavy snowfall at night. Each of these small densities is an atelectatic area of lung. At the hilar regions, and for some distance peripherally, dark streaks represent air-filled bronchi, which are easily discerned against the white background provided by the collapsed lung. These dark streaks are called air bronchograms. Hilar densities, a diffuse reticulogranular pattern, and air bronchograms are thus the cardinal radiologic features of hyaline membrane disease (Fig. 8-5).

Treatment

There is to date no definitive treatment for hyaline membrane disease. The therapeutic approaches of confirmed benefit are supportive in nature. This discussion is limited to the most successful ones. They are directly concerned with providing effective ventilation, correcting acid-base imbalance, providing optimal environmental temperature, and maintaining normal hematocrit and blood pressure.

Oxygen therapy. Nothing is more critical to tissue metabolism than an adequate supply of oxygen. The most important aspect of total therapy for hyaline membrane disease is the provision of oxygen. *Once the need for such therapy is apparent for any disorder, its adequacy must be ascertained and its hazards averted by continuous monitoring of arterial oxygen tensions.* In this section, before discussion of practical considerations, it seems fitting to discuss the physiologic principles that underlie rational oxygen therapy, its benefits, and its hazards.

Physiology of oxygen transport: the basis for rational oxygen therapy. The erythrocyte is the vehicle for transport of oxygen. Its basic function is to take up oxygen from the lungs and deliver it to the tissues, carrying sufficient quantities to effect rapid diffusion from capillaries to tissue cells. The performance of this function is dependent on a number of factors that include an adequate fraction of inspired oxygen ($F_{I_{O_2}}$), normal pulmonary function, blood volume, cardiac output, perfusion, and distribution of blood to tissues. Other aspects are intrinsic to blood. They involve arterial pH and temperature, hemoglobin concentration, and the affinity of hemoglobin for oxygen. Several definitions must be considered before continuing this discussion.

PARTIAL PRESSURE OF OXYGEN, OR OXYGEN TENSION (P_{O_2}). Management of oxygen therapy is based on monitored levels of arterial oxygen tensions ($P_{a_{O_2}}$), expressed in millimeters of mercury (mm Hg). The partial pressure of a gas is the measured force it exerts in its tendency to escape from a liquid to a gaseous medium or from one compartment to another, much like the pressure exerted by escaping bubbles in champagne. It is called "partial" when the gas in question is only one of several in a common liquid (or chamber) that exert pressure simultaneously. In arterial (or venous) blood, with the subject breathing room air, partial pressures are measurable for oxygen, carbon dioxide, nitrogen, and water vapor. Total pressure of these gases—that is, their aggregate driving force to escape—is approximately 750 mm Hg. The pressure exerted by oxygen itself, or partial pressure (arterial P_{O_2}), is about 90 mm Hg. The tension attributable to carbon dioxide, the arterial P_{CO_2}, is usually 40 mm Hg. The remaining partial pressures are exerted by nitrogen and by water vapor. The P_{O_2} is thus the driving force of oxygen, which will move it from one compartment to another—from alveoli to pulmonary capillaries if P_{O_2} is higher in alveoli than in capillaries, and from capillaries to tissues if partial pressure in the capillaries is higher than in tissue

fluid. The same principle is operative for movement of oxygen from tissue fluid to individual cells. Movement of C_{O_2} in the opposite direction, from tissues to blood and thence to alveoli, is governed by a similar pattern of pressure differences. Movement of gas from a higher to a lower partial pressure is movement governed by a *pressure gradient*. If normal arterial blood (P_{O_2}, 90 mm Hg) is exposed to room air (P_{O_2}, 160 mm Hg), oxygen will enter the blood until equilibrium is established, that is, until both have a P_{O_2} of 160 mm Hg. On the other hand, with arterial P_{CO_2} of 40 mm Hg and atmospheric P_{CO_2} of 0 (there is virtually no CO_2 in air), carbon dioxide will ultimately disappear from blood, having moved into room air. The pressure gradient for oxygen movement was from room air to blood; arterial P_{O_2} rose. For carbon dioxide it was in the opposite direction; arterial P_{CO_2} declined. This is precisely what occurs when blood collected for blood gas determination is inadvertently exposed to room air. Blood gas determinations in these circumstances are invalid.

OXYGEN CONTENT. The oxygen content of whole blood is the total amount of the gas in 100 ml of whole blood. Normal oxygen content is 20.6 ml (vol %). This includes 20 ml bound to hemoglobin and 0.6 ml (approximately 3% of the total) dissolved in plasma.

OXYGEN CAPACITY. Oxygen *capacity* must be distinguished from oxygen *content*. Oxygen-carrying capacity is the maximal amount of the gas that hemoglobin can theoretically hold. Oxygen content is the actual amount held. Most oxygen in blood is bound to hemoglobin. Each gram of hemoglobin has the capacity to bind 1.34 ml of oxygen. If the hemoglobin concentration of whole blood is 15 grams/100 ml, the calculated capacity at this concentration is 15×1.34, or 20.1 ml of oxygen/100 ml of blood.

OXYGEN SATURATION. Referring only to hemoglobin, oxygen saturation is given as a percentage value that is calculated by dividing the amount of oxygen bound to hemoglobin by the maximal amount that can be bound (oxygen capacity). Normal oxygen saturation is 96% to 98%. Oxygen saturation is governed by the P_{O_2} and by the affinity of hemoglobin for oxygen.

AFFINITY OF HEMOGLOBIN FOR OXYGEN. Fetal hemoglobin differs from adult hemoglobin. Among its unique attributes is the ability to bind more oxygen at any given P_{O_2}. Therefore, at any given P_{O_2}, oxygen saturation of fetal hemoglobin is higher than the adult's. Fetal hemoglobin thus has a greater affinity for oxygen than adult hemoglobin. The fetal red blood cell therefore takes up more oxygen in the lungs, but this phenomenon is of little overall significance. Of greater potential importance is the fact that increased affinity also causes less oxygen to be released to the tissues. Conversely, when oxygen affinity is reduced, as in the adult, more oxygen is unloaded to the tissues at any given P_{aO_2}. Hemoglobin releases bound oxygen in response to lowered oxygen tension (P_{O_2}). In the neonate, the tension must fall farther before fetal hemoglobin releases oxygen, since it is held more avidly than in the adult.

The molecular configuration of fetal hemoglobin differs from that of the adult. This difference, plus the quantity of organic phosphates in the red blood cell, determines the affinity of hemoglobin for oxygen. The principal organic phosphate in the erythocyte is 2,3-diphosphoglycerate (2,3-DPG). A diminished interaction between fetal hemoglobin and DPG in the neonatal erythrocyte results in greater affinity for oxygen. Greater interaction between adult hemoglobin and DPG results in less oxygen affinity. If the neonate is transfused with fresh adult blood, more oxygen is released to tissues.

OXYGEN-HEMOGLOBIN DISSOCIATION CURVE. Normally there is a predictable correlation

Fig. 8-6. Oxygen-hemoglobin dissociation curves. Cyanosis becomes apparent between 75% and 85% saturation, correlating to lower oxygen tension in neonates than that in adults. Scale at top shows the curves in relation to toxic levels. (From Klaus, M., and Meyer, B. P.: Pediatr. Clin. North Am. **13:**731, 1966.)

between oxygen saturation and P_{O_2}. Plotted on a graph in which the percentage of saturation is arranged vertically, and P_{O_2} horizontally, a typical S-shaped curve results when the plotted points are joined. Dissociation curves for fetal and adult hemoglobins are shown in Fig. 8-6. The saturation of fetal hemoglobin (vertical scale) is higher than the adult's at all P_{O_2} levels because there is a greater affinity for oxygen. Stated differently, the same percentage of saturation occurs at a lower P_{O_2} in fetal hemoglobin than in the adult's. This can be clearly discerned by reference to the two shaded vertical bars that indicate zones in which cyanosis is visible, corresponding to fetal and adult values for oxygen saturation of hemoglobin. Cyanosis is apparent when blood is between 75% and 85% saturated with oxygen. These saturations occur at P_{O_2} levels of 32 to 41 mm Hg in the neonate and 42 to 52 mm Hg in the adult. Fig. 8-6 demonstrates why the newborn is considerably less oxygenated than the adult when cyanosis first becomes discernible. The fetal dissociation curve is said to be shifted to the left of the adult's.

The position of the curve (shifted right or left) actually indicates the affinity of hemoglobin for oxygen. When the affinity is decreased, as in the adult, more oxygen is released to tissues at any given oxygen tension. Saturation at any oxygen tension is therefore less than in the neonate. Saturation at any given P_{O_2} decreases as affinity diminishes. The oxygen-hemoglobin dissociation curve is thus shifted to the right. If affinity is increased, as in the neonate, less oxygen is unloaded to tissues at any given P_{aO_2}. Saturation at any P_{aO_2} is therefore greater than in the adult. The curve is now said to be shifted to the left.

Two factors intrinsic to blood exert a major influence on affinity of hemoglobin for oxygen. Affinity diminishes as blood pH decreases and as temperature increases; the curve shifts to the right. Affinity increases as blood pH rises and as temperature falls; the curve shifts to the left. The increased affinity caused by lower temperatures explains a common phenomenon. In bitter cold weather, earlobes are bright red because the blood within them is chilled. Affinity for oxygen increases; saturation at any given P_{aO_2} is thus also increased, and the curve is shifted to the left, as in the neonate. The P_{O_2} of earlobe blood may be relatively low, but the increased saturation renders it bright red because hemoglobin retains more oxygen, releasing less to tissues as a result of its greater affinity for oxygen.

Practical aspects of oxygen administration

DOSE AND BLOOD LEVEL; MONITORING F_{IO_2} AND BLOOD GASES. Oxygen is like any drug; it must be administered in proper dosage. Unlike many drugs, however, the dose required for optimal and harmless effect varies widely from one infant to another and from time to time in the same infant. Appropriate doses of oxygen can be maintained only by monitoring its ambient concentrations and measuring the ultimate effect of such concentrations on the infant's arterial oxygen tension. The ultimate measure of optimal therapy is the arterial P_{O_2}. Carbon dioxide tension and pH are always determined on the same blood sample. A detailed record of these serial determinations must be kept, particularly in reference to the percentage of inhaled oxygen that is provided. The ambient concentration should always be measured when a blood sample is collected.

By any method of administration, from the simple oxygen hood to the complex mechanical ventilator, oxygen is a medication that requires proper dosage (F_{IO_2}) and repeated blood level determinations (arterial P_{O_2}). P_{aO_2} over 100 mm Hg is currently considered hyperoxemic; under 50 mm Hg it is hypoxemic. For sick babies who require supplemental oxygen, there is no P_{aO_2} that can be predictably correlated with any particular F_{IO_2}. In most neonatal intensive care units, current practice maintains P_{aO_2} between 50 and 70 mm Hg; some regulate at 60 to 80 mm Hg, others prefer as low as 40 to 60 mm Hg in small premature babies. These levels are achievable at widely varying inspired oxygen concentrations. An infant who is profoundly ill from hyaline membrane disease may require an F_{IO_2} of 1.00 (100% oxygen) to maintain a P_{aO_2} of 50 mm Hg. During recovery 5 days later, the same F_{IO_2} may produce a toxic P_{aO_2} of over 200 mm Hg. Similar radical changes in F_{IO_2} requirements can occur within an hour or less.

The dose of oxygen is always expressed as it's fraction of inspired air (F_{IO_2}). The day has long since passed when oxygen can properly be ordered in liters per minute. This designation merely expresses flow rate of the gas, not its concentration in inspired air. Orders for oxygen administration given as liters per minute betray a sad lack of information about adequate therapy.

The dose of oxygen must be monitored continuously. Use of any of several varieties of oxygen analyzers is mandatory for this purpose. At present we prefer an analyzer that is placed in line so that the air mixture is monitored continuously. The F_{IO_2} should be determined every hour. We provide prescribed oxygen concentrations through a blender that regulates simultaneous inflow of air and oxygen by adjusting an indicator to the desired level.

The arterial blood level of oxygen should be determined at least every 4 hours for sick babies, often at much shorter intervals (15 minutes) for the most acutely ill infants, and at least every 6 hours for babies who are not acutely ill. These scheduled assessments are particularly necessary for premature infants.

SITES OF BLOOD SAMPLING. For blood gas determinations, we use arterial blood samples exclusively. They are drawn from an umbilical artery catheter, or from the radial, brachial, or temporal arteries by needle puncture. In our laboratory at least two thirds of over 30,000 annual blood gas/pH determinations are drawn by puncture of those peripheral arteries. Determinations are made around the clock every day of the week.

Although the great majority of neonatal units use arterial blood for these assessments, a few facilities consider capillary blood samples to be adequate. Blood is collected by heel prick from a foot that has been warmed for 5 to 10 minutes. Others prick the lateral aspect of a finger, over one of the digital arteries. Capillary blood values of 35 to 55 mm Hg are said to correspond to arterial tensions of 40 to 65 mm Hg. If capillary P_{O_2} is above 65 mm Hg, the arterial level may exceed 150 mm Hg. Most centers do not rely on capillary samples for monitoring P_{O_2}.

Collection of arterial samples through an umbilical artery catheter is widely practiced. Most centers insert the catheter tip to a level between the third and fourth lumbar vertebrae, which is just above the aortic bifurcation and below the origins of the renal arteries. In sick infants who have a right-to-left shunt through the ductus arteriosus, blood taken from the descending aorta is a mixture of oxygenated blood from the left ventricle and deoxygenated blood from the right ventricle that has passed through the ductal shunt. It is a postductal specimen because it came from the descending aorta below (distal to) the ductus opening. If the ductal shunt is substantial, postductal arterial P_{O_2} is at least 10 mm Hg lower than preductal blood, sometimes lower by more than 30 mm Hg. Arterial blood collected from the right arm and from the temporal artery is preductal. The right subclavian artery (to the right arm) and the carotid arteries (to the head) branch from the proximal portion of the aortic arch. Aortic blood from the left ventricle passes these branches before it reaches the distal end of the arch where the ductus arteriosus connects to the aorta. It is thus unmixed with ductal blood. If a right-to-left shunt is present, ductus arteriosus blood empties into the aorta. This blood is from the right ventricle. It is deoxygenated (venous) blood that has not perfused the lungs. Its presence in postductal aortic blood may lower the P_{O_2} substantially. Arterial P_{O_2} levels in samples from the right radial and brachial arteries, and from either of the temporal arteries, are not mixed with postductal blood. These P_{O_2} levels are thus the same as in blood that perfuses the brain and the eyes. In severe hyaline membrane disease, with a right-to-left ductal shunt, the preductal P_{O_2} is considerably higher than the postductal one. Similarly, if an infant is hypotensive, the relatively higher pressure in the pulmonary circuit produces a significant shunt across the ductus. Postductal P_{O_2} in blood from the umbilical artery is therefore substantially lower than in blood from the right radial artery, and in many instances does not reflect oxygen tension of blood that perfuses the eyes. The P_{aO_2} in samples from the left radial artery may be similar either to the right radial artery or to postductal aortic samples, since the left subclavian artery (to the left arm) may originate from the aorta at the level of the ductus, slightly above it or slightly below. In the vast majority of infants, P_{aO_2} in the left arm is similar to that in postductal blood taken from an umbilical artery catheter.

MONITORING WITH TRANSCUTANEOUS OXYGEN TENSION MEASUREMENT ($\text{tc}P_{O_2}$). The necessity for frequent arterial blood gas samples ultimately requires repeated arterial punctures, usually taxing the ingenuity of staff and the well-being of babies. Furthermore, the resultant values are applicable to conditions that existed at the moment of sampling. We obviously have no idea what the oxygen tension is when blood is not taken. Neonatologists have long felt the need for a *noninvasive* technique by which blood gases can be monitored *continuously*. Several attempts to provide such devices have been concerned with P_{O_2} electrodes implanted at the tip of an indwelling umbilical artery catheter. Their limitations have restricted widespread use.

A device has been developed to measure oxygen tension by securing an electrode to the skin. The transcutaneous oxygen sensor can produce P_{O_2} values from the warmed skin ($\text{tc}P_{O_2}$) that are generally well correlated with arterial P_{O_2}. Continuous readout of oxygen tensions is possible. In addition, the device indicates the state of skin perfusion.

In healthy neonates a marked variation in $\text{tc}P_{O_2}$, mostly influenced by respiratory rate, is noted. An apneic episode causes a drop in $\text{tc}P_{O_2}$ in seconds, and if apnea is sustained, the rate of fall is constant at 30 mm Hg/min.

Crying infants have a marked drop in $\text{tc}P_{O_2}$, usually between 20 and 50 mm Hg. When crying ceases, the $\text{tc}P_{O_2}$ curve rises to normal. The difficulty in obtaining valid P_{aO_2} in crying infants by traditional methods of arterial blood sampling is well known.

Still in the laboratory stage of development is a transcutaneous sensor for $\text{tc}P_{CO_2}$ determination. The development of this technique for blood gas assessment is a major step toward improving total care of sick neonates.

WARMTH AND HUMIDITY OF OXYGEN. Oxygen must be warm and humid, regardless of the mechanism that is used to deliver it. This requires equipment that permits regulation of heat in a water reservoir through which oxygen flows before entering the respiratory tract. The infant pays dearly when cold, dry oxygen is thoughtlessly administered.

In an oxygen hood, ambient temperatures about the head and body should be similar. This cannot be accomplished unless oxygen is warmed. Prolonged oxygen therapy by mask is contraindicated, not only because F_{IO_2} cannot be regulated, but also because cold stress is inflicted on the face. Even if the oxygen is warm, the velocity of flow from the mask results in increased heat loss by convection (Chapter 4). The need for warmth and humidity is often overlooked when oxygen is administered by means of hood or mask. Most caretakers are not familiar with the exquisite thermal sensitivity of nerve endings in the skin of the face and forehead, believing that requirements for thermal environment are met by warming the rest of the body. *If face and forehead are chilled, the infant reacts as though totally cold stressed even when the rest of the body is kept warm.*

In the application of continuous positive airway pressure (CPAP) by either the nasal or endotracheal route, warmth and humidity are indispensable because oxygen is introduced directly over mucosal surfaces. Dry gas increases evaporative fluid loss from the extensive mucosal surfaces, thus augmenting evaporative heat loss. Additionally, mucosal integrity is threatened by the sustained drying effect of unhumidified oxygen. Secretory material, usually copious in small infants, becomes inspissated when humidity is lacking. Resultant obstruction of the respiratory passages, particularly the smaller ones, causes atelectasis.

HYPOXIA: DETECTION, PREVENTION, AND PENALTIES. Generally, a P_{aO_2} less than 50 mm Hg is considered hypoxemic. A number of infants may tolerate somewhat lower levels for some time, but it is unsafe to regularly maintain arterial tensions at these lower levels. The acute effects of hypoxemia must be understood; they are often difficult to identify with certainty from clinical manifestations. The clinical recognition of hypoxemia on the basis of *cyanosis* is far from a simple matter. Several factors influence the recognition of cyanosis, including color and thickness of skin, number of capillaries, hemoglobin level, and serum bilirubin. Add to these variables the type and intensity of light, as well as the differences in perception among observers, and one can readily appreciate the complexity of this clinical situation. In the neonate, acrocyanosis (including circumoral involvement) that is present 24 to 48 hours after birth is of no significance insofar as arterial oxygen tensions are concerned. Cyanosis is not uniformly discernible on all areas of the body, even when oxygen saturations in blood are as low as 70%. Cyanosis of the lips (and perhaps the tongue) is most reliably correlated with hypoxic P_{aO_2} levels; yet one in ten infants whose lips are not cyanotic may actually be hypoxic. Conversely, 28% of infants whose lips are blue are not hypoxic. They have no need for supplemental oxygen, and they will be needlessly exposed to the risk of pulmonary toxicity and retrolental fibroplasia if it is given. Hands, nailbeds, and circumoral areas are even less reliable. They frequently appear to be cyanotic in spite of normal oxygen saturations. The trunk and ears yield a high percentage of false-negative observations; they often appear pink in babies who are actually hypoxemic. *The clinical diagnosis of hypoxia is therefore unreliable. Cyanosis may be absent in hypoxic babies, and it may be present in those who are well oxygenated. Its presence over different parts of the body is variable, and there is little consistency among observers in the ability to recognize it.*

At this point in the discussion, it would be advisable to review the oxygen-hemoglobin dissociation curves (Fig. 8-6). Cyanosis is not visible until saturations fall between 75% and 85%. At these saturations the neonate's P_{aO_2} is between 32 and 42 mm Hg. Cyanosis in the older child and adult is identifiable at higher P_{aO_2} levels. The clinical message of the dissociation curve is clear. The pink baby in respiratory distress may be hypoxemic; when cyanosis finally appears, catastrophe may be at hand. The P_{aO_2} may already be as low as 32 mm Hg. *The ill effects of hypoxemia had transpired while the baby was pink.* The acute responses to hypoxia began as the P_{aO_2} fell below 50 mm Hg.

Diminished tissue oxygenation causes *metabolic acidosis* due to overproduction of lactic acid during anaerobic glycolysis. Peripheral vasoconstriction due to acidosis and hypoxemia may cause pallor and a transient rise in blood pressure.

Anaerobic glycolysis also depletes glycogen stores rapidly because more glycogen is required for glucose production. *Hypoglycemia* is therefore another penalty of hypoxia.

The most immediate response to a drop in oxygen tension is *constriction of pulmonary arterioles,* which is greatly accentuated if metabolic acidosis is also present. Hypoxemia worsens because ventilation is impaired by the resultant pulmonary hypoperfusion. Furthermore, surfactant production may diminish as a consequence of alveolar ischemia. One can now see that the fetal cardiopulmonary state is returning: pulmonary artery blood pressure rises, and a shunt is reestablished from the right to the atrium through the foramen ovale. In the extreme, as in sudden asphyxia from aspiration of a feeding, a right-to-left shunt also appears across the ductus arteriosus.

The thermogenic response to cold stress is reduced or eliminated at P_{aO_2} levels of 30 to

40 mm Hg. Thus *hypothermia* may develop while the baby is pink. Babies who are marginally hypoxic may become extremely restless. They cry continuously, and their aimless body movements are ceaseless.

The babies who are most often at risk without blood gas determinations are premature, dyspneic, but pink for several hours after birth, though their hyaline membrane disease is progressive. Alveoli collapse continually. They may receive unmeasured oxygen. They remain hypoxic, but there is no clinical indication of hypoxia. Pulmonary vasoconstriction progresses relentlessly. In this pink baby the meager supply of surfactant that was present at birth is dissipated quickly, and more alveoli collapse as time passes. At 8, 12, or perhaps 18 hours they are suddenly apneic, cyanotic, and hypotensive. Therapy should have been instituted while they were pink.

Brain damage due to hypoxia may be evident either while the baby is still in the nursery, or not until several months later. There is no $P_{a_{O_2}}$ level that can be regularly correlated with central nervous system damage. Acute and protracted episodes of hypoxia are known to injure brain tissue, but the duration of episodes, the extent to which arterial oxygen tension must decline, and the influence of other variables, such as acidosis and hypoglycemia, have not been defined precisely. There is agreement, however, that these factors produce signs of central nervous system dysfunction immediately after the hypoxic episode or chronically thereafter.

REDUCING THE $F_{I_{O_2}}$. In the presence of generalized cyanosis, it is advisable to abruptly increase the concentration of inspired oxygen. This is generally understood and widely practiced. However, it is not as generally appreciated that a reduced need for oxygen requires gradual diminution of ambient concentrations. Except for circumstances in which therapy is maintained for less than a few hours, an abrupt change to considerably lower concentrations is contraindicated. "Turning off the oxygen" after administering it in high dosage for some time is a dangerous practice. The longer the duration of therapy, the greater the hazard of abrupt discontinuation; sudden cyanosis and respiratory collapse may follow. This serious reaction is a result of sudden pulmonary vasoconstriction. Called "flip-flop," it is a retrogression that is sometimes more severe than the original disorder. It may persist for several hours or days, or it may be fulminant, leading to death. Usually a decrease of 5 or 10 percentage points every 3 to 4 hours is well tolerated, but variations should be expected. Infants who have received oxygen for over a week because of intrinsic lung disease may not adjust to such a regimen. They may require decrements as small as 3% to 5% every few hours, or even every 24 hours. On the other hand, infants with relatively normal lungs who have received oxygen for less than a few hours, and have recovered from perinatal asphyxia, may require—and will tolerate—a rapid decrease to avert hyperoxia.

HYPEROXIA: OXYGEN TOXICITY. The detection of oxygen overdosage is as sensitive as the identification of oxygen deprivation. Here the concern is with the etiologic relationship between retrolental fibroplasia and high arterial oxygen tensions. The absolute upper limit of safety and the length of time oxygen therapy is tolerated have not been documented. At present the concensus is that an arterial P_{O_2} in excess of 100 mm Hg increases the likelihood of eye injury and is of no value in the treatment of hypoxemia. There are no clinical signs to indicate when this limit has been surpassed. *During oxygen therapy the infant's future vision is therefore dependent on a careful monitoring regimen that includes frequent measurement of $F_{I_{O_2}}$ and arterial oxygen tensions.* The previously accepted criterion of 40% as the safe upper limit of $F_{I_{O_2}}$ is no longer acceptable. An infant with hyaline membrane disease, or any form of cardiorespiratory distress, may not survive in an environmental oxygen concentration of 40%. Yet such levels may cause dangerously high oxygen tensions in small premature infants whose respiratory difficulties are not so severe. To date, the principal toxic effects of oxygen in the neonate have been noted in the eyes and in the lungs.

Retrolental fibroplasia (RLF, retinopathy of prematurity) is a disease of the eyes related to hyperoxemia in premature infants. After its first description in 1942, and in the decade that followed, an intensive worldwide search for its cause took place. Approximately three dozen etiologic possibilities were investigated. The ophthalmologic and pediatric literatures were inundated with hopeful hypotheses and all sorts of apparent documentations, but not until 1951 was valid evidence presented for the destructive effects of oxygen. It emanated from Australia, and confirmation from England and the United States soon followed. Thus in the short course of 10 years, a disease was unearthed, its cause was defined, and a regimen for its prevention was established. Retrolental fibroplasia occurs primarily in premature infants; the shorter the gestational age, the greater the vulnerability. In these infants, therapeutic hyperoxygenation causes changes in the retinal vasculature that may ultimately destroy the normal architecture of the eye and result in total blindness. There is no doubt that the disease is caused by inordinately high levels of oxygen in retinal capillaries of premature infants. It also has been documented in full-term infants who received oxygen therapy and in premature infants who did not, but these instances are exceptional. Realization of the role oxygen overdosage was soon followed by rigid restriction of therapeutic oxygen to ambient concentrations below 40%, and as a result the disease virtually disappeared. However, in 1958 attention was called to an increased mortality rate in infants with hyaline membrane disease, and this increased rate was shown to be a function of the restrictive policies that came to govern oxygen administration. At just that time, the "do not disturb" attitude toward sick neonates had begun to yield to more aggressive approaches, and in this context the administration of oxygen was liberalized. It also became apparent that the relationship of arterial P_{O_2} to ambient oxygen concentrations was not fixed, but

that it was influenced by the infant's pulmonary function. A concentration of 40% was shown to be inadequate for many severely distressed babies. Today, mortality from hyaline membrane disease has indeed diminished, but at the cost of a resurgence of retrolental fibroplasia.

The disease begins during oxygen therapy. Oxygen does not diffuse through the cornea or sclera. RLF is therefore not directly related to a high $F_{I_{O_2}}$, as in bronchopulmonary dysplasia (see later), but rather it is a function of high $P_{a_{O_2}}$ levels. Retinal arterial constriction appears, and it persists during the therapeutic period as long as hyperoxemia is present. Within 1 or 2 months after treatment is terminated, the vessels dilate and proliferate; retinal edema then appears. At any time up to this stage, the process may come to a halt, with no resultant visual disturbance, or perhaps only a slight to moderate one. If extensive retinal detachment occurs, a scarring phase ensues within 1 or 2 months, and ultimately leads to blindness. This occurs in approximately 25% of infants with retinal vasospasm during early oxygen therapy. Thus, during the period of oxygen therapy, the only perceptible retinal change is vasoconstriction. Ideally, then, an ophthalmologist should examine the fundi periodically, and vigorous efforts should be exerted to reduce the dose of oxygen to a minimum if vasospasm is noted. Although the best practice is to maintain arterial P_{O_2} between 50 and 70 mm Hg, there is nevertheless no documented level of toxicity, nor are there data to indicate the length of time after which high levels become dangerous.

BRONCHOPULMONARY DYSPLASIA (BPD). When administered in high concentrations, oxygen is also injurious to the lungs. Lung damage is not related to blood oxygen tension but is a direct result of a high $F_{I_{O_2}}$, and perhaps other factors as well. Histologic damage is characterized by thickening and eventual necrosis of alveolar walls, basement membranes, and bronchiolar epithelial lining layers. Atelectasis and fibrosis are also present. Presumably these changes impair diffu-

Fig. 8-7. Radiologic appearance of bronchopulmonary dysplasia in advanced stage. White strands are seen throughout both lung fields, representing fibrosis. Lungs are overexpanded in the extreme; diaphragms are at a very low level, and intercostal spaces bulge.

sion of oxygen from alveolar lumens to capillaries. Respiratory dysfunction is thus prolonged, and the resultant abnormal radiologic appearance of the lungs may not resolve for several months (Fig. 8-7). The point of danger in the duration of therapy is not definitely known. The first report of bronchopulmonary dysplasia in neonates (1967) incriminated an F_{IO_2} over 0.80 for more than 150 hours. Soon thereafter, an F_{IO_2} of over 0.60 was noted to cause damage. Currently it appears that oxygen concentrations over 40% for more than 3 days are injurious. There is some evidence that bronchopulmonary dysplasia is not due to oxygen toxicity alone. It is unusual, for instance, to observe lung damage when a negative pressure ventilator is used without endotracheal intubation, even over prolonged time periods. It is equally unusual to find BPD in babies who have been managed only with CPAP. The importance of high concentrations of inspired oxygen in the production of this disorder should not be minimized, however, even if other factors are suspected. The use

of end-expiratory positive pressure, which permits lower levels of inspired oxygen, has been noted to diminish the incidence of BPD by 50%. A high F_{IO_2} is therefore critical, at least with use of positive pressure by means of an endotracheal tube. The three factors that may be implicated, then, are high F_{IO_2}, positive-pressure ventilation by means of an endotracheal tube, and duration of exposure to both these factors.

In summary, oxygen therapy may be lifesaving but blinding and damaging to lungs. Assiduous monitoring is required to ascertain the presence of effective arterial tensions and the absence of toxic ones. Oxygen must be administered in the smallest possible dose for the shortest possible time.

Methods of oxygen administration. The route of oxygen administration is determined by the infant's needs. If he breathes spontaneously, and diminished lung volume (atelectasis) is not a prominent problem, oxygen may simply be given in a head hood. If atelectasis is a major problem, as in hyaline membrane disease, but the baby can breathe spontaneously nevertheless, oxygen is given through a system that maintains some degree of positive pressure throughout the respiratory cycle. CPAP is an example of such a system. If the baby is unable to maintain respiration on his own, if apnea recurs frequently, or if adequate ventilation is not possible while the infant is breathing independently, oxygen must be administered by means of a mechanical ventilator.

Incubator and head hood. Concentrations of oxygen in an incubator cannot generally be raised beyond 60% to 70%. An imperfectly fitting plastic lid may allow significant escape of oxygen to further limit ambient concentrations. Opening portholes to gain access to the baby also depletes ambient oxygen concentration rapidly.

If environmental oxygen concentration must exceed 40% to 50% at a fairly constant level, a plastic head hood should be used. When a hood is used in an incubator, the portholes may be opened without affecting oxygen concentration in the hood. The head

Fig. 8-8. Effect of CPAP on radiologic appearance of lungs. **A,** Before CPAP. Infant had severe hyaline membrane disease. Lungs are dense, with air bronchograms visible. Right cardiac border is obscured. **B,** Twenty minutes after CPAP application. Lungs are not as dense, more air is retained, and the right cardiac border is clearly visible. With better aeration, air bronchograms are not discernible. **C,** One hour after CPAP was applied. Lungs appear normally aerated. Note bulging intercostal spaces indicating some overdistention resulting from CPAP. Cleared x-ray film on CPAP does not indicate disappearance of disease.

box is essential when infants are treated on an open table supplied with radiant heat from an overhead source. Oxygen delivered to a hood must usually be warmed to 31° to 34° C and must always be humidified. A constant blast of cold gas to the infant's face produces the responses to cold stress, even though the remainder of the body is in a thermoneutral environment, since thermal sensors of the face are more responsive than the skin sensors in any other part of the body.

Continuous positive airway pressure (CPAP). The application of CPAP has considerably diminished the morbidity and mortality of hyaline membrane disease. Normally, intrathoracic pressure at end-expiration is equal to atmospheric pressure. When alveolar stability is established, the lung remains expanded at end-expiration. In hyaline membrane disease, alveolar collapse is the rule (Figs. 8-3 and 8-4). CPAP provides varying degrees of alveolar stability (functional residual capacity) by maintaining positive pressure at end-expiration, thus keeping alveoli expanded when they would otherwise collapse; CPAP forces the alveoli to retain air. The results are often dramatic (Fig. 8-8). Increased ventilatory capacity is provided by virtue of the newly expanded alveoli. Respirations, if disorganized beforehand, become regular within several minutes thereafter. They increase in rate and depth, and the result is a rapid elevation of P_{aO_2}. Often there is also diminution of P_{aCO_2}, but at a slower rate. Recurrent apnea usually disappears. Normal levels of P_{aO_2} are attainable at a lower F_{IO_2}. Results are not as beneficial if hypoperfusion of the lung remains severe in spite of increased alveolar stability. Ventilating alveoli cannot be functional without adequate blood supply to take up oxygen and to deliver carbon dioxide for elimination.

CPAP is effective for any disorder that involves diminished lung compliance, including hyaline membrane disease, pulmonary edema from any cause, pulmonary hemorrhage, and postoperative thoracotomy. CPAP, as well as any other form of positive end-expiratory pressure, is dangerous if lung compliance is normal. Normally compliant lungs permit transmission of positive pressure to blood vessels in the lung itself and to the large veins that empty into the heart (inferior and superior venae cavae). In these circumstances the transmitted pressure diminishes pulmonary blood supply and impairs venous return to the heart. In the extreme, the heart is smaller on x-ray films. Cardiac output diminishes, and with less blood in the systemic circulation, there is a measurable fall in systemic blood pressure. On the other hand, when lung compliance is poor ("stiff lungs"), as in hyaline membrane disease or pulmonary edema, positive end-expiratory pressure is contained; it is not significantly transmissible to other intrathoracic structures.

Continuous positive airway pressure is also referred to as *continuous distending pressure*. It has been applied by means of a number of devices, all of which provide positive pressure at end-expiration and thus increased lung volume. CPAP was first administered through an endotracheal tube. Several variations have since been introduced; all of them apply positive pressure directly into the respiratory tract. Nasal CPAP is now widely utilized instead of the endotracheal tube. By applying a tightly fitted adapter to the external nares, and thus avoiding the necessity of tracheal intubation, nasal CPAP exploits the fact that the neonate is an obligate nose breather. Pressures and oxygen mixtures are administered in the same manner as by the endotracheal route. A positive-pressure hood and also a face mask for transmission of pressure through the nose have been used to avoid the endotracheal tube.

Positive end-expiratory pressure can also be achieved by maintaining continuous negative pressure (CNP) to the thorax. The devices that mediate this approach are designed to envelop the chest or the entire body below the neck. Sustained negative pressure expands the thorax and prevents its usual collapse at end-expiration. The net effect of this system is to maintain a continuous "pull" on the alveoli, preventing their collapse at end-expiration. This is in contrast to the methods that apply positive pressure directly into the respiratory tract and thus maintain alveolar distention by a constant "push." Continuous negative pressure eliminates the need for an endotracheal tube. The infant's head must be in an oxygen hood at an atmospheric pressure that is constantly higher than intrathoracic pressure. F_{IO_2} is regulated in the hood.

All methods of applying distending pressure have their undesirable side effects. They all produce pneumothorax, but with considerably less frequency than mechanical ventilation. There is some evidence that the incidence of pneumothorax due to CNP for hyaline membrane disease is no higher than that caused by the disease itself. The incidence of pneumothorax with endotracheal

Fig. 8-9. Displacement of endotracheal tube into right main bronchus causes collapse of left lung. In this case, bronchus to right upper lobe is also occluded, causing atelectasis there. Note position of tube deep into right main bronchus.

CPAP is 5% to 10%; with nasal CPAP it is somewhat lower.

Other noteworthy side effects are of an operational nature. The endotracheal tube is obviously irritating to the trachea. It virtually eliminates ciliary activity, and it is a source of respiratory tract infection. It frequently becomes displaced downward into the right main bronchus, causing atelectasis of the left lung (Fig. 8-9). Tube position must be monitored assiduously. The danger of laryngeal (subglottic) stenosis is small but real. These disadvantages are inherent in the use of endotracheal tubes, regardless of the type of respiratory support they mediate. Nasal CPAP has caused infections of the nose and disfigurement of the external nares, but these complications are rare. CNP also has disadvantages. Use of a positive pressure hood with a tight-fitting neck seal has caused transient unilateral Erb's palsy. The CNP body chamber does not permit free access to the infant without interrupting therapy, and the tight fit required around the infant's neck causes abrasion and troublesome cellulitis.

We have been impressed with the discomfort that nasal CPAP causes in a number of infants. The struggle that ensues may predispose them to pneumothorax. Prescribed pressures are sometimes difficult to stabilize. Sedation using chloral hydrate (50 mg/kg of body weight) is usually successful. Nasal CPAP is not usually effective if pressures higher than 10 cm H_2O are required. The infant's open mouth is a natural blowoff valve at this pressure.

At the onset of therapy with CPAP, nasal or endotracheal, we administer the same F_{IO_2} that failed to oxygenate the baby in a head hood (usually 0.60 to 1.00), with a distending pressure of 6 or 8 cm H_2O. In the extreme, pressures are increased to 14 cm H_2O (using tracheal intubation) in an F_{IO_2} of 1.00. When the P_{aO_2} is 70 or 80 mm Hg, the pressure is lowered to 10 cm H_2O in decrements of 1.0 cm every hour. F_{IO_2} is then diminished by 10 percentage points periodically, depending on the height of the P_{aO_2}. At an F_{IO_2} of 0.40, pressure is then gradually decreased. There can be no rigid procedures to raise or lower oxygen or pressure. Decisions must be based on arterial blood gas results.

What are the criteria for the initiation of CPAP? They vary from one center to another, virtually all of them using a designated P_{aO_2} at a given F_{IO_2}. Generally, if the P_{aO_2} is below 50 mm Hg in an F_{IO_2} of 0.70 or 0.60, CPAP is considered necessary. Recurrent apnea is another indication, regardless of the oxygen tension achieved at a prescribed F_{IO_2}. Apnea often disappears or is considerably diminished after the onset of CPAP therapy.

The nursing skill and close observation required for CPAP are no less demanding than for mechanical ventilation. The nursery that cannot maintain mechanical ventilation, cannot administer CPAP either.

Mechanically assisted ventilation; the use

of respirators. In general, the infants who require prolonged ventilatory assistance are severely depressed after perinatal asphyxia. It is indicated in babies with hyaline membrane disease who do not have sufficient vigor to breathe independently or who are repeatedly apneic for prolonged periods and do not respond to CPAP or CNP. These babies generally accumulate CO_2, with resultant severe respiratory acidosis. Administration of sodium bicarbonate is contraindicated in severe respiratory acidosis in which P_{CO_2} exceeds 60 mm Hg. Bicarbonate generates CO_2, which such babies cannot blow off. The result of sodium bicarbonate therapy is a heightened CO_2 and sometimes a worsened respiratory acidosis. Mechanical ventilation is the only effective treatment for hypercarbia. Infants whose P_{CO_2} is over 70 mm Hg are usually in need of mechanical ventilation.

Respirator therapy is a formidable undertaking that should not be attempted unless proper facilities, equipment, and trained personnel are on hand. The technical problems are numerous; they increase as the baby's size decreases, but they are not insurmountable. Scrupulous attention to detail is mandatory, and the major responsibility for these particulars belongs to the neonatal nurse. The endotracheal tube must be maintained in proper position. Once in place, it should not be allowed to slip into the trachea even for a distance of less than 1 cm, since it may then enter the right main-stem bronchus and occlude the left one in bypassing it (Fig. 8-9). The respirator must be observed repeatedly for proper settings. Respiratory difficulties in an infant with hyaline membrane disease are dynamic. Lung compliance may worsen rapidly or improve gradually, requiring adjustments in pressure or volume settings. Bronchial toilet and correct humidification of delivered oxygen must be maintained. Monitoring of blood gases and pH is essential at frequent intervals—so frequent in fact, that small, simple blood transfusions may be required periodically to replace the sampled blood.

Several types of apparatus are available. Positive-pressure respirators are used extensively. One type controls the volume of administered gas by limiting the inspiratory pressure created in the respiratory tract during its delivery; another type limits the volume of gas delivered and can be pressure restricted as well. It can provide a calculated volume of tidal air while ensuring that preset pressure limits are not exceeded.

Negative pressure respirators have been used successfully at some centers. However, they are apparently unsatisfactory for the most severely affected and the smallest infants. This type of respirator encloses the body from the neck down and moves gas in and out of the lungs by intermittently creating negative pressure around the trunk. Its great advantage is that it does not require endotracheal intubation. The oxygen content of inspired gas is determined by controlling its ambient concentration in the head chamber. Bronchopulmonary dysplasia is rare in babies treated with a negative-pressure ventilator.

Acid-base balance; fluid therapy. Metabolic acidosis inevitably develops in infants who are moderately or severely ill from hyaline membrane disease. Insofar as pulmonary function is concerned, the most direct deleterious effect of acidosis is constriction of pulmonary arterioles. Lung perfusion is thus diminished, and the right-to-left shunt increases. Serial measurements of pH and P_{CO_2} provide a basis for infusion of intravenous sodium bicarbonate. Base deficits less than 6 mEq/L do not generally require treatment. The dose of alkali is calculated and administered as described in Chapter 7.

Intravenous fluid is administered from the time of admission. It is given through the umbilical artery catheter if insertion was essential for blood gas monitoring. Umbilical artery catheters should not be used for the primary purpose of fluid administration. If the artery catheter has not been inserted, we use peripheral veins, frequently by placing an intravenous catheter. The umbilical vein is used only in an emergency for short time intervals. Infection, thrombosis, and cirrhosis later in life are reported from protracted fluid therapy through the umbilical vein.

We begin fluid therapy with 10% dextrose in water at a dose of 65 to 70 ml/kg of body weight per 24 hours. By the second day, a dose of at least 100 ml/kg is required. In small babies, particularly those on open beds heated by infrared lamps, insensible fluid loss is considerable. They may require 250 ml/24 hr or more. Hypotonic electrolyte solution is given on the second day. By the third day, if gastrointestinal feeding is not feasible, an amino acid–glucose–electrolyte solution is begun (peripheral alimentation).

Constant alertness to prevent excessive water loss is indispensable. The smaller the baby, the more precarious is water balance. The two principal routes of excessive losses are the skin (evaporative) and the kidneys (osmotic diuresis). The thin skin and relatively tremendous body surface of small infants pose as much hazard for water loss as for thermal dissipation. Administration of 10% dextrose solution sometimes causes osmotic diuresis when a substantial amount of glucose is excreted through the kidneys. We perform Clinitest determinations frequently. If the results are consistently 3+ or 4+, we reduce the concentration of intravenous dextrose solution. Recognition of impending dehydration is not difficult; accurate weighing, at least every 8 hours, is the keystone of caution. Losses greater than 10% of body weight during the first 3 days or 5% in any single day are excessive. Elevation of hematocrit and total protein are late signs of dehydration; these parameters are not acceptable as the only ongoing assessments of hydration. Serum sodium concentration plus simultaneous serum and urine osmolality are reliable laboratory parameters. Serum sodium in excess of 145 mEq/L indicates inadequate water therapy.

Provision of proper thermal environment. The deleterious effects of hypothermia are discussed in Chapter 4. Cold stress increases the need for oxygen in a baby who is already having difficulty with its intake. Furthermore, the increased metabolic rate that occurs in response to cold stress enhances metabolic acidosis in the presence of hypoxia by requiring overproduction of lactic acid. In aggravating hypoxia and enhancing acidosis, and by release of norepinephrine, cold stress causes increased pulmonary vasoconstriction, which probably also impairs the production and activity of surfactant. It is therefore crucial that proper temperature of incubator air and walls is maintained.

Maintenance of blood pressure and hematocrit. Systemic blood pressure is low in many infants with hyaline membrane disease. Because hypoxemia and acidemia have an early tendency to increase blood pressure, the hypotensive state is sometimes not detectable until they are corrected. Systemic hypotension increases right-to-left shunt through the ductus arteriosus, especially in the presence of inordinately high pulmonary artery pressure. Infants who are hypotensive cannot be oxygenated optimally. The diminished tissue perfusion and hypoxemia associated with shock cause oxygen deprivation of tissues. As a consequence, anaerobic glycolysis occurs, and lactic acid production causes severe metabolic acidosis. Ventilatory support is thus ineffective in optimal oxygenation if shock exists. Blood samples persistently demonstrate a low P_{aO_2} and a high base deficit. Sodium bicarbonate administration has little effect on the metabolic acidosis that accompanies shock.

Hypovolemia is often difficult to identify in the neonate. When blood pressure is low, the issue is straightforward. However, peripheral blood pressure does not decline until circulating blood volume is diminished by 25% to 40% of normal. Thus, many infants are hypovolemic despite normal peripheral blood pressure readings. In these circumstances, hypovolemia may be suggested by a rapid heart rate (over 160 beats/min).

We monitor blood pressure in the brachial or posterior tibial arteries with a Doppler ultrasound apparatus. Normal blood pressure varies with birth weight. The lower limit of normal mean blood pressure in babies whose birth weight is between 1001 and 2000 grams is 30 mm Hg; between 2000 and 3000 grams, it is 35 mm Hg; and between 3000 and 4000 grams, 43 mm Hg. In low birth weight babies we have found that these differences are not sufficiently large to be significant clinically. We therefore attempt to maintain *systolic* blood pressure at approximately 50 mm Hg. In babies weighing over 2500 grams, 60 mm Hg is our lowest acceptable level.

Having identified hypovolemia by clear-cut blood pressure readings, or surmised that it is present because of tachycardia even though blood pressure readings are normal, we immediately administer plasma as a volume expander. Packed red blood cells are ordered from the blood bank at the same time. Plasma is given rapidly in a dose of 10 ml/kg of body weight. Packed red blood cells are given in the same dose as soon as they are delivered to the nursery. If blood pressure remains low after the first dose of plasma, another dose is administered. Blood pressure is monitored at least every hour in the sickest babies.

Hematocrit must also be followed periodically. Most often, it is normal for the first 1 to 3 hours postnatally, even if hypovolemia is present. It falls, however, as the baby attempts to compensate for diminished blood volume by the transfer of tissue fluid into the vascular compartment; hemodilution ensues. We attempt to maintain the hematocrit at 45 to 50 vol %. It is determined at least twice daily during acute illness, and more often if indicated.

Blood sampling for laboratory data is an important and frequent cause of lower hematocrit readings. A record of the amount withdrawn should be kept at the incubator. When 10% of calculated blood volume (85 ml/kg) is withdrawn, a transfusion of packed cells is given.

Umbilical vessel catheterization

Umbilical artery. The risks of umbilical arterial catheterization are well known and very real. In spite of them, most neonatologists do not hesitate to employ these catheters *if the benefits derived significantly outweigh the risks entailed.*

The placement of arterial catheters is a surgical procedure that requires strict aseptic technique. Proper maintenance of the catheter, once it is in place, depends on the skills and knowledge of the nurse.

The safest location for the catheter tip in the aorta is below the origins of the renal arteries. If the tip is between the third and fourth lumbar vertebrae by x-ray films, it is situated below the renal arteries and above the aortic bifurcation. The catheter should have an end hole, rather than side holes, since the dead space at the tip of the latter type of catheter promotes thrombus formation. Furthermore, the catheter should be radiopaque so that its position can be ascertained by x-ray examination immediately after placement. If it is located above the desired level, it can be withdrawn an appropriate distance. If the tip is too low, *the catheter should not be inserted farther after the sterile insertion procedure has been terminated.*

Maintenance requires careful, constant attention to avert infection, to prevent hemorrhage because of loose fittings or accidental withdrawal, and to identify thromboembolic phenomena.

INFECTION. The incidence of infection varies from one report to another. The clinical significance of positive cultures from withdrawn catheter tips is questionable; yet a number of available reports cite such data. There is sound basis for applying antibacterial ointment at least once daily to the umbilical stump and to joints in the tubing system. Tubing and stopcock attached to the catheter should be changed daily. After withdrawal of blood from the stopcock, the open portal should be plugged with a sterile insert of some type. We use a syringe. The injection of medication through the stopcock should be meticulous. Care must be exercised to avoid contamination of the syringe tip that is inserted into the stopcock. Inadvertent contact of the syringe tip with contaminated objects (including fingers) prior to its insertion is a common occurrence. The incidence of infection probably increases with the length of time the catheter is left in place. The futility of prophylactic antibiotics for infants with umbilical vessel catheters has been well documented.

HEMORRHAGE. Massive fetal hemorrhage from the umbilical catheter is a real danger if fittings are loosened. Hemorrhage may also occur from the umbilical stump when the catheter is accidentally displaced from its insertion. Aortic blood pressure is high, and considerable blood loss may therefore occur rapidly. This possibility obviously makes constant attention and surveillance by the nurse imperative.

THROMBOSIS. Thromboembolic phenomena are the most frequent complications. Varying percentages (as high as 95%) are reported for the incidence of thrombi. In the vast majority of cases they have had no apparent clinical significance; their danger is not negligible, however. Thrombi that encase the catheter or are implanted onto the aortic wall are a potential source of embolization. Emboli are dislodged from these thrombi and released to the lower body, distal to the catheter tip. If they are of substantial size, they obstruct blood flow distal to the vessel they occlude. Necrosis of toes is the most frequent embolic phenomenon. The toes may become progressively cyanotic and ultimately gangrenous. If cyanosis persists for more than 15 minutes, the catheter should be withdrawn. Necrotic ulceration of the skin in the gluteal and perineal regions has been reported in a few infants.

The position of the catheter tip is critical. If the catheter is too high, thrombi may occlude the superior mesenteric artery or, more commonly, the renal arteries, causing infarction of intestines and kidneys, respectively. Opinion differs as to whether thrombi are more likely to occur as the duration of catheterization increases. Thrombosis is more likely in profoundly ill babies.

VASOSPASM. The commonest manifestation of interrupted blood flow is blanching, which may involve part of a toe, or both lower extremities in their entirety. It is attributed to arterial spasm, and it disappears promptly when the catheter is removed. There is no justification for the past practice of applying moist heat to the uninvolved extremity to relieve spasm of the opposite member.

INFUSIONS. Hypertonic solutions are probably tolerated, if they are infused at a slow rate, because the aorta is large and blood flow through it is rapid. The infused solution is therefore quickly diluted. Sodium bicarbonate should be diluted with equal parts of water or glucose solution and injected at a rate not exceeding 2 ml/min. Rapid injection of any material causes increased turbulence at the catheter tip and predisposes to thrombogenesis. Continuous infusion must be regulated by an automated pump. As a rule, we encounter backflow of aortic blood if the rate of infusion is less than 2 ml/hr.

Umbilical artery catheterization is indicated primarily for sampling in monitoring blood gases and pH. It should never be instituted for the sole purpose of fluid administration.

Umbilical vein. We use umbilical vein catheters only for exchange transfusion or for emergency administration of drugs, fluid, or volume expanders when no other route is immediately available. It is also used to monitor central venous pressure. The incidence of complications from protracted periods of catheterization is unacceptably high. Infection is more common in the vein than in the artery. Hepatic necrosis and thrombosis of the portal vein have also been reported. Portal hypertension at a later age has been attributed to portal vein thrombosis from umbilical vein catheterization during the newborn period.

Prevention of hyaline membrane disease

Hyaline membrane disease is a developmental disorder that centers about the maturation of metabolic pathways to surfactant production. Until prematurity itself can be prevented, the most promising approach seems to lie in attempts to stimulate the elaboration of surfactant in utero. Thus far, trials of corticosteroids (betamethasone) given to mothers between 24 hours and 7 days before delivery have yielded promising results. In this group of mothers, if offspring were less than 32 gestational weeks, the incidence of hyaline membrane disease was significantly reduced from that in controls. Mortality from the disease and the incidence of intraventricular hemorrhage were also reduced in babies of the same gestational age. However, even in the group that benefited from betamethasone, hyaline membrane disease occurred in 21%. In addition, betamethasone was ineffective for infants whose gestational age was 32 weeks or more. The betamethasone trial is not in itself a successful therapeutic effort, but the results are an encouraging indication that fetal medication is a promising approach to the problem.

Hydrocortisone has been administered postnatally to infants with hyaline membrane disease in a well-controlled trial. A beneficial effect was not demonstrated.

Outcomes

It was only a few years ago that we were frustrated spectators who could only observe hyaline membrane disease as it progressed along a predetermined, irrevocable course. Supportive therapy was meager. Those infants who survived had only minimal or moderate involvement. Many of them were afflicted with permanent brain damage and blindness. The most severely affected could only be offered very limited aid. They tired, with deepening cyanosis, from the struggle to expand their noncompliant ischemic lungs. Today our therapeutic regimens are still no more than supportive, but they are to some extent effective because they are directed against specific pathophysiologic mechanisms. It is the advent of newborn intensive care units and their concepts of neonatal care that must be credited with the encouraging results that have been recorded in recent years.

Neonatal survival. Compilation of the recent results from a number of centers indicates impressive improvement in the survival rate. The disease is, of course, still a serious, life-threatening process, but among infants who did not require mechanical support and who were given only constant distending pressure (CPAP), 93% survived. Of those who received only mechanical support, 47% survived. Among infants who were unsuccessfully treated with distending pressure and required subsequent mechanical support, 49% survived. Survival for all infants with the disease, regardless of type of treatment, with or without assisted respiration, was 61%.

Increased survival of mechanically ventilated babies has been well documented as more effective manipulation of ventilators has evolved. In Britain, for instance, survival of mechanically ventilated infants increased from 11% to 49% in recent years, and this figure represents the most severely affected group of infants. Intraventricular hemorrhage persists as a major problem. It is the most important cause of death among ventilated infants.

Postneonatal outcomes. Long-term developmental assessment is complicated by the possible role of intrauterine misadventure. Results vary from one institution to another, but overall, the majority of infants are developmentally normal. There are specific data to indicate that impaired development is not related to mechanical ventilation, but rather to gestational age, in the infants who were studied.

Cardiopulmonary abnormalities have persisted in a minority of infants, mostly among those in whom bronchopulmonary dysplasia was identified. Although abnormal x-ray films and pulmonary function studies occur in most infants, symptoms are nevertheless absent. Most follow-up studies report children up to 6 years of age. Full longitudinal study has yet to evolve.

The incidence of long-term pulmonary abnormalities seems to be lowest and mildest in children who were placed in negative-pressure respirators during their acute disease. These infants usually weighed over 1500 grams, and a number of them did not survive for want of more vigorous support with positive pulmonary pressure therapy. At 6 years of age, this same population developed normally, with only a few exceptions. As they approach school age however, perceptual problems are anticipated.

SYNDROMES DUE TO ASPIRATION OR FLUID RETENTION

Among the multiple causes of neonatal respiratory distress there is a spectrum of abnormalities presumably caused by aspiration of amniotic fluid and its contents into the respiratory tract or by retention of fetal lung fluid. The actual event of aspiration is believed to occur in utero or during delivery —undoubtedly a valid concept. However, in some infants the clinical signs of distress may be due to impaired evacuation of fetal lung fluid that would normally be absorbed into the pulmonary circulation during the first few breaths (p. 136). In either case, the end result is similar: the flow of air is obstructed in varying degrees by the presence of fluid, particulate matter, or both in the respiratory tract.

Most of the clinical signs that characterize these entities can be explained by two simple obstructive phenomena that may occur at any level of the respiratory tract. Fig. 8-10 illustrates both mechanisms: partial obstruction (check-valve, or ball-valve) and complete obstruction (stop-valve). The ball-valve mechanism permits entry of air past the obstruction during inspiration while obstructing its complete egress during expiration. This is possible because the calibers of bronchi and bronchioles become larger during inspiration and smaller during expiration. When bronchioles enlarge, air passes around the obstruction, but when they diminish in caliber during expiration, the lumen becomes completely occluded and air is trapped peripheral to the obstruction. By this mechanism progressive accumulation of trapped air may produce diffuse or regional overexpansion of the lungs (emphysema). On the other hand, a complete obstruction (stop-valve) does not permit entry of any air, and as a result, the portions of lung peripheral to it are collapsed. Both amniotic fluid, with its contents (principally vernix and meconium), and fetal lung fluid are each capable of producing either or both of these obstructive phenomena. The spectrum of abnormalities is thus characterized at one end by diffuse emphysema of both lungs without collapse and at the other end by collapse of large areas of the lungs. The clinical entity in which emphysema predominates has been called transient tachypnea of the newborn, respiratory distress syndrome type II, or obstructive emphysema of the newborn. The clinical condition in which occlusion and collapse are

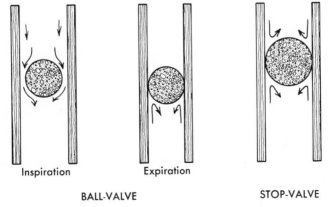

Inspiration   Expiration

BALL-VALVE   **STOP-VALVE**

Fig. 8-10. Mechanisms of airway obstruction. The ball-valve type allows entry of air peripheral to it but blocks air egress, resulting in emphysema. The stop-valve variety allows neither entry nor egress of air, resulting in atelectasis beyond the obstruction. (Modified from Caffey, J.: Pediatric x-ray diagnosis, ed. 5, Chicago, 1967, Year Book Medical Publishers, Inc.)

more prominent is known as meconium aspiration, or the massive aspiration syndrome.

Obstructive emphysema of the newborn (transient tachypnea, respiratory distress syndrome type II)

Affected infants may be born prematurely or at term. Respiratory distress begins at birth or shortly thereafter, and it is characterized by tachypnea, retractions, flaring of the nostrils, and expiratory grunt. Usually there is little or no difficulty with the onset of breathing. Rales are not heard. Cyanosis in room air may be noted, but it usually clears in relatively small increments of ambient oxygen concentration. Grunting and retractions may resolve within 24 to 48 hours, or they may persist for several days. As a rule, the duration of the clinical course is 2 to 4 days.

The roentgenogram is characterized by generalized overexpansion of the lungs, which is identifiable principally by a flattened contour of the diaphragm, in contrast to the distinctly domed configuration that is seen in normal infants. Dense streaks radiate from the hilar regions. Only occasionally are patches of density evident, representing areas of collapse.

The blood pH is moderately depressed; arterial P_{CO_2} is somewhat elevated, and the base deficit is usually 10 mEq/L or less. After initial correction with sodium bicarbonate, additional alkali therapy is seldom required, since these infants, despite respiratory dysfunction, seem to manage their alveolar gas exchange sufficiently well to maintain normal blood gas tensions. They do not require assisted ventilation of any type.

The clinical appearance of these babies suggests hyaline membrane disease, but transient tachypnea is a distinctly different abnormality with a far brighter prognosis. As a rule, affected babies recover, and there has thus far been no evidence of chronic lung disease among those who were followed to 5 or 6 months of age.

The grunting that occurs in this syndrome requires comment because it apparently serves a purpose that differs from the expiratory grunt of hyaline membrane disease. Since transient tachypnea involves diffuse emphysema (air trapping), the expiratory grunt probably represents an attempt to eject as much of the trapped alveolar air as possible. In hyaline membrane disease the grunt attempts to retain as much air as possible in an effort to maintain alveolar expansion.

Meconium aspiration (massive aspiration syndrome)

Meconium is passed into amniotic fluid in approximately 10% of all pregnancies, and it may be a sign of fetal distress. Some fetuses aspirate particles of meconium, which, during the first few breaths, may be inspired more deeply toward the alveoli, if this has not already occurred in utero. In contrast to transient tachypnea, affected infants often have difficulty establishing respiration. In a significant number, however, respiratory distress may be delayed for as long as several hours. It has been shown in puppies that delayed symptoms are associated with gradual progress of small particles toward the more peripheral airways with each breath. Presumably the same process operates in human infants. At least this explanation for the delayed distress observed in these babies is plausible. The signs of respiratory distress are similar to those described for transient tachypnea, except that rales are often present.

The radiologic appearance of the lungs is characterized by multiple patches of density, interspersed areas of emphysema, and thick streaks that emanate from the hilar regions. The patchy densities represent relatively large areas of atelectasis that are produced by complete obstruction (stop-valve). They are considerably more prominent and extensive than in transient tachypnea. In most instances, overdistention of the lung is predominant, even in the presence of widespread atelectasis. The x-ray film thus also shows flattened diaphragms and bulging intercostal spaces.

Respiratory abnormalities usually subside in 48 hours, although they may persist for 6 or 7 days. Death, though less frequent than in hyaline membrane disease, has been reported in 11% of affected infants. Pneumomediastinum and pneumothorax may complicate the course (see later).

Blood gas and pH determinations indicate varying degrees of mixed respiratory and metabolic acidosis. Alkali therapy and oxygen administration are necessary for severely ill babies.

We have managed a substantial number of very seriously ill infants with this syndrome. The intensity of respiratory and other types of support is often equal to that required for hyaline membrane disease. With rare exception, these infants are born at term; often they are post-term. In most, there is evidence of some sort of intrauterine distress. Apgar scores at 1 and 5 minutes are usually below 5. Pneumothorax and pneumomediastinum are not infrequent, though they appear in a minority of infants.

Meconium aspiration syndrome is a serious, important neonatal disorder that has understandably been preempted by the concentrated efforts that have been lavished on hyaline membrane disease. Recent data demonstrate that much of the morbidity and virtually all the mortality is avoidable by appropriate management in the delivery room. Thus, in one inquiry among meconium-stained infants whose tracheas were suctioned immediately, the incidence of respiratory distress was less than half of that in nonsuctioned infants. Death occurred in approximately 1% of the suctioned infants and 28% of the nonsuctioned infants.

In a prospective investigation involving tracheal aspiration of all cases of meconium-stained amniotic fluid, meconium was removed from the trachea in 57% of the babies. Abnormal x-ray films were noted in half of them. Postnatal respiratory distress was noted in every baby who had both an abnormal x-ray film and tracheal meconium. If either of these factors was absent, the infant's subsequent course was uneventful. Other babies, who were admitted from outlying hospitals and had not been suctioned, had an impressively higher morbidity rate. They also required assisted ventilation more often, and the incidence of pneumothorax and pneumomediastinum was higher.

The best contemporary management of meconium aspiration syndrome requires aspiration of the trachea in all babies who emerge from stained amniotic fluid with any degree of respiratory difficulty, humidification of inspired gas mixtures, and thoracic physical therapy during the first 8 hours for those who had tracheal meconium or an abnormal chest x-ray film that is diagnostic of the disorder.

EXTRANEOUS AIR SYNDROMES OF THE CHEST (AIR LEAK): interstitial emphysema, pneumothorax, pneumomediastinum, and pneumopericardium

These disorders have long been observed to occur spontaneously in neonates who are apparently otherwise normal or who have some underlying respiratory abnormality. Pneumothorax and pneumomediastinum are the most common expressions of the extraneous air syndrome (air leak).

Pneumothorax, and probably pneumomediastinum as well, occur with the first few breaths as a consequence of spontaneous alveolar rupture in normally expanded portions of a lung that fails to expand in other segments. In such circumstances, excessive distending pressure is applied to the normal alveoli during the forceful initial breaths. X-ray surveys have shown pneumothorax in 1% to 2% of all normal newborns who had no other difficulties and who were generally asymptomatic. They required no treatment. Spontaneous pneumothorax has long been reported also as a complication of meconium aspiration, hyaline membrane disease, pneumonia, and pulmonary hypoplasia associated with renal anomalies and with diaphragmatic hernia. Pneumothorax as a consequence of overzealous positive-pressure resuscitation is less frequent than is generally supposed.

Pneumothorax and its associated disorders have assumed a new significance in recent years, commensurate with the various types of respiratory support that are now in use

Interstitial emphysema

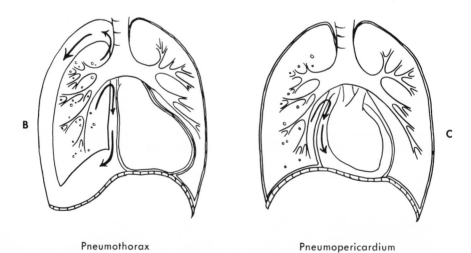

Pneumothorax   Pneumopericardium

Fig. 8-11. A, Air in interstitial lung tissue. Ruptured alveoli are indicated in framed alveoli at bottom. Air dissects from alveoli along vascular sheaths to hilus and thence to pleural space. (See x-ray film in Fig. 8-12, *A*.) **B,** Pneumothorax, indicating origin of air in lung tissue and its pathway to inflate pleural space. Heart shifts to left because of high pressure created in right chest. (See x-ray film in Fig. 8-12, *B*.) **C,** Course of air from lung to pericardial space. Distended pericardial space causes cardiac tamponade, small heart. (See x-ray film in Fig. 8-12, *C*.)

Interstitial emphysema

Pneumothorax   Pneumopericardium

Fig. 8-12. A, Interstitial emphysema. Multiple lakes of radiolucency (air), varying in size, impart a spongy appearance to lungs. (See Fig. 8-11, *A.*) **B,** Tension pneumothorax, right pleural cavity. The dense right lung is collapsed by pressure in pleural space created by air accumulation. Air-filled pleural cavity is darkest area that envelops right lung. (See Fig. 8-11, *B.*) **C,** Pneumopericardium. Dark halo of air fills pericardial space, outlining the heart itself. Note interstitial emphysema in right lung, indicated by large lakes of air. (See Fig. 8-11, *C.*)

for treatment of hyaline membrane disease. Their incidence has increased as the use of mechanical ventilation has become more widespread, and it has increased even more with the introduction of the various forms of continuous distending pressure. None of these conditions are in themselves new; they are simply more common than in the past. The incidence of these complications from assisted ventilation is reportedly 5% to 48%.

Interstitial emphysema, pneumothorax, pneumomediastinum, pneumopericardium, and, rarely, pneumoperitoneum unassociated with gastrointestinal disease, all have a common pathogenesis (Fig. 8-11). The process is initiated by rupture of overdistended alveoli. Escaping air enters the connective tissue between alveoli and then dissects along connective tissue sheaths of blood vessels to the hilar root *(interstitial emphysema)*, and from there into the mediastinum *(pneumomediastinum)*. It may also pass through the mediastinal wall and then enter the pleural space *(pneumothorax)* or, rarely, the pericardial space *(pneumopericardium)*. Occasionally when ruptured alveoli are situated just beneath the pleural membrane, air may burst through it directly into the pleural space. In a small number of instances *pneumoperitoneum* is associated with extraneous air in the chest. Presumably, air in the mediastinum dissects downward through foramens at the posterior margin of the diaphragm.

Interstitial emphysema regularly precedes the other extraneous air disorders. It is often not perceivable, however, if air does not accumulate in the pulmonary interstitial tissue. When it does, ongoing respiratory support becomes inadequate. The infant may suddenly become cyanotic; the P_{aO_2} falls and the P_{aCO_2} rises because transfer of gases between alveolar membranes and capillaries is impeded by intervening aggregations of air. The x-ray film is diagnostic. Rarely, only one lung is involved; as a rule both are involved. The lungs contain numerous small radiolucent areas (interstitial air) that create an overall spongy appearance (Fig. 8-12, *A*). The diagnosis can be made only by x-ray

examination. A substantial number of affected infants will soon develop pneumothorax and/ or pneumomediastinum, as interstitial air follows the pathogenetic course described above.

Because tension pneumothorax is life threatening and remediable if treated rapidly, the neonatal nurse must detect it as soon as it appears. Tension pneumothorax involves a massive accumulation of air in the pleural space that displaces the heart to the opposite side of the chest because of the high pressure that is produced. Pneumothorax and pneumomediastinum often occur in combination.

Some pneumothoraces are not symptomatic, or if symptoms appear, the course is often quite mild. They are usually severe when they occur as complications of ventilatory therapy. Tachypnea may be the only abnormal sign. On the other hand, the abrupt intrusion into the pleural space of a large volume of air is a dramatic life-threatening event. Tachypnea, grunting, and generalized cyanosis are immediately evident; sometimes the cyanosis appears more gradually. The affected hemithorax may bulge prominently. Tension displaces the hemidiaphragm downward, and severe abdominal distention appears immediately. The heart and mediastinum are displaced to the unaffected side of the chest, and, as a result, the cardiac sounds and impulses cannot be identified in their usual location. They may be perceived in the right chest if there is a left-sided pneumothorax, or far laterally against the left wall if the pneumothorax is on the right. The shift in apical impulse is the most valuable diagnostic sign. Confirmation is possible only by x-ray examination because an identical clinical appearance may be produced by diaphragmatic hernia (see later). On the radiograph of a pneumothorax, the lung on the affected side appears collapsed by air in the pleural space, and varying degrees of mediastinal displacement are apparent (Fig. 8-12, *B*).

Early recognition of pneumothorax is sometimes facilitated by changes in voltage on an electrocardiographic oscilloscope. The RS voltage decreases substantially (by 40%), often before clinical signs can be detected.

Another effective method for rapid diagnosis involves transillumination of the chest. If a significant amount of air has accumulated, the involved area clearly transilluminates when a high-intensity fiberoptic light source is applied to the chest. We have identified pneumothorax within 1 to 2 minutes with this method. (See Kuhns and others reference.)

In the evaluation of an infant with respiratory distress, locating the position of the cardiac impulse is of fundamental importance. If it is abnormal, a thoracentesis tray should be readied immediately. The release of pleural air is lifesaving. During the time preceding thoracentesis, the nurse should administer 100% oxygen by means of a hood or a tight-fitting mask. Positive-pressure ventilatory assistance through an endotracheal tube may increase the pneumothorax and should thus be avoided if possible pending establishment of continuous pleural suction through a chest tube. Breathing 100% oxygen may hasten the resolution of pleural air, or at least retard further accumulation. This response occurs over a 6- to 12-hour period, and although this therapy is extremely valuable, it should not be considered appropriate treatment for tension pneumothorax. After the emergency release of pleural air by needle aspiration, a chest tube must be inserted and connected to continuous suction under water.

Many infants with pneumothorax, particularly the spontaneous variety unassociated with pressure therapy, do not require pleural aspiration. Periodic administration of 100% oxygen is often effective. However, even if there is only slight distress, a thoracentesis tray should be placed at the cribside of any infant in whom a pneumothorax has been identified.

Pneumopericardium was a rare clinical entity until recently. Only thirteen cases had been reported in the English literature from 1942 to 1974. Now it probably occurs far more often than it is reported. It rarely appears alone, generally being associated with pneumomediastinum and/or pneumothorax. Of seventeen cases in the English literature,

eleven expired. Most of them also had hyaline membrane disease, and all but one had previously been resuscitated by bag. The infant becomes cyanotic abruptly. Because air in the pericardial space produces cardiac tamponade, the heart sounds are severely muffled or cannot be heard at all. In our four babies, all were receiving mechanical ventilation. There was thus no perceptible change in respiratory pattern. Cyanosis was profound, but the most impressive manifestation was total inaudibility of heart sounds in the presence of continued cardiac activity as seen on the oscilloscope. Cardiac tamponade causes pulse pressure to decrease; the pulses may not be palpable, and blood pressure is therefore low or unobtainable. The x-ray film (Fig. 8-12, *C*) is dramatic. A dark halo surrounds the heart, varying in thickness with the amount of accumulated air. It surrounds the heart completely, separating it inferiorly from the diaphragm. External to and encasing the halo, the parietal layer of the pericardium is often visible because the pericardial space is distended.

Treatment must be applied immediately, since untreated affected infants die in minutes. A pericardial tap must be done to evacuate the air. A repeat tap may be necessary, or a catheter may be required to provide for egress of air that continues to accumulate.

Pneumomediastinum usually produces mild, sometimes moderately disturbing, symptoms. Severe distress may result from a massive accumulation of air around the heart, which impairs venous return from the inferior and superior venae cavae by compression of these vessels. Tachypnea is the most frequent sign; occasionally cyanosis is apparent. Nurses often call attention to the possibility of pneumomediastinum by finding it difficult to locate the heartbeat. Cardiac sounds are distant and barely audible as a result of accumulation of air around the heart. There is no mediastinal shift; the breath sounds are normal. Sometimes air may spread to the subcutaneous tissue of the neck, where it causes visible swelling and a crunchy sensation when palpated (crepitus). The

Fig. 8-13. Pneumomediastinum. **A,** Anteroposterior view. The butterfly-shaped shadow of the thymus is above mediastinal air. The air (arrows) separates the thymic shadow and the cardiac shadow beneath it. **B,** Lateral view. Mediastinal air (arrow) is visible in the darkest area immediately beneath the sternum. Since air is situated between the heart and the anterior chest wall, the intensity of heart sounds is substantially diminished.

chest film is diagnostic. Lateral views reveal a collection of air directly beneath the sternum, displacing the cardiac shadow posteriorly. Sometimes a black halo, which is cast by mediastinal air, may be seen around the cardiac border in the frontal view. Since the thymus overlays the mediastinum, the thymus is frequently elevated by the air that is interposed between the thymic and cardiac shadows (Fig. 8-13). This is called the "batwing" sign on x-ray film.

Needle aspiration for removal of mediastinal air is ineffective, nor has any form of constant suction been shown to be valuable. Administration of 100% oxygen is the treatment of choice.

Acid-base imbalance and blood gas abnormalities may occur in pneumothorax or pneumomediastinum, particularly in the most profoundly affected babies. These biochemical deviations are similar to those of hyaline membrane disease. They are treated in the same fashion as described previously.

PNEUMONIA

Infection of the lungs may be acquired in utero (congenital pneumonia) or after birth. The congenital disease is more often lethal. Pneumonia is a common serious perinatal infection. It has a number of attributes that are unique to the neonate and is thus presented in Chapter 12 as a part of the general problem of perinatal infections.

CONGENITAL ANOMALIES

Malformations of the respiratory tract are numerous. A few of the major anomalies are discussed here.

Choanal atresia

The choanae are the posterior nares that open into nasopharynx. Atresia or stenosis is an uncommon malformation that produces dramatic symptoms and requires immediate recognition. Complete or partial obstruction of one or both apertures is caused by a membranous or bony structure covering them. Since the neonate can breathe only through his nose, catastrophic respiratory distress may result from obstruction. The first breath is usually normal because it is taken through the mouth. Cyanosis and severe retractions appear as the infant subsequently attempts to breathe through the nose. Thick mucoid secretions characteristically fill the nose. The anomaly can be demonstrated by failure to pass a catheter or probe through the nose into the nasopharynx. If a membrane covers the choanae, it can be punctured to open the airway. Most often this is not the case. An oral airway should be inserted to accommodate mouth breathing pending ultimate surgical correction of the obstruction. Occasionally respiration is possible only after endotracheal intubation. Choanal obstruction may impede the exhalation of carbon dioxide, and as a consequence, diffuse emphysema and an elevated arterial P_{CO_2} develop.

Tracheoesophageal fistula

Among the congenital malformations that cause neonatal respiratory distress, tracheoesophageal fistula is the commonest. Several variations have been recognized (Fig. 8-14). The most frequent form of this anomaly is atresia of a segment of the esophagus, which is thus divided into an upper blind pouch and a lower separated portion that communicates

Fig. 8-14. Three commonest types of tracheoesophageal fistula. A, Esophageal atresia with fistulous connection between the lower esophageal segment and the trachea. This is the commonest variety. B, Esophageal atresia with normal respiratory tract. C, Normal esophagus and trachea connected by a fistula (H type of malformation).

with the stomach in a normal fashion. A fistula connects this lower esophageal segment with the trachea. This lesion is present in 85% of infants with esophageal atresia. In another variety, which is far less common, esophageal atresia is the only malformation, the tracheo-bronchial tree being intact. A third type is characterized by a fistulous connection between an otherwise normal trachea and esophagus, the so-called H type of fistula. The other variations are extremely rare.

A distinctive triad of clinical signs is usually recognizable in the commonest variety of tracheoesophageal fistula: (1) accumulation of secretions in the mouth and hypopharynx, often requiring urgent and frequent suction, (2) continuous or sporadic respiratory distress, and (3) repeated regurgitation of feedings. The first two signs should immediately suggest this diagnostic possibility to the nurse. A trial of feeding should not be necessary; it could be dangerous because of aspiration. In affected infants, the mouth is full of bubbling saliva, and some degree of respiratory distress is clearly apparent. Often the abdomen is quite distended because air continually enters the stomach through the fistulous connection between the trachea and the lower esophageal segment. Pneumonia and atelectasis, particularly in the right upper lobe, are also rather frequent signs. The nurse should attempt to pass a catheter into the esophagus of any infant with these signs. The obstruction is not always perceived because the catheter may curl on itself in the esophageal pouch while it seems to pass with ease. One or 2 cc of air should be injected into the catheter while the nurse listens over the stomach for gurgling to indicate that the catheter tip is in the stomach. Listening for gurgling is not consistently reliable.

A chest film usually reveals the blind pouch filled with air. Instillation of dye contrast medium into the pouch, although frequently performed, is not necessary for the diagnosis because the air-filled pouch is plainly visible. If air is also present in the intestinal tract, and esophageal atresia has been demonstrated, a tracheoesophageal fis-tula is undoubtedly present. We use two techniques to demonstrate the pouch by x-ray film. The pouch is dramatically visible if it can be inflated with air at the moment the x-ray film is taken. The nurse uses bag and mask, insufflating five or six times. Then, with the next squeeze of the bag, the x-ray technician takes the film. Even more diagnostic is the passage of an umbilical artery catheter. It is radiopaque, and it loops within the blind pouch. In Fig. 8-15 are three films of a tracheoesophageal fistula. The first is a routine chest film in which the air-filled esophageal pouch is visible. Our clinical nurse supervisor suspected pathology from this film. The second is an x-ray film taken while the pouch was inflated by bag and mask. The third demonstrates the position of an umbilical artery catheter within the pouch.

Infants whose only anomaly is esophageal atresia (without a fistulous connection) have pooling of secretions and feeding difficulties. Respiratory symptoms, if they are present, are a consequence of aspirated secretions.

The H type of fistula is well known but rare; it is often suspected but seldom demonstrated early in the course. Respiratory distress is typically at its worst when the baby is fed, since milk enters the lung from the esophagus through the fistula. Tachypnea may persist between feedings, and pneumonia is almost a constant accompaniment. The tract must be demonstrated by feeding contrast medium while the baby is in a prone and somewhat oblique position. Fluoroscopic visualization is usually possible, but repeated attempts are often necessary because the fistula does not always fill with dye.

All forms of tracheoesophageal fistula must be repaired surgically. As technical surgical problems have been surmounted, pneumonia, septicemia, and associated anomalies have emerged as the major causes of death. For full-term infants without other anomalies or pneumonia, a 100% survival rate can be expected. Overall survival of full-term babies is approximately 70%, and for premature infants, 52%. From available data, it has been surmised that improved

Fig. 8-15. A, Tracheoesophageal fistula with esophageal atresia. Routine chest x-ray film. The radio-lucent pocket overlying the vertebrae just superior to the heart is the air-containing esophageal pouch. **B,** Inflated pouch during bagging with mask. **C,** Umbilical artery catheter looped in esophageal pouch.

management of pneumonia and septicemia would substantially diminish mortality. The later the diagnosis is made, the more hazardous are the procedure and postoperative course. Surgery can be delayed with impunity only if optimal supportive care is available. As a rule, the nurse is the infant's first attendant and thus can best direct initial attention to suspicious signs.

Diaphragmatic hernia

Incomplete embryonic formation of the diaphragm results in a congenital defect that allows displacement of abdominal organs into the thoracic cavity. Severe respiratory distress occurs at birth or shortly thereafter. The left side is involved five to ten times more frequently than the right side. Herniation occurs through one of several possible defec-

Fig. 8-16. A, Left diaphragmatic hernia immediately after birth. The left chest is opaque, filled with gasless intestine. The heart is displaced to the right chest. **B,** Intestine in left chest has begun to fill with air. The heart is now farther to the right. Fortunately, the infant was bagged with mask for only a short time. Longer periods fill the intestine to produce more tension in left chest, as seen in Fig. 8-17.

tive segments of the diaphragm; the commonest is at the posterolateral segment (foramen of Bochdalek). Defects at the anterior portion directly beneath the sternum (foramen of Morgagni) and at the esophageal hiatus are considerably less frequent.

In left-sided involvement the intestine, stomach, and spleen compress the lung. The gastrointestinal tract, distended with air, occupies most of the space preempted from the lung, and the mediastinum is dislocated to the right. In right-sided involvement the liver and/or intestine are the herniated abdominal organs; they displace the mediastinum to the left.

The severity of symptoms is related to the amount of lung compressed by the dislocated abdominal organs. The pattern of respiratory distress is no different from that caused by other neonatal disorders. The most severely affected babies gasp a few times at birth, never establishing respiration. If respiratory distress is not particularly severe at birth, it

frequently progresses alarmingly as the intestine in the chest expands with the normal entry of swallowed air (Fig. 8-16).

The diagnosis can sometimes be anticipated before birth if there is a history of polyhydramnios. Polyhydramnios occurs in over half of affected infants because the thoracic location of intestine is obstructive to intrauterine flow of amniotic fluid. The presence of a diaphragmatic hernia is invariably suggested by difficult respiration. Displacement of the cardiac impulse to one side of the chest is the most telling indication of the diagnosis, but pneumothorax can produce the same displacement. If the cardiac impulse is shifted to one side or the other, there should be an immediate realization that one is not dealing solely with the type of perinatal asphyxia in which resuscitative measures would be expected to alleviate much of the difficulty. The abdomen is sometimes sunken (scaphoid), but this condition depends on the displacement of a considerable amount of intestine.

Fig. 8-17. Diaphragmatic hernia. **A,** Lateral view. The cystic appearance in the chest (arrow) is caused by air-filled loops of intestine. **B,** Anteroposterior view. Gas-filled intestinal loops fill the left chest, displacing the heart (arrow) into the right chest. Heart sounds are thus heard in the right chest, and breath sounds in the left chest are virtually absent. (Courtesy Webster Riggs, M.D., Le-Bonheur Children's Hospital, Memphis, Tenn.)

More often, the abdominal contour is normal. Diminished breath sounds are the rule in the involved hemithorax.

A chest film confirms the diagnosis. The diaphragmatic margin is absent on the defective side, and the presence of inappropriate thoracic structures is readily discerned. The gas-filled intestines may impart a multicystic appearance to the left chest (Fig. 8-17). If the right side is affected, the liver casts a homogeneous density in the area it occupies. Absence or diminution of the normal liver shadow in the abdomen is another revealing radiologic sign.

The case fatality rate is high, being influenced by the rapidity of diagnosis and surgical correction. Even with optimal management, death is quite frequent because severe pulmonary hypoplasia precludes effective ventilation. Surgery is the only effective treatment, and it must be done with dispatch. Some infants expire before surgery can be initiated.

RESPIRATORY DISTRESS OF EXTRAPULMONARY ORIGIN

Respiratory distress may be the most prominent sign of a number of disorders of extrapulmonary origin. They fall into four broad categories: (1) congenital heart disease, (2) depression due to drugs, (3) metabolic acidosis of nonpulmonary origin, and (4) central nervous system disorders.

Congenital heart disease

In most instances, by the time respiratory difficulty appears in infants with major cardiac anomalies, congestive failure is well developed. In our experience, patent ductus arteriosus in small premature infants is the most common condition associated with congestive failure and pulmonary edema. A high mortality rate during the neonatal period among these infants is well documented. Of the many types of lesions involved in cardiac anomalies, approximately eight of them account for most deaths. Three of these eight anomalies are responsible for almost half the deaths: hypoplastic left heart syndrome (hypoplasia of the left ventricle, aortic atresia, and mitral atresia), coarctation of the aorta, and transposition of the great vessels. The remaining five conditions that are most frequently lethal in the first month of life include hypoplastic right heart syndrome with pulmonary arterial atresia or stenosis, tetralogy of Fallot, truncus arteriosus, endocardial cushion defect, and ventricular septal defect.

Respiratory distress of cardiac origin usually can be identified with the aid of a few simple observations. Breathing is rapid, but not often labored or obstructed. Heart sounds are loud and rapid. A gallop rhythm is particularly indicative of heart failure. Enlargement of the liver (more than 3 cm below the right costal margin), when present, is also a valuable sign. Enlargement of the heart can be seen on the chest film of almost all infants in congestive heart failure. These signs indicate primary cardiac dysfunction, and with few exceptions the electrocardiogram is abnormal in their presence.

Effects of drugs

Respiratory distress due to drugs is characterized by depressed function rather than the rapid, facile breathing associated with heart disease or the rapid, labored breathing so typical of intrinsic lung disorders. Drugs that depress neonates are administered to their mothers during labor; they are usually anesthetics and analgesics. Almost all these agents are known to cross the placenta. Affected infants usually initiate respiration, but the breathing that follows is shallow and slow. If depression is sufficiently deep, generalized cyanosis may be prominent. Cardiac activity is normal, unless hypoxemic bradycardia occurs as a result of depressed ventilation. The breath sounds are diminished, but only because respiration is shallow, thus reducing air intake. Painful stimuli cause little response in depressed infants, and, at best, the cry is feeble.

Barbiturates are notorious depressive agents. They cross the placenta rapidly. Infants who are born a few hours after maternal barbiturate administration have significant blood levels of the drug for several days after birth. Liberal use of barbiturates during labor and delivery has been curtailed.

Inhalational agents are often used in combination with other drugs during labor, and their individual effects are difficult to evaluate. Anesthetic concentrations of nitrous oxide over 75% generally produce asphyxiated infants. Maternal overdosage with any of these agents will cause depressed respiratory function in the neonate.

Narcotic analgesics are used extensively during the management of labor and delivery. Meperidine is most commonly employed, and its administration in doses that depress the infant is widespread. If it is given intramuscularly between 1 and 3 hours before delivery, some degree of neonatal depression is almost inevitable. If it is administered intramuscularly within an hour of birth in appropriate dosage, significant depression does not usually occur. The effects of meperidine are potentiated if barbiturates are used in combination with it.

Metabolic acidosis of extrapulmonary origin

Rapid respiration is stimulated by an abnormally low pH; if the lungs are normal, increased carbon dioxide excretion occurs and the arterial P_{CO_2} is reduced. Metabolic acidosis of extrapulmonary origin is most often caused by renal disorders, diarrhea, infection, and a peculiarity of protein metabolism in premature infants called "late metabolic acidosis." The respiratory rate usually subsides after proper alkali therapy for correction of the blood pH.

Central nervous system disorders

Intracranial hemorrhage occurs most frequently in premature infants in whom it is usually of intraventricular or subarachnoid origin. In full-term infants, subdural and intracerebral hemorrhages are more common. These episodes severely depress respiratory function. Sporadic apnea and irregular breathing are characteristic. Blood gas and pH alterations are identical to those of perinatal asphyxia.

SUMMATION

Respiratory problems are the most frequent cause of neonatal mortality and morbidity. Although most often attributable to intrinsic lung disease, some form of abnormal respiration is inevitable in any type of serious illness; the diagnostic possibilities suggested by breathing difficulties are thus numerous. Several situations require immediate diagnosis and therapy; such optimal management is often lifesaving. No one can better make the first discovery of serious respiratory dysfunction than the nurse, nor is anyone else better equipped to ascertain that therapy is proceeding effectively and without jeopardy to the infant.

References

Adams, F. H., Yanagisawa, M., Kuzela, D., and Martinek, H.: The disappearance of fetal lung fluid following birth, J. Pediatr. **78:**837, 1971.

Auld, P. A. M.: Oxygen therapy for premature infants, J. Pediatr. **78:**705, 1971.

Auld, P., Hodson, A., and Usher, R.: Hyaline membrane disease: a discussion, J. Pediatr. **80:** 129, 1972.

Avery, G. B., Fletcher, A. B., and O'Boyle, M. P.: Criteria for ventilatory assistance in hyaline membrane disease, Pediatrics **52:**623, 1973.

Avery, M. E.: Prevention of hyaline membrane disease, Pediatrics **50:**513, 1972.

Avery, M. E., and Fletcher, B. D.: The lung and its disorders in the newborn infant, ed. 3, Philadelphia, 1974, W. B. Saunders Co.

Avery, M. E., Gatewood, O. B., and Brumley, G.: Transient tachypnea of newborn, Am. J. Dis. Child. **111:**380, 1966.

Avery, M. E., and Said, S.: Surface phenomena in lungs in health and disease, Medicine **44:** 503, 1965.

Baden, M., Bauer, C. R., Colle, E., et al.: A controlled trial of hydrocortisone therapy in infants with respiratory distress syndrome, Pediatrics **50:**526, 1972.

Berg, T. J., Pagtakhan, R. D., Reed, M. H., et al.: Bronchopulmonary dysplasia and lung rupture in hyaline membrane disease: influence of continuous distending pressure, Pediatrics **55:**51, 1975.

Black, I. F. S., Kotrapu, N., and Massie, H.: Application of Doppler ultrasound to blood pressure measurement in small infants, J. Pediatr. **81:**932, 1972.

Boddy, K., Dawes, G. S., and Robinson, J.: Intrauterine fetal breathing movements. In Gluck, L., editor: Modern perinatal medicine, Chicago, 1974, Year Book Medical Publishers, Inc.

Briggs, J. N., and Hogg, G.: Perinatal pulmonary pathology, Pediatrics **22:**41, 1958.

Butler, J. N., and Claireaux, A. E.: Congenital diaphragmatic hernia as a cause of perinatal mortality, Lancet **1:**659, 1962.

Capitanio, M. A., and Kirkpatrick, J. A.: Roent-gen examination in the evaluation of the newborn infant with respiratory distress, J. Pediatr. **75:**896, 1969.

Chernick, V.: Modern therapy of hyaline membrane disease by stabilization of alveoli. In Gluck, L., editor: Modern perinatal medicine, Chicago, 1975, Year Book Medical Publishers, Inc.

Chernick, V.: Continuous distending pressure in hyaline membrane disease: of devices, disadvantages, and a daring study, Pediatrics **52:** 114, 1973.

Chernick, V., and Reed, M. H.: Pneumothorax and chylothorax in the neonatal period, J. Pediatr. **76:**624, 1970.

Comroe, J. H., Jr.: Physiology of respiration, ed. 3, Chicago, 1974, Year Book Medical Publishers, Inc.

Cowett, R. H., et al.: Foam-stability test on gastric aspirate and the diagnosis of respiratory distress syndrome, N. Engl. J. Med. **293:**413, 1975.

Cumarasamy, N., Nussli, R., Vischer, D., et al.: Artificial ventilation in hyaline membrane disease: the use of positive end-expiratory pressure and continuous positive airway pressure, Pediatrics **51:**629, 1973.

Daily, W. J. R., and Smith, P. C.: Mechanical ventilation of the newborn infant. I and II. In Current problems in pediatrics, Chicago, 1971, Year Book Medical Publishers, Inc.

Dawes, G. S.: Fetal circulation and breathing, Clin. Obstet. Gynecol. **1:**139, 1974.

De Leon, A. S., Elliot, J. H., and Jones, D. B.: The resurgence of retrolental fibroplasia, Pediatr. Clin. North Am. **17:**309, 1970.

Duc, G.: Assessment of hypoxia in the newborn, suggestions for a practical approach, Pediatrics **48:**469, 1971.

Emery, J. L., and Mithal, A.: The number of alveoli in the terminal respiratory unit of man during late intrauterine life and childhood, Arch. Dis. Child. **35:**544, 1960.

Fenner, R., Muller, H. G., Busse, M., et al.: Transcutaneous determination of arterial oxygen tension, Pediatrics **55:**224, 1975.

Gershanik, J. J.: Neonatal pneumopericardium, Am. J. Dis. Child. **121:**438, 1971.

Gluck, L.: Surfactant: 1972. In Nelson, N. M.: editor: Pediatr. Clin. North Am. **19:**325, 1972.

Goldman, H. I., Maralit, A., Sun, S., and Lanzkowsy, P.: Neonatal cyanosis and arterial oxygen saturation, J. Pediatr. **82:**319, 1973.

Gregory, G. A.: Respiratory care of newborn

infants, Pediatr. Clin. North Am. **19:**311, 1972.

Gregory, G. A., Gooding, C. A., Phibbs, R. H., and Tooley, W. H.: Meconium aspiration in infants: a prospective study, J. Pediatr. **85:**848, 1974.

Gregory, G. A., et al.: Treatment of the idiopathic respiratory distress syndrome with continuous positive airway pressure, N. Engl. J. Med. **284:**1333, 1971.

Hall, R. T., and Rhodes, P. R.: Pneumothorax and pneumomediastinum in infants with idiopathic respiratory distress syndrome receiving continuous positive airway pressure, Pediatrics **55:**493, 1975.

Harned, H. S.: Fetal physiology. In Barnett, H. L., editor: Pediatrics, New York, 1968, Appleton-Century-Crofts.

Harned, H. S., Jr., and Ferreiro, J.: Initiation of breathing by cold stimulation: effects of change in ambient temperature on respiratory activity of the full-term fetal lamb, J. Pediatr. **83:**663, 1973.

Harrison, V. C., Heese, H. de V., and Klein, M. B.: The significance of grunting in hyaline membrane disease, Pediatrics **41:**549, 1968.

Harrod, J. R., L'Heureux, P., Wangensteen, O. D., and Hunt, C. E.: Long-term follow-up of severe respiratory distress syndrome treated with IPPB, J. Pediatr. **84:**277, 1974.

Hartmann, A. F., Jr., Klint, R., Hernandez, A., and Goldring, D.: Measurement of blood pressure in the brachial and posterior tibial arteries using the Doppler method, J. Pediatr. **82:**498, 1973.

Indyk, L.: P_{O_2} in the seventies, Pediatrics **55:**153, 1975.

James, L. S., and Adamsons, K., Jr.: Respiratory physiology of the fetus and newborn infant, N. Engl. J. Med. **271:**1352, 1964.

Johnson, J. D., Malachowski, N. C., Grobstein, R., et al.: Prognosis of children surviving with the aid of mechanical ventilation in the newborn period, J. Pediatr. **84:**272, 1974.

Karlberg, P.: The adaptive changes in the immediate postnatal period, with particular reference to respiration, J. Pediatr. **56:**585, 1960.

Karlberg, P.: The first breaths of life. In Gluck, L., editor: Modern perinatal medicine, Chicago, 1974, Year Book Medical Publishers, Inc.

Kattwinkel, J., Fleming, D., Cha, C. C., et al.: A device for administration of continuous positive airway pressure by the nasal route, Pediatrics **52:**131, 1973.

Kitterman, J. A., Phibbs, R. H., and Tooley, W. H.: Aortic blood pressure in normal newborn infants during the first 12 hours of life, Pediatrics **44:**959, 1969.

Klaus, M. H.: Respiratory function and pulmonary disease in the newborn. In Barnett, H. L., editor: Pediatrics, New York, 1968, Appleton-Century-Crofts.

Klaus, M. H.: Cleansing the neonatal trachea, J. Pediatr. **85:**853, 1974.

Klaus, M. H., and Fanaroff, A. A.: Care of the high-risk neonate, Philadelphia, 1973, W. B. Saunders Co.

Klaus, M. H., and Meyer, B. P.: Oxygen therapy for the newborn, Pediatr. Clin. North Am. **13:**731, 1966.

Koop, C. E., Schnaufer, L., and Broennie, A. M.: Esophageal atresia and tracheoesophageal fistula: supportive measures that affect survival, Pediatrics **54:**558, 1974.

Krauss, D. R., and Marshall, R. E.: Severe neck ulceration from CPAP head box, J. Pediatr. **86:**286, 1975.

Kuhns, L. R., Bednarek, F. J., and Wyman, M. L.: Diagnosis of pneumothorax or pneumomediastinum in the neonate by transillumination, Pediatrics **56:**355, 1975.

Leonidas, J. C., Hall, R. T., Holder, T. M., and Amoury, R. A.: Pneumoperitoneum associated with chronic respiratory disease in the newborn, Pediatrics **51:**933, 1973.

Liggins, G. C.: The prevention of RDS by maternal steroid therapy. In Gluck, L., editor: Modern perinatal medicine, Chicago, 1974, Year Book Medical Publishers, Inc.

Liggins, G. C., and Howie, R. N.: A controlled trial of antepartum glucocorticoid treatment for prevention of the respiratory distress syndrome in premature infants, Pediatrics **50:**515, 1972.

Lippold, O.: Human respiration, San Francisco, 1968, W. H. Freeman & Co., Publishers.

Merenstein, G. B., Dougherty, K., and Lewis, A.: Early detection of pneumothorax by oscilloscope monitor in the newborn infant, J. Pediatr. **80:**98, 1972.

Morrow, G., III, Hope, J. W., and Boggs, R., Jr.: Pneumomediastinum: a silent lesion in the newborn, J. Pediatr. **70:**554, 1967.

Nelson, N. M.: Neonatal pulmonary function, Pediatr. Clin. North Am. **13:**769, 1966.

Northway, W. J., Jr., Rosan, R. C., and Porter, D. Y.: Pulmonary disease following respirator therapy of hyaline-membrane disease: bronchopulmonary dysplasia, N. Engl. J. Med. **276**:357, 1967.

Oski, F. A., and Delivoria-Papadopoulos, M.: The red cell, 2,3-diphosphoglycerate, and tissue oxygen release, J. Pediatr. **77**:941, 1970.

Outerbridge, E. W., Roloff, D. W., and Stern, L.: Continuous negative pressure in the management of severe respiratory distress syndrome, J. Pediatr. **81**:384, 1972.

Philip, A. G. S.: Oxygen plus pressure plus time: the etiology of bronchopulmonary dysplasia, Pediatrics **55**:44, 1975.

Pusey, V. A., Macpherson, R. I., and Chernick, V.: Pulmonary fibroplasia following prolonged artificial ventilation of newborn infants, Can. Med. Assoc. J. **100**:451, 1969.

Redmond, A., Isana, S., and Ingall, D.: Relation of onset of respiration to placental transfusion, Lancet **1**:283, 1965.

Reynolds, E. O. R., and Taghizadeh, A.: Improved prognosis of infants mechanically ventilated for hyaline membrane disease, Arch. Dis. Child. **49**:505, 1974.

Rhodes, P. G., Hall, R. T., and Leonidas, J. C.: Chronic pulmonary disease in neonates with assisted ventilation, Pediatrics **55**:788, 1975.

Robert, M. F., Neff, R. K., Hubbell, J. B., Tacusch, H. W., and Avery, M. E.: Maternal diabetes and the respiratory distress syndrome, N. Engl. J. Med. **294**:357, 1976.

Rooth, G.: Transcutaneous oxygen tension measurements in newborn infants, Pediatrics **55**: 232, 1975.

Rowe, R. D., and Mahrizi, A.: The neonate with congenital heart disease, Philadelphia, 1968, W. B. Saunders Co.

Rudolph, A. J., Desmond, M., and Pineda, R. G.: Clinical diagnosis of respiratory difficulty in the newborn, Pediatr. Clin. North Am. **13**:669, 1966.

Rudolph, A. M.: Congenital diseases of the heart, Chicago, 1974, Year Book Medical Publishers, Inc.

Scarpelli, E.: Pulmonary surfactants and their role in lung disease. In Schulman, I., et al., editors: Advances in pediatrics, vol. 16, Chicago, 1969, Year Book Medical Publishers, Inc.

Sinclair, J. C.: Prevention and treatment of the respiratory distress syndrome, Pediatr. Clin. North Am. **13**:711, 1966.

Stahlman, M.: Recovery from the respiratory distress syndrome, Pediatrics **52**:280, 1973.

Stahlman, M., Hedvall, G., Dolanski, E., et al.: A six-year follow-up of clinical hyaline membrane disease, Pediatr. Clin. North Am. **20**:433, 1973.

Stahlman, M. T., Young, W. C., Gray, J., et al.: The management of respiratory failure in the idiopathic respiratory distress syndrome of prematurity, Ann. N.Y. Acad. Sci. **121**:930, 1965.

Stern, L.: Therapy of the respiratory distress syndrome, Pediatr. Clin. North Am. **19**:221, 1972.

Stern, L.: The use and misuse of oxygen in the newborn infant, Pediatr. Clin. North Am. **20**: 447, 1973.

Stiehm, E. R., and Rich, K.: Recognition and management of shock in pediatric patients. In Current problems in pediatrics, vol. 3, Chicago, 1973, Year Book Medical Publishers, Inc.

Strang, L. B.: The lungs at birth, Arch. Dis. Child. **40**:575, 1965.

Strang, L. B.: The pulmonary circulation in the respiratory distress syndrome, Pediatr. Clin. North Am. **13**:693, 1966.

Sundell, H., et al.: Studies on infants with type II respiratory distress syndrome, J. Pediatr. **78**: 754, 1971.

Thibeault, D. W., Lachman, R. S., Laul, V. R., and Kwong, M. S.: Pulmonary interstitial emphysema, pneumomediastinum, and pneumothorax, Am. J. Dis. Child. **126**:611, 1973.

Ting, P., and Brady, J.: Tracheal suction in meconium aspiration, Pediatr. Res. **7**:398, 1973.

Turner, T., Evans, J., and Brown, J. K.: Monoparesis: complication of constant positive airways pressure, Arch. Dis. Child. **50**:128, 1975.

Walsh, S. Z., Meyer, W. W., and Lind, J.: The human fetal and neonatal circulation, Springfield, Ill., 1974, Charles C Thomas, Publisher.

Weller, M. H.: The roentgenographic course and complications of hyaline membrane disease, Pediatr. Clin. North Am. **20**:381, 1973.

Yeh, T. F., Vidyasagar, D., and Pildes, R. S.: Neonatal pneumopericardium, Pediatrics **54**: 429, 1974.

Yu, V. Y. H., Liew, S. W., and Roberton, N. R. C.: Pneumothorax in the newborn: changing pattern, Arch. Dis. Child. **50**:449, 1975.

Chapter 9

Hematologic disorders

PERPLEXING HEMATOLOGIC PROBLEMS are more frequent during the neonatal period than at any other time in childhood. The commonest manifestations of neonatal blood disorders are anemia, hemorrhage into tissues, hyperbilirubinemia, and polycythemia (plethora). Anemia may be the end result of hemolysis, blood loss, or impaired red cell production. Hemorrhage into tissues is produced by disorders of the clotting mechanism. Hyperbilirubinemia follows intravascular hemolysis, or the degradation of extravasated blood. Polycythemia is the result of an oversupply of blood to the fetus.

HEMOGLOBIN IN NORMAL NEONATAL BLOOD

The normal neonate's blood volume at birth is somewhat influenced by the quantity of blood allowed to flow from the placenta before the cord is clamped. The placental circulation contains approximately 75 to 125 ml at term, comprising one fourth to one third of total fetal blood volume. The infant's blood volume may be increased significantly by allowing the placenta to empty. At birth, infants held at levels below the placenta tend to acquire blood, and those held above it may lose some. In normal circumstances approximately 25% of the placental blood is transfused into the infant within 15 seconds after birth; at the end of 1 minute 50% of blood is transferred. If a term infant is held below the level of the placenta, and clamping of the cord is delayed several minutes, blood volume can be increased by 40% to 60%. The increase is greater in a premature infant. Whether this added volume has a salutary effect on the baby's subsequent course has not been well

defined. Thus some studies indicate a lower incidence of respiratory distress if cord clamping is delayed, whereas others do not demonstrate such an association. In any event, during the first few days of life, hemoglobin concentrations are higher in babies whose cords are clamped late, but there is no evidence that the additional hemoglobin is of any particular benefit.

Hemoglobin and hematocrit determinations may vary according to sampling site. At birth and for several days thereafter, hemoglobin concentration is higher in capillary than in venous blood. Normal hemoglobin concentration in cord blood ranges from 16 to 19 grams/100 ml (mean, 16.8 grams/100 ml), whereas capillary values may be at least 2 grams/100 ml higher. Even higher capillary levels may result from peripheral circulatory stasis, in which slowed blood flow causes stasis of the red blood cells, thereby increasing their concentration.

Normally, hemoglobin concentrations rise somewhat during the first few hours of life, particularly if the cord is clamped late. This rise is due to shifts of fluid that result in decreased plasma volume. After 24 hours they decline slightly, and by the end of the first week hemoglobin levels are at least equal to that of cord blood. A normal decrease continues after the first week.

ANEMIA DUE TO HEMOLYSIS

An abnormally rapid rate of red cell breakdown causes anemia and hyperbilirubinemia. Ordinarily, erythropoiesis increases in response to hemolysis, thus augmenting the number of reticulocytes and nucleated red cells in circulating blood. The hallmarks of hemolysis are anemia, hyperbilirubinemia, reticulocytosis, and increased numbers of nucleated red cells. The commonest causes of fetal and neonatal hemolysis are isoimmunization (maternofetal blood incompatibility) and infection. Less frequently, hemolytic anemia is due to toxic drug effects, erythrocyte enzyme defects, or abnormal red cell morphology.

Isoimmunization: Rh incompatibility (erythroblastosis fetalis)

Erythroblastosis fetalis is also known as hemolytic disease of the newborn. Before the widespread use of anti-Rh gamma globulin to prevent fetal disease, approximately one third of all cases of isoimmunization involved Rh incompatibility; this form of the disease is often serious. Most cases of isoimmunization are now due to ABO incompatibility, which is generally mild, occasionally severe.

Antigens and blood group factors. The terms *blood group antigens* and *blood group factors* are used interchangeably. There are a number of blood group systems, of which the Rh and ABO systems are the most significant. Other antigenic systems are only rarely involved in maternofetal blood incompatibilities. An antigen is a substance that stimulates the production of antibodies. Thousands of discrete patches of red cell antigens are situated on or in the covering cell membrane. The Rh system is comprised of six factors: C,c, D,d, and E,e. Although the terms *Rh positive* and *Rh negative* strictly indicate the presence or absence of any Rh factor, in common usage these terms refer to the D factor, which is involved in 95% of Rh incompatibilities.

Pathogenesis. In the pathogenesis of Rh disease, fetal red cells pass across the placenta to an Rh-negative mother, who produces antibodies to Rh antigen on fetal red cell surfaces. These antibodies are transmitted across the placenta to the fetus; they become attached to fetal red cells, and hemolysis follows. This course of events requires maternal antibody production, which can occur only in the presence of incompatibility between mother and fetus (Rh-negative mother, Rh-positive fetus). *The mother produces antibodies to fetal antigens only if her own cells lack these antigens.* This is the basis of Rh incompatibility. Thus an Rh-negative mother (whose cells lack D factor) is the recipient of erythrocytes from her Rh-positive fetus. She responds by generating anti-D antibodies, which pass across the placenta and become attached to the D antigen on fetal red cells, causing their eventual dissolution.

During normal pregnancy, small quantities of fetal blood (0.1 to 0.2 ml) may cross the placenta into the maternal circulation, whereas larger amounts are transferred during placental separation. During a first pregnancy, initial sensitization to D antigens does not occur prior to the onset of labor because at least 0.5 to 1 ml is required for a sensitizing maternal immune response. Thus the minute leakage of fetal blood before labor is insufficient to sensitize a primigravida, but the larger amount of blood transferred during placental separation is sufficient to cause sensitization. During the second pregnancy with an Rh-positive fetus, the usual small amount of fetal blood leakage now acts as a booster dose because the mother has been previously sensitized, and her antibody production increases remarkably. Offspring of this and all subsequent pregnancies may thus be affected. Firstborn babies may be erythroblastotic if maternal sensitization has occurred after past transfusion of Rh-positive blood or if there was previous abortion of an Rh-positive fetus, but these events are unusual.

Clinical manifestations. The disease begins in utero, at which time its severity can be estimated by analysis of amniotic fluid (p. 9). In response to hemolysis, the rate of erythropoiesis is accelerated, and immature red cells (erythroblasts) appear in the fetal circulation. Red cell destruction releases hemoglobin, thus increasing the formation of bilirubin, which is largely, although not entirely, excreted across the placenta into the maternal circulation. At birth most affected infants have slightly elevated bilirubin levels, but jaundice is rarely evident. Anemia is present in proportion to the severity of hemolysis.

If amniocentesis has not been performed, the first visible indication of the severity of the disease may be the color of amniotic fluid at the time of membrane rupture. Straw-colored fluid is usually associated with mild or absent fetal disease; deep yellow fluid indicates a severely involved fetus. Intrauterine death may be associated with green- or brown-tinted fluid.

Most mildly affected infants appear to be normal at birth, although the liver and spleen may be somewhat enlarged. If the fetus is profoundly affected, pallor is obvious because of anemia.

The hemolytic process that originated in utero continues after birth. Bilirubin production increases as a function of hemolysis, and now it accumulates in the infant because placental excretion is precluded. Anemia is progressive, and the number of nucleated red cells increases. Although jaundice is usually not apparent at birth, it may appear 30 minutes later in the most severely affected babies. As a rule, it is evident within 24 to 36 hours. The liver and spleen may be enlarged so extensively as to reach well below the level of the umbilicus.

Hydrops fetalis is the most severe expression of Rh disease. Progressive anemia due to intense hemolysis leads to fetal hypoxia, cardiac failure, generalized edema, and effusion of fluid into the pleural, pericardial, and peritoneal spaces. Hydrops is a frequent cause of intrauterine death among infants with Rh disease. It generally appears between the thirty-fourth and fortieth gestational weeks. Intrauterine transfusion apparently supports some of these infants until an exchange transfusion can be performed after delivery. At birth, the most striking findings of hydrops fetalis include universal edema (anasarca) and alarming pallor. The edema may be so extensive that the infant is almost twice the expected birth weight for gestational age. Respiratory distress is sometimes severe. Jaundice is usually not apparent until later. Immediate exchange transfusion is urgent, but hydropic infants seldom survive.

Laboratory diagnosis. Fetal diagnosis of the disease and an accurate estimate of its severity are accomplished by analysis of amniotic fluid for bilirubin (p. 9). Repeated amniocentesis is usually essential to monitor the extent of fetal involvement. Erythroblastosis can also be anticipated by demonstrating a rising titer of anti-D antibodies in maternal serum during pregnancy, but this is not as reliable as amniotic fluid studies. These antibodies are produced by the mother in response to D factor on fetal cells that leaked through the placenta into her circulation. In the infant, the diagnosis is made postnatally by demonstrating these same antibodies on the surface of red blood cells. These maternal antibodies crossed the placenta to enter the fetal circulation. The diagnosis is accomplished by the direct Coombs' test. If anti-D antibody has become attached to D antigen on the infant's erythrocytes, the addition of Coombs' reagent causes visible agglutination of the cells, thus establishing the diagnosis of erythroblastosis. The diagnosis can be excluded if the Coombs' test is negative.

Treatment: exchange transfusion. The most effective treatment is exchange transfusion. Details of this procedure are well described in monographs devoted to erythroblastosis. Although the indications for exchange transfusions can be complex and equivocal, they are generally performed when bilirubin concentrations reach 20 mg/100 ml in term infants, 15 mg/100 ml in larger premature infants, and lower levels in smaller ones. The goal of treatment is to prevent the most sinister complication of the disease, kernicterus (p. 198), and to eliminate the possibility of progressively severe anemia. A "two-volume" exchange is utilized. This term refers to the exchange of an amount of donor blood that is twice the infant's blood volume. Donor blood is thus given at 170 ml/kg of body weight. This volume replaces 85% of the infant's blood. Fresh Rh-negative blood is used, either type O or the infant's own type.

The transfusion is given through a catheter in the umbilical vein by alternately removing 7 to 20 ml of blood, depending on the size of the infant, and infusing like amounts of donor blood. The procedure should be completed in little over an hour. Careful attention to thermal balance is essential. The procedure thus should be performed under a source of radiant heat. In experienced hands the mortality rate from the complications of exchange transfusion is less than 1%.

The nurse must keep scrupulous records of the amount of blood transfused. Constant attention to cardiac and respiratory rates is essential, and this is greatly facilitated by the use of heart rate and apnea monitors. The nurse must be familiar with the potential hazards of an exchange transfusion.

Hazards of exchange transfusion. The possibilities for misadventure during exchange transfusion are numerous. *Heart failure* may occur as a result of transfusion overload if the infused blood volume is miscalculated. *Cardiac arrest due to hyperkalemia* may follow the use of old donor blood (over 48 hours) because its serum potassium content is considerably higher than normal. Recent reports have demonstrated that the traditional practice of administering calcium gluconate after each 100 ml of exchanged blood is neither necessary nor effective. Reduction of ionized calcium during exchange transfusion is related to binding of calcium by citrate in the ACD solution that is generally used as an anticoagulant in donor blood. Calcium levels do indeed fall gradually and considerably during the procedure. They return to normal a very short time later, sometimes within 10 minutes. The infants studied (term and premature) had no symptoms that could be related to hypocalcemia. Occasionally the nurse may encounter repeated bursts of *irregular cardiac rhythm* caused by contact of the catheter tip with myocardium or by rapid injection of blood directly into the heart when the catheter is inserted too deeply. *Air embolus* may occur when large amounts of air are

sucked into an open-ended catheter if the infant gasps deeply. The catheter should be filled with saline solution and attached to a stopcock before insertion. *Perforation of the umbilical vein* during vigorous attempts to force catheter passage may cause hemorrhage into the liver. Negligent technique adds to the hazard of *bacterial infection.* *Acidemia* may be severe during the exchange transfusion and for some time thereafter because the pH of donor blood is often 6.8 or less. At some centers, alkali is added to donor blood to avert acidemia, which is increased in the presence of cold stress, for want of an external heat source. *Hypoglycemia* occurs in Rh disease independently of exchange transfusion, but it may be aggravated by the procedure (Chapter 11). It is more frequent in severe than in mild erythroblastosis. Blood sugar determination, or a screening test such as Dextrostix, should be part of the overall evaluation of these babies before exchange transfusion. Dextrostix testing should be done every hour after the procedure for 2 to 4 hours. The treatment of hypoglycemia is described in Chapter 11.

Perforation of the intestine, primarily the colon, occurs in 1% to 2% of infants. The symptoms are those of a perforated gut or peritonitis. They include abdominal distention, bloody stools, bilious vomiting, gastric retention, respiratory distress, hypotension, pallor, and cyanosis. Abdominal distention appears first, usually within 48 hours of the last exchange transfusion. X-ray examination reveals free air in the peritoneal space in most instances, but perforation of the intestine often occurs without this sign. Intestinal dilatation and peritoneal fluid are also visible on x-ray films. Most infants require surgery, and postoperative recovery has been reported in 90%. Intestinal perforation after exchange transfusion is attributed to ischemia of the gut. Blood flow to the intestine may be profoundly disrupted during the procedure as a result of back pressure created in the portal venous system during the injections of blood. Whereas the catheter tip should pass through the ductus venosus into the inferior vena cava, in fact this maneuver is not possible in the majority of cases. As the catheter passes through the umbilical vein in the liver, it is deflected into the portal vein. Blood is thus exchanged directly in and out of this vessel. Since the portal vein drains blood from the intestine, disruption of normal vascular pressure during exchange transfusion precludes normal blood flow to and from the intestinal wall. Diminished blood supply causes ischemia and necrosis. Perforation of the wall is the result of this process.

Phototherapy. The use of intense fluorescent lights for reduction of serum bilirubin levels is discussed in Chapter 10. Phototherapy is not recommended for treatment of Rh disease because the rate of hemolysis usually exceeds the rate of bilirubin diminution brought about by phototherapy.

Prevention. Erythroblastosis has recently become a preventable disease. Maternal sensitization can be prevented by the administration of high-titered, anti-D gamma globulin to unsensitized mothers (primigravidas) within 48 hours after delivery or abortion. The effectiveness of this vaccine is based on the fact, previously described, that fetal red cells enter the maternal circulation in greatest quantity at the time of delivery. In the presence of injected anti-D antibody, fetal cells passing into the maternal circulation are destroyed before they can exert their immunogenic effect. In essence, the mother is temporarily immunized against her fetus' invading red cells, and she is thus protected from sensitization. Administration of anti-Rh gamma globulin must be repeated after each delivery. This procedure is effective. The incidence of rhesus disease has declined remarkably.

Isoimmunization: ABO incompatibility

The disorder produced by incompatibility in the ABO groups is usually considerably milder than Rh disease. Group A or B infants of group O mothers are most commonly involved; group B infants of group A mothers are only occasionally affected.

Group O infants are never affected, regardless of the mother's blood type.

ABO incompatibility differs from Rh disease in several respects. Preexistent natural anti-A and anti-B antibodies from group O mothers pass to the fetus without previous sensitization by leakage of fetal blood. As a result, firstborn infants are frequently involved, and there is no relationship between the appearance or severity of disease and repeated sensitization from one pregnancy to the next. Stillbirth and hydrops fetalis are rare. Jaundice is common; hepatosplenomegaly occurs inconsistently. Reticulocytosis indicates a hemolytic process, but significant anemia during the neonatal period and later is rare. The direct Coombs' test on the infant's cells may be negative or mildly positive, but the indirect Coombs' test utilizing infant's serum on adult red cells may be strongly positive. Infants whose direct Coombs' test is positive are more likely to be jaundiced, with bilirubin in excess of 10 mg/100 ml. An affected group A infant has demonstrable anti-A antibody in his serum. A blood smear reveals increased numbers of spherical, plump, mature erythrocytes called *spherocytes*. These cells are thicker and smaller in diameter than normal red cells. They are not observed in abnormally increased numbers on smears from infants with Rh disease. The usual indication for exchange transfusion for ABO incompatibility is progressive elevation of serum bilirubin concentration to 20 mg/100 ml in term infants and 15 mg/100 ml in premature infants. The donor blood must be group O; it should never be the infant's own type.

Hemolysis due to infection

Infectious diseases, bacterial and nonbacterial, are associated with hemolytic anemia. Hyperbilirubinemia, and to a lesser extent anemia, are often prominent signs of septicemia and neonatal renal infection. The nonbacterial infections that cause hemolysis are of intrauterine origin. They include cytomegalic inclusion disease, toxoplasmosis, rubella, herpesvirus, and coxsackievirus infections. Congenital syphilis also causes hemolysis. Hyperbilirubinemia during infections is due to hepatocellular damage as well as to hemolysis. Infections are discussed in Chapter 12.

Other causes of hemolysis

A number of enzymatic deficiencies in red cells are known to cause hemolytic anemia. *Glucose-6-phosphate dehydrogenase (G-6-PD) deficiency* is the commonest. It occurs primarily among blacks, Filipinos, Sephardic (not Ashkenazic) Jews, Sardinians, Greeks, and Arabs. It is genetically transmitted, occurring predominantly in males, rarely in females. The disorder is manifest during the newborn period in only a fraction of affected individuals. Jaundice and anemia are the presenting signs. A large number of drugs have been reported to cause hemolysis in G-6-PD–deficient patients. Most of these substances are rarely, if ever, used in the newborn infant.

Large doses of water-soluble vitamin K analogue (Synkavite, Hykinone) may produce severe jaundice. Doses of 1 mg do not cause such an effect. Vitamin K_1 is generally utilized rather than the water-soluble analogue because it appears to be safer in respect to hemolysis.

Vitamin E deficiency has been demonstrated as a cause of moderately severe hemolytic anemia in premature infants. Reticulocytosis and a tremendous number of platelets (thrombocytosis) are associated with the anemia. The most profoundly affected infants are severely edematous, often in association with cardiovascular difficulties and hypoproteinemia. Administration of vitamin E (tocopherol) produces a rapid response. However, administration of alpha-tocopherol is effective only when the infant is chronologically at term. Until then, intestinal absorption is inefficient. Furthermore, simultaneous oral administration of iron preparations or of milk with iron results in impaired absorption of both.

Abnormal morphology of erythrocytes occurs in several varieties; they are uncommon causes of hemolytic anemia. *Hereditary spherocytosis* is the most frequent of these conditions. The red cells are abnormally fragile and thus are predisposed to premature breakdown. The life span of these cells is therefore abnormally short. They are remarkably susceptible to deposition and dissolution in the spleen. The responsible molecular abnormality has not been identified. A substantial number of affected individuals have hemolytic anemia in the newborn period. Jaundice and pallor due to anemia are the outstanding signs of the disease. The blood smear reveals a preponderance of spherocytes. They are small and round, and they stain densely as a result of their spherical configuration. These cells are similar in appearance to those observed in ABO incompatibility. Treatment during the newborn period includes exchange transfusion for high bilirubin levels or simple transfusion if anemia is the only difficulty.

Hemolytic anemia has also been described in the rare entity known as *hereditary elliptocytosis*. Most of the red cells in affected infants are a bizarre elliptical shape, and those of one of the parents have a similar appearance. Treatment during the newborn period is the same as that for hereditary spherocytic anemia.

ANEMIA DUE TO LOSS OF BLOOD
Prenatal blood loss

CAUSES OF FETAL AND NEONATAL
BLOOD LOSS

I. *Cord*
   A. Rupture of varices or aneurysms
   B. Traumatic rupture of normal cord
   C. Torn vessels with velamentous insertion
II. *Placenta*
   A. Incision into fetal side during cesarean section
   B. Placenta previa
   C. Abruptio placentae
   D. Multilobed placenta with interlobar vessels
III. *Fetal blood loss*
   A. Fetomaternal (acute or chronic blood loss)
   B. Fetofetal (into twin, acute or chronic blood loss)

IV. *Enclosed hemorrhage*
   A. Intracranial
   B. Ruptured liver
   C. Ruptured spleen
   D. Adrenal hemorrhage
   E. Retroperitoneal
   F. Subaponeurotic (scalp)
   G. Cephalhematoma
   H. Pulmonary (massive)

The fetus may lose blood before or during parturition. In utero it may bleed into the mother's circulation, into the vessels of a twin, or as a result of mishap during the birth process. The latter is usually due to some factor in the placenta or cord that predisposes to ruptured vessels or to operative complication during cesarean section.

Fetomaternal transfusion is a common phenomenon, but resultant abnormal clinical signs in the neonate are infrequent. Loss of fetal blood presumably occurs at the intervillous spaces. The precise site of placental leak has not been demonstrated. Fetal blood cells in maternal circulation have been detected in as many as 50% of pregnancies; yet in only 1% of them is blood loss sufficient to cause neonatal anemia. Fetal red cells are easily detected in maternal circulation by the acid elution technique. They do not disappear completely for several weeks after delivery.

Fetofetal transfusion occurs in monochorionic (identical) twins through arteriovenous anastomoses in the common placenta. This condition is also known as the *intrauterine parabiotic syndrome*. The effect of blood loss on the donor twin depends on the size of the transfusion and its duration. Clinical signs of acute or chronic blood loss may therefore occur (see later). In the extreme, death occurs in utero early in pregnancy. In approximately 15% of monochorionic twins, or perhaps more, significant anemia occurs in the donor. Hemoglobin has been reported as low as 5 grams/100 ml. Signs of acute or chronic hemorrhage are observed. The donor twin is often considerably smaller than the recipient and may be severely undergrown for dates. All the physical attributes of in utero undergrowth are in evidence. Oligohydramnios and hypotension are also common. Postnatal hypoglycemia occurs as a result of intrauterine malnutrition. Pallor is impressive proportional to the anemia. The recipient twin is polycythemic, with a significantly increased blood volume. Hemoglobin concentration may be 20 to 30 grams/100 ml volume. A deep red complexion contrasts dramatically with the pallor of the donor sibling. Polyhydramnios and hypertension are common. The recipient sibling may be strikingly larger than his twin, often appearing overnourished by comparison. The size of twins differs little if the transfusion occurs late in pregnancy. Thus, gross differences may exist in blood volume and other hematologic attributes in the absence of other discrepancies of size and development. The cardiovascular, pulmonary, and central nervous system signs of polycythemia (see later) are noted in the recipient baby.

Obstetric misadventure may cause life-threatening fetal blood loss. In all instances the signs of acute hemorrhage are in evidence. Placenta previa and abruptio placentae are sometimes associated with fetal as well as maternal hemorrhage. Anomalous vessels at the insertion of the cord (velamentous) are vulnerable to disruption and hemorrhage. Even the normal cord can be torn if it is inordinately short, or regardless of length during unattended delivery. Severe acute hemorrhage may complicate cesarean section if the placenta is inadvertently incised during the procedure. In multilobular placentas, the vascular connections between lobes rupture easily, which may result in severe fetal hemorrhage. During cesarean section, delayed clamping of the cord causes anemia *if the baby is above the level of the placenta*. The infant is usually placed on the mother's abdomen, or is held at approximately that level, when the cord is clamped and cut. A significant amount of blood thus passes from fetus to placenta by virtue of gravity if clamping is delayed. Furthermore, unlike the situation in vaginal deliveries, the uterus is not contracted; it is atonic. This enhances backflow of blood to the placenta because low vascular resistance persists. The result is reduction in blood volume, red blood cell volume, and plasma volume. These values are significantly higher, however, if delayed clamping occurs *while the infant is held below the level of the placenta.*

Acute hemorrhage. Acute hemorrhage may result from any of the conditions listed previously; fetomaternal and fetofetal transfusions are most often chronic. The signs of acute hemorrhage are those of hypovolemia (shock) and anemia. They are generally present at birth and include pallor, cyanosis, tachycardia, feeble or absent pulses, gasping, tachypnea, and retractions. The cry is weak, spontaneous activity is absent or diminished, and flaccidity is severe. Superficially these infants appear to be asphyxiated, but three differentiating clinical signs are helpful. First, babies who are in shock from acute blood loss have a rapid heart rate (over 160 beats/min) unless they are also profoundly hypoxic; infants who are only asphyxiated usually have bradycardia as a result of profound hypoxemia. Second, infants in shock remain cyanotic in spite of oxygen therapy; asphyxiated babies respond to it. Third, infants who are in shock usually breathe rapidly; asphyxiated infants breathe slowly. Acute blood loss should be suspected in the presence of these differentiating signs. Suspicion is the initial step; without it the baby is lost. The diagnosis is more assured if there is knowledge of an obstetric accident. Low hemoglobin and hematocrit values are diagnostic, but they are sometimes misleadingly normal at birth. The hematocrit may remain normal immediately after acute blood loss because often 3 or 4 hours must pass before hemodilution occurs from the influx of interstitial fluid into the circulation in an attempt to maintain blood volume. Hemoglobin values in capillary blood may be a source of error; they can be spuriously high because of severe stasis of peripheral circulation. Venous blood samples are preferable. Immediate transfusion is lifesaving.

Chronic blood loss. Protracted fetomaternal or fetofetal hemorrhage is associated with slowly developing anemia and compensatory adjustment of blood volume. At birth, affected infants are pale and anemic, but misleadingly vigorous. Several reports have described pale babies, otherwise apparently well, whose hemoglobin concentrations were as low as 5 grams/100 ml. After chronic intrauterine blood loss, hemoglobin at birth may range from 5 to 12 grams/100 ml. The temptation to immediately transfuse a chronically anemic baby is irresistible. If signs attributable to severe anemia (tachycardia, hypoxia) are evident, a packed-cell transfusion is indeed indicated. There is no need to rapidly restore hematocrit or hemoglobin values to normal levels, certainly not to levels higher than 35 vol % or 12 grams/100 ml, respectively. Two characteristics of chronic intrauterine blood loss must be kept in mind for their critical therapeutic implications. Most important is that generally there is no diminution in blood volume in chronic loss that can compare to that of acute loss. Rapid, overzealous transfusion is thus dangerous; it may overload the vascular space and cause failure of a heart that already functions marginally because of severe anemia. Second, chronic blood loss involves iron deficiency. Therefore many of these babies do not require transfusion at all; they need only elemental iron, 5 to 10 mg/kg of body weight daily. The iron therapy should be maintained for a year.

Postnatal blood loss

Postnatal hemorrhage most often occurs into enclosed spaces (see list on p. 186). Defects of the clotting mechanism, also responsible for serious postnatal blood loss, are discussed later. Enclosed hemorrhage is a common cause of anemia during the first 3 days of life. *Intracranial hemorrhage* (subarachnoid, subdural, and intraventricular) may be sufficiently severe to cause a significant drop in hemoglobin, although signs of central nervous system dysfunction are predominant. *Hemorrhage into the scalp* may be extensive, resulting in massive blood loss and a hemoglobin concentration as low as 3 grams/100 ml. The scalp is boggy and thick, obscuring the sutures and fontanelles of the skull, and extending over the forehead to impart a blue suffusion to the skin. Deficiency of vitamin K–dependent and other clotting factors is often present in affected infants. We have encountered severe scalp hemorrhage in an infant with hemophilia. In addition, a high incidence of difficult labor and delivery has been noted. Scalp hemorrhage is first apparent from 30 minutes to 4 hours after birth. Pallor increases as blood continues to accumulate in the scalp, and if hemorrhage is severe, shock ensues. Transfusion is urgent, and intravenous sodium bicarbonate is also necessary because of severe metabolic acidosis. Vitamin K_1 or any other coagulation factor shown to be deficient should be given intravenously.

After traumatic labor, especially in breech deliveries, hemorrhage may occur into the liver, spleen, adrenals, and kidneys. Hemorrhage into the liver is particularly pernicious. It may also follow vigorous external cardiac massage. Blood accumulates beneath the liver capsule for a day or two while the infant appears quite well, although perhaps somewhat pale. When the capsule ruptures and pressure is released, bleeding from the liver becomes copious, and sudden shock ensues. Liver enlargement is easily palpated, and the upper abdomen appears distended, particularly after rupture of the capsule. Rupture of the spleen may occur during traumatic delivery, from severe enlargement in erythroblastosis fetalis, or during exchange transfusion.

Enclosed hemorrhage, in addition to causing shock, often gives rise to hyperbilirubinemia from degradation of the extravasated blood. Treatment first consists of simple transfusion for blood loss, and then if the bilirubin rises to 10 mg/100 ml, phototherapy is indicated (p. 199). Exchange transfusion is necessary if bilirubin continues to accumulate beyond serum levels of 20 mg/100 ml and at lower levels in preterm infants.

DISORDERS OF COAGULATION

Hemorrhage may result from inherited disorders of the clotting mechanism, from clotting defects created by other disease processes, or from exaggerations of physiologic neonatal clotting deficiencies. Platelet abnormalities are also an important cause of hemorrhage. When trauma is superimposed on coagulation defects, serious hemorrhage may result, as exemplified by massive bleeding into the scalp. A complete presentation of the coagulation defects would not be appropriate here; discussion is thus restricted to the most prominent of these disorders, vitamin K deficiency, and platelet abnormalities.

Hemorrhagic disease of the newborn: vitamin K deficiency

Hemorrhagic disease of the newborn is a bleeding disorder during the first few days of life that is caused by a deficiency of vitamin K, which is in turn responsible for a deficiency of prothrombin and other coagulation factors (factors II, VII, IX, and X). These factors are generated in the liver, and their production is also dependent on normal hepatic function.

Vitamin K–dependent factors are substantially reduced from adult values at birth. In normal infants, particularly those fed cow's milk early, these levels are gradually restored. Hemorrhagic disease is rare in infants who receive cow's milk on the first day of life. Hemorrhage is most common in breast-fed infants. In a few babies (less than 0.5%), hemorrhage occurs as a result of sustained low levels. The babies of mothers who have taken phenobarbital and diphenylhydantoin (Dilantin) are especially at risk for vitamin K deficiency with severe hemorrhagic complications. They should not be treated in a routine fashion with vitamin K but rather should be treated as though actively bleeding; 1 to 2 mg of the vitamin are thus administered intravenously immediately after birth. Coagulation studies are obtained prior to treatment and should be repeated subsequently. As a rule, the hemorrhagic manifestations become apparent on the second or third day. Bloody or black stools (melena), hematuria, and oozing from the umbilicus are the most frequent signs. Hemorrhage from the nose, from the circumcision site, and into the scalp and skin (ecchymosis) is also visible. The most characteristic laboratory feature of the disease is a prolonged prothrombin time.

Prophylactic administration of vitamin K at birth prevents deficiencies of the involved clotting factors. Vitamin K_1 is the preferred preparation. The recommended intramuscular dose is 0.5 to 1 mg. Larger doses do not exert an increased prophylactic effect. Cow's milk contains approximately 6 mcg of vitamin K per 100 ml, and breast milk contains only one fourth as much. The consumption of 10 ounces of cow's milk formula during the first 48 hours thus tends to restore the prothrombin time toward normal: In premature infants, the response to vitamin K administration and to early feedings is less pronounced, presumably because of immature liver function.

Vitamin K is effective in the treatment, as well as the prevention, of hemorrhagic disease. Intravenous administration of 1 to 2 mg is preferred to intramuscular injection in bleeding infants because the latter route results in large hematomas. This precaution applies to any bleeding diathesis. The coagulation defect is ordinarily corrected within 2 to 4 hours after vitamin K administration. Bleeding may be sufficiently pronounced to require blood transfusion for correction of diminished blood volume, or fresh-frozen plasma to supply the deficient coagulation factors.

THROMBOCYTOPENIA

Platelets are the smallest cells in the blood. They do not possess nuclei and are normally visible on a routine blood smear in small aggregations. Formed from megakaryocytes in the bone marrow, platelets are indispensable to effective coagulation. They function in the earliest stages of hemostasis by aggregating at points of vascular injury, where they literally act as a plug. They also release substances that are essential for coagulation in its later stages.

Clinical manifestations of platelet deficiency

Petechiae and ecchymoses are the characteristic lesions produced by platelet deficiencies. They are present at birth, or they appear any time thereafter. Typically, new lesions continue to form in crops if the deficiency persists. Central nervous system hemorrhage is always a potential hazard in the presence of platelet deficiency, but fortunately it occurs infrequently. Although bleeding can sometimes be massive, it is usually insufficient to cause a significant decline in hemoglobin concentration. However, the breakdown of extravasated blood sometimes results in serious hyperbilirubinemia. The principal disorders that produce thrombocytopenia are infectious, pharmacologic, or immunologic in nature.

Thrombocytopenia due to infection

Thrombocytopenia is a frequent accompaniment of perinatal infection. Among the bacterial infections, septicemia is by far the most prominent. Congenital syphilis also produces platelet deficiency. Thrombocytopenia, petechiae, and ecchymoses are major clinical signs of congenital rubella, toxoplasmosis, cytomegalovirus infection, and herpesvirus infection (Chapter 12). These bacterial and nonbacterial infections may produce a constellation of signs comprised of hepatosplenomegaly, jaundice, anemia, and thrombocytopenia.

Thrombocytopenia induced by drugs

A number of drugs taken by the mother during pregnancy may destroy her platelets and the platelets of her fetus as well. The sulfonamides and quinine are of significance because of their widespread use in the past. These and other drugs stimulate the production of maternal antibodies, which destroy maternal platelets and cross the placenta to exert identical effects in the fetus.

Thrombocytopenia is also produced by the thiazides, a group of diuretics used for the treatment of preeclamptic edema. In these circumstances, platelet antibodies are not produced in the mother; her own platelets remain intact, but those of the fetus are destroyed by toxic effects of the drug. Thrombocytopenia may persist for as long as 3 months after birth in some infants. In a few babies, hemorrhage may be extensive, primarily involving the gastrointestinal tract, brain, and lungs.

Thrombocytopenia induced by immune mechanisms

Fetal platelets may be destroyed by placental passage of antibody from the mother. This destruction is rare, and it is produced by two distinct mechanisms. In one type, antiplatelet antibodies are the result of maternal disease. They destroy her platelets and cross the placenta to destroy those of her fetus. This mechanism is operative in maternal idiopathic thrombocytopenic purpura and systemic lupus erythematosus. In another type of immune mechanism, the mother's platelets are unaffected. This pattern is similar to that described for erythroblastosis fetalis. Platelets are serologically distinct because of the different antigens they possess. When fetal platelets enter the maternal circulation, the mother produces antibodies to them that cross the placenta to destroy fetal platelets. The resultant disease varies widely in severity. Intracranial hemorrhage is apparently more common in this type of thrombocytopenia than in most others. Firstborn infants are frequently affected. The clinical signs are otherwise similar to any other type of platelet deficiency.

Thrombocytopenia and giant hemangioma

Congenital hemangiomas, usually large ones, may reduce the number of circulating platelets considerably. These vascular tumors trap and destroy tremendous numbers of platelets, thereby creating thrombocytopenia, which causes generalized bleeding. The platelet count of blood within the hemangioma is higher than in blood taken from other sites. Generalized hemorrhage is usually preceded by abrupt swelling and tenseness of the hemangioma. Treatment consists of irradiation of the hemangioma, which usually shrinks in several days. Removal of the tumor may be urgent if it compresses the trachea when situated in the neck. Irradiation should be given first, surgical excision may follow a few days later.

Disseminated intravascular coagulation (DIC)

Intravascular coagulation is produced by a diversity of factors that themselves are associated with a multiplicity of disease states. It is therefore the symptom complex that results from a number of serious disorders. It is characterized by inappropriate activation of the clotting process. Inordinately rapid consumption of clotting factors and platelets occurs during intravascular coagulation, and DIC is thus also referred to as *consumption coagulopathy*. The resultant depletion of these factors leads to a paradoxic hemorrhagic diathesis, which constitutes the most serious threat of this syndrome.

Any disorder that introduces a stimulus to clotting into the bloodstream can cause DIC. In the neonate, infections of bacterial and viral origin are the most common sources of such stimuli. Bacterial septicemia due to gram-negative rods, disseminated herpesvirus, and rubella are particularly noteworthy. It has been noted in association with abruptio placentae, presumably in response to the entry of amniotic fluid into the fetal circulation. Severe antigen-antibody reactions, as in Rh disease, also seem to be responsible for triggering this process.

Clinical signs are variable and widespread because bleeding may occur anywhere in the body. Bleeding from venipunctures is a very common initial sign, even from the punctures inflicted 24 hours previously. Life-threatening hemorrhage into vital organs is cause for considerable anxiety when coagulation factors and platelets are extremely depressed.

The presumptive diagnosis can be made

by demonstrating prolonged prothrombin time (PT) and partial thromboplastin time (PTT), thrombocytopenia, and a decreased fibrinogen level. Strong evidence for the diagnosis is the presence of fragmentation of red cells on a routine blood smear. Their architecture is disrupted as they pass through the smallest vessels in which fibrin thrombi have formed as a result of intravascular coagulation. The red cells are sheared by the microthrombi. Treatment, to be ultimately effective, must be directed against the underlying disorder. With few exceptions such treatment is too time-consuming; something more immediate must be done to reverse the life-threatening hemorrhagic tendency. Heparin is usually given to interrupt the ongoing coagulation. When effective, it halts consumption of platelets and clotting factors that are being incorporated into the intravascular clots. Bleeding then ceases. Heparin is given intravenously, 100 units/kg/4 hr. Exchange transfusion blood is also effective.

POLYCYTHEMIA AND INCREASED BLOOD VOLUME

Increased blood volume and hematocrit values may arise from four possible sources: (1) prolonged emptying of placental blood into the infant after birth, (2) continuous transfer of maternal blood to the fetus (maternofetal transfusion), (3) transfusion from a donor twin in utero (fetofetal transfusion), and (4) increased red cell production. In the last category are small-for-dates babies, infants who experienced intrauterine hypoxia, and babies with certain chromosomal abnormalities.

The normal, benign upper limits of hemoglobin and hematocrit values are difficult to define precisely. Infants with high levels are often asymptomatic, whereas some are quite ill from less extensively elevated levels. As a rule, difficulties should be anticipated if the hemoglobin concentration exceeds 23 grams/100 ml and the hematocrit is over 70%. Some authors have noted symptoms at 60% or over. Increased blood volume and viscosity seem to be related to several clinical signs. Respiratory distress occurs, and there is some

evidence that it is a consequence of diminished pulmonary compliance because engorged vasculature probably stiffens the lungs. Cardiac decompensation may result from an increased blood volume. Convulsions, which have been observed in association with hypervolemia and polycythemia, are presumably caused by suboptimal brain perfusion associated with increased blood viscosity. Finally, hyperbilirubinemia often follows polycythemia at birth because larger amounts of bilirubin are formed by the breakdown of increased numbers of red cells. Treatment requires withdrawal of blood in amounts determined by the extent of plethora and size of the infant. This is accomplished by small exchange transfusions in which plasma replaces blood, volume for volume.

SUMMATION

Most of the blood disorders discussed in this chapter are a threat to the infant's intact survival, although they usually constitute only a transient threat. In the majority of instances, early recognition and rapid treatment can avert tragedy. A nurse's role in the early recognition of difficulty cannot be overestimated. With knowledge of the course of pregnancy and labor she can anticipate many of the described abnormalities before birth. Thus, if a preeclamptic woman has taken thiazides during pregnancy, it is possible that thrombocytopenia will appear in her offspring. If placenta previa or abruptio placentae were present, or if cesarean section was performed, shock due to fetal blood loss is a distinct possibility. If twins are delivered, plethora in one and severe anemia in the other are potential threats. Recognition of abnormal clinical signs, combined with the history of pregnancy, provides the nurse with alertness to the problems that may arise. The most gratifying results of such alertness are realized in instances of acute blood loss, when prompt action is an absolute necessity. The potential danger of this occurrence is suggested by the history; its presence is indicated by clinical signs and confirmed by laboratory results. As in so many other aspects of neonatal disease, the nurse is in a position to initiate appropriate management of blood disorders, if only by calling attention to their presence.

References

Allen, F. H., and Diamond, L. K.: Erythroblastosis fetalis, Boston, 1958, Little, Brown & Co.

Barrow, E., and Peters, R. L.: Exsanguinating hemorrhage into scalp in newborn infants, S. Afr. Med. J. **42**:265, 1968.

Bleyer, W. A., Hakami, N., and Shepard, T. H.: The development of hemostasis in the human fetus and newborn infant, J. Pediatr. **79**:838, 1971.

Danks, D. M., and Stevens, L. H.: Neonatal respiratory distress associated with a high hematocrit reading, Lancet **2**:499, 1964.

Gatti, R. A., et al.: Neonatal polycythemia with transient cyanosis and cardiorespiratory abnormalities, J. Pediatr. **69**:1063, 1966.

Gershanik, J. J., Levkoff, A. H., and Duncan, R.: Serum ionized calcium values in relation to exchange transfusion, J. Pediatr. **82**:847, 1973.

Gross, G. P., Hathaway, W. E., and McGaughey, H. R.: Hyperviscosity in the neonate, J. Pediatr. **82**:1004, 1973.

Gross, S., and Melhorn, D. K.: Exchange transfusion with citrated whole blood for disseminated intravascular coagulation, J. Pediatr. **78**:415, 1971.

Gross, S., and Melhorn, D. K.: Vitamin E, red cell lipids and red cell stability in prematurity, Ann. N.Y. Acad. Sci. **203**:141, 1972.

Hathaway, W. E., Mull, M. M., and Pechet, G. S.: Disseminated intravascular coagulation in the newborn, Pediatrics **43**:233, 1969.

Immunohematology; principles and practice: a programmed instruction course, Raritan, N.J., 1965, Ortho Pharmaceutical Corp.

Maisels, M. J., Li, T., Piechocki, J. T., and Werthman, M. W.: The effect of exchange transfusion on serum ionized calcium, Pediatrics **53**:683, 1974.

Michael, A. F., and Mauer, A. M.: Maternal-fetal transfusion as a cause of plethora in the neonatal period, Pediatrics **28**:458, 1961.

Naeye, R.: Human intrauterine parabiotic syndrome and its complications, N. Engl. J. Med. **268**:804, 1963.

Naiman, J. L.: Current management of hemolytic disease of the newborn infant, J. Pediatr. **80**:1049, 1972.

Orzalesi, M.: ABO system incompatibility: relationship between direct Coombs' test positivity and neonatal jaundice, Pediatrics **51**:288, 1973.

Oski, F. A., and Naiman, J. L.: Hematologic problems in the newborn, Philadelphia, 1966, W. B. Saunders Co.

Queenan, J. T.: Modern management of the Rh problem, New York, 1967, Harper & Row, Publishers.

Sacks, M. O.: Occurrence of anemia and polycythemia in pheno-typically dissimilar single-ovum human twins, Pediatrics **24**:604, 1959.

Saigal, S., O'Neill, A., Surainder, Y., et al.: Placental transfusion and hyperbilirubinemia in the premature, Pediatrics **49**:406, 1972.

Schulman, I.: Anemias due to increased destruction of red cells. In Barnett, H. L., editor: Pediatrics, New York, 1968, Appleton-Century-Crofts.

Sisson, T. R. C., Knutson, S., and Kendall, N.: The blood volume of infants. IV. Infants born by cesarean section, Am. J. Obstet. Gynecol. **117**:351, 1973.

Touloukian, R. J., Kadar, A., and Spencer, R. P.: The gastrointestinal complications of neonatal umbilical venous exchange transfusion: a clinical and experimental study, Pediatrics **51**:36, 1973.

Usher, R., and Lind, J.: Blood volume of the newborn premature infant, Acta Paediatr. Scand. **54**:419, 1965.

Chapter 10
Neonatal jaundice

ACCORDING TO ADULT STANDARDS, all neonates have hyperbilirubinemia; their serum bilirubin levels exceed 1 mg/100 ml at some time during the first few days of life. These elevations of serum bilirubin levels produce visible jaundice in only half of all newborn infants, and for the majority of these babies the icterus is a normal event; in others it may indicate a number of disorders of diverse etiology (see outline, p. 195).

BILIRUBIN IN THE NORMAL NEONATE
Types of bilirubin (conjugated and unconjugated)

The existence of direct- and indirect-reacting bilirubin has been known for over 50 years, but the chemical differences that characterize them were first demonstrated in the 1950s. Direct-reacting bilirubin is bilirubin glucuronide, which is also referred to as conjugated bilirubin because the free bilirubin molecule undergoes conjugation with a glucuronide radical in the liver. Because the resultant complex is water soluble, it is normally excreted through the biliary tree and also through the kidneys if serum levels are abnormally high. Indirect-reacting bilirubin is unconjugated bilirubin because it has not been converted to the glucuronide form in the liver. Since it is fat soluble and not water soluble, it cannot be excreted in bile or through the kidneys. Because it is fat soluble, unconjugated bilirubin has a high affinity for extravascular tissue, particularly fatty tissue and brain. In plasma it is complexed to albumin. A laboratory report of total bilirubin includes the direct and indirect fractions and does not distinguish between them unless the direct fraction is specifically determined.

Formation of bilirubin

Most of the body's bilirubin is formed from the breakdown of erythrocytes. The life span of a normal neonatal red cell is estimated at 80 to 100 days by different investigators (adult life span is 120 days); its fragility increases as the cell ages, and it is then sequestered from the blood. Hemoglobin is then split into 2 fragments, heme and globin. The globin fraction is a protein, and it is utilized as such by the body. Unconjugated bilirubin is formed from the heme fraction in reticuloendothelial cells that are primarily located in the spleen and liver. One gram of hemoglobin yields 35 mg of unconjugated bilirubin. The normal neonate produces bilirubin at a rate of 6 to 8 mg/kg/24 hr.

Bilirubin in plasma (albumin binding)

Once formed, bilirubin is transported in plasma to the liver, where it is conjugated with glucuronide (see later). In plasma, unconjugated bilirubin is bound to albumin; 1 gram of albumin binds 16 mg of bilirubin. Bilirubin that is complexed to albumin cannot leave the vascular space. A minute amount of the pigment is unbound, in which state it is free to leave the blood and permeate tissues. It is in the unbound state that bilirubin also diffuses into liver cells, where conjugation with glucuronide takes place. When not bound to albumin, bilirubin permeates other extravascular tissues, including the brain. The quantity of unbound bilirubin is increased if albumin-binding capacity is reduced, which may occur in several circumstances. Thus, unconjugated bilirubin may accumulate to levels that surpass albumin-binding capacity. This accumulation generally occurs at serum bilirubin levels of 20 mg/100 ml or more, but it is quite variable, depending on maturity and illness of the baby. Furthermore, at any serum level, bilirubin is displaceable from albumin-binding sites by several substances having a greater affinity for these sites. These substances include metabolities such as free fatty acids, or drugs such as sulfonamides, salicylates, and sodium benzoate. Albumin-binding capacity is also reduced in the presence of an acid blood pH. Hypoalbuminemia causes low binding capacity, whereas binding capacity can be increased by giving albumin intravenously. Neonatal serum albumin does not bind bilirubin as effectively as adult serum albumin. Thus, gram for gram, "fetal albumin" has a lower binding capacity than that of the adult. Binding capacity increases with age to approximately adult levels by 5 months. The binding capacity of purified human serum albumin, administered at the time of exchange transfusion to augment bilirubin removal, is half that of circulating serum albumin in adults. Neonatal serum albumin falls between the two.

Bilirubin in the liver; conjugation and excretion

The conjugation of bilirubin with a glucuronide radical takes place within liver cells through a series of reactions that culminates in the transfer of glucuronic acid from uridine diphosphate glucuronic acid (UDPGA) to bilirubin. This last reaction is catalyzed by the transfer enzyme, glucuronyl transferase. The steps that precede the formation of UDPGA require oxygen and glucose. Oxygen deprivation and hypoglycemia may thus impair UDPGA production and contribute to hyperbilirubinemia. Bilirubin glucuronide is passed from the liver cell into the biliary tree and thence into the gastrointestinal tract.

The fetal and neonatal small intestinal mucosa contains a considerable amount of the enzyme beta-glucuronidase. This substance can convert the bilirubin glucuronide that has entered the intestine back to unconjugated bilirubin by splitting off the glucuronide. Bilirubin is now fat soluble once again, and it is absorbed across the intestinal wall into the portal (enterohepatic) circulation. Meconium contains 0.5 to 1 mg of bilirubin per gram. Delayed meconium passage thus increases the amount of bilirubin reabsorbed across intestinal mucosa because more bilirubin glucuronide is converted to the unconjugated reabsorbable form. This "enterohepatic shunt" contributes significantly to physiologic jaundice: it may explain the high incidence of hyperbilirubinemia in some cases of upper intestinal obstruction. It is the mechanism by which late feeding, because it promotes intestinal stasis, results in higher mean serum bilirubin levels than does early feeding. The old practice of withholding feedings for 48 hours has long been discontinued for this and several other good reasons as well. During the first few days of life the neonate's capacity to excrete bilirubin is only 1% or 2% that of the adult's. This is apparently related to deficient activity of glucuronyl transferase, which increases gradually after a few days, probably attaining adult levels at 2 to 4 weeks of age.

Physiologic jaundice

Although a deficiency of glucuronyl transferase has been said to be the major cause of physiologic jaundice, the diminution in activity of this enzyme is not as profound as previously believed. Glucuronyl transferase deficiency is not the sole cause of physiologic jaundice; a number of immature functional difficulties are accountable. First, an excessive amount of bilirubin is delivered to the liver because synthesis is increased and because there is significant reabsorption of the pigment from the intestine via the enterohepatic shunt (see previous discussion). Second, there is a diminished capacity of the liver to excrete the excessive bilirubin delivered to it because uptake by hepatic cells is inhibited and because there is diminished conjugation of the pigment that enters the liver cell. Hyperbilirubinemia is therefore a regular occurrence in all neonates, but jaundice occurs in only half of them because serum bilirubin levels must exceed 4 to 6 mg/100 ml before it is visible as pigment in the skin. In term infants a peak unconjugated bilirubin level is reached on the third or fourth day of life; in premature infants it is attained on the fifth or sixth day. This is physiologic jaundice. Physiologic jaundice is a useful clinical concept because it implies a normal state that does not require therapy. However, the limitations of functional immaturity may persist, and bilirubin may accumulate to hazardous levels. As a rule, physiologic jaundice fulfills the following specific criteria: (1) the infant is otherwise well; (2) in full-term infants, jaundice first appears after 24 hours and disappears by the end of the seventh day; (3) in premature infants, jaundice is first evident after 48 hours and disappears by the ninth or tenth day; (4) serum unconjugated bilirubin concentration does not exceed 12 mg/100 ml, either in term or preterm infants; (5) hyperbilirubinemia is almost exclusively of the unconjugated variety, and conjugated (direct) bilirubin should not exceed 1 to 1.5 mg/100 ml; (6) daily increments of bilirubin concentration should not surpass 5 mg/100 ml. Bilirubin levels in excess of 12 mg/100 ml may indicate either an exaggeration of the physiologic handicap or the presence of disease. At any serum bilirubin level, the appearance of jaundice during the first day of life or persistence beyond the ages previously delineated usually indicates a pathologic process.

CAUSES OF NEONATAL JAUNDICE

The following list presents the most prominent disorders associated with neonatal jaundice categorized by the mechanisms involved. Most of these conditions also entail some degree of anemia, particularly in the presence of intravascular hemolysis or blood loss into enclosed spaces.

CAUSES OF PATHOLOGIC NEONATAL JAUNDICE*

I. *Intravascular hemolysis (unconjugated hyperbilirubinemia)*
   A. Hemolytic disease of the newborn (Rh, ABO, others)
   B. Polycythemia (large placental transfusion, fetofetal transfusion, maternofetal transfusion)
   C. Abnormalities of red cells
      1. Hereditary spherocytosis
      2. Enzyme deficiencies (G-6-PD deficiency and others)
      3. Elliptocytosis
      4. Pyknocytosis
      5. Hemoglobinopathy (Barts, Zurich)
   D. Chemical hemolysins (vitamin K analogues, maternal naphthalene ingestion in G-6-PD deficiency)
II. *Extravascular hemolysis; enclosed hemorrhage (unconjugated hyperbilirubinemia)*
   A. Petechiae, ecchymoses
   B. Hematoma
   C. Hemorrhage
   D. Intraventricular hemorrhage
III. *Impaired hepatic function*
   A. Deficient glucuronyl transferase (unconjugated hyperbilirubinemia)
      1. Familial nonhemolytic jaundice, types I, II
      2. Transient familial neonatal hyperbilirubinemia (Lucey-Driscoll syndrome)
   B. Infection (conjugated, unconjugated hyperbilirubinemia)
      1. Bacterial (septicemia, syphilis, pyelonephritis)
      2. Nonbacterial
         a. Toxoplasmosis
         b. Cytomegalovirus
         c. Rubella
         d. Herpes simplex
         e. Coxsackievirus
         f. Neonatal hepatitis
   C. Metabolic factors (unconjugated hyperbilirubinemia)
      1. Infants of diabetic mothers
      2. Galactosemia

*Modified from Odell, G. B.: Postnatal care. In Cooke, R. E., editor: The biologic basis of pediatric practice, New York, 1968, McGraw-Hill Book Co.

3. "Breast milk jaundice"
4. Hypothyroidism
D. Biliary obstruction (conjugated, unconjugated hyperbilirubinemia)
   1. Biliary atresia

Intravascular hemolysis

Isoimmune hemolytic disease of the newborn (p. 181). Maternofetal blood group incompatibility (Rh, ABO) is the most frequent cause of pathologic jaundice. Hemolysis is intravascular by virtue of an antigen-antibody reaction on the surface of the red cells.

Polycythemia (p. 191). An increased quantity of erythrocytes results in sequestration of greater numbers of aged cells, which, when broken down, yield excessive amounts of bilirubin. The accumulation of pigment is occasionally sufficiently pronounced to necessitate an exchange transfusion. Hyperbilirubinemia occurs in the absence of maternal blood group incompatibility or any other disorder that accelerates hemolysis.

Intrinsic red cell abnormalities. Enzymatic deficiencies, the most prominent of which is G-6-PD deficiency (p. 185), are responsible for hemolysis and jaundice because of disrupted erythrocyte metabolism; this is particularly noteworthy in premature black infants.

Abnormal contours of erythrocytes also render them vulnerable to early dissolution and the occasional production of jaundice. Hereditary spherocytosis is the commonest disorder in this category. Rare abnormalities of red cell morphology that may also cause icterus are hereditary elliptocytosis (p. 185) and pyknocytosis. In pyknocytosis the red cells are small; they stain rather deeply, and the cell borders are irregular. Their life span is abnormally short, thereby increasing the rate of hemolysis.

Drug toxicity (chemical hemolysins). Excessive doses of vitamin K produce hyperbilirubinemia in premature infants. Hemolysis is more severe and more likely to occur in the presence of G-6-PD deficiency. Hyperbilirubinemia has also been reported in infants whose mothers received large doses of vitamin K to protect the infant from hemorrhagic disease of the newborn. Vitamin K should be administered to the infant, preferably in the form of K_1, only in an intramuscular dose of 0.5 to 1 mg. Ingestion or inhalation of naphthalene is a rare but fascinating example of drug-induced icterus. It has been reported in G-6-PD–deficient infants whose mothers ingested or inhaled fumes from mothballs.

Extravascular hemolysis (unconjugated hyperbilirubinemia)

Degradation of blood in enclosed spaces is relatively rapid. Perhaps the most graphic example is the hyperbilirubinemia that follows the formation of petechiae in the skin from any cause. One gram of hemoglobin is transformed into 35 mg of bilirubin; the added pigment from rapid hemolysis of a small amount of blood thus overtaxes the neonate's limited capacity to conjugate bilirubin. Extensive ecchymosis from traumatic delivery is not uncommon in small premature infants; an inordinately high level of serum bilirubin often occurs as a result. Large cephalhematomas produce the same effect, particularly if they are bilateral.

Impaired hepatic function

Deficient glucuronyl transferase activity. Two rare entities that involve glucuronyl transferase deficiency are worthy of mention. *Familial nonhemolytic jaundice,* (Crigler-Najjar syndrome) is a heritable, permanent deficiency of glucuronyl transferase that does not involve hemolysis. Unconjugated hyperbilirubinemia persists throughout life because of an inability to form bilirubin glucuronide. The syndrome occurs in a serious, often lethal form (type I) and in a milder form that is apparently a partial deficiency of glucuronyl transferase type II. Type I bilirubinemia ranges upward from 20 to 25 mg/100 ml. Numerous exchange transfusions are often required in the neonatal period. In contrast to type II, it resists phenobarbital therapy. Kernicterus and death are common. Serum bilirubin in type II disease is generally under 20 to 25 mg/100 ml, and small amounts of bilirubin glucuronide are in bile. Response to phenobarbital is usually satisfactory. Kernicterus is less likely to occur in the milder expression of the syndrome. Most survivors suffer severe brain damage as a result of bilirubin toxicity. Occasionally kernicterus develops later in childhood.

Transient familial neonatal hyperbilirubinemia (Lucey-Driscoll syndrome) affects all the offspring of one mother. Severe unconjugated hyperbilirubinemia appears during the first few days and subsides during the second or third week. An unidentified factor in the sera of affected mothers and in their infants has been shown to impair glucuronyl transferase activity in vitro.

Infection. Bacterial and nonbacterial infections are often associated with jaundice. Some degree of conjugated (direct) hyperbilirubinemia is frequent, indicating impaired liver function and often actual destruction of hepatic tissue. Septicemia and renal infection produce hemolysis as well. The nonbacterial infections and syphilis probably do likewise; structural liver damage occurs more frequently in them than in the bacterial diseases.

Metabolic factors

Infants of diabetic mothers. The basis for increased incidence of hyperbilirubinemia in infants of diabetic mothers is unknown. The frequency of prematurity and respiratory distress among these babies is probably the most important factor. Depression, by asphyxia, of hepatic function that is already immature seems plausible. Furthermore, severe illness diminishes intestinal mobility, thereby enhancing reabsorption of bilirubin from the small intestine.

Galactosemia. Protracted bilirubinemia, with either moderately or severely elevated levels, may occur in galactosemia as the only clinical manifestation. Jaundice may persist for over 10 days. The bilirubin is unconjugated at first, but later, as liver damage begins, conjugated bilirubin is retained in the blood.

"Breast milk jaundice." Breast milk jaundice is an interesting condition in which unconjugated hyperbilirubinemia appears during the second week in breast-fed infants. Milk from mothers of affected babies contains a compound (a form of pregnanediol) that inhibits the activity of glucuronyl transferase. Discontinuation of breast feeding is followed by clearance of jaundice, which occasionally persists for 3 to 10 weeks. Serum bilirubin concentrations vary from 15 to 25 mg/100 ml. There is usually a history of jaundice in previously breast-fed infants of the same mother.

Hypothyroidism. Persistent low-grade hyperbilirubinemia may be, as in galactosemia, the only sign of hypothyroidism in the first 2 to 4 weeks of life. Only unconjugated bilirubin is involved.

Biliary obstruction

Developmental failure of the biliary tree is not common. It has been noted in congenital rubella infection, but other causes, still unknown, are operative as well. Jaundice appears during the first week or later; half the affected infants are not icteric until the second week. Conjugated hyperbilirubinemia always develops eventually, although some degree of unconjugated bilirubin accumulation also occurs, particularly at the onset of jaundice. The conjugated hyperbilirubinemia progresses relentlessly in the months or few years left of life. Biliary cirrhosis eventually becomes so extensive as to virtually eliminate most of the liver functions.

Biliary atresia has traditionally been considered a congenital anomaly. It generally referred to absence of a lumen in the extrahepatic ducts, the bile ducts that emerge from the liver and join to form the common duct, which inserts into the second part of the duodenum. Usually, obliteration of at least some of intrahepatic bile ducts is also identified. The only lesion that was thought to be amenable to surgery was the one in which there was preservation of bile ducts within the liver and those immediately outside of it, but with obliteration of the common duct. It has also been a dictum that an infant with obstructive jaundice should not be operated on before 4 months of age because the postoperative mortality was said to be 50%; yet no laboratory test could distinguish neonatal hepatitis from biliary atresia with consistency. Exploration was the only procedure that permitted a definitive diagnosis of either of these disorders. Jaundice worsened, livers enlarged and became more cirrhotic, and, by the time surgery was elected at 4 months of age, the process was irreversible. Yet surgeons have closed the abdomens of such children with a pronouncement of hopelessness, only to find that the jaundice cleared months later and that the child was eventually normal.

This view of biliary atresia is in the process of revision. The "4-month rule" has been abrogated. The lesion is perhaps a dynamic one in which obliterative bile duct changes (fibrosis) begin in utero and progress to completion postnatally. An important stimulus to this changing concept is the "Japanese operation" (Kasai operation), in which small intestine is anastomosed to the liver at the site of emergence of bile ducts (the porta hepatis). It may be successful if there is microscopic evidence of bile ducts with lumens. Whether or not this or some other operation proves to be definitive, of fundamental importance is the changing view in which biliary atresia is considered a dynamic process that can perhaps be halted. Exploration may therefore be indicated in selected babies by 2 months of age.

KERNICTERUS (BILIRUBIN ENCEPHALOPATHY)

Kernicterus, the most serious complication of neonatal hyperbilirubinemia, is caused by deposition of unconjugated and unbound bilirubin in brain cells. Neurologic signs appear between the second and tenth days of life. They produce depression (coma, lethargy, diminished or absent Moro reflex, hypotonia, and absent sucking and rooting reflex) followed by excitation (twitching, generalized seizures, opisthotonos, hypertonia,

and a high-pitched cry). Occasionally the anterior fontanelle bulges. Many affected infants die in the neonatal period, and those who survive usually have impaired intellectual or motor function. The effects of these neurologic deficits in later childhood may vary from severe to subtle dysfunction. Morphologic changes in affected brain cells suggest that damage from kernicterus impairs learning, memory, and adaptive behavior. In some children perceptual function may be diminished even in the absence of subnormal IQ or motor deficits. Deafness is not infrequent.

Serum bilirubin concentrations in excess of 20 mg/100 ml in term infants and 15 mg/100 ml in preterm babies are generally accepted as the levels at which kernicterus is likely to occur. This rule of thumb has traditionally provided the clinician with a simple guide for deciding whether to perform an exchange transfusion. Actually, the extent to which bilirubin is bound to albumin is even more important than its concentration in the serum. Bilirubin encephalopathy is caused by the migration of unbound bilirubin into brain substance. Therefore it may not occur at high serum bilirubin levels if the pigment is albumin bound. Conversely, it can occur at serum levels considerably below 20 mg/100 ml if significant quantities of bilirubin are not albumin bound. The causes of diminished albumin binding have been described on p. 193. Respiratory or metabolic acidosis, drugs administered by the physician, and hypothermia are impediments to albumin binding. Acidosis impairs the capacity of albumin to hold bilirubin, and some drugs competitively displace the pigment from its binding site. The metabolic response to cold stress releases free fatty acids that dislocate bilirubin from albumin. Kernicterus has been reported in small premature infants at serum bilirubin levels below 10 mg/100 ml, but more often between 10 and 15 mg/100 ml. The factors that increase the vulnerability of these infants are stated by Lucey as follows:

Birth weight less than 1500 grams
Hypothermia
Asphyxia, severe prenatal or postnatal
Hypoalbuminemia
Septicemia
Meningitis
Drugs that affect albumin binding
Serum bilirubin above 10 mg/100 ml

Yet in spite of these variables and the importance of unbound bilirubin, total serum bilirubin determination rather than assessment of albumin-binding capacity is currently the most practical guide for evaluating the need for exchange transfusion.

THERAPY FOR HYPERBILIRUBINEMIA
Exchange transfusion

Exchange transfusion is the classic therapeutic procedure for hyperbilirubinemia of any etiology. The two-volume exchange removes approximately 85% of the infant's red blood cells. In the case of erythroblastosis the offending cells are thus eliminated. In cases of drug toxicity the circulating drug may be largely removed. Exchange transfusion is less effective for the removal of total body bilirubin, although it remains the most valuable form of therapy for this purpose. Whereas most of the bilirubin in plasma is indeed eliminated by the procedure, pigment in extravascular tissue rapidly migrates back into the blood after the transfusion. As a rule, serum bilirubin at the end of an exchange transfusion is approximately 50% of preexchange levels. However, as a result of the diffusion of bilirubin from tissues, these levels promptly rise to 70% or 80% of their previous values, and the process may continue so that bilirubin concentrations soon equal or surpass preexisting levels. The rapidity and extent of this rebound phenomenon depend on the amount of pigment stored in tissues and the remaining vigor of the hemolytic process that caused hyperbilirubinemia. Serum bilirubin may thus reaccumulate after the first transfusion, so that one or more additional transfusions are frequently necessary. (Exchange transfusion is also discussed on p. 182.)

Administration of albumin

Since albumin-binding capacity is a crucial determinant of the development of kernicterus, it would seem rational to enhance it. The use of albumin before or during the exchange transfusion does indeed increase binding capacity and therefore results in removal of larger amounts of bilirubin, because the additional circulating protein pulls bilirubin out of extravascular tissue to bind it. Intravenous administration of 1 gram of albumin in a 25% salt-poor preparation 1 or 2 hours before exchange transfusion exerts such a measurable effect. Other investigators have given 6 to 12 grams of albumin during the transfusion by adding it to donor blood. By attracting bilirubin from the tissues into the blood during this procedure, albumin causes higher posttransfusion serum levels of the pigment. However, the resultant values may spuriously indicate the need for another transfusion when this is in fact not the case, since binding capacity has been enhanced by continuous addition of albumin during the exchange transfusion. The issue can be resolved only by determination of albumin-binding capacity, a procedure that is not yet generally available. There has been a recent report of a fluorescent dye method for determination of bilirubin binding capacity of serum albumin that holds promise of widespread application. It is a simple, rapid procedure that requires less serum than is required for routine bilirubin determination. A considerable amount of data, especially long-term follow-up results, will be essential before this test can be applied clinically. For the time being, when albumin is given, most clinicians use serum values somewhat in excess of 20 mg/100 ml as an indication for a repeat transfusion.

Phototherapy

The use of intense fluorescent light to reduce serum bilirubin gained widespread acceptance in the United States after a decade of general use abroad. Blue light decomposes bilirubin by photooxidation. When light is applied to jaundiced infants, shielded skin remains more icteric, which suggests that decomposition transpires in the skin. The products formed in the breakdown of bilirubin are not toxic. There is no doubt that serum unconjugated bilirubin concentrations are reduced by phototherapy. Numerous precautions have been urged by investigators whose experience with lights is extensive. Long-term outcomes have not been completely evaluated, nor have the theoretic effects of intense light on a wide spectrum of biologic processes been assessed. Many of the objections that have been raised are hypothetical; significant immediate adverse effects have not been demonstrated, nor have any long-term adverse effects. Yet the "light controversy" rages on. The use of lights must be regarded with the same caution as the use of a new drug; the potential dangers of the unknown should not outweigh the benefit expected. However, it will be a rare new drug indeed that can be withheld from the neonate until its long-term effects are totally known. For both patient and physician, life is too short. The etiology of jaundice must be sought before and during therapy. In the presence of a mild hemolytic process, hemoglobin determination is essential at frequent intervals because anemia may develop in spite of diminishing bilirubin levels.

Phototherapy is applied by exposing the nude infant to fluorescent daylight bulbs that supply 200 to 400 footcandles at the skin surface. Although light intensity continues to be expressed in footcandles, the total inappropriateness of this unit of measurement has been pointed out recently. Our interest is the amount of energy delivered by the blue part of the light spectrum, which is photodestructive to bilirubin. The term "footcandles" actually expresses the observer's *sensation* of brightness produced by a given light source. The appropriate unit of measurement is called flux (energy in watts per square centimeter). It will be the pervasive unit of measurement in the future.

Optimal light intensity and duration of therapy have not been determined. Phototherapy should not be used for routine prophylaxis against hyperbilirubinemia in any infant, full term or premature. In ABO incompatibility, it is useful for infants who are candidates for exchange transfusion, but in whom there is as yet no clear indication for its performance. Phototherapy has recently been utilized increasingly for Rh disease, and the data indicate that fewer early (first 12 hours of life) and late transfusions are necessary. One must be mindful that in removing bilirubin with phototherapy, the vulnerable red cells remain in circulation for ultimate hemolysis. The result is progressive anemia at safe levels of serum bilirubin. There is frequent prolongation of hospital stay for close observation of precipitous decline in hemoglobin. In our experience, a need arises for multiple simple transfusions because of progressive anemia. We still believe it best *in Rh disease* to observe for hyperbilirubinemia, perform the first exchange transfusion, and then apply phototherapy.

For hyperbilirubinemia from any cause, lights should never be used to delay an exchange transfusion once the serum bilirubin approaches levels that require it. If indicated, phototherapy should be instituted when the bilirubin concentration reaches 10 mg/100 ml in premature infants and sometimes at even lower levels in smaller babies. The average fall in pigment concentration is 3 to 4 mg/100 ml after 8 to 12 hours of therapy. Rebound elevations of several milligrams per 100 ml are the rule after therapy is discontinued.

In the day-to-day management of infants, the most important immediate untoward effects of phototherapy include increased metabolic rate, hyperthermia, loose stools, and significantly increased loss of water through the skin. Metabolic rate increases, and the caloric requirement thus rises. There may be difficulty in meeting caloric needs if intestinal transit time is increased to cause loose stools. Hyperthermia (and the loose stools) increases water losses, and the daily fluid requirement thus increases.

The effect of phototherapy on growth of premature infants during the neonatal period has been assessed, and the data negate the previous conclusion (from the same investigator) that long-term growth is impaired. There is indeed diminished growth during the period of phototherapy, but there is also a catch-up period during the second and third weeks of life. The reason is probably that phototherapy causes increased metabolic demands and decreased intestinal absorption of milk (because intestinal transit time is increased).

That natural light conditions affect serum bilirubin levels has been demonstrated in a study from Finland, where, through the year, seasonal daily duration of daylight varies from 3 to 22 hours. Premature babies born during the "light" half of the year had significantly lower bilirubin levels than those born during the "dark" half of the year. None of them received phototherapy. Environmental light undoubtedly also influences the effect of phototherapy. Factors such as the number of windows in a nursery, the light they admit, the position of the baby in relation to windows, and the geographic location of the hospital all must be reckoned with in evaluating the results of light therapy.

A warning issued by the Federal Drug Administration called attention to the protective effect of a plastic barrier between phototherapy lights and babies. Without a plastic shield, ultraviolet light from fluorescent bulbs has caused skin erythema in two babies. Commercial lights have Plexiglas shields built into the apparatus. The plastic walls of an incubator are also protective. Phototherapy should be used only with plastic interposed between the light and the baby. The erythematous skin caused by ultraviolet light suggests that the retina would also be jeopardized in the absence of a surface that filters out the ultraviolet light.

Because blue light is the effective segment of the spectrum that acts on bilirubin, narrow-spectrum blue lights have been used for phototherapy. Reduction of serum bilirubin levels was greater than with the usual fluorescent bulbs. However, as one might anticipate, it was impossible to detect cyanosis. The generally utilized "cool white" fluorescent bulbs are still preferred.

The "bronze baby syndrome" has received wide attention. It occurs in light-treated babies with liver disease whose hyperbilirubinemia has a significant direct component. A gray-brown discoloration of skin, serum, and urine was observed. The discoloration cleared 3 weeks after therapy was discontinued. "Tanning" of black infants has been also reported. This is distinct from the "bronzing" effect. The skin simply becomes more deeply pigmented during exposure to the lights. A maculopapular rash has also been noted as one of the side effects of therapy.

The infant's eyes are shielded from the intense light he receives during phototherapy. No evidence from human eyes has indicated that the light is injurious, but microscopic injury to retinal cells has been observed in monkeys exposed to phototherapy (without shielding eyes) for 3 to 7 days. The extent of the damage was well correlated with duration of exposure. *There is thus now strong evidence to justify conscientious maintenance of eye patches during treatment.* The nurse should be certain that the lids are closed when the blindfold is applied. It should be removed daily to inspect the eyes for conjunctivitis. Failure to change the eye shields has resulted in unsuspected severe purulent conjunctivitis.

Phenobarbital

Phenobarbital has been successfully used to diminish serum unconjugated bilirubin. It apparently promotes hepatic clearance of the pigment by increasing the capacity for conjugation. With this as a goal it has been given to mothers continuously for several days before delivery, to babies several days afterward, and to mothers and babies perinatally. Phenobarbital is not usually employed for hyperbilirubinemia due to blood incompatibility, since it requires a relatively long time to exert effects. There is no real indication for its use in treatment or prevention of neonatal hyperbilirubinemia.

References

Anttolainen, I., Simila, S., and Wallgren, E. I.: Effect of seasonal variation in daylight on bilirubin level in premature infants, Arch. Dis. Child. **50:**156, 1975.

Behrman, R. E.: Summary of a symposium on phototherapy for hyperbilirubinemia, J. Pediatr. **75:**718, 1969.

Behrman, R. E., and Fisher, D. E.: Phenobarbital for neonatal jaundice, J. Pediatr. **76:**945, 1970.

Boggs, T. R., and Bishop, H.: Neonatal hyperbilirubinemia associated with high obstruction of the small bowel, J. Pediatr. **66:**349, 1965.

Broughton, P. M. G.: The effectiveness and safety of phototherapy. In Bergsma, D., Hsia, D. Y-Y, and Jackson, C., editors: Birth defects: bilirubin metabolism in the newborn, vol. VI, no. 2, White Plains, N.Y., June, 1970, National Foundation–March of Dimes.

Diamond, I.: Bilirubin binding and kernicterus. In Schulman, I., et al., editors: Advances in pediatrics, vol. 16, Chicago, 1969, Year Book Medical Publishers, Inc.

Diamond, L. K.: A history of jaundice in the newborn. In Bergsma, D., Hsia, D. Y-Y, and Jackson, C., editors: Birth defects: bilirubin metabolism in the newborn, vol. VI, no. 2, White Plains, N.Y., June, 1970, National Foundation–March of Dimes.

Food and Drug Administration (HEW): Comment: Hazard of ultraviolet radiation from fluorescent lamps to infant during phototherapy, J. Pediatr. **84:**145, 1974.

Gellis, S. S.: Biliary atresia, Pediatrics **55:**8, 1975.

Hodgman, J. E., and Teberg, A.: Effect of phototherapy on subsequent growth and development of the premature infant. In Bergsma, D., Hsia, D. Y-Y, and Jackson, C., editors: Birth defects: bilirubin metabolism in the newborn, vol. VI, no. 2, White Plains, N.Y., June, 1970, National Foundation–March of Dimes.

Kapitulnik, J., Horner-Mibashan, R., Blondheim, S. H., et al.: Increase in bilirubin-binding affinity of serum with age of infant, J. Pediatr. **86:**442, 1975.

Keenan, W. J., Perlstein, P. H., Light, I. J., and Sutherland, J. M.: Kernicterus in small sick premature infants receiving phototherapy, Pediatrics **49:**652, 1972.

Koop, C. E.: Biliary atresia and the Kasai operation, Pediatrics **55:**8, 1975.

Kopelman, A. E., Brown, R. S., and Odell, G. B.: The "bronze" baby syndrome: a complication of phototherapy, J. Pediatr. **81:**466, 1972.

Kwang-sun, L., Gartner, L. M., and Zarafu, I.: Fluorescent dye method for determination of the bilirubin-binding capacity of serum albumin, J. Pediatr. **86:**280, 1975.

Lester, R., Jackson, B. T., and Smallwood, R. A.: Fetal hepatic function. In Bergsma, D., Hsia, D. Y-Y, and Jackson, C., editors: Birth defects: bilirubin metabolism in the newborn, vol. VI, no. 2, White Plains, N.Y., June, 1970, National Foundation–March of Dimes.

Lilly, J. R.: The Japanese operation for biliary atresia: remedy or mischief? Pediatrics **55:**12, 1975.

Lucey, J. F.: The unsolved problem of kernicterus in the susceptible low birth weight infant, Pediatrics **49:**646, 1972.

Lucey, J. F.: Light: a time for change to "radiant flux," or microwatts per square centimeter (μW/CM^2), Pediatrics **50:**5, 1972.

Lucey, J. F.: Comment: Another view of phototherapy, J. Pediatr. **84:**145, 1974.

Lucey, J. F., Ferreiro, M., and Hewitt, J.: Prevention of hyperbilirubinemia of prematurity by phototherapy, Pediatrics **41:**1047, 1968.

Messner, K. H., Leŭre-Dupree, A. E., and Maisels, M. J.: The effect of continuous prolonged illumination on the newborn primate retina (abstr.), Pediatr. Res. **9:**368, 1975.

Moller, J., and Ebbesen, F.: Phototherapy in newborn infants with severe rhesus hemolytic disease, J. Pediatr. **86:**135, 1975.

Nakai, H., and Margaretten, W.: Protracted jaundice associated with hypertrophic pyloric stenosis, Pediatrics **29:**198, 1962.

Odell, G. B.: "Physiologic" hyperbilirubinemia in the neonatal period, N. Engl. J. Med. **277:**193, 1967.

Odell, G. B.: The distribution and toxicity of bilirubin, Pediatrics **46:**16, 1970.

Odell, G. B., Storey, B., and Rosenberg, L. A.: Studies in kernicterus. III. The saturation of serum proteins with bilirubin during neonatal life and its relationship to brain damage at five years, J. Pediatr. **76:**12, 1970.

Page, I. H., Gartner, L. M., and Arias, I. M.:

Formation, transport, metabolism and excretion of bilirubin, N. Engl. J. Med. **280:**1339, 1969.

Poland, R. L., and Odell, G. B.: Physiologic jaundice: the enterohepatic circulation of bilirubin, N. Engl. J. Med. **284:**1, 1971.

Shennan, A. T.: The effect of phototherapy on the hyperbilirubinemia of rhesus incompatibility, Pediatrics **54:**417, 1974.

Sisson, T. R. C., Kendall, N., Shaw, E., and Kechavarz-Oliai, L.: Phototherapy of jaundice in the newborn infant. II. Effect of various light intensities, J. Pediatr. **81:**35, 1972.

Woody, N. C., and Brodkey, M. J.: Tanning from phototherapy for neonatal jaundice, J. Pediatr. **82:**1042, 1973.

Wu, P. Y. K., Lim, R. C., Hodgman, J. E., et al.: Effect of phototherapy in preterm infants on growth in the neonatal period, J. Pediatr. **85:** 563, 1974.

Zuelzer, W. W., and Brown, A. K.: Neonatal jaundice, Am. J. Dis. Child. **101:**113, 1961.

Chapter 11

Metabolic disorders

HYPOGLYCEMIC SYNDROMES
Glucose balance in the normal neonate

THE FETUS DERIVES GLUCOSE directly from maternal blood by a process of diffusion through the placenta that requires some energy for its accomplishment (facilitated diffusion). During early gestation glycogen, which is the stored source of glucose, is primarily hoarded in the placenta as an additional source of fetal glucose. At about the twentieth to twenty-fourth gestational weeks the fetal liver becomes the primary storage site for glycogen while placental deposits gradually diminish. Glycogen stores in the fetal heart and skeletal muscle simultaneously increase as pregnancy proceeds to term. These glycogen supplies, particularly those of the liver and heart, are indispensable sources of energy. If they are suboptimal for any reason, the ability to withstand perinatal asphyxia is impaired. Cardiac glycogen is rapidly depleted during asphyctic episodes; a direct relationship exists between the quantity stored at birth and the capacity to survive. At birth, hepatic glycogen is normally twice the adult concentration, cardiac stores are ten times as great, and skeletal muscle quantities are three to five times greater.

After birth, the infant's caloric needs are supplied from external sources, and it may be hours or days before the expended glycogen is even partially replenished. In the meantime, the energy cost of respiration, thermoregulation, and muscle activity causes abrupt diminution of glycogen stores. It follows, then, that intrauterine malnutrition and the low stores of glycogen which it entails, poses a serious threat to the asphyxiated infant in terms of depleted carbohydrate. Even in normal infants, approximately 90% of liver glycogen is consumed by the end of the third hour after birth, rising gradually thereafter to attain adult concentrations by the end of the third week. The effects of respiratory distress on energy expenditure are well illustrated by the virtually complete depletion of glycogen stores found in postmortem analysis of the heart, liver, and diaphragm. The normal newborn infant can tolerate a relatively short period of fasting without chemical derangement. Carbohydrate stores are consumed during the first 2 or 3 days; later, fat is probably the principal source of energy.

At any given moment, blood sugar concentration is a reflection of two principal balancing functions: hepatic release of glucose and utilization of glucose by tissues. In the liver, glucose is primarily produced by breakdown of glycogen and production from noncarbohydrate substances (gluconeogenesis). Normal output of glucose from the liver also depends on adequate glycogen stores and effective activity of enzymes and hormones concerned with its production. Utilization of glucose by tissues is abnormally increased by the metabolic response to cold stress, acidosis, and hypoxia.

Neonatal hypoglycemia

Normal blood sugar concentrations range from 30 to 125 mg/100 ml in term babies over 2500 grams and from 20 to 100 mg/100 ml in low birth weight infants. The diagnosis of hypoglycemia during the first 72 hours of life is established when true blood sugar is diminished beyond these lower limits in two consecutive blood samples. The diagnostic requirement of two low determinations is necessary because blood sugar levels normally fluctuate widely. The restriction of diagnostic criteria to laboratory data is unavoidable because the symptoms associated with hypoglycemia occur with similar frequency in normoglycemic infants with unrelated disorders. After the third day of life, normal blood sugar is at least 40 mg/100 ml. We do not play the "numbers game" with these prescribed normal levels of glucose. With or without symptoms, if blood sugar values are close to the designated low levels in an infant who is at known risk for hypoglycemia, we begin treatment.

The symptoms attributable to hypoglycemia from any cause may also occur in infants with central nervous system disorders, septicemia, hypocalcemia, hypomagnesemia, cardiorespiratory disorders, and a multiplicity of other abnormalities. There are no pathognomonic clinical signs of hypoglycemia. The signs associated with low blood sugar include apnea, cyanosis, rapid and irregular respirations, tachypnea, tremors, jitters, twitches, convulsions, lethargy, coma, abrupt pallor, sweating, upward rolling of the eyes, weak cry, and refusal to feed. The etiologic relationship of these signs to hypoglycemia is credible if they clear within 5 minutes after intravenous glucose administration; if they

do not clear, a cause other than hypoglycemia is undoubtedly operative.

Blood sugar falls to abnormally low levels if glycogen stores are suboptimal, if gluconeogenesis (glucose from lipids and protein) in the liver is diminished, if available insulin is excessive, or if carbohydrate-regulating hormones such as cortisol, epinephrine, and glucagon are insufficient. In rare circumstances, enzyme deficiencies in the liver impair the release of glucose, thus causing hypoglycemia.

These pathophysiologic mechanisms are responsible for four broad clinical categories. The first category is comprised of small-for-dates infants who were subjected to intrauterine malnutrition. The second category includes infants of diabetic mothers and erythroblastotic infants. The third category includes infants with birth weights below 1250 grams who are subjected to such severe stress that their metabolic requirements exceed their glycogen stores. The fourth category includes infants with rare developmental and genetic disorders such as glycogen storage disease, galactosemia, and tumors of the pancreatic islets (insulinomas). In any of these clinical groupings an additive hypoglycemic effect may be exerted by severe respiratory

Table 11-1. Causes of neonatal hypoglycemia

Clinical entity	Mechanism	Duration
Intrauterine malnutrition	Low liver glycogen store	Transient
Fetal asphyxia	Glycogen depletion	Transient
Cold stress	Glycogen depletion	Transient
CNS hemorrhage	Unknown	Transient
CNS malformation	Unknown	Transient
Adrenal hemorrhage, insufficiency	Ineffective catecholamine response	Transient
Infants of diabetic mothers	Increased plasma insulin activity	Transient
Erythroblastotic infants	Increased plasma insulin activity	Transient
Maternal tolbutamide, chlorpropamide	Hyperinsulinism	Transient
Abrupt stop of intravenous glucose, $\geq 10\%$	Hyperinsulinism	Transient
Glycogen storage disease (types I and II)	Defective glycogen breakdown	Protracted
Galactose intolerance (galactosemia)	Defective conversion of galactose to glucose	Protracted
Islet cell tumor	Hyperinsulinism	Protracted
Cyanotic congenital heart disease with congestive failure	Unknown	Transient
Hypopituitarism	Adrenal insufficiency	Protracted
Septicemia	Unknown	Transient

distress, hypoxia, and hypothermia. Table 11-1 lists the most important clinical entities associated with hypoglycemia and the mechanisms involved.

Hypoglycemia and intrauterine malnutrition. Hypoglycemia occurs in approximately 20% of infants with intrauterine growth retardation. The incidence is higher in males (twice as frequent as in females) and in the smaller of twins if the birth weight discrepancy exceeds 25% and the weight of the affected infant is less than 2000 grams. Symptoms occur in 50% to 90% of hypoglycemic infants. Small-for-dates babies have diminished stores of hepatic glycogen and diminished capacity for gluconeogenesis. They also possess a relatively increased mass of glucose-consuming tissue because the brain is least affected by growth retardation and is closest to normal weight compared to other organs, especially the liver. In normally grown neonates the liver, which is the principal glucose supplier, weighs one third as much as the brain, which is an active glucose consumer. In malnourished infants the liver weighs only one seventh as much as the brain. The hepatic source of glucose is thus quite reduced in malnourished babies. Most glycogen-depleted hypoglycemic infants are below the tenth percentile on the Colorado growth charts. Other hypoglycemic infants are affected for unknown reasons, although many seem to be subjected to excessive metabolic demands resulting from some type of stress.

Symptoms usually appear between 24 and 72 hours of age; occasionally they begin as early as 3 hours and as late as 7 days of age. Severely hypoxic, hypothermic small-for-dates infants are most likely to become hypoglycemic within 6 hours after birth.

Monitoring blood sugar is thus important in small-for-dates infants and in any other stressed baby. Infants who place below the tenth percentile should have blood sugar assessment at least twice during the first 24 hours and at least three times daily thereafter until 4 days of age. Screening for low values is feasible with Dextrostix. A laboratory determination for blood sugar should be requested if the Dextrostix color change indicates a level less than 45 mg/100 ml. The Dextrostix is exquisitely sensitive, and because it is such a simple procedure it is commonly performed inaccurately. The blood must remain on the reactive tip for precisely 1 minute. Shorter periods do not permit a complete reaction; longer periods allow too much reaction. The blood must be rinsed off by a forceful stream of water from a plastic squeeze bottle. Care must also be exercised in touching the strip to the capillary blood flowing from a heel prick because the delicate membrane that covers the tip is easily disrupted by contact with the skin. Treatment of hypoglycemia is discussed later in this chapter.

Infants of diabetic mothers. Before the introduction of insulin over 40 years ago, few diabetic women conceived, and among those who did, the outcome of pregnancy was often catastrophic. Pregnancy in diabetic women is now commonplace, and in recent years screening during pregnancy has also identified women whose gestational diabetic tendencies were unsuspected in the nonpregnant state. As a result of more effective management of diabetes, particularly during gestation, the offspring of diabetic mothers are now numerous, constituting a significant problem and a major challenge to the caretakers of high-risk infants. One in 500 to 1000 pregnant women is diabetic. The incidence of gestational diabetes is considerably higher—one in 120 pregnancies. Perinatal infant mortality and morbidity rates are inordinately high among infants of diabetic mothers. There is general agreement that diabetic pregnancies should be interrupted between the thirty-sixth and thirty-seventh weeks because earlier deliveries are associated with a high rate of neonatal mortality, whereas later ones are associated with a higher incidence of stillbirth. Fetal monitoring in diabetic and other high-risk pregnancies is discussed in Chapter 1.

The classification of diabetes during pregnancy that was introduced by Dr. Priscilla White is a universal reference for grading the

Table 11-2. White's classification of diabetes in pregnancy

Class A	Highest probability of fetal survival No insulin, little dietary regulation Includes gestational diabetes and pre-diabetes
Class B	Onset at age 20 or more Duration less than 10 years before pregnancy No vascular disease
Class C	Onset between 10 and 19 years of age Duration between 10 and 19 years Minimal vascular disease (retinal arteriosclerosis, calcification of vessels in the legs only)
Class D	Onset before age 10 years Duration 20 years or more Moderately advanced vascular disease (diabetic retinopathy, transient albuminuria, and hypertension)
Class E	Characteristics of class D plus calcification of pelvic vessels
Class F	Characteristics of class D plus nephritis

severity of the maternal disease (Table 11-2). It differentiates severity according to duration of diabetes before pregnancy, age at onset, and extent of vascular involvement. Class A is the commonest variety; it includes gestational diabetes. Gestational diabetes is characterized by an abnormal glucose tolerance curve in an asymptomatic mother, which reverts to normal within 6 weeks after delivery. Whereas mortality in babies born of Group A mothers is higher than in those of nondiabetic mothers, it is the lowest of all the groups in White's classification. The most unfavorable neonatal outcomes occur in classes D through F. Toxemia of pregnancy is more likely to occur in women with vascular disease (classes D through F), and this is probably an additional contributory factor to poor pregnancy outcome. Class A and B mothers give birth to large-for-dates babies; mothers in class C and below deliver small-for-dates babies (Chapter 5).

There is no well-defined explanation for all the abnormalities in infants of diabetic mothers. The hypoglycemia that commonly occurs within hours after birth is associated with increased insulin activity in the blood. Furthermore, hyperplasia and increased insulin content of the pancreatic islet cells are demonstrated at necropsy in virtually all these infants. Current concensus holds that fetal hyperglycemia, which results from high maternal levels of blood sugar, provides a relentless stimulus to the islets for insulin production, as evidenced by their hyperplasia. Sustained fetal hyperinsulinism and hyperglycemia ultimately lead to excessive growth and deposition of fat. This may explain the high incidence of infants who are large for gestational age. When the generous supply of maternal glucose is eliminated after birth, continued islet cell hyperactivity leads to hyperinsulinism and depletion of blood glucose. Within 2 to 4 hours hypoglycemia occurs. Although this hypothesis is plausible, it does not explain the obesity of offspring from mothers who are prediabetic, that is, those who are genetically predisposed to diabetes but have none of the characteristic abnormalities; nor does it explain the multiplicity of other abnormalities in infants of diabetic mothers.

The disorders that befall infants of diabetic mothers include hypoglycemia, hypocalcemia, hyperbilirubinemia, hyaline membrane disease (as a function of prematurity), renal vein thrombosis, and a considerably higher incidence of congenital anomalies than in infants of nondiabetic mothers.

At birth, blood glucose concentration is 80% or more of the maternal level. Within an hour in normal infants, it falls to a mean of 40 to 50 mg/100 ml, but in infants of diabetic mothers, hyperinsulinism causes a greater decline. Levels below 20 and 30 mg/100 ml usually occur from 2 to 4 hours after birth, sometimes sooner, occasionally later. This decline is followed by a spontaneous rise between 4 and 6 hours of age. Approximately half the infants of treated diabetic mothers (classes B through F) develop glucose levels below 30 mg/100 ml. Among infants of gestational diabetic mothers (class A) approximately 20% are affected. Occasionally hypoglycemia is protracted. Rarely it appears as late as 12 to 24 hours of age.

Hypocalcemia (serum calcium below 7 mg/100 ml or 3.5 mEq/L) often occurs with or without hypoglycemia. Low serum calcium is often present soon after birth. It is thought to be caused by depressed fetal parathyroid function that persists in the neonate temporarily. Symptoms are usually imperceptible; those which do appear are not specific for hypocalcemia and are also seen in normocalcemic infants. They include irritability, coarse tremors, twitches, and convulsions. Low serum calcium levels are also frequently observed in stressed premature infants of nondiabetic mothers. The treatment of hypocalcemia is described later.

Hyperbilirubinemia is more frequent among infants of diabetic mothers than in babies of like gestational age who are born of nondiabetic mothers. The characteristics and treatment of this disorder are identical in all premature infants.

Renal vein thrombosis is a rare occurrence. It may be unilateral or bilateral and is sometimes associated with radiologic evidence of calcification. The involved kidney is palpably enlarged, and hematuria and proteinuria are the rule. The survival of affected infants is in grave doubt. Nephrectomy is indicated if involvement is unilateral.

The incidence of all types of congenital anomalies is two to three times greater than in the general population. The incidence of congenital heart disease is increased threefold compared to infants of nondiabetic mothers.

Whether or not they are overtly ill, infants of diabetic mothers must be managed in an intensive care facility. Approximately half of them have an undisturbed course, but careful observation is necessary nevertheless. The severity of the maternal diabetes should be known and recorded as early as the first prenatal visit. The nursery should be notified when a diabetic woman begins labor.

The schedule for blood glucose monitoring of infants of diabetic mothers is different from that of small-for-dates infants because the timing of hypoglycemia differs. Since the lowest blood glucose levels in infants of diabetic mothers occurs at 2 to 4 hours of age, blood glucose determinations should be done on cord blood at birth and at 1, 2, 4, and 6 hours of age. Distressed infants, and all infants of classes B through F mothers, should be given 10% dextrose intravenously immediately after birth at a rate of 65 to 70 ml/kg of body weight.

Hypoglycemia and erythroblastosis fetalis. For years the danger of hypoglycemia in erythroblastotic infants was obscured by a preoccupation with the dramatic hematologic, cardiopulmonary, and central nervous system aspects of the disease. Low blood glucose levels may occur in almost a third of moderately or severely affected infants and in 5% of all erythroblastotic infants, regardless of severity. When cord hemoglobin is less than 10 grams/100 ml, the incidence of hypoglycemia is comparable to that in small-for-dates infants. As in the latter group, symptoms are often absent. When present, they are identical to those of hypoglycemia from other causes. Blood sugar levels may fall transiently before or after exchange transfusion, most often during the first day of life but occasionally later. Islet cell hyperplasia and increased insulin content of the islets and blood are similar to those of infants of diabetic mothers. Their cause is unknown. Blood glucose levels should be monitored every 4 to 6 hours during the first day and regularly for the ensuing 3 days. Therapy is the same as for all forms of hypoglycemia.

Hypoglycemia in very small premature infants. Low blood sugar levels are not uncommon in infants whose birth weight is less than 1250 grams. Hypoglycemia may occur during the hours after birth and during the days that follow. Intravenous 10% dextrose is given routinely after birth and for variable periods thereafter. Presumably liver glycogen stores are low in these very immature infants, and the increased metabolic demands imposed by extrauterine life deplete glycogen supplies rapidly. The process is accentuated by cold stress, asphyxia, and respiratory difficulty, all of which are frequent in these small infants. Blood sugar data should be followed every 4 to 8 hours for the first 2 days of life and periodically thereafter. Since pH and blood gas determinations are usually necessary at frequent intervals, it is advisable to obtain glucose determinations simultaneously.

Treatment of hypoglycemia. Hypoglycemia requires treatment with intravenous glucose, whether symptoms are present or not. The method for administering glucose is identical for the hyperinsulinemic (infants of diabetic mothers, erythroblastotic infants) and the glycogen-depletion types of hypoglycemia (small-for-dates infants, smaller of twins). If a low blood sugar level is found in the first sample, a second is collected for confirmation, and treatment is begun immediately. A 25% glucose solution is given in a dose of 2 to 4 ml/kg of body weight, followed by a 15% solution by continuous infusion at a rate that delivers 65 to 75 ml/kg of body weight every 24 hours. If the blood glucose level remains low after two subsequent determinations within 2 to 3 hours after onset of treatment, steroids should be added. Hydrocortisone, 5 mg every 6 to 12 hours, or 1 mg of prednisone every 6 to 12 hours, is generally used for this purpose. Oral milk feedings are started as soon as the infant tolerates them. Blood sugar level should stabilize at normal values for 24 or 48 hours before the concentration of the glucose infusion is lowered to 10% and then 5%, giving each for a 12-hour period. Except in the most protracted cases, steroids can usually be discontinued after 2 or 3 days.

At some centers hypoglycemic infants of diabetic mothers are first treated with glucagon, 300 mg/kg of body weight. Glucagon acts on glycogen to increase the formation of glucose. It is therefore of doubtful use in small-for-dates infants who are hypoglycemic because of glycogen depletion.

Prognosis of neonatal hypoglycemia. Untreated symptomatic hypoglycemia in the neonate may cause death. Later in childhood the incidence of central nervous system dysfunction varies from 30% to 60% of untreated symptomatic small-for-dates infants. The incidence of later neurologic abnormality in asymptomatic infants may be considerably lower, but nevertheless significant. The destiny of asymptomatic small-for-dates babies with hypoglycemia is not known, since there are no well-controlled follow-up studies available. Clearly defined outcomes of well-treated hypoglycemic small-for-dates babies are also wanting. Data from a recent well-planned inquiry suggest that these infants still do not fare as well as normoglycemic controls, but many other unanswered questions have left the issue beclouded. Outcome of the asymptomatic hypoglycemic infant has not been clarified. Until it is, the recommendation to treat such infants rapidly is virtually universal. The outcome for hypoglycemic infants of diabetic mothers has not been defined precisely. Some investigators have not found central nervous system abnormalities later in childhood; others have noted a low incidence of brain abnormalities, but no well-controlled, follow-up studies are available. At some centers, infants of diabetic mothers are treated for hypoglycemia, whether or not symptoms are evident; at others no treatment is instituted.

HYPOCALCEMIA

The causes of neonatal hypocalcemia are multiple, and for the most part the mechanisms by which it is produced have yet been unequivocally defined. Normal serum calcium levels vary from 8 to 10 mg/100 ml (4 to 5 mEq/L). Calcium levels below 7 mg/100 ml are considered abnormally depressed. The etiologic association of clinical signs with hypocalcemia, as with hypoglycemia, is difficult to establish because the symptoms occur in other unrelated disorders, and they are often nonexistent in hypocalcemic infants.

Two peaks of incidence occur, one during the first 48 hours and another between the fifth and tenth days of life. Typically, the infant with early hypocalcemia is premature or small-for-dates and has experienced perinatal asphyxia. The early variety is thought to be related to temporary neonatal hypoparathyroidism. Serum calcium is low, phosphorus is high, and magnesium is sometimes diminished. Serum calcium is also related to gestational age: the shorter the gestation, the lower the calcium. Infants of diabetic mothers are often hypocalcemic. A history of abruptio placentae or placenta previa is not unusual. The symptoms of this early form of hypocalcemia, if any are discernible, often do not include neuromuscular involvement. Rather, they may be characterized by apnea, cyanotic episodes, edema, high-pitched cry, and abdominal distention; even these manifestations, however, have not been proved to be of hypocalcemic origin.

The form of hypocalcemia that begins during the fifth to tenth days is called neonatal tetany. It occurs in well-nourished infants who are fed milk formulas. Some of these preparations, notably evaporated milk, contain diminished concentrations of calcium in relation to phosphorus, compared to concentrations in human milk. An increase in serum phosphorus follows several days of feeding, and the resultant hyperphosphatemia depresses activity of the parathyroid gland. The effect of this suppression is to diminish serum calcium. Most proprietary brands of milk formula now contain a ratio of calcium to phosphorus closely simulating that of human milk. The signs of neonatal tetany are characterized by neuromuscular irritation—twitching, tremors, jitters, and focal or generalized convulsions. Convulsions frequently begin as the infant is taken up for a feeding. They vary in duration from a few seconds to as long as 10 minutes. Minor stimuli often provoke tremors or convulsive episodes, whereas in the undisturbed interim only restlessness may be apparent.

Maternal hyperparathyroidism is rare, but when it exists, the infant is quite likely to be hypocalcemic. A number of reports describe the diagnosis of maternal hyperparathyroidism only after identification of hypocalcemia in her newborn infant. Mothers of hypocalcemic infants should be investigated for this possibility.

Hypocalcemia is treated initially with intravenous injection of 10% calcium gluconate, 1 to 1.5 ml/kg of body weight. The injection must be given slowly over a period of at least 5 minutes because sudden bradycardia frequently occurs during rapid administration. The heart rate should be monitored electronically or by auscultation. If it drops below 100 beats/min, the injection should be discontinued immediately. It may be resumed after a normal cardiac rate is maintained for approximately 30 minutes. Intramuscular administration of calcium gluconate is contraindicated because calcium precipitates rapidly; a calcemic mass and necrosis result. Caution is also required during intravenous infusion because accidental escape to extravascular tissue produces local calcification and sloughing. Calcium gluconate thus should not be administered through scalp veins. Orally administered calcium, added to formula, is begun as soon as feasible. Calcium chloride is the most effective preparation; it is added to make a concentration that does not exceed 2% of the formula volume. Higher concentrations cause irritation of gastric mucosa and vomiting. The total daily dose should not exceed 1 gram. Blood pH must be determined at least every 6 hours because acidemia from calcium chloride is a frequent occurrence. It usually need not be administered for more than 2 or 3 days. Serum calcium levels rise rapidly soon after the initiation of therapy. Calcium lactate is often used in preference to calcium chloride; its effect is not as rapid, but acidemia is less likely to occur. It is added to feedings to constitute a concentration not in excess of 5%. The total daily dose should not be greater than 2 to 3 grams.

HYPOMAGNESEMIA

Reports of tetany due to low magnesium levels have appeared with increasing frequency in the past few years. Normal serum magnesium concentration in the neonate is 1.2 to 1.8 mg/100 ml. Hypomagnesemia usually accompanies hypocalcemia. It occurs during or after exchange transfusions because magnesium becomes bound to the citrate in donor blood. For unknown reasons, it may also occur in infants of diabetic mothers. Serum magnesium determinations are essential for proper evaluation of babies with signs of neuromuscular excitability. They are especially important in hypocalcemic infants who do not respond to calcium therapy. If the signs are caused by magnesium deficiency, tetany and convulsions disappear promptly after appropriate therapy. An intramuscular dose of 50% magnesium sulfate (0.2 ml/kg of body weight) is given every 4 hours for the first day. The need for subsequent therapy is determined by serial serum magnesium determinations.

HYPERMAGNESEMIA

Magnesium sulfate is a preparation of choice for the treatment of preeclampsia. When it is administered by either the intramuscular or intravenous routes, serum magnesium levels in maternal and cord blood are higher than normal. The maternal normal range is 1.2 to 2.2 mEq/L; normal values in cord blood are 0.9 to 2.6 mEq/L. Most cases of neonatal hypermagnesemia reported to date have not been associated with clinical abnormalities, and there is some doubt that high magnesium levels are responsible for abnormal signs. However, there are several instances of severe neonatal illness associated with high serum magnesium concentrations. At high levels magnesium causes peripheral neuromuscular block (curare-like effect) and central nervous system depression as well. Clinical abnormalities in the neonate are believed by some authors to include hypotonia, weak or absent cry, and severe respiratory depression with apnea and cyanosis. The respiratory difficulty has necessitated mechanically assisted ventilation. Several investigators have used intravenous calcium in attempts to antagonize the depressive effects of excessive magnesium, but with little evidence of benefit. The consensus is that calcium therapy is not effective. However, a dramatic response to exchange transfusion has been well documented. Magnesium toxicity should be suspected in a symptomatic infant whose mother was treated vigorously with magnesium sulfate for preeclampsia.

References

Adam, P. A. J., and Schwartz, R.: Diagnosis and treatment: Should oral hypoglycemic agents be used in pediatric and pregnant patients? Pediatrics **42**:819, 1968.

Anderson, J. M., Milner, R. D. G., and Strich, S. J.: Pathological changes in the nervous system in severe neonatal hypoglycemia, Lancet **2**:372, 1966.

Avery, M. E., Oppenheimer, E. H., and Gordon, H. H.: Renal-vein thrombosis in newborn infants of diabetic mothers, N. Engl. J. Med. **265**:1134, 1957.

Barrett, C. T., and Oliver, T. K.: Hypoglycemia and hyperinsulinism in infants with erythroblastosis, N. Engl. J. Med. **278**:1260, 1968.

Beard, A. G., Panos, T. C., Marasigan, B. V., et al.: Perinatal stress and the premature neonate. II. Effect of fluid and calorie deprivation on blood glucose, J. Pediatr. **68**:329, 1966.

Beard, A. G., et al.: Neonatal hypoglycemia: a discussion, J. Pediatr. **79**:314, 1971.

Brady, J. P., and Williams, H. C.: Magnesium intoxication in a premature infant, Pediatrics **40**:100, 1967.

Chantler, C., Baum, J. D., and Norman, D. A.: Dextrostix in the diagnosis of neonatal hypoglycemia, Lancet **2**:1395, 1967.

Clarke, P. C. N., and Carre, I. J.: Hypocalcemic, hypomagnesemic convulsions, J. Pediatr. **70**:806, 1967.

Cornblath, M., Joassin, G., Weisskopf, B., et al.: Hypoglycemia in the newborn, Pediatr. Clin. North Am. **13**:905, 1966.

Cornblath, M., and Schwartz, R.: Disorders of carbohydrate metabolism in infancy, Philadelphia, 1966, W. B. Saunders Co.

Craig, W. S.: Clinical signs of neonatal tetany; with especial reference to their occurrence in newborn babies of diabetic mothers, Pediatrics **22**:297, 1958.

Craig, W. S., and Buchanan, M. F. G.: Hypocalcemic tetany developing within 36 hours of birth, Arch. Dis. Child. **33**:505, 1958.

Davis, J. A., Harvey, D. R., and Yu, J. S.: Neonatal fits associated with hypomagnesemia, Arch. Dis. Child. **40**:286, 1965.

Driscoll, S. G., Benirschke, K., and Curtis, G. W.: Neonatal deaths among infants of diabetic mothers, Am. J. Dis. Child. **100:**40, 1960.

Ertel, N. H., Reiss, J. S., and Spergel, G.: Hypomagnesemia in neonatal tetany associated with maternal hyperparathyroidism, N. Engl. J. Med. **280:**260, 1969.

Farquhar, J. W.: Prognosis for babies born to diabetic mothers in Edinburgh, Arch. Dis. Child. **44:**36, 1969.

Fischer, G. W., Vazquez, A. M., Buist, N. R. M., et al.: Neonatal islet cell adenoma: case report and literature review, Pediatrics **53:**753, 1974.

From, G. L. A., Driscoll, S. G., and Steinke, J.: Serum insulin in newborn infants with erythroblastosis fetalis, Pediatrics **44:**549, 1969.

Gentz, J., Persson, B., and Zetterstrom, R.: On the diagnosis of symptomatic neonatal hypoglycemia, Acta Paediatr. Scand. **58:**449, 1969.

Gittleman, I. F., et al.: Hypoglycemia occurring on the first day of life in mature and premature infants, Pediatrics **18:**721, 1956.

Griffiths, A. D.: Association of hypoglycaemia with symptoms in the newborn, Arch. Dis. Child. **43:**688, 1968.

Haworth, J. C.: Carbohydrate metabolism in the fetus and the newborn, Pediatr. Clin. North Am. **12:**573, 1965.

Haworth, J. C.: Neonatal hypoglycemia: how much does it damage the brain? Pediatrics **54:**3, 1974.

Haworth, J. C., and McRae, K. N.: The neurological and developmental effects of neonatal hypoglycemia: a follow-up of 22 cases, Can. Med. Assoc. J. **92:**861, 1965.

Hubbell, J. P., Muirhead, D. M., and Drorbaugh, J. E.: The newborn infant of the diabetic mother, Med. Clin. North Am. **49:**1035, 1965.

Johnson, J. D., Hansen, R. C., et al.: Hypoplasia of the anterior pituitary and neonatal hypoglycemia, J. Pediatr. **82:**634, 1973.

Keen, J. H.: Significance of hypocalcemia in neonatal convulsions, Arch. Dis. Child. **44:**356, 1969.

Lee, F. A., and Gwinn, J. L.: Roentgen patterns of extravasation of calcium gluconate in the tissues of the neonate, J. Pediatr. **86:**598, 1975.

Lipsitz, P. J.: The clinical and biochemical effects of excess magnesium in the newborn, Pediatrics **47:**501, 1971.

Lubchenco, L. O., and Bard, H.: Incidence of hypoglycemia in newborn infants classified by birth weight and gestational age, Pediatrics **47:**831, 1971.

Lucey, J. F., Randall, J. L., and Murray, J. J.: Is hypoglycemia an important complication in erythroblastosis fetalis? Am. J. Dis. Child. **114:**88, 1967.

Medovy, H.: Outlook for the infant of the diabetic mother, J. Pediatr. **76:**988, 1970.

Milner, R. D. G.: Neonatal hypoglycaemia: a critical reappraisal, Arch. Dis. Child. **47:**679, 1972.

Mizrach, A., London, R. D., and Gribetz, D.: Neonatal hypocalcemia: its causes and treatment, N. Engl. J. Med. **278:**1163, 1968.

Naeye, R. L.: Infants of diabetic mothers; a quantitative, morphologic study, Pediatrics **35:**980, 1965.

Neligan, G. A., Robson, E., and Watson, J.: Hypoglycemia in the newborn: a sequel of intrauterine malnutrition, Lancet **1:**1282, 1963.

O'Sullivan, J. B.: Gestational diabetes: unsuspected, asymptomatic diabetes in pregnancy, N. Engl. J. Med. **264:**1082, 1961.

Pedersen, J.: The pregnant diabetic and her newborn, Baltimore, 1967, The Williams & Wilkins Co.

Pildes, R., et al.: The incidence of neonatal hypoglycemia: a complete survey, J. Pediatr. **70:**76, 1967.

Pildes, R. S., Cornblath, M., Warren, I., et al.: A prospective controlled study of neonatal hypoglycemia, Pediatrics **54:**5, 1974.

Pildes, R. S., Forbes, A., and Cornblath, M.: Studies of carbohydrate metabolism in the newborn infant. IX. Blood glucose levels and hypoglycemia in twins, Pediatrics **40:**69, 1967.

Raivio, K. O.: Neonatal hypoglycemia. II. A clinical study of 44 idiopathic cases with special reference to corticosteroid treatment, Acta Paediatr. Scand. **57:**540, 1968.

Raivio, K. O., and Halman, N.: Neonatal hypoglycemia. I. Occurrence of hypoglycemia in patients with various neonatal disorders, Acta Paediatr. Scand. **57:**517, 1968.

Raivio, K. O., and Osterlund, K.: Hypoglycemia and hyperinsulinemia associated with erythroblastosis fetalis, J. Pediatr. **43:**217, 1969.

Reisner, S. H., Forbes, A. E., and Cornblath, M.: The smaller of twins and hypoglycemia, Lancet **1:**524, 1965.

Sanerkin, N. G., Edwards, P., and Jacobs, J.: Pulmonary thrombo-embolic phenomena in the newborn, J. Pathol. Bact. **91:**569, 1966.

Saville, P. D., and Kretchmer, N.: Neonatal tetany: a report of 125 cases and review of the literature, Biol. Neonatol. **2:**1, 1960.

Scott, J. M.: Iatrogenic lesions in babies following umbilical vein catheterization, Arch. Dis. Child. **40:**426, 1965.

Shelley, H. J.: Carbohydrate reserves in the newborn infant, Br. Med. J. **1:**273, 1964.

Shelley, H. J.: Carbohydrate metabolism in the foetus and the newly born, Proc. Nutr. Soc. **28:**42, 1969.

Tsang, R. C., Chen, I., Hayes, W., et al.: Neonatal hypocalcemia in infants with birth asphyxia, J. Pediatr. **84:**428, 1974.

Tsang, R. C., Chen, I-W., Friedman, M. A., et al.: Parathyroid function in infants of diabetic mothers, J. Pediatr. **86:**399, 1975.

Tsang, R. C., Kleinman, L. I., Sutherland, J. M., and Light, I. J.: Hypocalcemia in infants of diabetic mothers, J. Pediatr. **80:**384, 1972.

Tsang, R. C., Light, I. J., Sutherland, J. M., and Kleinman, L. I.: Possible pathogenetic factors in neonatal hypocalcemia of prematurity, J. Pediatr. **82:**423, 1973.

Tsang, R. C., and Oh, W.: Neonatal hypocalcemia in low birth weight infants, Pediatrics **45:**773, 1970.

Yeung, C. Y., Lee, V. W. Y., and Yeung, C. M.: Glucose disappearance rate in neonatal infection, J. Pediatr. **82:**486, 1973.

Zucker, P., and Simon, G.: Prolonged symptomatic neonatal hypoglycemia associated with maternal chlorpropamide therapy, Pediatrics **42:**824, 1968.

Chapter 12

Perinatal infection

ALTHOUGH OF DIVERSE ETIOLOGY, perinatal infections have many attributes in common that distinguish them from infections in later life. Whether of bacterial, viral, or protozoan causation, the tissue damage wrought by these infections and the patterns of disease they produce are remarkably different from those observed in more advanced age groups. For instance, the bacteria generally implicated in fetal and neonatal disease are not ordinarily pathogenic in older children. Conversely, organisms that cause serious disease in mature patients, such as pneumococci, *Haemophilus influenzae,* group A streptococci, and meningococci, are rarely encountered during the perinatal period. Diseases caused by rubella virus, cytomegalovirus, herpesvirus, and *Toxoplasma* are usually mild or asymptomatic in later life, but in the fetus and neonate these organisms produce extensive devastation of tissue, often resulting in death or dysfunctional survival.

In the pathogenesis of antepartal or intrapartal infection, maternal involvement, usually asymptomatic, always precedes fetal disease. The fetus may acquire disease from infected amniotic fluid, from the maternal bloodstream across the placenta, or by direct contact with infected maternal tissue in the birth canal. After birth the neonate must contend with the possibility of acquiring infection from other infants or from personnel or objects that surround him, particularly the equipment designed to save his life. The neonate's vulnerability to these hazards is determined by a number of variables, of which prematurity is clearly the most significant.

Another distinctive feature of perinatal infection is the immunologic response it stimulates. Special procedures are necessary to differentiate antibodies generated by the fetus and neonate from those received through the placenta from the mother. Serologic techniques that diagnose infections in older children are of little value in the newborn infant.

Physical signs of infectious disease, if any are indeed perceptible, are unique in their subtlety and their lack of specificity. Early in the course of infection one may not be aware of any disturbance, yet the disorder soon becomes rapidly fulminant and uncontrollable. Thus a severely septicemic premature infant may merely be hypoactive and refuse feeding. Furthermore, fever, the hallmark of infectious disease later in life, is often absent in the infected newborn. Coughing, which is almost universal in older children with pneumonia, is rare.

The choice of therapeutic antibiotics must usually be made before results of cultures are known. Such choices must be influenced by knowledge of the bacterial organisms most likely to cause disease. Their incidence is unique to the neonate. Equally important in the choice of therapy is an understanding of the immature pharmacologic response of the newborn infant. During the first 2 or 3 weeks of life, the absorption, metabolism, and excretion of drugs vary considerably from those observed in older patients, and the uninformed use of some drugs may have serious results. The disastrous consequences of neglecting these differences were exemplified by the widespread use of sulfisoxazole (Gantrisin) and chloramphenicol, which were administered in complete ignorance of the special hazards they imposed on the neonate. Sulfisoxazole caused an unexpectedly high incidence of kernicterus, and chloramphenicol caused numerous deaths.

This chapter discusses the salient aspects of perinatal infection, the fundamental reasons for its uniqueness, and the characteristics of its most important clinical entities.

ETIOLOGY
Bacterial agents

Most bacterial infections are caused by organisms comprising the flora of the mother's genital and intestinal tracts; beyond early infancy these agents are rarely pathogenic. Although varying lengthy lists of etiologic agents have emerged from numerous studies; a rather uniform pattern is apparent for the three major clinical entities: pneumonia, septicemia, and meningitis. Gram-negative rods produce 75% to 85% of these bacterial infections; *Escherichia coli* is pre-dominant among them. *Pseudomonas aeruginosa* is the next most common agent. It is usually acquired postnatally; nursery equipment is a major source of its propagation. The remaining 15% to 25% of these major infections are caused principally by gram-positive cocci, of which streptococci are the commonest. These are generally group B streptococci, which have increased markedly in incidence recently. Staphylococci cause septicemia and pneumonia. They are infrequently implicated in meningitis. During the worldwide nursery epidemics of the late 1950s and early 1960s, they were a prominent cause of pneumonia, and although still an important factor, they are now encountered with less frequency (see later). *Listeria monocytogenes* is a maternally derived gram-positive rod that also causes septicemia and meningitis. Most pediatric infections from this organism occur during the newborn period.

Table 12-1. Vertically transmitted viruses implicated in fetal and neonatal infection*

Virus	*Fetal/neonatal disorders*
Rubella virus	Microcephaly, meningoencephalitis (chronic), cataracts, microphthalmia, glaucoma, deafness, hepatitis, jaundice, hepatosplenomegaly, pneumonitis, cardiovascular anomalies, myocardial necrosis, thrombocytopenia, anemia, purpura, inguinal hernia
Cytomegalovirus	Microcephaly, cerebral calcification, hydrocephalus, encephalitis, chorioretinitis, hepatitis, jaundice, hepatosplenomegaly, pneumonitis, cardiac anomalies, thrombocytopenia, purpura, anemia, inguinal hernia
Herpesvirus hominis	Meningoencephalitis, microcephaly, cerebral calcification, herpetic rash, hepatitis, jaundice, pneumonitis, thrombocytopenia, anemia, coagulopathy, keratoconjunctivitis, chorioretinitis
Coxsackievirus group B	Meningoencephalitis, myocarditis, hepatitis, jaundice, thrombocytopenia
Varicella-zoster	Chickenpox rash, pneumonitis, hepatitis
Variola poxvirus	Smallpox rash, pneumonitis, hepatitis, meningoencephalitis
Vaccinia virus	Vaccinia rash, pneumonitis, hepatitis, stillbirth
Poliomyelitis	Spinal or bulbar polio similar to adult, myocarditis, pneumonitis, stillbirth, abortion
Rubeola	Measles as in later life (usually benign), stillbirth, abortion
Western equine encephalomyelitis	Meningoencephalitis
Myxovirus (mumps)	Congenital parotitis, ? congenital malformations
Hepatitis virus B	Neonatal hepatitis

*Modified from Sever, J. L., and White, L. R.: Intrauterine viral infections, Annual Rev. Med. **19:**471, 1968.

Viral agents

Viral diseases in the fetus and neonate are far less frequent than bacterial diseases, but they comprise an important cause of morbidity and mortality. They are generally transmitted from the mother but may also be acquired postnatally. Data on postnatally acquired viral disease are relatively meager, but considerable interest has been focused on infections acquired in utero. Thirteen viral agents are known to be vertically transmitted (from mother to fetus). These are listed in Table 12-1, accompanied by the prominent clinical findings for each. The importance of these perinatal viral diseases lies not only in the mortality they produce but in the more numerous infants who survive them with varying degrees of central nervous system damage.

Protozoan agent

Toxoplasma gondii is the most important protozoan agent involved in perinatal infection. Toxoplasmosis is discussed in detail later in this chapter.

PATHOGENESIS
Bacterial infections

Bacterial infections are acquired in utero, during descent through the birth canal, and after birth in the delivery room or nursery.

Intrauterine bacterial infection acquired by the ascending route. With few exceptions bacterial infections are acquired prenatally by the ascending route; that is, organisms from the perineum and vagina gain entry into the uterine cavity through the cervix. Amniotic fluid is infected after passage of bacteria through a ruptured amniotic membrane, but sometimes the organisms permeate an intact one. They then gain entry into the fetus through the oral cavity and move to the lungs, gastrointestinal tract, and middle ear. Occasionally they enter the bloodstream from these sites.

The presence of organisms in amniotic fluid triggers an inflammatory response in the membranes consisting of infiltrates of polymorphonuclear leukocytes, which ultimately enter the amniotic fluid. Interestingly, the reaction begins in the maternal tissue and then spreads to the amniotic membrane, which is a fetal structure. The resultant lesion is known as chorioamnionitis. Benirschke and Driscoll have aptly pointed out that this is a unique example of response by one organism (maternal) to infection in another (fetal). The presence of bacteria in amniotic fluid thus produces chorioamnionitis and an outpouring of leukocytes into amniotic fluid. Chorioamnionitis and infected amniotic fluid do not always cause fetal disease. They merely expose the fetus to intrauterine infection. Based on the development of chorioamnionitis, several diagnostic procedures have been devised to identify exposure to intrauterine bacterial infection.

Identification of fetal infection. At birth three procedures are of value in identifying the risk imposed by exposure to infection, even though most exposures do not produce active disease. These procedures are especially applicable to premature infants. At a number of neonatal facilities, antibiotics are given to premature infants so identified, even though they are asymptomatic. The most widely used procedure involves examination of gastric contents for the presence of neutrophils. A second useful test employs microscopic examination of frozen sections of the umbilical cord immediately after birth. Infiltration of the cord by polymorphonuclear leukocytes is part of the overall response that characterizes chorioamnionitis. A third test utilizes microscopic examination of a section of amniotic membrane for the presence of infiltrate. It must be emphasized that positive results from these procedures do not prove fetal disease. For newborn infants in whom infection is documented, however, these tests are positive with few exceptions.

Rupture of membranes and prolonged labor. There is general agreement that early rupture of amniotic membranes predisposes to chorioamnionitis and umbilical vasculitis (inflammation of the cord and its vessels) and that the possibility of fetal infection is thus enhanced. Most investigators consider that membrane rupture is early if it occurs at least 24 hours before delivery. Beyond this time the risk of infection increases as the interval between rupture of membranes and birth is prolonged. However, for reasons as yet unknown, numerous infections occur even when membranes rupture closer to delivery than 24 hours. Length of labor is not as clearly correlated with the incidence of infection. There is little doubt that the hazard is most serious when early membrane rupture and prolonged labor are combined. For the nurse, this type of information is valuable in anticipating and detecting the signs of infection. When an infant with a history of exposure to infection in utero is admitted to the nursery, cultures should be taken. The best sites for specimen collection are the throat, axillae, inguinal folds, and external auditory canals. If these cultures are taken within 1 or 2 hours after birth, the results reveal organisms to which the infant was exposed. If signs of illness appear subsequently, the results of cultures provide some basis for the selection of therapeutic antibiotics.

Gestational age and fetal infection. A strong positive association between short gestational age and increased incidence of chorioamnionitis, umbilical vasculitis, and neonatal infection has been cited universally. The shorter the gestational age, the higher their incidence. The incidence of septicemia, meningitis, and pneumonia is considerably higher among premature than among term infants.

Intrauterine bacterial infection acquired transplacentally. Syphilis and occasionally *Listeria monocytogenes* are transmitted across the placenta. Fetal tuberculosis is a rare infection, but when it occurs, it too is acquired through the placenta. Fetal infection from transplacentally derived pneumococcus, streptococcus, staphylococcus, and *Salmonella* is also rare. Before antibiotics were available, maternal septicemia due to these organisms was more frequent, and fetal infection by the placental route was an occasional sequel.

Bacterial infection acquired postnatally. Nursery personnel, infant cohorts, fixtures, and equipment utilized for care of the neonate comprise important sources of postnatal infection. In this respect the lessons learned from the worldwide scourge of staphylococcal epidemics are important to recall. Causative strains of staphylococci were repeatedly cultured from attendants, from other infants, and from articles in the environment such as airborne particles, linen, diapers, and blankets. An exchange between infants and environmental components was postulated by numerous investigators, and indeed the general pattern that emerged from most studies indicated as much. However, disagreement arose about the relative importance of each of these factors, and more fundamentally, about the original source of organisms. The bitter experience with staphylococcal epidemics over a period of several years led to a multiplicity of stringent hygienic measures and isolation techniques, some of which have been relaxed considerably because epidemiologic strains of staphylococci seemed to disappear from the nursery. The influence exerted by these stringent nursery practices is impossible to estimate. It is possible that a phase in the long-term natural life cycle of staphylococci has passed, largely unrelated to our feverish efforts to eliminate them. Infection control practices in the nursery are discussed later in this chapter.

Commensurate with the decline of staphylococcal disease, there was a rise in the incidence of postnatally acquired gram-negative rod infections. The increased use of mechanical equipment for the care of high-risk neonates has certainly been a factor in the upsurge of these infections. Epidemics caused by organisms such as *Pseudomonas aeruginosa, Klebsiella, Aerobacter, Proteus, Achromobacter, Flavobacterium,* and *Alcaligenes faecalis* have been traced to a variety of unsuspected sources in the environment. Most of these organisms proliferate and thrive in water alone, and for this reason Wheeler has aptly dubbed them "water bugs." Epidemics of septicemia, meningitis, pneumonia, and conjunctivitis due to these organisms have arisen from one or more of the following sources:

> Suction machines
> Face masks
> Resuscitation apparatus
> Humidifying systems in incubators
> Plastic sleeves on incubator portholes
> Aerators on sink faucets
> Dripping sink taps
> Submerged water supply inlets in sinks
> Cross connections between water inlets and waste lines
> Dirty soap dispensers and soap trays
> Bathing pans
> Solutions used for eye irrigation
> Benzalkonium (Zephiran) and other solutions used for cold sterilization

The lesson from the experience in recent years is clear: Vigilance in maintaining cleanliness of the physical environment is indispensable to the survival of all neonates.

Viral and protozoan infections

Fetal viral disease and toxoplasmosis are transmitted from the mother across the placenta. The only known exceptions are herpesvirus and cytomegalovirus infections, which are often acquired by the ascending route. Cytomegalovirus is also acquired transplacentally. The viruses listed in Table 12-1 have a presumed or proved capacity to permeate the placenta and enter the fetal bloodstream. Fetal infections may occur at any time during pregnancy. Rubella begins during the first trimester, occasionally slightly later. Cytomegalovirus infection may begin at any time in pregnancy, and in most cases herpesvirus disease is acquired in the third trimester.

Host defenses (immune response)

The mechanisms that comprise the host's defense against invasion by infectious agents are interdependent and multiple. Nonspecific factors include surface protection provided by the skin and mucous membranes, activity of phagocytic cells, and the inflammatory response. Specific factors involve the production of antibodies. They are specific in that they counteract a single organism and are effective against none other; in contrast the skin barrier, phagocytosis, and inflammation are active against any organism that encounters them.

Antibodies. The definitions of antibody and antigen are mutually dependent. An antibody is a protein synthesized by specific types of cells in response to antigenic stimulation; an antigen is a substance of any kind that stimulates the production of antibodies. One type of antibody is bound to cells, and another circulates in plasma (humoral antibodies); the latter are the immunoglobulins.

Most of the available data on the perinatal immune response concern the immunoglobulins. They are secreted into body fluids by lymphocytes and plasma cells, which are specialized cells in tissues. There are several varieties of immunoglobulins, the three major ones being IgG, IgM, and IgA (or gamma-G, gamma-M, gamma-A).

IgG. The IgG fraction contains antibodies to the majority of bacterial and viral organisms previously encountered by the mother. Of the three major immunoglobulins, only IgG crosses the placenta from the maternal to the fetal circulation. Maternally derived IgG first appears in the fetus during the third gestational month, accumulating progressively thereafter. Placental transfer is markedly increased during the last trimester. Length of gestation is thus a significant determinant of the IgG level at birth, which is lower in premature infants than in term infants. At 32 weeks, for example, a premature infant's cord blood contains only 400 mg/100 ml of IgG. In term infants the IgG concentration is at least equal to maternal levels, approximately 1000 mg/100 ml. Since most of the mother's circulating antibodies to bacterial and viral agents are in the IgG fraction, the fetus receives an ample supply of them from her. These antibodies are in effect an imprint of her own lifetime experience with infections. The uninfected neonate has virtually no other IgG at birth.

After birth, maternal IgG antibodies are

catabolized, with resultant depletion over the first 3 months of life. The infant's synthesis of IgG increases gradually during the same period, and at approximately 3 months of age it is sufficient to supplant the loss of maternal IgG. The premature infant's IgG level reaches its lowest point much sooner because there was a low concentration at birth. There is thus a longer period of lower IgG levels until such time as the infant can generate significant amounts of the immunoglobulin. The fact that levels of protection are lower over a longer period of time may be a significant cause of the premature infant's greater susceptibility to infections, and the high incidence of rehospitalization they entail, during the early months of the first year. Total IgG concentration in term babies thus falls from about 1000 mg/100 ml at birth to 400 mg/100 ml at 3 months, at which time a gradual increase begins as a result of the infant's accelerated synthesis. The mother's protection against infection is thus bestowed on her baby, and these protective effects are extended well beyond intrauterine life. IgG contains specific antibodies against most of the common infectious agents, including gram-positive cocci (pneumococcus, streptococcus), meningococcus, and *Haemophilus influenzae,* the viruses, and the toxins of diphtheria and tetanus bacilli. This extended protection may explain partially, at least, the low incidence of these infections during the neonatal period, since most mothers possess antibodies to them. It should be noted in this connection that IgG does not contain antibodies against the enteric gram-negative rods; thus the infant is not protected against these infections by maternal antibody.

IgM. The fetus can produce significant amounts of IgM at about the twentieth gestational week. Since IgM does not cross the placenta, concentrations detected in the neonate clearly represent his own synthesis of it. At birth the normal serum IgM concentration is below 20 mg/100 ml. Normal adult levels are 75 to 150 mg/100 ml. Intrauterine infections of all sorts may produce an immunologic response in the fetus that often results in higher levels. Measurement of IgM has therefore been used to establish the presence of infection. However, IgM determinations are nonspecific indicators; they are no more specific for a particular type of infection than the erythrocyte sedimentation rate in older individuals. Diagnosis of some specific infections is possible by identifying their antibodies within the IgM fraction. These infections include syphilis, toxoplasmosis, cytomegalovirus, rubella, and herpesvirus. In the mother, IgM contains antibodies against gram-negative bacteria and a scattered variety of other antigens. In the neonate, IgM production is stimulated during the initial immunologic response to virtually all infectious agents.

IgA. IgA does not cross the placenta, and it is not detectable in most normal infants at birth. The fetus and neonate are slower to generate IgA than IgM, and it is thus found less regularly in serum of infected infants at birth. Normal adult levels are 200 to 400 mg/100 ml. The function of serum IgA is not altogether clear, but it is found over surfaces of intestinal and respiratory mucosa, as well as over renal epithelial surfaces in a form called "secretory IgA." At these sites it is notably active as an antibody. Its role in the intestine is best known. Secretory IgA is present in breast milk in significant concentrations. Unlike serum IgA, IgM, and IgG, secretory IgA resists enzymatic digestion of gastric and intestinal juices. It therefore imparts immunity to mucosal surfaces of the intestine. For example, oral polio vaccine depends, for its effectiveness, on multiplication in the intestinal tract. The vaccine fails to immunize babies on breast milk from mothers with high antibody titers to poliovirus. Vaccine virus is eliminated in the gut by secretory IgA from breast milk.

SPECIFIC BACTERIAL INFECTIONS
Pneumonia

Pneumonia is the commonest of the serious neonatal infections. It has been cited as a cause of death in 10% to 20% of autopsies. Its peak incidence occurs during the second and third days of life. Pneumonia may be acquired in utero (congenital pneumonia) or from the nursery environment.

Congenital pneumonia is usually associated with obstetric abnormalities such as early rupture of membranes, prolonged duration of labor, maternal infection, and uncomplicated premature delivery. The bacteria most frequently involved are *Escherichia coli* and other enteric organisms and group B streptococci. Symptoms are evident at birth or within 48 hours thereafter. When affected infants are in distress at birth, they are flaccid, pale, or cyanotic. Resuscitation is often necessary. Once respirations are established, they are rapid and shallow. Slight retractions may be present, but they may not be as striking as those of hyaline membrane disease. If the infection is severe, repeated apneic episodes occur. Crepitant rales are sometimes audible. Temperature elevation is more likely in full-sized infants. Premature infants often have subnormal body temperature.

Postnatally acquired pneumonia is generally caused by *Pseudomonas aeruginosa,* penicillin-resistant staphylococci, and enteric organisms. Clinical signs usually appear after 48 hours of life. A substantial number of infants are hypoxic at birth for reasons unrelated to infection. The commonest presenting signs are rapid respiration, poor feeding, or aspiration during feeding. Vomiting and aspiration sometimes occur during feeding because previously unsuspected pneumonia is already present. The chest film in such instances reveals densities that cannot be attributed with certainty to effects of aspirated formula or to preexisting pneumonia. Recovery from postnatal pneumonia is more frequent than from congenital pneumonia.

Antibiotic therapy for pneumonia and other bacterial infections is discussed on p. 224.

Septicemia

Septicemia is a generalized infection characterized by the proliferation of bacteria in the bloodstream. The incidence of septicemia has not diminished since the introduction of antibiotics, but the etiologic agents have changed and survival has increased. Before the antibiotic era, group A streptococci were predominant. Currently, coliform organisms and group B streptococci are the most frequent etiologic agents. The use of antibiotics has diminished mortality from 90% to a range of 13% to 45%, depending on the reporting investigator. Premature infants are most commonly involved; males are affected twice as often as females.

The early symptoms are vague and nonspecific. One expects chills, fever, and prostration in older infants, but the neonate may merely lose vigor, refuse feedings, or lose weight. The nurse may simply note that he is "doing poorly." Other abnormal signs are less subtle and as wide ranging as the bloodstream itself. Vomiting and diarrhea occur in approximately 30% of patients. Abdominal distention may be prominent. Abnormal respiration (apnea, tachypnea, and cyanosis) occurs in 20% to 30% of affected infants. Jaundice is a frequent finding. Hyperbilirubinemia may involve a high concentration of conjugated (direct) bilirubin, mostly in infants over a week of age. Hypoglycemia is not uncommon, being associated with gram-negative rod infection almost exclusively. It responds to increased concentrations of intravenous glucose, as described on p. 209. A wide variety of skin lesions occur. Pustules, furuncles, and subcutaneous abscesses are most often associated with streptococcal and staphylococcal infections, and less often with *Escherichia coli* and *Pseudomonas aeruginosa*. The latter organism also produces localized purplish cellulitis that breaks down into a black, gangrenous ulcer. Petechiae and ecchymoses are not common.

Meningitis occurs in a third of septicemic infants, although clinical signs are evident in only half the infants with this complication. The symptoms include convulsions, altered state of consciousness, irritability, spasticity, and fullness of the anterior fontanelle (see later).

The diagnosis of septicemia can be documented only by recovery of organisms from blood culture, which requires at least 24 hours for growth. Since organisms are also present in the spinal fluid and urine, lumbar taps and suprapubic aspiration of the bladder are essential components of the diagnostic approach. By applying Gram's stain to centrifuged spinal fluid and urine, the morphologic identity of the bacteria may be established, thus affording a rational basis for immediate choice of antibiotics. Cultures of blood, spinal fluid, and urine must be taken before treatment is begun. If there is nothing to suggest the identity of the offending organism, kanamycin (Kantrex) or gentamicin (Garamycin) plus ampicillin are given immediately (p. 224).

Multiple exchange transfusions, one every 12 hours, are reportedly effective for septicemia with sclerema. We have seen dramatic disappearance of sclerema and obvious overall improvement. Sometimes four to six transfusions are required.

Other laboratory data are helpful in making the diagnosis. Leukocytes in peripheral blood, less than 4000/cu mm, in combination with clinical findings, are highly suggestive of septicemia. White blood cell counts over 30,000 are suggestive, but not as strongly suggestive as leukopenia. Thrombocytopenia (platelet count less than 150,000 cu mm) with or without associated evidence of disseminated intravascular coagulation (p. 190) is a common hematologic abnormality. IgM (p. 219) determination often reveals elevated levels (over 20 mg/100 ml in the first week of life). Usually the elevation is not evident for 3 to 7 days after onset of symptoms. High IgM levels generally confirm a diagnosis of bacterial infection days after the decision to treat with antibiotics has been made.

Meningitis

Almost half of all cases of meningitis in children occur during the first year of life, and the incidence is highest during the neonatal period. It is considerably more frequent in premature than in term infants, and in males rather than in females. The causative organisms and the obstetric complications associated with meningitis are the same as those cited for septicemia.

Systemic symptoms cannot be differentiated from those of septicemia. Fullness of the anterior fontanelle is the most specific sign of meningitis. Stiffness of the neck (Kernig's sign), which is so frequent in older infants and children, is rare in the neonate. Opisthotonos occurs in one fourth of the infected infants; coma and convulsions occur in half of them.

The diagnosis must be confirmed by spinal fluid abnormalities and isolation of the organism from a cultured specimen. White cell content of spinal fluid may vary from 20 to several thousand per cubic millimeter. Polymorphonuclear leukocytes predominate. If the infection is due to *Listeria monocytogenes,* mononuclear cells are in the majority. Sugar content is usually low, and protein is elevated. Organisms are evident on Gram-stained smears of centrifuged spinal fluid. Blood cultures yield the etiologic agent in 75% of cases. Fatality rates vary from approximately 35% to 60%, and in approximately half of the survivors severe central nervous system handicaps persist.

Treatment of meningitis is the same as that for septicemia. However, if polymyxin is utilized, it must be given intrathecally as well as parenterally, since the drug cannot cross the blood-brain barrier to spinal fluid when given by the latter route. The addition of intrathecal gentamicin by lumbar puncture to systemic administration was shown to be no more effective than systemic therapy alone. There was no less mortality or residual central nervous system abnormality among survivors.

Group B streptococcal disease

Special mention is made of group B streptococcal infection because of its startling increase in frequency during the past several years. The major diseases it produces are septicemia, meningitis, and pneumonia, but otitis media and conjunctivitis also occur.

Group B streptococcus was previously believed to be significant only in its causation of mastitis of cattle. It behaves in man, however, very much like the more familiar *Listeria monocytogenes*. Both organisms can be recovered from the cervices of asymptomatic pregnant women, and both are sometimes recovered from the urethras of asymptomatic male partners of such women. Maternal colonization during pregnancy may result in spontaneous abortion, severe neonatal septicemia, or a normal baby.

Two clearly defined syndromes occur, depending on their time of onset. The early-onset disease (so-called septicemic form), in which meningitis can nevertheless occur, is seen in the first few days after delivery. It is apparently acquired by the ascending route in utero or by contact with infected tissue during birth. It generally progresses rapidly and relentlessly to cause death in 1 or 2 days. The lungs are heavily involved, and septicemia is almost the rule. In most instances meningitis is absent. Not all cases are so hopeless, however. We have been pleasantly surprised to encounter a number of affected infants who responded to therapy. The most frequent symptoms are respiratory distress, coma, shock, and jaundice. The organism can be cultured from any number of sites, including the nasopharynx, skin, the external ear canal, meconium, and blood. Mortality ranges from 40% to 100%. The late-onset, or meningitic, form occurs several days to 3 months after discharge from the nursery. It almost invariably involves the meninges; its onset is not as abrupt as the early form, and its prognosis for survival is better. Mortality is approximately 20%.

From 4% to 6% of asymptomatic pregnant women have cervical cultures positive for group B streptococci. Cultures of the vulva and vagina have been positive more frequently, with up to 14% of vaginal cultures having been reported as positive. About 1% to 2% of all neonates are colonized with the organism, but colonization does not necessarily lead to disease. Approximately one in ten colonized babies becomes diseased.

The organisms recovered from babies are usually identical to those grown from their mothers.

Group B infection departs from the usual pattern of perinatal infections in two ways: Maternal complications are not necessarily increased (although in some uncontrolled series complications were said to be increased), and the term infant may be as vulnerable as the premature. In fact, in some series the incidence of the disease was higher in the full-term infants.

The organism is exquisitely sensitive to penicillin and ampicillin. Group B disease has thus not been a problem in which the appropriate drug is not available. Most authors agree that the early form is an example of vertical transmission (mother to baby). The epidemiology of the late form is not yet clarified, but there are data suggestive of the role of nursery personnel in transmission of the late variety of the disease. Mother-to-infant transmission may also play a role, or the colonized infant may leave the hospital in health only to become ill later. This phenomenon is common in staphylococcal disease.

Prenatal treatment of maternal carriers eradicates the organism. Because group B streptococcal disease is now a significant public health problem, it has been suggested that routine vaginal cultures be taken during the third trimester and that all positive gravidas be treated with penicillin to eliminate the organism.

Diarrhea

Several bacterial agents can produce primary diarrhea. The most important is enteropathogenic *Escherichia coli* (EEC). Salmonella, shigella, and staphylococci are infrequent causes. Serologic techniques have identified 140 groups of *E. coli*; somewhat over a dozen have been implicated in nursery epidemics of diarrhea.

Regardless of etiology, the early signs of infection consist of refusal to feed, weight loss, and hypoactivity. These may precede the diarrhea itself by a day or two. Blood and pus in the stool are rare, except in shigellosis, which itself is rare. As diarrhea continues, the infant becomes toxic, dehydrated, and acidotic (metabolic acidosis). These signs may appear abruptly during the early phase of explosive diarrhea. Dehydration is even more rapid if vomiting is also present. An ashen gray color, or pallor, is indicative of vasomotor collapse and impending death. Rapid correction of metabolic acidosis and dehydration is therefore crucial. Milder forms of the disease are not unusual, being characterized by protracted diarrhea with fewer stools and a refusal to feed.

Institutional outbreaks are almost inevitable if an infected infant is in the nursery. The disease spreads from one bassinet to the next. Feces of infected babies contain an enormous quantity of organisms, and contamination occurs easily, mostly from unwashed hands of personnel and from gowns. Enteropathogenic *E. coli* has been cultured from the nasopharynx, thus suggesting that airborne spread occurs in some instances.

Diarrheal stools must be cultured as soon as they are evident. Most often a bacterial agent is not causative, and the microbiology laboratory will report that no pathogens are identifiable. When viral cultures are performed, they, too, are often negative. Enteropathogenic *E. coli* may cause explosive epidemics. For this reason oral neomycin or polymyxin, which constitutes effective therapy, is administered even before the results of cultures are returned. If these are positive, the infant should be removed from the nursery, and all other babies should be cultured and treated with the same antibiotics.

Urinary tract infection

Neonatal urinary tract infections have been observed to occur as frequently as septicemia. For unknown reasons, renal infection in the neonate has received relatively scant attention. It is far more common in males than in females, the reverse of sex distribution in later childhood. Furthermore, its occurrence in a male does not strongly suggest underlying anomaly, as it does in older children.

Suspicion of infection should be aroused if more than 10% of body weight is lost during the first 5 days in an infant who is not especially ill. Fever is not unusual, particularly if the onset of symptoms is later than 5 days. A significant number of babies appear gray or cyanotic; abdominal distention and jaundice occur in relatively few. During the second week of life, however, jaundice with a high level of direct bilirubin is commonly associated with renal infection, almost always in males. Convulsions, in the absence of meningitis, occur in a small number of infants.

The organisms are gram-negative enteric rods with few exceptions. Blood cultures may be positive in up to 30% of affected babies. Two consecutive urine cultures, obtained by suprapubic aspiration, are diagnostic. Treatment is effective with appropriate antibiotics. Death occurs from complications of septicemia such as meningitis. Sometimes clinical symptoms, bacteriuria, and pyuria all disappear spontaneously, before treatment is begun.

Conjunctivitis

Infection of the conjunctivae may be acquired during the birth process or from the nursery environment. Bacterial conjunctivitis is usually due to staphylococcus, *Pseudomonas aeruginosa,* and enteric organisms. Clinical signs include swelling and redness of the conjunctiva, with varying amounts of purulent exudate. In its mildest form conjunctivitis causes "sticky eyes," with little or no swelling.

Gonorrheal infection causes the most serious form of conjunctivitis. It is acquired during delivery by direct contact with infected maternal tissue. Initial symptoms are noted between the second and fifth days of life, sometimes later. Severe conjunctival redness, swelling of the eyelids, and copious pus are typically evident. Untreated, the infection may spread to the eyes, causing panophthalmitis and extensive destruction of ocular tissue. It also causes severe arthritis. Rapid diagnosis is possible from a Gram-stained smear of exudate from the eye, which reveals gram-negative cocci within pus cells.

Gonorrheal infection is treated with intramuscular penicillin. Conjunctivitis due to other organisms is effectively controlled by local instillation of an eye ointment containing polymyxin, bacitracin, and neomycin.

Omphalitis

Severe infection of the umbilical stump causes edema, redness, and purulent exudate in the region of the umbilicus. In milder infections there is no visible exudate, but redness and induration of the periumbilical skin are evident. Slight periumbilical erythema without induration is not pathologic. Inflammation of the umbilical stump may herald septicemia. Culture of the blood and the umbilicus is indicated, and treatment for septicemia should be started immediately.

ANTIMICROBIAL TREATMENT

The antibiotics of choice for neonatal infections are listed in Table 12-2. In most instances they must be chosen before results of cultures are available. It is thus essential that they be effective against most of the organisms likely to infect the neonate. Major consideration must be given to the bacterial infections acquired in utero and during birth; they are derived from normal maternal intestinal flora (coliforms, group B streptococci). Penicillin-resistant staphylococci and *Pseudomonas aeruginosa* are more likely to be etiologic in postnatally acquired infections than in congenital ones. When onset of symptoms occurs after 48 to 72 hours, additional consideration must be given to these possibilities.

The overall effectiveness of some antibiotics has diminished through the years. About two decades ago streptomycin was highly active against coliform infections, but it ultimately lost its effectiveness and was replaced by kanamycin (Kantrex). Now the

Table 12-2. Antibiotics of choice (1976)

Drug	Dose	Schedule	Route
Kanamycin	15 mg/kg/24 hr	q. 8 to 12 hours	IM
Gentamicin (Garamycin)	5 mg/kg/24 hr	q. 12 hours (up to 7 days of age)	IM or IV
	7.5/mg/kg/24 hr	q. 8 hours (over 7 days of age)	
Penicillin G (aqueous crystalline)	100,000 U/kg/24 hr	q. 12 hours (up to 7 days of age) q. 6 hours (over 7 days of age)	IM or IV
Ampicillin	100 to 200 mg/kg/24 hr	Same as for penicillin	IM or IV
Methicillin (or oxacillin)	100 to 200 mg/kg/24 hr	Same as for penicillin	IM or IV
Nafcillin	50 mg/kg/24 hr	Same as for penicillin	IM or IV
Polymyxin B	3 to 4 mg/kg/24 hr 10 to 20 mg/kg/24 hr 1 mg (in 1 ml saline solution)	q. 12 hours q. 6 to 8 hours q. 24 hours	IM or IV Oral Intrathecal
Colistimethate sodium	8 mg/kg/24 hr	q. 12 hours	IM
Neomycin	50 to 100 mg/kg/24 hr	q. 6 hours	Oral

activity of kanamycin against *E. coli* has begun to decline significantly. In the years immediately following its introduction, kanamycin was active against 90% to 95% of *E. coli* strains; currently it eliminates approximately 60% in some hospitals. In the early phases of their use both streptomycin and kanamycin were also effective against staphylococci, and this effectiveness, too, was soon lost. Diminished activity of these drugs is related to their widespread use. At present, gentamicin (Garamycin) is a satisfactory replacement for kanamycin. Interestingly, it too is effective against penicillin-resistant staphylococci and at least 90% of *E. coli* strains. Gentamicin is also effective against *Pseudomonas aeruginosa,* thus offering a decided advantage in the treatment of bacterial infection.

For over two decades penicillin has remained useful against most strains of staphylococci that are not hospital acquired, streptococci, syphilis, *Listeria monocytogenes,* and gonorrheal organisms. However, ampicillin has largely replaced penicillin because it is active against the same organisms and a majority of *E. coli* strains as well. The staphylococci that are resistant to penicillin must be treated with nafcillin or a similar type of drug specifically active against penicillin-resistant strains.

Infections manifest during the first 48 hours are best treated with kanamycin or gentamicin plus ampicillin because they are probably congenitally acquired. Onset at a later age implies that hospital-acquired organisms may be etiologic. For these infections a combination of polymyxin and nafcillin may be used, but as more data accumulate, gentamicin ultimately may be favored over polymyxin.

SPECIFIC VIRAL INFECTIONS

The viruses implicated in perinatal infections are listed in Table 12-1. They are transmitted across the placenta from mother to fetus, except for herpesvirus, which is usually acquired by the ascending route, and cytomegalovirus, which is sometimes acquired similarly. Maternal transmission may occur early in pregnancy, causing chronic intrauterine infections such as rubella or cytomegalovirus, or closer to delivery, causing postnatal onset of infections such as herpesvirus, Coxsackievirus, varicella, and smallpox. One of several consequences may befall the fetus or neonate as a result of maternal infection: (1) death may occur in utero or after birth as a result of fetal disease; (2) intrauterine death may follow severe maternal toxicity; (3) survival may occur despite infection but with congenital malformations or destruction of tissue (brain and liver), or often with no apparent aftermath; (4) the virus may not be transmitted to the fetus.

The intrauterine infections of primary importance are rubella, cytomegalovirus infection, and herpesvirus infection.

Rubella

The congenital rubella syndrome is a chronic virus infection of the fetus and neonate that begins during the first trimester of pregnancy and usually persists for months after birth. The virus has been recovered from abortuses, placentas, and amniotic fluid. At autopsy it has been grown from virtually every organ of the body. In life it has been cultured from the throat, urine, meconium, conjunctival secretion, and spinal fluid, from surgically removed segments of the ductus arteriosus, from cataractous lenses, and from liver specimens. The majority of infants may harbor virus as long as 3 months. In some infants the virus persists for several months or years longer. Virus has been recovered from the lens of a 3-year-old child. Persistently infected infants may be a source of contagion; small epidemics among hospital personnel have been traced to them. Pregnant women are thus at risk when exposed to these infants.

Approximately 10% to 20% of gravid women are susceptible to rubella. Estimates of the risk of fetal disease after maternal infection have varied through the years from one epidemic to the next. In general, maternal infection during the first gestational month causes disease in 33% to 50% of exposed fetuses; during the second month 25% are affected, and during the third month 9% are affected. There is a distinct but smaller risk during the fourth month of pregnancy; 4% of exposed fetuses may be affected, primarily by lifelong hearing impairment.

Whether positive or negative, a history of infection is unreliable because at least half the infected older children and adults are asymptomatic. Furthermore, the clinical signs of rubella are difficult to interpret during nonepidemic periods, since they mimic several other virus infections. During the extensive epidemic of 1964, half the mothers of diseased infants were unaware of infection during pregnancy. Fetal disease is no less severe in the asymptomatic mother than in the symptomatic one.

The cardinal clinical signs are intrauterine growth retardation, congenital heart disease, and cataracts. The organs of growth-retarded infants are hypoplastic because rubella virus impairs the proliferative (mitotic) phase of growth (p. 84). Several types of cardiac malformation have been noted; the commonest are patent ductus arteriosus and stenosis of the peripheral pulmonary arteries. Severe myocardial degeneration also occurs in a few infants. Cataracts may be bilateral or unilateral; they are usually present at birth, but occasionally they develop days or weeks later. Other eye abnormalities include microphthalmia and glaucoma. Thrombocytopenia and petechiae are present in 40% to 80% of infected neonates. Enlargement of the liver and spleen is common, and unconjugated hyperbilirubinemia, largely due to hemolysis, is also frequent. When hepatitis occurs, it further contributes to the retention of unconjugated bilirubin, but it also causes elevations of direct bilirubin as well (obstructive jaundice). Occasionally rubella hepatitis progresses to cirrhosis. Interstitial pneumonia is not uncommon, the virus having been recovered from affected lungs. Neurologic abnormalities are present in a minority of neonates; they usually appear later in in-

fancy. Microcephaly, for instance, ordinarily develops after the newborn period. Spinal fluid abnormalities consist of elevated protein concentration and increased white cells, usually lymphocytes. In the neonate they are more frequent than clinical neurologic abnormalities.

The diagnosis of congenital rubella is strongly suggested by the combined presence of cataracts and congenital heart disease. Elevated IgM levels are not regularly detectable at birth. Serologic documentation is possible by demonstrating rubella antibody in serum IgM. Other serologic tests are not helpful because they measure maternal IgG antibody, which may be present as a result of an infection that preceded pregnancy by many years.

The immune status among nursery personnel of childbearing age should be determined at the onset of employment. If serologic tests indicate susceptibility, attenuated rubella virus vaccine should be administered. Infected infants are contagious; susceptible personnel who are exposed while unknowingly pregnant are at risk of having an infected fetus.

Cytomegalovirus (CMV) infection

The cytomegaloviruses are ubiquitous agents that cause infections in populations of all ages throughout the world. Perinatal infections are acquired transplacentally from asymptomatic mothers or by the ascending route from the cervix. In the presence of acute maternal infection, 50% of fetuses are affected. The acutely infected mother is more likely to transmit the disease early in pregnancy than later. Early gestational transmission also seems to be associated with greater severity of fetal disease. Beyond the neonatal period, acquired cytomegalovirus infections are usually asymptomatic; the excretion of virus in urine (viruria) is thus required for the identification of infected individuals. Maternal viruria at the time of delivery has been noted in 3% to 4% of apparently normal women. Positive cultures from the cervix at the time of delivery have been demonstrated in 4.5% of women in Pittsburgh and as many as 28% in Japan. Similar studies have identified viruria in 1% of randomly selected newborns, most of them apparently normal, in whom viruria often persists through the first year of life. Cytomegalovirus has been recovered from an abortus as early as the twelfth gestational week. The fate of apparently healthy viruric neonates has not been documented, but estimates of later central nervous system damage range from 10% to 25%. The only report of postnatal acquisition of the disease in the nursery concerns two premature infants who may have become infected from blood transfusions.

The results of congenital infection range from widespread tissue damage that is incompatible with life, to survival associated with extensive brain damage, and to complete absence of signs during the neonatal period. Diseased infants are often small-for-dates and hypoplastic. The principal target organs are the blood, brain, and liver, although virtually every organ of the body can be affected. Hemolysis causes anemia and unconjugated hyperbilirubinemia. Thrombocytopenia with petechiae and ecchymoses in the skin is quite frequent. Obstructive jaundice (direct hyperbilirubinemia) is a consequence of liver damage. Enlargement of the liver and spleen are common. Cytomegalovirus also produces encephalitis; the resultant clinical signs vary from lethargy and hypoactivity to convulsions. Microcephaly may be present at birth, or it may develop over the ensuing few months. Skull x-ray examinations may reveal calcification in the brain, which is also present in infants with toxoplasmosis. Chorioretinitis is discernible in 10% to 20% of symptomatic infants; this lesion, too, is similar to the eye findings in infants with toxoplasmosis. Pneumonia occurs occasionally.

The diagnosis is best established by recovery of virus from urine. There is considerable diagnostic value in the demonstration of elevated IgM levels, and more specifically in the identification of cyto-megalovirus antibodies within the IgM fraction. Although several antiviral drugs have been utilized for treatment, their efficacy has not been clearly established.

Herpesvirus infection

Herpesvirus has recently been classified into type 1 and type 2 varieties, each with distinctive serologic attributes and clinical implications. Type 1 causes the common, and often recurrent, lesions in the lips of older children and adults. It also produces gingivostomatitis and skin lesions above the waist. Type 2 causes the vast majority of lesions in the cervix, vagina, and external genitalia. Most neonatal infections are due to type 2 virus. The fetus acquires herpesvirus by the ascending route from infected genitalia or by direct contact with these tissues during the birth process. Neonatal herpesvirus is thus a venereal disease acquired by the infant in a manner similar to gonorrhea. Transplacental acquisition probably occurs, but it is apparently rare, having been reported in only a few suggestive cases. Delivery by cesarean section has been recommended for infants whose mothers are known to have genital herpes. The value of this prophylactic approach is not established. If membranes rupture 6 hours or more before section is performed, ascent of virus may infect the fetus. A number of instances have been reported in which herpes infection followed delivery by cesarean section.

Like most other infectious agents that affect the neonate, herpesvirus produces a broad spectrum of clinical signs. The neonatal disease exists in disseminated and nondisseminated forms. The disseminated variety is fatal to 96% of affected infants. Although microscopic lesions may be found in every organ of the body, the most extensive involvement occurs in the adrenals, liver, brain, blood, and lung. Initial symptoms may be present at birth, or they may not appear until 3 or 4 weeks of age. Fever is detectable in approximately one third of infected infants. Other common signs include hepatosplenomegaly, hepatitis with jaundice (associated with direct hyperbilirubinemia), bleeding diathesis, and neurologic abnormalities. These neurologic signs are described later. Vesicular skin lesions are almost pathognomonic, but unfortunately they occur in only one third of the patients. They are usually sparsely distributed over the entire body; occasionally they appear in clusters. Sudden bleeding from the gastrointestinal tract, needle punctures, and circumcision sites portends death within 48 hours. Most infants so affected have been shown to have disseminated intravascular coagulation.

Several nondisseminated forms are composed of central nervous system, skin, and eye abnormalities, which occur singly or in combination. In none of them is there visceral involvement. These varieties of the disease cause death in 25% of the infants, but over half the survivors have residual damage to the brain and eyes. Neurologic abnormalities are the most frequent. They include convulsions (focal or generalized), abnormal muscle tone, opisthotonos, a bulging fontanelle, and lethargy or coma. The spinal fluid contains an elevated protein concentration and increased leukocytes (predominantly lymphocytes). The eye signs include cloudy corneas (keratitis), conjunctivitis, and chorioretinitis. In a substantial proportion of infants with nondisseminated infection, skin involvement is the sole manifestation. As a rule they survive, but psychomotor damage is residual in some. New skin lesions continue to appear for several days; occasionally they recur sporadically up to 2 years of age. These recurrences may be associated with routine immunizations, unrelated febrile disease, or trauma. Most often the lesions appear for no known reason.

The most seriously disabling sequelae among surviving infants are neurologic. They consist of microcephaly or hydrocephalus and varying degrees of psychomotor retardation. Ocular residua may cause total or partial blindness as a result of scars in the cornea (from keratitis) and retina (from chorioretinitis).

In the absence of skin lesions, the diagnosis is elusive because the symptoms are otherwise nonspecific, most often being confused with septicemia. Cultures of virus from skin vesicles and the throat or identification by electron microscopy are the most reliable diagnostic procedures. Positive culture results are observable within 24 to 48 hours.

Antiviral drugs have been used as therapy for neonatal herpesvirus infection, but their efficacy has not been determined. They include iododeoxyuridine (IDU), cytosine arabinoside (ara-C), and adenine arabinoside (ara-A). They are toxic, particularly to the hematopoietic system, and all of them are immunosuppressive. Ara-A appears to be least toxic of the three drugs. A controlled trial of these drugs is now in progress among twenty centers in the United States, and a preliminary evaluation of ara-A has been encouraging. Eight infants were given the drug, and all survived with no demonstrable neurologic defect at 6 months to 1 year of age. There was no toxicity for bone marrow, liver, or kidney.

PROTOZOAN INFECTION
Toxoplasmosis

Toxoplasmosis, caused by the protozoan *Toxoplasma gondii,* is usually an asymptomatic infection in older individuals. It is widespread to varying degrees among different populations over the world. In the United States it occurs in 1 to 4 per 1000 live births—approximately 3000 infected infants annually. It is an important perinatal infection, being transmitted across the placenta from an apparently healthy, but infected, mother. The acutely infected mother is more likely to transmit the organism to her fetus in late rather than early pregnancy. Fetal infection from maternal illness is 17%, 24%, and 62% in the first, second, and third trimesters, respectively. The reasons for this phenomenon are unknown. Symptoms appear in the infant at birth or soon thereafter, but many infants are asymptomatic for the first several weeks of life. The organism has been found in every cell type in the body except the red blood cell, and the resultant clinical signs are thus variable. An array of neurologic abnormalities includes convulsions, coma, severe generalized hypotonia, microcephaly, or hydrocephalus. Skull films may reveal diffuse, comma-shaped intracranial calcifications. Chorioretinitis occurs in most symptomatic infants; microphthalmia is also common. Other signs include hepatosplenomegaly, jaundice (direct and indirect hyperbilirubinemia), petechiae and ecchymoses of the skin (thrombocytopenia), and pallor (anemia). The fatality rate among diseased neonates is 12%. Neurologic deficits are extremely common in survivors.

Serologic diagnosis is feasible immediately after birth by demonstration of specific IgM antibodies. Other serologic procedures, if they reveal sufficiently high titers, also establish the diagnosis (hemagglutination inhibition and Sabin-Feldman dye tests).

CONTROL OF NURSERY INFECTION

Because of continuous presence in the nursery and involvement with hour-by-hour care, the nurse is the baby's most supportive caretaker. However, a lack of concern for hygienic practices can become a serious threat to the infant's survival. The prenatal acquisition of bacterial infection is in large measure unpreventable, but with few exceptions postnatally acquired infectious disease can indeed be avoided. Quite aside from the strict sterility that is obviously required during administration of parenteral fluids and medications, or in preparation of formulas, the practices of nursery personnel need only be predicated on a few simple rules of hygiene. Realistically there is nothing aseptic about these practices; rather, they are clean to the utmost. The provision of a continuously germ-free environment is impossible, even in the most sophisticated nurseries; nor does it seem desirable when one considers that animals maintained in such environments experience a significant delay in their capacity to produce antibodies because of the absence of antigenic stimuli.

Traditionally the practices advocated for prevention of infections have also tended to make the nursery a forbidding place to enter. Such an atmosphere is particularly inadvisable for neonatal intensive care units because the infants in them require greater attention from more people than any other type of patient in the hospital. Surgeons, cardiologists, neurologists, hematologists, anesthesiologists, x-ray technicians, laboratory technologists—all these individuals, besides the nursery staff itself, must regularly converge on sick infants. The resultant traffic is often something to behold. This type of care requires unimpeded access to the nursery, but careful hygienic demeanor is mandatory for all concerned. The simpler and more rigid the rules, the more consistently they are followed. A number of studies have provided a scientific basis for discarding needless and obstructive so-called aseptic techniques. The nurse's role in all this is pivotal. Daily practices must protect patients from exposure to infection, and, in addition, the nurse should be the most effective and vociferous promulgator of established rules of hygienic technique.

Infections are propagated by people and by things. In addition to a predisposition to infection because of illness, the sick neonate is also at great risk because a large cohort of personnel must use a multiplicity of objects in giving care. Furthermore, the nature of a special care nursery is such that it attracts referrals from other institutions. As a consequence, a relatively large number of profoundly ill infants are housed in one facility for extended periods of time, thus increasing the hazard of cross-contamination. The practices to be described are applicable to any nursery—routine or special care. The risks they are designed to minimize are greater in special care facilities.

Propagation of infection by personnel

Personnel carriers of various organisms have been studied extensively, and their role in epidemics has been conjectural. There is some evidence that they may spread infection by the airborne route, but the current concensus is that direct contact by contaminated hands is the principal modality.

Most published studies concern the spread of staphylococci and their colonization among infant cohorts. Colonization of staphylococci occurs when organisms settle on the skin, in the nose, and in the throat without producing disease. The colonized infant is at considerably higher risk of subsequent disease than the noncolonized one. For instance, staphylococcal skin infection has been noted in 20% of infants who become colonized in the first 2 days of life, whereas only 1.4% of noncolonized infants are similarly afflicted. Colonization has been noted in as many as 100% of infants in a single nursery during epidemic years, but high rates also occur during nonepidemic periods. The significance of staphylococcal colonization is not restricted to the diseases that may subsequently appear during the nursery stay; discharged infants often become ill at home. They may also spread the organism to cause household epidemics, even though they remain healthy.

It thus follows that the effects of various procedures for minimizing nursery infections can be gauged from colonization rates and the incidence of overt disease. A number of excellent studies have in fact utilized this approach, and they are in general agreement on the validity of some of these procedures. In each instance the investigators caution that the conclusions reached are directly applicable to conditions in their respective facilities and that universal adoption of their practices may or may not be valid.

Failure to wash hands properly between handling of different infants is undoubtedly the principal mode of spread of infection by any organism. Nothing is more fundamental to proper nursery hygiene than handwashing. On first entering the nursery, personnel should wash to a level above the elbows for at least 2 minutes. Between patients, washing for 15 seconds should be adequate. Currently the use of any type of soap or an iodinated detergent is recommended. The iodinated preparations are preferable, at least for the initial 2-minute scrub, because they are active against gram-positive cocci and

gram-negative rods as well, but they sometimes cause skin sensitivity.

In December, 1972, statements from the Food and Drug Administration and the American Academy of Pediatrics recommended that routine total body bathing of infants, utilizing hexachlorophene-containing detergents, be discontinued. Although clinical signs of toxicity in human infants had not been documented, diffuse cystic lesions were observed in the brains of monkeys who were bathed daily for 90 days with a detergent containing hexachlorophene. Furthermore, blood levels of hexachlorophene in human newborns had been demonstrated, presumably absorbed from the skin. Several weeks after these statements were issued, the Center for Disease Control (Atlanta) reported approximately sixty nursery outbreaks of staphylococcal disease throughout the nation. Whether or not these outbreaks were related to the discontinuation of hexachlorophene bathing is still conjectural. The temporal relationship between the two events suggests as much, although documentation is lacking. The original statements of the Food and Drug Administration and the American Academy of Pediatrics were subsequently modified to recommend that hexachlorophene bathing may be utilized in the presence of a staphylococcal outbreak, but it is unlikely to halt the spread of infection. The modified statements also emphasized the fundamental importance of handwashing and the necessity to investigate all nursery practices to determine the sources of staphylococcal colonization and disease. The preferred method of skin care is now "dry skin care" (see Skin Care of Newborns, Statement, Fetus and Newborn Committee, American Academy of Pediatrics).

Nursery personnel should wear short-sleeved scrub dresses to accommodate washing to the elbows. At some facilities the use of gowns by physicians and other personnel has been discontinued if infants are not removed from incubators. However, long-sleeved gowns should be worn and changed between handling infants if they are taken from an incubator or bassinet, whether to feed or to perform a procedure (individual gown technique). Caps, masks, and hairnets are no longer recommended.

Isolation and suspect nurseries are not considered essential, but infants with diarrhea and draining infections must be removed from the nursery. Infants with bacterial meningitis, septicemia, and pneumonia need not be isolated, nor is there a need to remove infants if amniotic membranes have ruptured early (even if the fluid is purulent), if there is a history of antepartum or postpartum maternal fever, or if the baby was born anywhere outside the delivery room.

Several studies have revealed that colonization rates and the incidence of infectious disease are not increased when parents are permitted entry into the nursery. This development is particularly important in light of the recent realization that a profound impact is exerted on the mother by protracted separation from her sick newborn; it may significantly alter her attitude for some time afterward (Chapter 13). The precautions regarding handwashing and gowning for personnel are similarly applicable to parents.

The trend has thus been toward simplification of techniques for the control of infection by documenting the uselessness of certain procedure that have apparently been more ritualistic than scientific. However, most of the conclusions from these rather recent studies were evolved during an era when the incidence of staphylococcal epidemics declined. Although currently there is sound basis for relaxation of previously needless rigidities, it remains to be seen whether the easier, new approach will withstand the recurrence of extensive staphylococcal epidemics that were the bitter experience of the late 1950s and early 1960s.

Details of nursery techniques and measures for the management of nursery epidemics are fully presented in a recent revision of *Standards and Recommendations for Hospital Care of Newborn Infants* (1976), published by the American Academy of Pediat-

rics. A copy of this publication should be available at every facility that cares for newborn infants.

Infection from equipment and fixtures

The recently increased use of indwelling catheters, at the umbilical site and in peripheral veins, has added another potential source of serious infection. The risk of infection entailed in umbilical vessel catheters is well known. It is not generally appreciated, however, that catheters in peripheral veins cause a considerably higher incidence of bacteremia and local infections. These catheters must be placed with meticulously aseptic technique. They should be managed in the same fashion as the deep vein catheters that are used for total parenteral alimentation.

A group of gram-negative organisms, aptly dubbed by Wheeler as "water bugs," has been identified as an important cause of individual and epidemic infection. These organisms are spread primarily from contaminated equipment. Infants are infected by an enormous inoculum of bacteria capable of proliferating in clear water. Illness usually begins several days after birth or some time later if the nursery stay is protracted.

Pseudomonas is the most prevalent of these organisms. Other frequent offenders are *Aerobacter, Alcaligenes, Achromobacter, Flavobacterium, Serratia,* and *Erwinia* (implicated in contaminated caps on bottles of intravenous fluids). The epidemics caused by these bacteria may be widespread in the nursery during a short period of time, or the infections may occur sequentially in one or a few infants over a protracted interval. They emanate from any piece of equipment, particularly those associated with high humidity or moisture of any kind. Plumbing fixtures are also important sources of contamination. A list of these objects is presented on p. 218.

Regularly obtained cultures from most of these articles are an essential component of bacteriologic surveillance. Furthermore, autoclaving or gas sterilization is indicated for all items that lend themselves to these processes.

Water in the reservoirs of incubators has been discontinued in many nurseries. Oxygen humidifiers are changed daily, and the water within them is changed every 8 hours. Disposable plastic tubes from oxygen outlets are discarded every 24 hours. Mist generators that provide clouded moisture in incubators for infants in respiratory distress are avoided because such treatment is useless, and it increases the incidence of "water bug" infections. Sterile distilled water from previously unopened bottles that is used in ultrasonic nebulizers is changed every 8 hours. Cotton balls are not stored in solutions of benzalkonium chloride (Zephiran) because in these circumstances *Pseudomonas* has been repeatedly recovered from the disinfectant. It is disconcerting to realize that bacteriologists use compounds related to benzalkonium chloride in their media to encourage the growth of *Pseudomonas* by impairing proliferation of other organisms.

The sources of infection in the nursery have multiplied commensurate with recent advances in the care of sick infants. It is essential for the nurse supervisor to execute a program of bacteriologic surveillance and sterilization of equipment. The staff nurse must be certain that the equipment she is using has been cleaned or sterilized in accordance with this program. These programs must be planned in conjunction with the physician in charge of the nursery, an infectious disease expert, an epidemiologist, and a representative from the hospital bacteriology laboratory.

The spread of organisms from people and from things must be eliminated, or at least minimized, by applying sensible techniques of proved value. As in so many other aspects of newborn care, the nurse can assure or destroy the success of infection control procedures better than any other staff member. Close and continuous contact with the babies qualifies the nurse as a perceptive monitor of the incidence of infection, and repeated contacts with physicians and other personnel provide the opportunity to appraise and regulate their demeanor in regard to infection control.

References

Ablow, R. C., et al.: A comparison of early-onset group B streptococcal neonatal infection and the respiratory distress syndrome of the newborn, N. Engl. J. Med. **294**:65, 1976.

Alford, C. A., Neva, F. A., and Weller, T. H.: Virologic and serologic studies on human products of conception after maternal rubella, N. Engl. J. Med. **271**:1275, 1964.

Alford, C. A., et al.: A correlative immunologic, microbiologic and clinical approach to the diagnosis of acute and chronic infections in the newborn infant, N. Engl. J. Med. **277**:437, 1967.

Alford, C. A., Jr., Polt, S. S., Cassady, G. E., et al.: Gamma-M-fluorescent antibody in the diagnosis of congenital syphilis, N. Engl. J. Med. **280**:1086, 1969.

Altemeier, W. A., and Smith, R. T.: Immunologic aspects of resistance in early life, Pediatr. Clin. North Am. **12**:663, 1965.

Anderson, G. S., et al.: Congenital bacterial pneumonia, Lancet **2**:585, 1962.

Baker, C. J., Barrett, F. F., Gordon, R. C., and Yow, M. D.: Suppurative meningitis due to streptococci of Lancefield group B: a study of 33 infants, J. Pediatr. **82**:724, 1973.

Barrie, D.: Incubator-borne Pseudomonas pyocyanea infection in a newborn nursery, Arch. Dis. Child. **40**:555, 1965.

Barton, L. L., Feigin, R. D., and Lins, R.: Group B beta-hemolytic streptococcal meningitis in infants, J. Pediatr. **82**:719, 1973.

Benirschke, K.: Routes and types of infection in the fetus and the newborn, Am. J. Dis. Child. **99**:714, 1960.

Benirschke, K., and Clifford, S. H.: Intrauterine bacterial infection of the newborn infant: frozen section of the cord as an aid to early detection, J. Pediatr. **54**:11, 1959.

Benirschke, K., and Driscoll, S. G.: The pathology of the human placenta, New York, 1967, Springer-Verlag New York, Inc.

Bergstrom, R., Larson, H., Lincoln, K., and Winberg, J.: Studies of urinary tract infections in infancy and childhood. XII. Eighty consecutive patients with neonatal infection, J. Pediatr. **80**:858, 1972.

Blanc, W. A.: Pathways of fetal and early neonatal infection, viral placentitis, bacterial and fungal chorioamnionitis, J. Pediatr. **59**:473, 1961.

Brunell, P.: Antiviral drugs for the neonate: the risk-benefit ledger, J. Pediatr. **86**:317, 1975.

Cabrera, H. A., and Davis, G. H.: Epidemic meningitis of the newborn caused by flavobacteria. I. Epidemiology and bacteriology, Am. J. Dis. Child. **101**:289, 1961.

Ch'len, L. T., Whitley, R. J., Nahmias, A. J., et al.: Antiviral chemotherapy and neonatal herpes simplex virus infection: a pilot study—experience with adenine arabinoside (ara-A), Pediatrics **55**:678, 1975.

Davies, P. A.: Bacterial infection in the fetus and newborn, Arch. Dis. Child. **46**:1, 1971.

Davies, P. A., and Aherne, W.: Congenital pneumonia, Arch. Dis. Child. **37**:598, 1962.

Davis, L. E., et al.: Cytomegalovirus mononucleosis in a first trimester pregnant female with transmission to the fetus, Pediatrics **48**:200, 1971.

Desmond, M. M., et al.: Congenital rubella encephalitis, J. Pediatr. **71**:311, 1967.

Desmonts, G., and Couvreur, J. Quoted in Remington, J. S.: Toxoplasmosis and congenital infection. In Bergsma, D., editor: Birth defects: intrauterine infections, vol. 4, no. 7, White Plains, N.Y., December, 1968, National Foundation–March of Dimes.

Eichenwald, H. F.: Congenital toxoplasmosis: a study of 150 cases, Am. J. Dis. Child. **94**:411, 1957.

Eickhoff, T. C., Klein, J. O., Daly, A. K., et al.: Neonatal sepsis and other infections due to group B beta-hemolytic streptococci, N. Engl. J. Med. **271**:1221, 1964.

Ermocilla, R., Cassady, G., and Ceballos, R.: Otitis media in the pathogenesis of neonatal meningitis with group B beta-hemolytic streptococcus, Pediatrics **54**:643, 1972.

Evans, H. E., Akpata, S. O., and Baki, A.: Bacteriologic and clinical evaluation of gowning in a premature nursery, J. Pediatr. **78**:883, 1971.

Foley, J. F., et al.: Achromobacter septicemia—fatalities in prematures, Am. J. Dis. Child. **101**:279, 1961.

Franciosi, R. A., Knostman, J. D., and Zimmerman, R. A.: Group B streptococcal neonatal and infant infections, J. Pediatr. **82**:707, 1973.

Gehibach, S. H., Gutman, L. T., Wilfert, C. M., et al.: Recurrence of skin disease in a nursery: ineffectuality of hexachlorophene bathing, Pediatrics **55**:422, 1975.

Gitlin, D., Kumate, J., Urrusti, J., et al.: The selectivity of the human placenta in the transfer of plasma proteins from mother to fetus, J. Clin. Invest. **43**:1938, 1964.

Gluck, L., and Wood, H. F.: Staphylococcal colonization in newborn infants with and without antiseptic skin care; a consideration of epidemiologic routes, N. Engl. J. Med. **268**:1265, 1963.

Gotoff, S. P.: Neonatal immunity, J. Pediatr. **85**:149, 1974.

Gotoff, S. P., and Behrman, R. E.: Neonatal septicemia, J. Pediatr. **76**:142, 1970.

Hanshaw, J. B., Steinfeld, H. J., and Cherie, J. W.: Fluorescent antibody test for cytomegalovirus macroglobulin, N. Engl. J. Med. **279**:566, 1968.

Hardyment, A. F., et al.: Observations on the bacteriology and epidemiology of nursery infections. I. Staphylococcal skin infections, Pediatrics **25**:907, 1960.

Hildebrandt, R. J., et al.: Cytomegalovirus in the normal pregnant woman, Am. J. Obstet. Gynecol. **98**:1125, 1967.

Hoffman, M. A., and Finberg, L.: Pseudomonas infections in infants associated with high humidity environments, J. Pediatr. **46**:626, 1955.

Horn, K. A., Zimmerman, R. A., Knostman, J. D., and Meyer, W. T.: Neurological sequelae of group B streptococcal neonatal infection, Pediatrics **53**:501, 1974.

James, L. S.: Hexachlorophene, Pediatrics **49**:492, 1972.

Kohen, D. P.: Neonatal gonococcal arthritis: three cases and review of the literature, Pediatrics **53**:436, 1974.

Kopelman, A. E.: Cutaneous absorption of hexachlorophene in low-birth-weight infants, J. Pediatr. **82**:972, 1973.

Korones, S. B., Ainger, L. E., Monif, G. R., et al.: Congenital rubella syndrome: new clinical aspects with recovery of virus from affected infants, J. Pediatr. **67**:166, 1965.

Korones, S. B., Roane, J. A., Gilkeson, M. R., et al.: Neonatal IgM response to acute infection, J. Pediatr. **75**:1261, 1969.

Korones, S. B., Todaro, J., Roane, J. A., et al.: Maternal virus infection after the first trimester of pregnancy and status of offspring to 4 years of age in a predominantly Negro population, J. Pediatr. **77**:245, 1970.

Kresky, B.: Control of gram-negative bacilli in a hospital nursery, Am. J. Dis. Child. **107**:363, 1964.

Light, I. J., Brackvogel, V., Walton, R. L., and Sutherland, J. M.: An epidemic of bullous impetigo arising from a central admission-observation nursery, Pediatrics **49:**15, 1972.

Light, I. J., and Linnemann, C. C., Jr.: Neonatal herpes simplex infection following delivery by cesarean section, Obstet. Gynecol. **44:**496, 1974.

Lockhart, J. D.: How toxic is hexachlorophene? Pediatrics **50:**229, 1972.

McCracken, G. H.: Changing pattern of the antimicrobial susceptibilities of Escherichia coli in neonatal infections, J. Pediatr. **78:**942, 1971.

McCracken, G. H., Hardy, J. B., Chen, T. C., et al.: Serum immunoglobulin levels in newborn infants. II. Survey of cord and follow-up sera from 123 infants with congenital rubella, J. Pediatr. **74:**383, 1969.

McCracken, G. H., and Shinefield, H. R.: Changes in the pattern of neonatal septicemia and meningitis, Am. J. Dis. Child. **112:**33, 1966.

McCracken, G. H., Shinefield, H. R., Cobb, K., et al.: Congenital cytomegalic inclusion disease: a longitudinal study of 20 patients, Am. J. Dis. Child. **117:**522, 1969.

McCracken, G. H., Jr.: Group B streptococci: the new challenge in neonatal infections, J. Pediatr. **82:**703, 1973.

McCracken, G. H., Jr., and Eichenwald, H. F.: Antimicrobial therapy: therapeutic recommendations and a review of newer drugs. I. Therapy of infectious conditions, J. Pediatr. **85:**297, 1974.

McCracken, G. H., Jr., and Eichenwald, H. F.: Antimicrobial therapy: therapeutic recommendations and a review of the newer drugs. II. The clinical pharmacology of the newer antimicrobial agents, J. Pediatr. **85:**451, 1974.

Miller, D. R., Hanshaw, J. B., O'Leary, D. S., and Hnilicka, J. V.: Fatal disseminated herpes simplex virus infection and hemorrhage in the neonate: coagulation studies in a case and a review, J. Pediatr. **76:**409, 1970.

Monif, G. R. G.: Viral infections of the human fetus, New York, 1969, The Macmillan Co.

Monif, G. R. G., Avery, G. B., Korones, S. B., et al.: Postmortem isolation of rubella virus from three children with rubella-syndrome defects, Lancet **1:**723, 1965.

Monif, G. R. G., Egan, E. A., Held, B., and Eitzman, D. V.: The correlation of maternal cytomegalovirus infection during varying stages in gestation with neonatal involvement, J. Pediatr. **80:**17, 1972.

Nahmias, A. J., Alford, C. A., and Korones, S. B.: Infection of the newborn with herpesvirus hominis, Adv. Pediatr. **17:**185, 1970.

Nahmias, A. J., and Tomeh, M. O.: Herpes simplex virus infection. In Current problems in pediatrics, vol. 4, Chicago, 1974, Year Book Medical Publishers, Inc.

Olding, L.: Bacterial infection in cases of perinatal death, a morphological and bacteriological study based on 264 autopsies, Acta Paediatr. Scand. **171**(supp.)**:**1, 1966.

Overall, J. C., Jr.: Neonatal bacterial meningitis: analysis of predisposing factors and outcome compared with matched control subjects, J. Pediatr. **76:**499, 1970.

Overbach, A. M., Daniel, S. J., and Cassady, G.: The value of umbilical cord histology in the management of potential perinatal infection, J. Pediatr. **76:**22, 1970.

Peter, G., Lloyd-Still, J. D., and Lovejoy, F. H., Jr.: Local infection and bacteremia from scalp vein needles and polyethylene catheters in children, J. Pediatr. **80:**78, 1972.

Powell, H., Swarner, O., Gluck, L., and Lampert, P.: Hexachlorophene myelinopathy in premature infants, J. Pediatr. **82:**976, 1973.

Prod-hom, L. S., Choffat, J. M., Frenck, N., et al.: Care of the seriously ill neonate with hyaline membrane disease and with sepsis (sclerema neonatorum), Pediatrics **53:**170, 1974.

Remington, J. S.: Toxoplasmosis and congenital infection. In Bergsma, D., editor: Birth defects intrauterine infections, vol. 4, no. 7, White Plains, N.Y., Dec., 1968, National Foundation–March of Dimes.

Remington, J. S., Miller, M. J., and Brownlee, I.: IgM antibodies in acute toxoplasmosis. I. Diagnostic significance in congenital cases and a method for their rapid demonstration, Pediatrics **41:**1082, 1968.

Rosen, F. S.: Immunity in the fetus and newborn. In Gluck, L., editor: Modern perinatal medicine, Chicago, 1974, Year Book Medical Publishers, Inc.

Sever, J. L.: Possible role of humidifying equipment in spread of infections from the newborn nursery, Pediatrics **24:**50, 1959.

Sever, J. L.: Perinatal infections affecting the fetus and newborn, Proceedings of a Conference on Mental Retardation Through Control of Infectious Diseases, June 9-11, 1966, Public Health Service Publication no. 1962, Washington, D.C., 1966, Government Printing Office.

Sherman, J. D., et al.: Alcaligenes faecalis infection in the newborn, Am. J. Dis. Child. **100:** 212, 1960.

Shuman, R. M., Leech, R. W., and Alvord, E. C.: Neurotoxicity of topically applied hexachlorophene in the young rat, Arch. Neurol. **32:**315, 1975.

Shuman, R. M., Leech, R. W., and Alvord, E. C., Jr.: Neurotoxicity of hexachlorophene in humans. II. A clinicopathological study of 46 premature infants, Arch. Neurol. **32:**320, 1975.

Silverman, W. A., and Homan, W. E.: Sepsis of obscure origin in the newborn, Pediatrics **3:** 157, 1949.

Silverman, W. A., and Sinclair, J. C.: Evaluation of precautions before entering a neonatal unit, Pediatrics **40:**900, 1967.

Skin care of newborns, Statement, Fetus and Newborn Committee, American Academy of Pediatrics, Pediatrics **54:**682, 1974.

Smith, R. T., Platon, E. S., and Good, R. A.: Septicemia of the newborn, current status of the problem, Pediatrics **17:**549, 1957.

Snowe, R. J., and Wilfert, C. M.: Epidemic reappearance of gonococcal ophthalmia neonatorum, Pediatrics **51:**110, 1973.

South, M. A.: Enteropathogenic Escherichia coli disease: new developments and perspectives, J. Pediatr. **79:**1, 1971.

Sprunt, K., Redman, W., and Leidy, G.: Antibacterial effectiveness of routine hand washing, Pediatrics **52:**264, 1973.

Starr, J. G., and Gold, E.: Screening of newborn infants for cytomegalovirus infection, J. Pediatr. **73:**820, 1968.

Stern, H., and Tucker, S. M.: Prospective study of cytomegalovirus infection in pregnancy, Br. Med. J. **2:**268, 1973.

Swartzberg, J. E., and Remington, J. S.: Transmission of toxoplasma, Am. J. Dis. Child. **129:** 777, 1975.

Van Furth, R., Schutt, H. R. E., and Hijmans, W.: The immunological development of the human fetus, J. Exp. Med. **122:**1173, 1965.

Watson, D. G.: Purulent neonatal meningitis: a study of forty-five cases, J. Pediatr. **50:**352, 1957.

Weller, T.: The cytomegaloviruses: ubiquitous agents with protean clinical manifestations, I and II, N. Engl. J. Med. **285:**203, 1971.

Wheeler, W. E.: Water bugs in the bassinet, Am. J. Dis. Child. **101:**273, 1961.

Wilson, M. G., et al.: New source of Pseudomonas aeruginosa in a nursery, J.A.M.A. **175:** 1146, 1961.

Yeung, C. Y.: Hypoglycemia in neonatal sepsis, J. Pediatr. **77:**812, 1970.

Chapter 13

Impact of intensive care on the maternal-infant relationship

Jean Lancaster

EARLY IN THIS CENTURY several investigators documented the devastating effects on young children of the total absence of a mother or mother surrogate. Later, concern was focused on children subjected to interruption of normal mother-child relationships. Because separation from the mother during a child's hospitalization was common practice, the hospital became a focus for these investigations. With the recent development and proliferation of specialized centers for the care of high-risk neonates, concern has arisen about separation of the mother from her baby at birth. Now, however, attention is directed toward the impact of separation on the mother and her subsequent capacity for mothering, rather than the effects of separation on the child.

PHYSICAL SEPARATION

Although there is a dearth of data on the separation of mother and newborn child, several animal studies and a number of human studies are now available. The animal studies have indicated that early separation is detrimental to the mother-child relationship. For instance, if lambs were separated from their mothers immediately after birth and reunited several hours later, the mothers were either unable or unwilling to recognize their offspring. Some of the ewes fed their lambs indiscriminately; others butted them away. Among rats and mice, total rejection of the young did not occur, but mothering skills were less proficient when early separation had occurred. In contrast, when lambs were kept with their mothers

for 4 days, then separated and later reunited, the mothers always returned to their own lambs to exhibit normal maternal behavior. It seems that for many animal species physical contact with the young in the immediate postnatal period is essential for the development of normal mothering behaviors. Whether a similar critical period exists for humans is conjectural, but one recent study suggests such a possibility. In this study, groups of mothers were allowed differing amounts of physical contact with their infants in the newborn period. A month later, follow-up observations indicated that mothers who had the most frequent contact with their babies were more sensitive to their infants' needs. These mothers also made the greatest effort to meet their infants' needs.

For both animals and humans, touch seems to play a very important role in the establishment of the relationship. The human mother first uses touch to become acquainted with her baby, and later she employs it to express love. She explores his body with her fingertips, gradually using more of her hands, and finally enfolding him in her arms, holding him closely to her body. Mothers of premature infants, having been separated from their babies since birth, often express difficulty in believing that they have a child.

Eye-to-eye contact between human mothers and their children seems to play a very important part in eliciting maternal affection. Similarly the performance of caretaking activities and the perception of satisfaction from the child seem to be necessary preludes to the development of maternal love.

Prolonged physical separation of mother and child precludes the natural evolution of these phenomena.

PSYCHOLOGIC SEPARATION

Besides physical separation there is evidence that a mother suffers psychologic estrangement from her high-risk infant. The causes of these feelings are varied and complex. She has lost the normal child she anticipated during pregnancy, and the realization that her baby is less than perfect initiates a grief reaction.

First, the mother is in a state of shock. The baby born to her was not the normal, healthy one she expected. During this period of shock, denial is very evident in her reaction. Occasionally this denial takes extreme forms, as exemplified by the mother in premature labor who does not recognize she is in labor until birth is imminent. As shock and denial are replaced by awareness of reality, strong feelings of anger, guilt, and shame may emerge. These feelings, or the depression that often accompanies them, may divert the mother from the establishment of a normal relationship with her baby. Absence of anxiety and concern for the baby's outcome may well signal an unhealthy future for the maternal-child relationship. If the baby has a visible congenital anomaly, the mother's feeling of anger and guilt may delay for some time any desire to establish a relationship with him. If a long interval elapses between the time she is told of the anomaly and the moment she actually sees her baby, fantasies, which are characteristically much worse than the actual anomaly, may develop. The mother then has the additional burden of eliminating these fantasies before she can begin relating to the reality of her child.

If the baby's survival is in doubt, the mother may be reluctant to invest in a relationship with him. Anticipatory grief is evident at the time. She begins to prepare herself for the death of her infant, while at the same time she continues to have hope that the baby will live. Withdrawal from a close relationship is common. In our experience, delay in naming the baby until survival is assured constitutes the most common manifestation of anticipatory grief. With her baby surrounded by electronic monitors, catheters, and other sorts of equipment, the mother is understandably unable to focus on her baby; her attention becomes fixed on the equipment and the threatened loss it symbolizes. Initiation of a close relationship to the baby is unlikely until a favorable outcome is certain.

In addition to the equipment that surrounds the baby and the infant's responses, the numbers and specialized skills of personnel may also constitute a barrier for the mother. Often, for instance, she sees nurses who are so skilled and knowledgeable that in comparison she feels totally incapable of learning to care for her baby. This impression may undermine her self-esteem to an extent that causes total withdrawal.

IMPLICATIONS FOR ACTION

Although none of the foregoing factors are conclusive, they do suggest the need for some action to lessen the impact of separation of mother and child. There are several ways to decrease the effects of physical separation. Although it is not rational to discontinue the management of high-risk infants in specialized units, it is possible to bring mothers into the nursery. The mother must see her infant at the earliest opportunity. Prior to the first visit, the nurse must prepare parents for the baby's appearance and the equipment attached, explaining, at the bedside, the function of each item and its role in promoting recovery. Comments about the baby's individuality are particularly helpful, and statements such as, "He likes to hold my finger while I feed him," or "She is very active," will also assist the mother to see her baby beyond the equipment. Phototherapy should be temporarily discontinued and eye patches should be removed for short periods of time to permit eye-to-eye contact between parents and child, except when the baby is so ill that he cannot open his eyes. The nurse must be present with the parents when they first visit; however, I have found it advantageous to leave the parents alone with their baby for a short period of time. Constant supervision tends to inhibit mothering responses such as touch and eye-to-eye contact. Some mothers can tolerate only brief visits in the beginning. When they indicate a need to leave, they should be reassured that their reactions are normal and that they are welcome to return at will.

For the mother who has been hospitalized elsewhere, we have found it helpful to send a Polaroid picture of the baby. The picture provides some visual contact that is otherwise impossible. She is encouraged to call the nursery at any time to talk with the nurse who cares for her baby. Night hours are extremely stressful for parents; we receive many telephone calls between 10 P.M. and 1 A.M.

In our center, mothers are encouraged to visit their babies and fondle them while they are still in incubators. Observations at several centers have not demonstrated an increased risk of infection if parents are allowed to visit the nursery. In fact, one investigator noted that mothers observed isolation precautions more carefully than medical personnel. Mothers are encouraged to touch and fondle their babies when they visit. In the case of a premature infant, the nurse must prepare parents for the characteristic generalized startle reaction to touch, instead of the expected localized physical response. They must also be apprised of the lack of response of a depressed infant, regardless of maturity. For example, when the premature infant who is touched by his mother simply exhibits a Moro reflex and cries, the mother may perceive the response as displeasure. She is not unwanted by her baby; he has not repelled her attention. She should be told of this expected response to spare her the agony of a misinformed reaction.

As soon as it is appropriate, our mothers are asked to perform caretaking activities under the supervision of nurses. Some mothers engage in limited caretaking during the period of intensive care. These activities should elicit positive reinforcement of the mother's endeavors. She must be protected from feelings of incompetence lest she withdraw further from her baby. All mothers are encouraged to feed and bathe their babies repeatedly before discharge. Since a mother may interpret poor feeding, sleeping during feeds, or regurgitation as indications of her own ineptness, she should be forewarned of the normal nature of these occurrences. The nurse should not immediately take the infant who feeds poorly from the mother and then feed the baby successfully in her presence. The resultant maternal feelings of both inadequacy and resentment are needlessly imposed on her already existing emotional difficulties. Rather, the nurse should help the mother to feed her infant by demonstrating techniques such as gentle rotation of the nipple or stroking of the infant's cheek to initiate a sucking reflex.

Diminishing the impact of psychologic separation is somewhat more difficult. Some understanding of the mother's feelings is prerequisite to any attempt to alleviate them. In essence she is experiencing a grief reaction. She has experienced a loss—the lost expectation of a perfect child—as well as a blow to her self-esteem as a woman and a mother, because the child she produced was imperfect. Since the child she bore survived, her grief is different from the woman's whose baby has died. She must surrender the baby of her fantasies to form a relationship with her real child, who may be normal or handicapped. The mother (and father as well) usually progresses through shock, a developing awareness of reality, and finally an acceptance of reality. During the phase of shock she cannot comprehend what is said to her. She frequently claims that everything is unreal or dreamlike. She may deny the reality of her predicament. Although the neonatal nurse rarely encounters the mother at this stage of her grief process, she can, in collaboration with nurses on the maternity floor, keep the mother continuously informed about the baby's status. However, it is important to realize that a mother in this phase of grief can ill afford to be overwhelmed with too much information. An honest, simple explanation is all that is needed; it is certainly all she can understand for the time being. Problems at hand should be discussed; predicting problems such as jaundice, pneumothorax, retardation, or possible death must be avoided in an attempt to prevent completion of the grief process. Once the grief process is completed, parents must reestablish a relationship with a baby who is perceived as dead and buried; frequently, the reestablishment of this relationship is never accomplished.

Active intervention into the grief process by describing reality and by encouraging the mother to express her feelings will assist her progress. She must not be pushed into discussing her feelings. With a developing awareness of reality, the mother has moved into the second stage of grief. Now she may be overcome with feelings of anger, guilt, and shame. She may lash out at those who come to her aid; she may berate herself or her spouse for her dreadful failure. Transfer of parental guilt and anger to medical and nursing staff is common. It is a great temptation of the staff to categorize such a mother as "difficult." The result of this categorization is well known to anyone who reads these pages with interest. Personnel withdraw from the mother in question; in fact, complete abandonment is not uncommon. Yet the patient has merely grasped at anger and hostility as an immediately available mode of coping with her catastrophy. No greater harm can be inflicted at that moment than abandonment by the only individuals who could be supportive and who could thereby avert a potentially long-term attitudinal difficulty. The mother must be encouraged to express these negative emotions; they indicate attempts to cope with a stressful situation. Only as she externalizes them can she begin to move toward acceptance of reality, and only then can she begin to establish the bonds of relationship with her baby.

One indication of progress is the development of an interest in the infant and his care. However, when she asks the same questions over and over again in her struggle to grasp the situation, those who work with her should be genuinely concerned and patient. It is during this time that she can first be taught to care for her baby and thus relate to him. Impatience with frequent questions turns her away and impedes ultimate acceptance of her baby. Several studies have shown that mothers who fail to visit or call about their baby, who exhibit little anxiety in relation to the child's prematurity or illness, who seek little information about their baby, and who are unable or unwilling to share their own fears and concerns are destined for a difficult, if not pathologic, relationship with their child. Identification of such behavior urgently requires parental counseling by others besides the nurse. A significant correlation between lack of interest and a paucity of telephone calls and visits has been observed. Further, the incidence of children who are destined for parental battering increases in the face of these signs of detachment or neglect.

If survival of the infant is in doubt, the mother may be unable to form a relationship. At this time, the parent is preparing for death while simultaneously maintaining hope for survival. Parents may physically withdraw from their infant during such crises; yet they usually maintain contact by phone. They must begin to accept the reality of an uncertain prognosis. It is important for both parents to be accurately informed about the baby's condition. Cautious optimism must be utilized in counseling parents about their infant's condition. Informing them that death is a certainty or that mental retardation is a likelihood will be detrimental to the establishment of an acceptable relationship should the baby survive. When death is imminent, this information must be imparted by the physician first, and then by a supportive nurse. The situation is even more pressing, and requires more time, if brain damage is certain. In these circumstances the nurse is continuously the support figure, the one who consoles, and the one who can best help in constructing some sort of future from shattered expectations. Parents must not be allowed to develop unrealistic optimism, but close contact should nevertheless be encouraged. Close early contact with an infant who later dies does not cause a dangerous increase in grief among mothers with no history of emotional difficulty. The last stage of the grief process (acceptance of reality) may take several months and indeed may never be accomplished, particularly if the infant is handicapped.

Mothers need frequent praise and reassurance as they learn to care for their babies. The nurse should guide a mother who has difficulty with a caretaking activity, rather than supplant her. The impressive competence of the nurse may well discourage the mother from trying to learn.

Nurses can evaluate a mother's emotional state by being alert to signs of tension, such as rapid breathing, muscle tension, perspiration, and rapid or stilted conversation. When the mother is participating in care of her baby, her approach to touching and holding him often reveals a great deal about her emotional state. During the learning period, if she is unsure of herself, she will handle the baby rather stiffly and awkwardly, tending to hold him away from her body. At first she prefers only to touch him with her fingertips rather than enfold him in her arms. A distant sort of handling and holding is often manifest during feeding. The mother who is at ease with her baby holds him closely, with his head resting in the crook of her elbow in proximity to, or touching, her breast. She usually holds him turned toward her, and she seeks repeated eye contact with him. Both baby and mother are relaxed in a comfortable position. In contrast, the mother who is uneasy and anxious usually assumes an awkward, uncomfortable position. Her arm is stiff and it tires easily. In her insecurity she is preoccupied with the mechanics of the feeding process, and thus

makes no attempt to estabish eye contact with her infant. She seeks reassurance from the nurse repeatedly and must receive positive responses from her baby, such as consuming all of the offered formula or sleeping postprandially. She is visibly upset if the baby fails to take all of the milk or if he regurgitates. This behavior reinforces feelings of incompetence and is often perceived as rejection. Eventually, with support from an adept nurse, this mother will develop a comfortable relationship with her baby.

An occasional mother, for one reason or another, fails to establish a firm bond with her baby. She holds him on her knee with his head on her forearm but at a distance from her breast. The baby will likely be on his back or perhaps turned away from her. Instead of making eye contact, she gazes around the room, apathetic and disinterested. Because she pays little attention to the baby, the bottle is tilted incorrectly, so that the nipple is filled with air rather than milk. This mother needs counseling if she is ever to form a healthy relationship with her baby. Identifying such a mother in the early phase of her relationship with the baby and referring her for help may prevent multiple problems in the future. It should be noted that most mothers transiently exhibit some signs of discomfort with their babies; it is the predominant and persistent behavior patterns that are important.

As mother and baby become acquainted, she seeks some indication that she is successfully meeting his needs. Relaxation and sleep are the commonest early signs of such success. Unfortunately, because of their biologic difficulties, high-risk babies are often at first unable to respond favorably to the mother's ministrations. Mothers should be taught that this lack of response is not a reflection of poor mothering, so that the baby's inability to respond does not further jeopardize the relationship.

SUMMATION

Several courses of action may successfully reduce the undesirable effects of prolonged separation of mothers and babies after birth.

Preliminary studies suggest that early separation interferes with the development of normal mothering skills, attitudes, and relationships. Most of the approaches suggested here are supportive. All of them are primarily nursing functions. The nurse's continuous presence in the neonatal unit and knowledge of normal behavioral patterns and supportive techniques place the nurse in a key position to assist mothers in overcoming the problems of separation.

References

Barnett, C. R., Leiderman, P., Grobstein, R., and Klaus, M.: Neonatal separation: the maternal side of interactional deprivation, Pediatrics **45**:197, 1970.

Bibring, G. L.: Some considerations of the psychological processes in pregnancy, Psychoanal. Study Child **14**:113, 1959.

Blau, A., Slaff, B., Easton, K., et al.: The psychogenic etiology of premature births, Psychiatry Med. **25**:201, 1963.

Cohen, R. L.: Some maladaptive syndromes of pregnancy and the puerperium, Obstet. Gynecol. **27**:562, 1966.

Deutsch, H.: The psychology of women: a psychoanalytic interpretation. II. Motherhood, New York, 1945, Grune & Stratton, Inc.

Dubois, D. R.: Indications of an unhealthy relationship between parents and premature infant, JOGN Nursing **4**:21, 1975.

Fanaroff, A. A., Kennell, J. H., and Klaus, M.: Follow-up of low birth weight infants: the predictive value of maternal visiting patterns, Pediatrics **49**:287, 1972.

Green, M., and Solnit, A. J.: Reactions to the threatened loss of a child: a vulnerable child syndrome. III. Pediatric management of the dying child, Pediatrics **34**:58, 1964.

Hersher, L., Richmond, J., and Moore, A.: Maternal behavior in sheep and goats. In Rheingold, H., editor: Maternal behavior in mammals, New York, 1963, John Wiley & Sons, Inc.

Johnson, S. H., and Grubbs, J. P.: The premature infant's reflex behaviors: effect on the maternal-child relationship, JOGN Nursing **4**:15, 1975.

Kahn, E., Wayburne, S., and Fouche, M.: The Baragwanath Premature Baby Unit: an analysis of the case records of 1,000 consecutive admissions, S. Afr. Med. J. **28**:453, 1954.

Kaplan, D., and Mason, E.: Maternal reactions to premature birth viewed as an acute emotional disorder, Am. J. Orthopsychiatry **30**:539, 1960.

Kennedy, J. C.: The high-risk maternal-infant acquaintance process, Nurs. Clin. North Am. **8**:549, 1973.

Kennell, J. H., and Klaus, M. H.: Care of the mother of the high-risk infant, Clin. Obstet. Gynecol. **14**:926, 1971.

Kennell, J. H., and Rolnick, A. R.: Discussing problems in newborn babies with their parents, Pediatrics **26**:832, 1960.

Klaus, M. H., Jerauld, R., Kreger, N. C., et al.: Maternal attachment: importance of the first postpartum days, N. Engl. J. Med. **286**:460, 1972.

Klaus, M. H., and Kennell, J. H.: Mothers separated from their newborn infants, Pediatr. Clin. North Am. **17**:1015, 1970.

Klaus, M. H., Kennell, J. H., Plumb, N., and Zuehike, S.: Human maternal behavior at the first contact with her young, Pediatrics **46**:187, 1970.

Leifer, A. D., Leiderman, P. H., Barnett, C. R., and Williams, J. A.: Effects of mother-infant separation on maternal attachment behavior, Child Dev. **43**:1203, 1972.

Lindemann, E.: Symptomatology and management of acute grief, Am. J. Psychiatr. **101**:141, 1944.

Mason, E. A.: A method of predicting crisis outcome for mothers of premature babies, Public Health Rep. **78**:1031, 1963.

McFarland, M. B., and Reinhart, J. D.: The development of motherliness, Children **6**:48, 1959.

Newton, N., and Newton, M.: Mothers' reactions to their newborn babies, J.A.M.A. **181**:206, 1962.

Owens, C.: Parents' reactions to defective babies, Am. J. Nurs. **64**:83, 1964.

Ribble, M. A.: The rights of infants, New York, 1943, Columbia University Press.

Robson, K. S.: The role of eye-to-eye contact in maternal-infant attachment, J. Child Psychol. Psychiatry **8**:13, 1967.

Rose, J., Boggs, T. R., Jr., Adlerstein, A., et al.: The evidence for a syndrome of "mothering disability" consequent to threats to the survival of neonates: a design for hypothesis testing including prevention in a prospective study, Am. J. Dis. Child. **100**:776, 1960.

Rubenstein, J.: Maternal attentiveness and subsequent exploratory behavior in the infant, Child Dev. **38:**1089, 1967.

Rubin, R.: Basic maternal behavior, Nurs. Outlook **9:**683, 1961.

Rubin, R.: Maternal touch, Nurs. Outlook **11:** 828, 1963.

Solnit, A., and Stark, M.: Mourning the birth of a defective child, Psychoanal. Study Child **16:** 523, 1961.

Spitz, R. A.: Hospitalism, Psychoanal. Study Child **1:**53, 1945.

Thaler, O. F.: Grief and depression, Nurs. Forum **5:**8, 1966.

Ujhely, G. B.: Grief and depression: implications for preventive and therapeutic nursing care, Nurs. Forum **5:**23, 1966.

Chapter 14
Organization and functions of a neonatal special care facility

ADVANCED DIAGNOSTIC AND THERAPEUTIC TECHNIQUES during the past decade have resulted in the evolution of a new type of facility for the care of sick neonates. Prior to the 1960s, infants were admitted to a full-term or a premature nursery. Infected babies were deported to a separate, irregularly staffed nursery that was reserved solely for contagious disease. Uninfected sick infants were managed in the premature or full-term nursery to which they were originally admitted. In many hospitals an observation nursery was set aside for infants with unproved but suspected infection. Postoperative neonates were treated in surgical areas along with children of all ages, and in many instances with adults as well.

The contemporary special care facility arose in response to an awareness of the singular characteristics of perinatal disorders. A newly acquired understanding of pathophysiologic phenomena during this period of life, and the capacity to apply this knowledge clinically, required an appropriate setting in which the severely ill baby could be managed. These developments occurred simultaneously with advances in electronics and biochemistry. Practical methods for the evaluation of numerous crucial parameters of fetal and neonatal illness were thus made available. Continuous monitoring of cardiorespiratory function became a reality. The performance of multiple biochemical determinations on minute quantities of blood was facilitated by new microtechniques. Conservation of body heat became feasible with the availability of radiant heaters and servocontrolled incubators. With confidence in improved methods for the control of infec-

tion, a direct impetus was provided for housing all medically and surgically ill infants in a common area, whether they were premature or mature, infected or noninfected. This new approach revolutionized requirements of nursery architecture, fixtures, and equipment, but more important, a need was created for specially trained personnel in several disciplines who must function cohesively if lives were to be saved. Today, optimal performance by all personnel requires a spirit of camaraderie in which traditional ideas of hierarchy are minimized in the nursery organization. Every worker in a special care unit is indispensable to its successful operation.

Although survival is an obvious end point by which to gauge the success of these new, vigorous efforts, *intact* survival is the overriding consideration. There is good reason to assume that diminished mortality and decreased incidence of central nervous system damage among survivors go hand-in-hand. The factors that contribute to perinatal mortality may, if present to a less severe degree, result in central nervous system dysfunction rather than death. By minimizing the effects of these deleterious factors, diminished mortality is probably associated with a decreased incidence of dysfunctional survival.

Do mortality rates decrease when intensive care is applied? There is excellent evidence that they do indeed. In the Province of Quebec, among hospitals with special care units or with access to them by transfer of sick infants, mortality during the first week of life was approximately half that of hospitals without such services. Similar benefits have been reported from Nova Scotia and from several large centers in the United States. In the state of Arizona the mortality of babies with hyaline membrane disease who were *not* transported to an intensive care unit was 59% (1967 to 1970); among those who *were* transported the mortality was 32%. In the same state, in intensive care institutions themselves, the mortality of babies between 1000 and 2500 grams fell from 11.5% in 1964 to 5.9% in 1970. At Vanderbilt University Hospital, mortality of babies in the same weight bracket was 11.8% before intensive care; it was 6.5% afterward. At Mount Zion Hospital in San Francisco, mortality of low birth weight infants was 21.8% before intensive care, and 6.6% after it was introduced. At the Robert B. Green Hospital in San Antonio, Texas, in just 2 years (1969 to 1971), the mortality of infants who weighed 1500 to 2500 grams was reduced from 18% to 7.8%. There is little doubt that intensive care programs have indeed increased survival.

What has happened to the survivors? Follow-up studies have been encouraging. From Britain, follow-up of only the smallest survivors (birth weights below 1000 grams) reveals 90% without any handicap, 4% with physical handicaps only, and 5% with mental handicaps. For infants below 1500 grams, studied outcomes reveal some sort of neurologic defect in 7% to 10% of infants. Although these figures are still high, the outlook is not as dismal as it was once considered. For the specific handicap called spastic diplegia, in which intellectual function is seldom impaired, the fall in incidence is dramatic. From Sweden, a decline of 50% is recorded. From Britain an incidence of 10.3% fell to zero. From other centers in that country and elsewhere, the incidence is 3.6% or less. There has been a reduction in *all* forms of cerebral palsy among children of very low birth weight reported from virtually all centers in which such data have been recorded. An improvement in IQ has been associated with the decline in physical handicaps among low birth weight babies, although IQ is still below the norms for term infants.

During the first year of our own special care program at the University of Tennessee, there was a decline of 28% in the mortality rate of low birth weight infants from the average of the preceding 8 years. We attribute this decline to the training of personnel; new equipment was not acquired until the last 5 or 6 months of that period. Although electronic monitors, mechanical respirators, and other such items are important, they are nevertheless a secondary consideration. *The care of sick babies cannot be intensive unless personnel perform with intensity.* Without this ingredient, complex equipment is useless. The heavy staffing requirements imposed by special care units should preclude indiscriminate establishment of these facilities by hospitals that merely seek to enhance or maintain their community images. Special care units must ultimately operate as regional centers. As such, they must accept responsibility for the transfer of infants, and they must sponsor extensive educational programs for their own personnel and for those of the referring hospitals in their respective regions. Thus the functions of these centers should include service to the community, education of personnel, ongoing evaluation of currently utilized techniques, and the production of new information through research.

This chapter is devoted to a description of the functions of a neonatal special care center and of the structural characteristics and equipment that are required for the performance of these functions. Optimal staffing patterns and appropriate educational programs are also discussed.

INFANTS IN NEED OF SPECIAL CARE

Special care is composed of a spectrum of activities ranging from close observation of apparently well infants who may not require therapy but are at risk of serious illness, to intensive treatment of infants whose survival is in doubt. A special care facility should thus provide different levels of graduated management for a high-risk infant population. The requirements for admission to this unit will necessarily vary from one hospital to another. Each institution must apply criteria that will select the greatest number of high-risk infants that can be accommodated in its facility. At our facility we admit infants delivered in our hospital whose birth weight is less than 1500 grams, as well as any distressed infant, regardless of birth weight. We also admit all infants of diabetic mothers and those with histories of certain obstetric difficulties. Sick babies less than 28 days of age are admitted by referral from the region and from our hospital clinic. Postoperative surgical patients are also managed in our special care unit. Since exigencies arise repeatedly, these criteria are often altered according to an infant's condition on the one hand and the census of our unit on the other.

Many of the specific conditions that qualify an infant for admission to the special care facility are listed on p. 24. No claim is made for the completeness of these tables; a few exceptional unlisted situations may also require special attention.

CLINICAL FUNCTIONS

The clinical functions performed in a special care unit include direct observation of patients by nursing personnel and physicians, physiologic monitoring with electronic equipment, biochemical monitoring by laboratory personnel, diagnostic and therapeutic procedures, and promotion of maternal-child contact to the fullest feasible extent. The success of the last-mentioned function is almost exclusively dependent on skillful nursing. (See Chapter 13.)

Direct observation of infants

The components of direct observation of sick infants have been described throughout this book. This phase of special care is reiterated to emphasize its fundamental importance. It is thus unwise to provide electronic equipment for remote observation of sick babies from centrally located consoles similar to those in adult intensive care units. Severe difficulty can be better detected in the earliest stages by an alert nurse who notes slight cyanosis, even though uninterrupted respirations and heart rate have not yet tripped the alarms of monitors. A monitor cannot signal the regurgitation of a feeding until the baby becomes apneic after aspiration of milk. Optimal outcomes are basically dependent on constant scrutiny of infants by personnel rather than by gadgets. The crucial factors listed here are direct observations that can be made only by well-trained nurses. *None of them is detectable by monitors:*

1. Acceptance of feedings; course of weight gain
2. Early detection of regurgitation to prevent aspiration of vomitus
3. Abdominal distention; frequency and character of stools
4. Changes in activity (lethargy, convulsive phenomena, hyperactivity)
5. Jaundice
6. Pallor and early cyanosis
7. Skin lesions that indicate infection
8. Deviations from prescribed volumes of intravenous infusions
9. Edema
10. Respiratory distress characterized by tachypnea, retractions, flaring of alae nasi, and grunting
11. Quality of breath sounds
12. Character and location of heart sounds

Physiologic monitoring and therapy: electronic and other types of equipment

Electronic monitoring has greatly facilitated the detection of cardiovascular and respiratory difficulties. *These instruments are intended for use by skillful personnel; they are not intended to replace them.* In addition to cardiorespiratory monitoring, the control of temperature and ambient oxygen concentrations is also feasible with appropriate instrumentation. Following are the general categories of equipment required for intensive neonatal care:

I. *Monitors*
  A. Respiration (apnea)
  B. Heart rate
  C. Blood pressure
  D. Temperature (rectal or skin probes), with or without controller

E. Electrocardiogram (oscilloscopes, writers)
F. Oxygen analyzers (ambient), with or without controllers

II. *Therapeutic equipment*
A. Incubators, with servocontrolled temperature
B. Infusion pumps for intravenous fluid administration
C. Phototherapy lamps
D. Radiant heaters over treatment tables

III. *Oxygen administration*
A. Plastic head hoods
B. Humidifier warmers, preferably with variable temperature control
C. Repirators (positive pressure with pressure or volume limiters; negative pressure)
D. CPAP apparatus

IV. *Resuscitation equipment*
A. Insufflation bags with masks
B. Endotracheal tubes and adapters
C. Laryngoscopes with premature blades

Biochemical monitoring

The special care unit should have its own laboratory staffed by technologists who are aware of the clinical significance of their efforts. At the very least, blood gas and pH determinations should be available within minutes after they are ordered for infants in respiratory distress and for periodic monitoring of other conditions such as late metabolic acidosis of prematurity. Since large units are usually located in sprawling hospital complexes whose central laboratories are at some distance from the nursery, the special care unit's laboratory should provide as many biochemical parameters as possible. Reliability and immediate availability of results are best assured when laboratory personnel are involved with newborn medicine on a full-time basis and are thus familiar with the special problems of sick infants. Blood glucose, bilirubin, and electrolyte determinations are indispensable. Hemoglobin and hematocrit determinations, stained blood smears, and Gram stains are also important.

Radiologic diagnosis

Chest films are the most frequent radiologic need in the nursery. They are best procured with minimal disturbance to the infant and thus should be taken by portable x-ray equipment, with the infant in an incubator. Films of the skull, abdomen, and extremities also can be taken with portable equipment. Gastrointestinal series and intravenous pyelograms should be performed in an x-ray room within the special care unit. If such a room is not available, the infant should be transported to the hospital radiology department only if accompanied by a nurse or a physician. A transport incubator with its own battery to provide heat, and its own portable source of oxygen, must be available for this purpose.

STRUCTURAL COMPONENTS

The complete special care unit contains areas designed for intensive, intermediate, and minimal care. Infants are admitted directly to these areas, depending on their status, or they may be moved from one section to another according to changes in conditions. Thus an infant who was successfully treated for hyaline membrane disease, perhaps with ventilatory assistance, can be transferred with ease from the intensive care to the intermediate care area. Minimal care sections are generally devoted to convalescent growing infants.

Special care facilities should be as close as possible to the labor and delivery rooms. Currently, most new neonatal units are constructed by remodeling existing facilities, thus imposing severe limitations on optimal location, floor plan, and space. A number of notable units in the United States and in Canada are housed in children's hospitals rather than in general hospitals. These centers function solely as referral units, since they are usually at some distance from obstetric facilities.

The ideal center should accommodate thirty-five to forty-five infants who are distributed among the three graduated care areas. Complete units for fewer than fifteen to twenty infants who are similarly distributed may be too expensive to operate. They may also fail to provide sufficient clinical

Fig. 14-1. Floor plan of the Newborn Center at the City of Memphis Hospital, University of Tennessee. (Courtesy Bruce M. Thogmartin and Michael D. Tyne, Consultants, Ross Planning Associates, Ross Laboratories, Columbus, Ohio.)

material to maintain the interest and skill of personnel.

The number of bassinets and incubators within each of the three graduated care areas must be determined individually for each institution. These calculations depend on the population to be served. In some hospitals or communities the incidence of low birth weight is 7% of live births; in others, such as our own, it may be 15% to 17%. Since the principal source of infants requiring special care is the low birth weight group, the number of maximal care stations is largely determined by the incidence of small babies. The extent of referrals from the community is another important consideration in these calculations.

Current trends are toward housing all infants who need special care in a single large room, with sections organized administratively for the three levels of graduated care. Such an arrangement permits assignment of personnel according to their respective skills while providing ease of movement of patients and personnel from one area to another. An average of at least 80 square feet per infant should be allocated. More space is provided for each infant in the maximal care area than in the other sections.

The Newborn Center at the University of Tennessee Center for the Health Sciences (City of Memphis Hospital) will be briefly described because it is an example of a modern special care unit. It is comprised of a single large room that accommodates forty infants (2000 square feet) and a number of other rooms for ancillary functions (Figs. 14-1 and 14-2). The plan was developed to conserve nursing energy by minimizing walking distances entailed in use of the telephone, procurement of instruments and supplies, and recording of notes in charts that are otherwise stored at a central desk. The diagram of our floor plan (Fig. 14-1) shows the disposition of incubators or bassinets and the placement of wall cabinets and other cabinets throughout the room. Supplies are stored as close to the infant as possible, permitting the nurse to remain in the area to which she is assigned. Ready-made milk formula in individual bottles is stored in the cabinets. Extensive work surface adjacent to each infant is provided by the counter tops. Daily notes are made

Fig. 14-2. Recently constructed Newborn Center at the City of Memphis Hospital, University of Tennessee. The baby being fed is in the intermediate care area. The maximal care section is in the background. The facility houses forty infants.

at the cribside. The area contains ten sinks operated by foot pedals for convenient hand-washing. Telephone extensions are placed at each corner of the room. At least ten electrical outlets are available for each of the seventeen maximal care stations. Two oxygen lines and a suction and air outlet serve each incubator. In addition to copious illumination from lighting fixtures, an adjustable work light is suspended from the ceiling over each maximal care incubator. With a "panic button" at each maximal care incubator, the nurse can signal for help without leaving the infant. Infant stations in the intermediate care areas are provided with fewer service attachments. A nurse supervisor's office and a treatment and x-ray room are located at one end of the large room for infants. Two central desks for ward secretaries serve the entire area.

Rooms for ancillary services are located off the central corridor that leads to the infant area. The floor plan shows two feeding rooms, equipped with sinks and incubator outlets, in which mothers may tend their convalescent babies in privacy or with nurse supervision if necessary. A large scrub area contains three sinks just outside the nursery proper. Clean and dirty utility rooms with autoclave, house officer sleeping quarters, a nurses' lounge, and the laboratory are also shown. A conference room with library accommodates teaching sessions for nurse personnel, medical students, house officers, fellows, and groups of mothers. Offices for the physician in charge, for fellows, and for social service personnel are located in an adjacent building. Social service interviews are generally conducted in mothers' rooms during their hospitalization or in the unit's conference room.

A baby-viewing area was not provided. Based on the concepts presented in Chapter 13, parents are encouraged to visit their infants in the nursery.

The delivery suite is located two floors above the special care unit. An express elevator transports infants from the delivery room directly to the nursery. The facility for normal term infants is one floor above the special care nursery.

STAFF

No problem is more vexing than the procurement of adequate numbers of qualified personnel. The heavy staffing requirement of these units invariably taxes hospital budgets. Administrative officials thus find it difficult to provide funds for the ideal staffing pattern.

A corps of registered nurses, practical nurses, and nurse assistants or technicians must be deployed to match training and skill with the level of care required for each infant. For every shift, optimal staffing should provide one nurse for two infants in the maximal care area, and one nurse for three to six infants in the other sections. In calculating the total number of personnel required for 24 hours, the needs for each shift must be multiplied by a factor of 4.4 to allow for vacations, sickness, and off days. Ward secretaries, laboratory technologists, social workers, and housekeeping personnel are essential for complete staffing. In a large center the physician-in-charge must be a full-time neonatologist; in a smaller center a pediatrician may be employed part time. Large units are also staffed with residents who rotate through the nursery during their pediatric training and with fellows in neonatology. Nursing students and postgraduate nurse trainees are regularly present in units that are affiliated with schools of nursing and medicine.

EDUCATIONAL PROGRAMS

The special care center that proposes to manage high-risk infants who are born in a large hospital as well as those referred from the community is committed to an extensive educational program of high quality. Training should be provided for the unit's nurses and for other nurses from hospitals throughout the region. In-service programs should begin with a series of lecture sessions devoted to the principles of perinatal medicine, combined with cribside instruction in the various sections of the unit. This initial phase of training requires at least 3 months. Ongoing education must thereafter include periodic sessions devoted to case presentations and to special subjects such as the basic principles of electricity and their application to the prevention of shock hazards, demonstration and practice of endotracheal intubation utilizing models specially made for this purpose, and discussions of important current literature. Training sessions are given by the physician in charge, by neonatology fellows, and by the clinical nurse supervisor or someone designated. The unit must also participate in advanced degree programs sponsored by the school of nursing and in the instruction of student nurses according to the school's curriculum.

The education of other members of the nursing team (assistants, practical nurses) is also indispensable. This phase of the program should be administered primarily by the clinical nurse supervisor and staff.

We have been gratified by our weekly social work conferences, which are supervised by social service personnel and are attended by medical students, house officers, fellows, nurses, and laboratory technologists. Environmental factors, family relationships, and economic problems of the families of selected infants are discussed at each meeting. The goal of these conferences is to assess the infant's home environment before he is discharged and to apply community resources to the alleviation of existing problems. It is not unusual to defer discharge of an infant until our social workers have attempted to minimize the problems that may jeopardize his health at home. Medical aspects of the hospital course are related to the home environment that awaits the baby in question. All available personnel are encouraged to attend. The importance of total infant care plus social concern is effectively projected by the nature of the discussions during these sessions.

Laboratory technologists should attend all training sessions along with nurses. They thus acquire perspective regarding the importance of their role in the successful operation of the unit and an understanding of the clinical significance of the data they produce every day.

Training programs for medical students,

house officers, and fellows are a part of the curriculum of the school of medicine. The fully staffed unit should also sponsor refresher courses for practicing physicians.

Although these training programs must necessarily be diverse if they are to serve the needs of all types of personnel, they are unified by their emphasis on each staff member's importance to the intact survival of sick infants.

References

Davies, P. A., and Stewart, A. L.: Low-birth-weight infants: neurological sequelae and later intelligence, Br. Med. Bull. **31**:85, 1975.

Desmond, M. M., Rudolph, A. J., and Phitaksphraiwan, P.: The transitional care nursery: a mechanism for preventive medicine in the newborn, Pediatr. Clin. North Am. **13**:651, 1966.

Desmond, M. M., Rudolph, A. J., and Pineda, R. G.: Neonatal morbidity and nursery function, J.A.M.A. **212**:281, 1970.

Gluck, L.: The newborn special care unit: its role in the large medical center, Hosp. Pract. **3**:33, 1968.

Gluck, L.: Design of a perinatal center, Pediatr. Clin. North Am. **17**:777, 1970.

Lucey, J. F., editor: Problems of neonatal intensive care units, Report of the Fifty-ninth Ross Conference on Pediatric Research, Columbus, Ohio, March, 1968, Ross Laboratories.

Lucey, J. F.: Why we should regionalize perinatal care, Pediatrics **52**:488, 1972.

Schlesinger, E. R.: Neonatal intensive care: planning for services and outcomes following care, J. Pediatr. **82**:916, 1973.

Segal, S.: Neonatal intensive care: a prediction of continuing development, Pediatr. Clin. North Am. **13**:1149, 1966.

Segal, S., and Pirie, G. E.: Equipment and personnel for neonatal special care, Pediatr. Clin. North Am. **17**:793, 1970.

Silverman, W. A.: Intensive care of the low birth weight and other at-risk infants, Clin. Obstet. Gynecol. **13**:87, 1970.

Stewart, A. L., and Reynolds, E. O. R.: Improved prognosis for infants of very low birth weight, Pediatrics **54**:724, 1974.

Swyer, P. R.: The regional organization of special care for the neonate, Pediatr. Clin. North Am. **17**:761, 1970.

Index